NOVEMBER 1975

NOVEMBER 1975

THE INSIDE STORY OF
AUSTRALIA'S GREATEST POLITICAL CRISIS

PAUL KELLY

ALLEN & UNWIN

© Paul Kelly, 1995

This book is copyright under the Berne Convention.
No reproduction without permission.

First published in 1995
Allen & Unwin Australia Pty Ltd
9 Atchison Street, St Leonards, NSW 2065 Australia
Phone: (61 2) 9901 4088
Fax: (61 2) 9906 2218
E-mail: 100252.103@compuserve.com

National Library of Australia
Cataloguing-in-Publication entry:

Kelly, Paul, 1947– .
  November 1975: the inside story of Australia's greatest political crisis.

  Includes index.
  ISBN 1 86373 987 4.

  1. Whitlam, Gough, 1916– . 2. Fraser, Malcolm, 1930– .
  3. Kerr, John, Sir, 1914–1991. 4. Australia—Politics
  and government—1972–1975. I. Title.

320.994

Set in 10.5/12 pt Baskerville by DOCUPRO, Sydney
Printed by Australian Print Group, Maryborough, Vic.

10 9 8 7 6 5 4 3 2 1

Contents

Preface vii

1 Whitlam 1
2 Fraser 23
3 1974 43
4 Kerr 66
5 The loan 86
6 The deadlock 104
7 The battle 131
8 Failed compromises 168
9 The solution 196
10 Dismissal 245
11 1975 281

Appendices
A A statement by Opposition front-bencher
   Mr R J Ellicott, QC 318
B Opinion dated 4 November 1975 and signed by
   Maurice Byers 322
C Letter from the Chief Justice of the High Court
   to the Governor-General 343
D Sir John Kerr's letter of dismissal 345
E Governor-General's statement of reasons 346
F Malcolm Fraser's caretaker commission 350
G Proclamation 351
H Letter from the Queen's private secretary to the Speaker 353

Notes 354
Index 378

For my son, Daniel

Preface

THIS BOOK IS a fresh account of Australia's political and constitutional crisis in 1975. It is published to coincide with the twentieth anniversary of the Dismissal. My intention is to provide a comprehensive narrative of this story for a younger generation of readers, and also fresh insights for those readers familiar with these events. I have drawn upon the published accounts by or on behalf of the principal figures—Gough Whitlam, Malcolm Fraser, Sir John Kerr and Sir Garfield Barwick. I have also conducted about thirty new interviews with a range of participants, some of whom have never previously spoken publicly about this story.

I believe that the story can only be understood in terms of the personal relationships between the principals, in addition to the political and constitutional dynamics. Having reported on the 1975 crisis at the time and having written a book on the Dismissal the following year, I believe, twenty years later, that the story is more fascinating and extraordinary than ever. It remains the most dramatic event in our political history.

I would like to thank my publisher, Patrick Gallagher, and the staff at Allen & Unwin. But my greatest thanks are extended to my family—my sons Joseph and Daniel for their support, and above all my wife Margaret for her personal support and her assistance with the ideas in the manuscript, the sources, logistics and index.

Paul Kelly
9 September, 1995

1
Whitlam

The mandate of 1972 was the most positive and precise ever sought and ever received by an elected government in Australian history.

Gough Whitlam on his mandate[1]

THE 1975 POLITICAL and constitutional crisis was a product not only of the contest between the Labor Government and the Liberal–Country Party Opposition but also of competing views of Australian democracy. The underlying issues raised by the crisis remain unresolved today. They are merely disguised by the current debate over federalism, republicanism and individual rights. As Australia approaches its centenary of Federation in 2001 and contemplates changes to its democracy to reflect a growing national confidence, the legacy of 1975 hangs like a skeleton in its constitutional cupboard, out of sight but still denied interment.

The events of 1975 constitute a story of men, parties and institutions. The men were Gough Whitlam, Malcolm Fraser and Sir John Kerr; the parties were the Australian Labor Party and the Liberal and Country Parties; and the institutions were those defined in section 1 of the Constitution, a 'Federal Parliament, which shall consist of the Queen, a Senate, and a House of Representatives', and in section 2 which specifies that a 'Governor-General appointed by the Queen shall be Her Majesty's representative in the Commonwealth', along with the respective powers of these offices and institutions as defined in that document.

There was a battle for power conducted in terms of political convention and constitutional provision. But its essence was personal.

The key to 1975 lies in the personalities and characters of Whitlam, Fraser and Kerr and their judgements of each other. The contest can be comprehended only in terms of the dynamics of personal relations.

The Whitlam Government period of 1972–75 is unique because of the level of conflict it witnessed between the House of Representatives and the Senate. The Senate rejected a series of government bills; it blocked Supply to the government in effect in 1974, and in fact in 1975; it contemplated this with a frequency that threatened to convert an unprecedented action into a mundane tactic. This conflict produced two double dissolution elections within 19 months, granted on a total of 27 bills, in comparison with the two previous double dissolutions in 1914 and 1951, granted on each occasion on only one bill. Finally, the Whitlam era generated the greatest confrontation between the two Houses and the greatest parliamentary struggle between the parties, which culminated in the Governor-General's dismissal of the Prime Minister. The climate of politics was filled with unusual rancour, even by Australia's robust standards.

The definitive event that transformed Australia's political landscape and initiated this fateful conflict was the election on 2 December 1972 of the Whitlam Labor Government. This election was more significant than a normal transfer of power. It was hailed as a watershed at the time and, despite divergent interpretations of the Whitlam era, it will probably endure as a turning point in policy innovation and cultural assertion. The Whitlam Government, in its achievements and its excesses, generated powerful emotions within both the professional political corps and the wider community. The initial questions to be posed are: why was Whitlam's victory a watershed event, and what was it in the nature of his government that provoked such hostility?

The answers are threefold. The win was a celebration of Labor's relevance and recuperative capacity after 23 years in opposition, the longest such period for a major party, during which Labor's ability to govern again was in doubt. As a consequence the Labor Government possessed a strain of euphoria, induced by vindication after prolonged denial. Members at their party meeting after victory were described by Labor veteran Fred Daly as 'excited like children on their first day back at school'. Daly himself was infected, declaring the first time he moved a successful gag motion, 'I've waited almost 30 years to do that'.[2]

Second, Labor's return to power was driven by a compelling political figure bound to arouse passions, Gough Whitlam: a self-styled man of destiny who represented a synthesis in leadership technique between the didactic impulse of the parliamentary tradition and the fashion of political charisma that had arisen in America with the

Kennedy mystique. Whitlam was a flawed hero, writ large. The character, style and temperament of the Labor Government was made in his image; its achievements and its dismissal can be grasped only in terms of the Whitlam phenomenon. Whitlam was a visionary without design skills; a statesman philosopher unable to master the technique of personnel management.

Finally, under Whitlam's influence the ALP was elected on a vast government-directed reform program that discarded the old axioms of socialism and nationalisation, and promised instead to pilot Australia onto a path of equality and modernisation based upon a revitalisation of institutions. The theatre of Whitlamism was to dramatise the impact of change, a risky tactic; its substance was to replace systematically the old order of process and policy with a new order. The effect was to exaggerate the real threat Whitlam posed to established interests.

During its three years in office many hopes were shattered by Labor's blunders. But this should not obscure the expectation and inspiration that surrounded Whitlam's 1972 ascension. Such expectations were matched by an equally firm and then fierce resistance to Whitlam's government founded upon the Menzian-induced belief within the non-Labor parties that they and only they were Australia's legitimate rulers. The Coalition's response to Whitlam was antagonistic, not just because he won thereby terminating a generation of non-Labor rule. Whitlam was a threat because, for the first time in 23 years, Labor had an opportunity to challenge the central tenet of postwar politics—that the Coalition had the legitimate charge of the national direction.

The Whitlam personality

Whitlam is testimony to the great man theory of history. Without Whitlam there would have been no ALP Government in 1972; equally, there would have been no dismissal in 1975. Whitlam's character is the essential ingredient in both events and in the fantastic odyssey that connected them.

It was the chemistry within Whitlam of a wilful personality and a profound intellectual conviction that made him such an explosive figure. His strengths were his logic, knowledge, oratory, energy, optimism, idealism, vision, dedication and self-belief. Whitlam was an instructor rather than a politician. He was half-way towards the prophet; and prophets, prone to rejection in their own time, find solace in awaiting vindication by history.

Whitlam had a fresh electoral strategy for the ALP—adding the middle class vote to its eroding working class base. Whitlam was a champion of middle class politics. He sought not to attack capitalism but to redistribute its benefits; to make Labor the political patron of the rising technocratic elite; and to promote education as a credential for individual progress.

A boyhood spent in Canberra as the son of a distinguished public servant and creative mother who instilled the virtues of intellectual attainment and the values of personal excellence meant, as Freudenberg says, that Whitlam was imbued with a belief in the federal government and parliament.[3] After war service as an airforce navigator Whitlam pursued the law at the New South Wales bar, but only as a prelude to entry into politics. Whitlam had no inclination to 'make his pile' first; he was ambitious and addicted already to his lifelong search for a better, more rational method of government in the interests of the community. His decision to join the ALP was inspired by John Curtin's 1944 referendum to secure greater Commonwealth powers for postwar reconstruction—a theme that would dominate Whitlam's career.

From his entry into Parliament as a 36-year-old in 1952—just three years after the start of the 23-year Coalition ascendancy—Whitlam devoted his best 20 years to resurrecting Labor's fortunes, to restructuring its machinery and to devising its policy program. Between his February 1967 election as ALP leader and his December 1972 election as Prime Minister, Whitlam redefined some of the ends and much of the means of Australia's oldest political party.

Whitlam made the ALP almost relevant to the world of the 1970s—a considerable achievement. He gave Labor both the indispensable tonic of hope and a rationalist mindset. He is the father of the modern ALP which would experience its greatest electoral successes after his enforced departure.

Upon his election as ALP leader Whitlam confronted Labor with the possibility of its own extinction: 'Our actions in the next few years must determine whether it [Labor] continues to survive as a truly effective parliamentary force, capable of governing and actually governing . . . the alternative . . . is the collapse of the two-party system as we know it'.[4] Labor's agony during the 1950s and 1960s was more intense even than that of the Coalition in the 1980s and 1990s.

Whitlam was a born political optimist who in office grew almost inured to flirting with danger. Whitlam's own description of his approach to deadlocked issues was acute: 'When you are faced with an impasse, you've got to crash through or you've got to crash'. It is an essential insight.[5] He oscillated between the library and the rollercoaster.

Gough Whitlam saw himself as an agent of historical progress.

Equipped with a vast knowledge, he was not reluctant to depict himself on an epic stage. When the Liberal Prime Minister, Sir William McMahon, announced the 2 December 1972 election, Whitlam had a typical riposte: 'It is the anniversary of Austerlitz. Far be it from me to wish or appear to wish to assume the mantle of Napoleon; but I cannot forget that 2 December was a date on which a crushing defeat was administered to a coalition, another ramshackle, reactionary coalition'.[6]

Whitlam was a visionary leader who had waited so long for the chance to implement that vision that he tended towards impatience with all critics, friend and foe alike. Blessed with stature, intellect and philosophy, Whitlam's prime ministership was shaped and then overwhelmed by his sense of mission. The flaw, finally, was that Whitlam's vision of his program and himself was too large and too egocentric for the country to handle. Many voters concluded that 'this bastard is too big for his boots'.

There are three traits in the complex Whitlam personality which, influential in his career, proved decisive in the 1975 crisis. They were his resort to confrontation as a technique to secure his dominance; his reluctance to compromise his long-cherished objectives; and his inability to master 'face-to-face' dialogue, which meant that he was an innocent in the most ancient of political arts—personal persuasion, negotiation and manipulation.

Each trait contributed to the greatest blunder of Whitlam's career—his misjudgement of Sir John Kerr as a man. It was this misjudgement which led directly to Whitlam's dismissal by Kerr. The 1975 crisis was a triangular struggle of will, persuasion and judgement. Whitlam, facing the impasse of his career, acted on his purest instincts.

The first was to confront—to crash through or crash. It was the rule by which Whitlam had lived and prospered. Whitlam had turned brinkmanship into a refined technique. As a true leader, he operated on his own terms, not those of others.

The technique was first applied in Whitlam's great pre-1972 struggle to reform the ALP to allow representation of the parliamentary leadership at Federal Executive and Federal Conference. It is an illustration of Whitlam's fatalism. In 1966, as deputy leader, he was almost expelled from the party over the fused issues of State Aid and the authority of the parliamentary party. Defying the attempt by the Federal Executive to lay down an anti-State Aid stance to the parliamentary wing, Whitlam declared that 'this extremist group breaches the party's policy; it humiliates the party's parliamentarians; . . . it will and must be repudiated'. Whereupon he soon branded the executive 'the twelve witless men'. An authorisation from ALP leader, Arthur

Calwell, to have Whitlam expelled from the ALP came to the very brink of success.

Whitlam put his political life on the line because he felt the provocation was so great and the issues so fundamental. The incident, which almost terminated Whitlam's leadership before it was launched, invites comparison with the 1975 crisis that terminated his prime ministership. Whitlam took a stand not sure that he could prevail but prepared to accept the dangers. In both cases he increased the stakes involved in order to intimidate his opponents. He was prepared to *stake all and lose*—thereby maximising the result of a victory.[7]

In fact, Whitlam repeated the tactic in 1968, two years later. Faced with a Federal Executive refusal to seat a Tasmanian delegate, Brian Harradine, a move which Whitlam interpreted as designed to thwart his campaign to reform the Victorian party, Whitlam pulled the plug. He resigned as leader, attacked the Federal Executive and stood for re-election seeking a mandate to intervene and reform the left wing-dominated Victorian executive. Dr Jim Cairns contested the leadership on the platform: 'Whose party is this—ours or his?'. Whitlam won, just, 38–32, a smaller margin than expected. It was another two years before federal intervention occurred in Victoria.

But Whitlam operated on the premise that the Cairns question had been answered—it was Whitlam's party. He had no doubt how that authority had been established—by risking all to achieve victory.

As Prime Minister, Whitlam had even greater leverage. He blackmailed the caucus into submission by putting his leadership on the line. In the process Whitlam helped to institutionalise a climate of internal confrontation. He dismissed several senior ministers after a contest of wills and he forced the resignation of the Speaker of the House of Representatives on the floor itself. He was not prepared to accept the limits imposed upon his supreme objectives by the party, the cabinet or, finally, the Governor-General's interpretation of the Constitution. When the gravest threat materialised—a strike by the Fraser-led opposition to destroy his government—Whitlam's response was a massive retaliation: he went into 'crash through or crash' mode with the purpose of crippling Fraser's leadership and winning a greater victory. A compromise or negotiation in this context fell outside Whitlam's psychological range. At this point he crashed fatally into the immovable nexus of the Senate and the Governor-General.

The second trait that shaped Whitlam's response to the crisis was his refusal to compromise on his government's objectives. Whitlam in fact saw these objectives as quintessentially his own. Despite his hyperbole it is probably true that the program he put before the people in the 1972 campaign was the most comprehensive—though far from the most viable—that had been offered to that point. The 1972 policy speech was based upon Whitlam's reform of the ALP federal platform conducted at the three Federal Conferences— Adelaide in 1967, Melbourne in 1969 and Launceston in 1971. Whitlam, proud of his transformation of the platform, declared that it 'is studded with things I was the first to suggest'.[8]

Freudenberg said the best description of Whitlam's thinking was 'programmatic', by which he implied that Whitlam had a grand schema into which he slotted the individual policy parts.[9] Whitlam's mind was highly organised but inflexible; a caucus cynic once said that Gough would have been a superb organiser of the German train system. This inflexibility could be manifested as either dogmatism or determination. When Whitlam's inflexible adherence to his program was linked with his conviction that his program was the indisputably correct course for Australia, then he began to embrace a brand of dysfunctional politics. It was a condition once described by Menzies 'in which to be logical is to be right and to be right is its own justification'. Menzies' critique of this condition is that it overlooked the need for 'the common touch'—a failure which Whitlam, unlike Menzies, never addressed.[10]

Whitlam's philosophy of reform was that 'once a compromise was made, once the spirit and pace of reform slackened, it was quite likely lost forever'.[11] This extreme view was tied to his determinist belief that the electoral standing of his government was directly proportional to the pace at which his program was being implemented. Whitlam said that Labor's re-election in 1974 occurred only because so much of his program had been implemented so swiftly.[12] There was truth in this claim. But it was also true that the voters were bewildered and frightened by the pace of change, much of which was unexplained and the subject of effective opposition propaganda.

The nexus between Whitlam and his program was unbreakable. He would not retreat, compromise or negotiate on his life's work. In a sense he was apolitical; his real purpose was to leave behind a society demonstrably different from that which he had inherited.[13] When this life's work was threatened at midpoint by Fraser, Whitlam's inflexibility reached its zenith. He would never negotiate. Whitlam quoted Winston Churchill's war speeches to rally the nation; but Fraser was merely a ruthless conservative, not a Hitler.

The third element that Whitlam brought to both the 1975 crisis and the nature of his government was an inadequate management of personal relationships, the lubricant without which the engine will stall.

Whitlam's mind was an encyclopaedia of dates, names, facts,

quotations, arcane references and trivia, all part of what he once called his authoritative knowledge of history from the time of King David to the present.[14] Yet the quest for knowledge is not risk-free; the downside for Whitlam was that he mastered the Bourbons but rarely understood his own colleagues.

The essential element in the rise of Gough Whitlam is that it was achieved on merit. Whitlam won party support because of his performance, not because he assembled votes. Never a numbers man or backroom negotiator, Whitlam was inept at deal-making. His inclination was to productivity at his desk, not the social round or comraderie at the bar. The risk in this disposition was that Whitlam was too uninterested in the opinions of his colleagues and, eventually, the opinion of the people. He was a solo operator, working with a tight staff, who referred to him only as their 'Leader', an implicit acceptance of his remarkable status.

Whitlam alienated a majority of the senior ministers with whom he worked—right and left, young and old, old friend or old enemy. The list includes Jim Cairns, Frank Crean, Rex Connor, Clyde Cameron, Kim Beazley, John Wheeldon, Moss Cass, Ken Wriedt, Lionel Bowen and Rex Patterson. Some were difficult individuals. But the list transcends politics and enters the realm of the personal. Whitlam lacked introspection in his handling of colleagues—a condition induced by his narcissistic tendency to discount the value of their contribution to his political vision.[15]

Whitlam rarely applied himself to people with the application that he brought to policy. The man of such fluency and sway with language grew uneasy in direct and intimate dialogue. His private secretary, John Mant, said: 'Gough was a magnificent parliamentarian but he had difficulty engaging in a dialogue with people as equals'.[16] Whitlam tended to speak at people, not to them; colleagues tended to have an audience with Gough, not a discussion. His magnificent self-effacing humour sometimes only reinforced the gap: 'I don't care how many *prima donnas* there are, as long as I'm the *prima donna assoluta*'.

Whitlam was deficient in management skills, a function of both his lack of interest in people and his conception of politics as a series of grand decisions. He was weak on implementation, administration and follow-through. Whitlam's notion of reform was limited to the high ground of executive and legislative decision-making. Yet this decision-making was merely the start of a complicated process in which his ministers had to 'make the reform work' by administration, consultation and juggling competing interests, an activity Whitlam often found tedious. Above all, Whitlam failed to instil within his team a sense of coherent purpose and joint participation. They were, rather, satellites around his sun.

It is no surprise that such a leader was guilty of severe personal misjudgements: putting Cairns into the Treasury; trusting Connor over the loans affairs; accepting campaign funds from Iraq; allowing Lance Barnard to retire, precipitating the Bass by-election; denying Hayden the Treasury for so long; and basing his political future in the 1975 crisis upon John Kerr.

Kerr was Whitlam's last and greatest blunder in personnel management.

Whitlam and the constitutional conundrum

The 1975 crisis was the most spectacular struggle in the long war between Labor and the Constitution. The crisis was not just about Whitlam's fight to survive. Whitlam used the crisis to try to change the Constitution to accord with the ALP's version of Australian democracy. It became, in effect, an extension of his reform program. This is the key in understanding Whitlam's approach to the 1975 crisis and its resolution.

Gough Whitlam's entire career had been devoted to bringing Labor and the Constitution into harmony. Whitlam grasped from the 1950s that unless this was achieved then Labor's social democratic goals were doomed. It was this lifetime struggle that drove Whitlam during the 1975 crisis that culminated in his dismissal on 11 November—an event that is merely the most sensational in the long battle by the ALP since Federation to combat the constitutional and institutional limits on Labor's reformism. The conflict between Labor and the Constitution was as old as the Commonwealth of Australia; the 1975 crisis was remarkable only for its form and intensity.

From the start of his career Whitlam perceived the great institutional obstacle which had crippled Labor—that the Constitution, the Federation and the Parliament had been established from 1 January 1901 by non-Labor politicians and approved by the people by referendum before the emergence of the ALP as a dominant voice in national politics.

This meant that the organs of Australian democracy were cast in the non-Labor political values of the late nineteenth century before the rise of class politics, popular sovereignty, and central economic and social planning, all of which were the essence of twentieth century Labor ideology. From 1901 onwards Labor was handicapped by the conservative nature of the Constitution and the parliamentary balance it ordained which gave the Senate virtually equal power with the House of Representatives. If the ALP had succeeded in delaying the Federation then a constitution written some years later would have given more weight to Labor objectives.

The Constitution, in effect, posed two great obstacles to the ALP. Whitlam's career leading to 11 November can be interpreted as a sustained effort to circumvent or to combat these obstacles. The first lay in the limits imposed by the Constitution, as interpreted by the High Court, on the Commonwealth Government's legislative power. The Constitution created not just a Commonwealth; it created powerful States dedicated to checking the Commonwealth's powers—the precise powers basic to Labor's national reform purposes. Over time the Court expanded the interpretation of the Commonwealth's power at the expense of the States—but it also ruled as unconstitutional the Labor Party's socialist objective of the nationalisation of industry. This made the delivery of Labor's central platform provision a political impossibility. The Court in its interpretation of section 92 favoured the operation of private enterprise across State lines, thereby backing the non-Labor view of Australia's future and rejecting Labor's instinct for socialism.

The second obstacle for Labor originated in the method by which the Constitution gave effect to Australian democracy, notably the power of the Senate in relation to the House of Representatives. The Senate became one of the most powerful Upper Houses in the English-speaking world, able to check the people's will expressed by a popular vote in the House of Representatives. The Senate, elected by the people but with equal representation between States, was destined to collide with a reformist ALP Government. Only Labor's dismal record at federal elections and a 'winner-take-all' Senate voting system before 1949 had delayed the onset of such a battle.

It is a matter of public record that the Whitlam Government was successful in surmounting the first obstacle but fell at the second. Neither the High Court nor the Constitution posed any inhibition to the Whitlam Government's 1972–75 legislative program—despite fears during the previous 20 years that the Constitution would not permit Labor to implement its policies. Whitlam's experience in this respect was different from that of his ALP prime ministerial predecessor, Ben Chifley.

It was the constitutionally ordained balance between the Senate and the House of Representatives which proved fatal for Whitlam. The Whitlam legislative program was under repeated assault from the Senate, an attack which began on Labor's legislation but then shifted decisively via the Supply bills to the government's very existence and became the means, eventually, by which the government was sunk.

The issue of 'Labor versus the Constitution' on legislative powers was put and resolved during the Chifley era—the non-Labor side, the High Court and the Constitution won. The ultimate test was the Court's rejection of Chifley's bank nationalisation, the purest attempt by Labor to implement socialism.[17]

Labor's inability to fashion a successful program between Chifley's defeat and Whitlam's arrival resulted from its failure to address the policy consequences arising from the High Court's decisions. When ALP leader Arthur Calwell promised not to raise nationalisation in the 1961 campaign Whitlam was disgusted. Either Labor believed in its platform or it did not; the ALP was socialist or it was not. If the policy was self-defeating then it should be replaced.

The solution Whitlam eventually devised was not to change the Constitution but to change Labor policy; to find a new ALP reform model.[18] His answer was to revive Labor reformism on a workable basis both through creating public corporations to rival private corporations and through section 96 which allowed the Federal Government to provide grants to the States 'on such terms and conditions as the Parliament thinks fit'.[19]

Whitlam pledged to expand the role of the national government to promote equality of opportunity—the philosophical rock upon which he based his 1972 program. It was the core of his democratic socialism. He used equality of opportunity, first, to replace the ALP's doctrinal but moribund attachment to socialism through nationalisation and, second, as the basis to win an election. Whitlam exploited the flaw in non-Labor politics: it was too static, despite Sir Robert Menzies' occasional flourishes and John Gorton's bungled attempt at modernisation.

Whitlam recognised that the needs of urban Australia were unattended. He devised a more moderate and workable model for the ALP which accommodated the conservative structure of the Constitution. It was based on a planning and financial role for the national government on the national issues that shaped people's lives. Accordingly, the Whitlam Labor Party promised a universal health insurance scheme; a new commission to fund schools on the basis of need; a new urban affairs ministry; grants for sewerage extension, public transport and regional development; full federal responsibility for tertiary education; use of federal power to establish Aboriginal land rights; a hospitals commission; and a series of new social welfare pledges.

The shift that Whitlam engineered in social policy was paralleled by a similar shift in Labor's attitude towards federalism. In the period after World War I, Labor changed its platform to support a unified rather than a federal Australia; it was pledged to abolish federalism. The abolition of the Senate became an official objective.[20] This stance was incompatible with the federal nature of the Constitution; it defied the original compact between the colonies which had made the Commonwealth achievable; its assumption that Australia could be reconstituted as a nation without a federal compact was certainly wrong.

Whitlam secured the removal of the unification position at the 1971 conference and its replacement with a policy to 'balance the functions and finances of the Commonwealth, State and local governments to ensure adequate services and development of resources'. His agenda still required changes in federalism—a leadership role for the Commonwealth Government and a greater role for local government, a mixture certain to antagonise the States.

Whitlam's historic role, therefore, was to moderate and modernise the platform of the ALP by reconciling it with the Constitution. Yet the consequence was to make his party more threatening to the non-Labor side and to the States. Whitlam had buried the objectives of nationalisation and unification which were incompatible with the Constitution, unacceptable to the people and unachievable for Australia. (But it was not until after the Whitlam era, at the 1979 conference, that abolition of the Senate was finally dropped from the platform.)

At this point there were two responses from the Liberal and Country Parties—a reluctance to believe that Labor had changed its core values, and a determination to counter the challenge from the ALP to their ascendancy. Whitlam's pragmatism had made him electable; but his principles threatened the Menzian order which, while crumbling, was still largely intact. After the 1972 election the non-Labor parties and the States feared a pragmatic ALP Government, liberated from the grip of its doctrinaire positions, but still committed to its program through a greater Commonwealth role.

It was possible for Whitlam to accommodate his program to the Constitution; but he could not adjust the program to bypass the Parliament. The problem confronting Whitlam would lie in the instrument through which he had to realise his reforms—the Federal Parliament, which consisted of a Senate and a House of Representatives, and a Governor-General who acted as the Queen's representative. Whitlam believed in Parliament with a passion; it was the forum of his dominance. But Whitlam's vision of the Parliament ended at Kings Hall: he saw the Parliament only in terms of the House of Representatives; his inability to think beyond Kings Hall proved fatal on 11 November 1975.

Graham Freudenberg declared:

> Television, radio, the press, party meetings, conferences, seminars, public meetings were all important, but Parliament remained the supreme forum . . . Menzies had a greater presence over the House; Ward was more feared; McEwen commanded greater authority; Allan Fraser could be a better debater; Kim Beazley could be more eloquent; but in his recognition of Parliament's teaching and informing role, and in his sustained use of Parliament for the expression of a cause, Whitlam can well lay claim to the title of the supreme parliamentarian of his time.[21]

The conundrum of Whitlam's career is that he strove to tie Labor reformism to the chariot wheels of the Parliament yet the Parliament proved a less than satisfactory vehicle with which to secure reforms during the 1972–75 period.

Gough Whitlam on 11 November 1975 became the greatest casualty of the Parliament since Federation. He fell on the issue of the Senate's powers as defined in the Constitution and enforced in this instance by the power of the Governor-General. It was the most dramatic moment in the ongoing battle between Labor and the Constitution. The battle had been resolved decisively against Labor's socialism policy and for private enterprise during the Chifley era. But in the Whitlam era another battle was fought—between Whitlam's view of the supremacy of the House of Representatives and the Coalition's insistence upon the equal powers of the Senate. Whitlam brought all his passion to this contest. It was the great test on the central theme of his career. Labor lost when the Governor-General, backed by the Chief Justice of the High Court, interpreted the Constitution in favour of the Coalition's position and against Labor's.

Whitlam and Australian democracy

The feature of the December 1972 election was not that Whitlam defeated McMahon; that had been widely predicted. It was, rather, the relatively narrow margin. The Whitlam Government had a nine seat majority and, since there was no Senate election at this time, it inherited an Upper House with a decisive non-Labor majority. A more cautious leader than Whitlam would have decided that his reform agenda had to be tempered by the need for further electoral consolidation at subsequent polls. But such temporising was foreign to Whitlam's nature. He had waited, planned, prepared for too long; so he rushed towards his reforms.

Whitlam had no interest in the mere occupation of office. He was a idealist who thought in straight lines and precise timetables. From the first hours after his election win he thought only about the implementation of his program—and he did not slacken for the next three years. Whitlam saw his success as a turning point, conceivably *the* turning point, in Australia's history.[22]

From the start Whitlam displayed a predilection for political, administrative and constitutional innovation—a theme which would characterise his administration and which was inseparable from its doom. Labor's inaugural performance was a two man government which saw Whitlam and his deputy, Lance Barnard, sworn to 13 and 14 portfolios respectively. Whitlam later told Parliament that this 'was the smallest ministry with jurisdiction over Australia since the Duke of Wellington formed a ministry with two other Ministers 138 years previously'. He joked privately that its defect was having one minister too many.

The duumvirate, as it was called, was created for one purpose—as an instrument by which Whitlam could dramatically chart Australia's new course. Whitlam's theatrical sense was engaged. This was not just a transfer of power; it was a watershed. Yet it was the institutional innovation and reform freneticism of the duumvirate that told Labor's opponents that Whitlam's judgement would fall victim to his vision.

The duumvirate was the first expression of Whitlam's theory of the mandate—a theory that would dominate his administration. The Governor-General, Sir Paul Hasluck, commissioned the duumvirate on Tuesday 5 December 1972 on advice from Whitlam that the people's will, as expressed in his election victory, was a command to immediate action. The duumvirate was 'the apotheosis of the mandate'.[23]

The Whitlam Government rose and fell amid the breaking of political precedent; the rationale in each case was the doctrine of the mandate. The 14 day duumvirate in 1972, like the 26 day constitutional crisis in 1975, was sustained from Whitlam's perspective by the doctrine of the mandate which he understood as the essential expression of a parliamentary democracy.

The decisions of the duumvirate symbolised the creation of Whitlam's new order. They involved the termination of the national service call-up system, under which conscripts had been sent previously to fight in Vietnam, and the release of seven men who had been gaoled for 18 months under the National Service Act. Others included the reopening of the equal pay case before the Arbitration Commission, the appointment of a woman, Ms Elizabeth Evatt, to the Commission, the removal of the sales tax on the contraceptive pill, and major new grants for the arts. The foreign policy changes were dramatic—the opening of talks in Paris to establish diplomatic relations with China, the exclusion from Australia of racially selected sporting teams, and a change in Australia's voting at the United Nations to take a firm pro-sanctions line against the minority white regimes in South Africa and Rhodesia. In three social areas far-reaching moves were made—the establishment of an interim committee of the Australian Schools Commission to begin granting funds to private schools on a 'needs' basis, the first moves towards a system of Aboriginal land rights, and the initial moves to establish a growth centre at Albury–Wodonga.[24]

The two man government captured the public's imagination. But it created a false impression about the ease with which government could bring lasting change.

Whitlam saw a link between himself and Sir Robert Menzies—as leaders who cast long shadows. Yet they were divided by emotion. Menzies believed in the settlement of time, the serenity of power, of measured action, of waiting for opportunity to present itself and ignoring your opponents until their vulnerability invited a strike. Whitlam by contrast was consumed by his grand vision and by attention to trivial details. Unable or unwilling to restrain his predilections, he indulged too often his passion for reform at the expense of community confusion.

While the political trigger for the duumvirate was the election victory, its moral basis was Whitlam's mandate. Over the next three years he would use the mandate to empower his government, to impose discipline upon the ALP caucus, to confront the Senate, to challenge the Opposition and, ultimately, to intimidate the Governor-General.

Whitlam later declared: 'The mandate of 1972 was the most positive and precise ever sought and ever received by an elected government in Australian history. The program was the most comprehensive, its promulgation and popularisation the most intense and extensive in Australian political history'.[25]

The problem for Whitlam was that his mandate theory based in the House of Representatives was defective. It was not fully sustained by the Constitution. The mandate was a political device which arose from *Labor's* interpretation of the Constitution and democracy, an interpretation not universally shared.

The 1975 crisis sprang from a deepseated contradiction in Australia's Constitution. The founding fathers established the Commonwealth of Australia as a unique system of government. They drew upon two great ideas—responsible government from Westminster and federalism from the United States—and fused these two ideas into a new Constitution. The problem was that the two ideas were in conflict, a fact which the founders realised but could not resolve. They left the resolution to history, and 75 years later Whitlam and Malcolm Fraser were to struggle with this inherited contradiction.

Responsible government was well understood by the founding fathers and was the system of government that applied in the Australian colonies. Under responsible government the leader who enjoyed the confidence of the Lower House was commissioned by the Crown or the Crown's representative to form a government. This was the system that led directly to Whitlam's mandate theory.

At Westminster the notion of responsible government reached its zenith following the great conflict from 1909 to 1911 when the Lords denied Supply to the Commons. The resolution of this conflict established the ascendancy of the Commons over the Lords. This triumph for responsible government—thereby ensuring that the leader who enjoyed the confidence of the Lower House would prevail against a hostile Upper House—was repeatedly raised by Whitlam to justify his own stance during the 1975 crisis. The essence of responsibility under the Westminster system is that the government is responsible only to the Lower House—the popularly elected house—and not to the Upper House. It is the Lower House that makes and breaks governments. The founding fathers sought to enshrine this practice in the Constitution, and Quick and Garran in their annotation on the Constitution declare: 'for better or for worse, the system of Responsible Government as known to the British Constitution has been practically embedded in the Federal Constitution . . .'[26]

However, the story did not end there. If it had, then Whitlam would have prevailed in 1975.

The price for persuading the six colonies to federate in a Commonwealth—thereby founding a nation upon a continent in defiance of distance, geography and regionalism—was the creation of a Senate to represent the States and protect their interests against the Commonwealth. The Senate made the Commonwealth achievable; without the Senate there would have been no agreement to surrender power to a new central authority, a Federal Parliament. The Senate, above all, symbolises the federal nature of the Constitution. The founding fathers had looked to the United States where they found a model of democracy and federalism and whose Senate provided equal representation on a State basis.[27] Australia's founders used the Senate to lock the former colonies into the new Commonwealth.

Quick and Garran described Australia's Senate as:

> . . . not merely a second chamber of revision and review representing the sober second thought of the nation . . . it is that, but something more than that. It is the chamber in which the States, considered as

separate entities, and corporate parts of the Commonwealth, are represented. They are so represented for the purpose of enabling them to maintain and protect their constitutional rights against attempted invasion.[28]

The Senate was designed with virtually equal powers with the House of Representatives, including the power to reject Appropriation bills. This decision, taken at the 1891 Convention, endured because 'the issue simply came to this: either the Senate be given power to reject any bill, or the Federation process would end'.[29]

The founding fathers, or at least some of them, knew they had implanted a contradiction at the heart of the Constitution. How could responsible government co-exist with federalism? The power over Appropriation meant that, if it had the will, the Senate could make the government responsible to it. How could the government be made and unmade in the Lower House if the Upper House could vote against Supply? This dilemma exercised the minds of the Convention delegates and, reviewing the debates, Quick and Garran observed: 'In the end it is predicted that either Responsible Government will kill the Federation and change it into a unified State or the Federation will kill Responsible Government and substitute a new form of Executive more compatible with the Federal theory'.[30]

In 1975 Whitlam acted as killing agent on behalf of Responsible Government.

Britain enjoyed responsible government but it was not a federation. The United States was a federation but it did not embrace responsible government, relying instead upon a separation of legislature and executive. But Australia had attempted a synthesis. An overwhelming majority of the founding fathers saw the Senate as a States House and this is the reason it was given such power over money bills. Only a minority had the insight to grasp that this was wrong, an insight expressed by Alfred Deakin: 'The contest will not be, never has been and cannot be between States and States . . . It is certain that once this Constitution is framed it will be followed by the creation of two great national parties'.[31]

Whitlam's party, the ALP, took its stand on responsible government as the correct interpretation of the Constitution. When Whitlam enunciated the mandate theory after his 1972 election victory he had the Westminster principles, 'embedded' in the Constitution, to sustain his stance. In the 1975 crisis Whitlam emerged in Australian history as the great champion of responsible government. But when his opponents struck they had an equal constitutional weight behind them; they attacked as a party—the other great party as predicted by Deakin—

using the Senate's power over Supply which owed its very existence to the federal compact. The Coalition, employing the Senate's powers, sought to make the government responsible to it. So it happened in 1975 that the timebomb implanted in the Constitution from its inception was detonated.

Whitlam and the people

Politics does not run on theory. Such constitutional contradictions are dormant until awakened and such political theories are forgotten until there is opportunity to resuscitate them. It was the ineptitude of the Whitlam Government that rendered it electorally vulnerable to a hostile Senate. Whitlam's reform ambitions were not matched by popular support. When his opponents smelt his political blood they gathered for the kill. Whitlam's ability as a politician could not sustain his aspirations as a statesman. It is appropriate to review the factors that turned the people against him, since this turning was the vital ingredient that made the crisis possible.

Whitlam's government suffered from three difficulties, the combined impact of which it could not surmount.

First, its economic policy was inappropriate for the times—a detailed program of public sector expansion at the onset of the international stagflation of the 1970s. The Whitlam program was a product of the age of postwar Keynesianism, a freakish period that combined economic growth, low unemployment and price stability. Whitlam's complacent belief was that permanent economic growth would finance his program by delivering greater revenues through the effortless transference of taxpayers into higher tax brackets.

Yet the climate in which Whitlam tried to implement that program was transformed after the first OPEC oil shock in mid-1973 sent oil prices to record levels and inaugurated a phase of international inflation and severe domestic adjustment. This was a contingency which Whitlam had never envisaged and for which he had never planned. His tragedy was that the ALP did not win the 1969 election and so enjoy a relatively benign economic climate for its first term.

The inflation of the early 1970s had an historic significance—it destroyed the postwar 'golden age' enjoyed by social democratic and Western liberal governments in which economic growth underwrote a massive expansion of welfare and social initiatives. The unravelling came earlier in the United States—when President Lyndon Johnson blundered into believing that he could both have his Great Society and prosecute the Vietnam War. In Australia Whitlam believed that he could enjoy sustained economic growth and implement his own social utopia.

His experience of office was dominated by his adjustment to the fact that the central policy assumption of his political career was no longer operative.

These punishing circumstances would have demanded a substantial rethink from any government. That Labor had so many big spending programs only accentuated the pain. The economic policy changes that the government attempted in 1974 and 1975 then produced deep divisions within the cabinet and the caucus.

The Whitlam 'It's Time' slogan of 1972 depicted a vote for Labor as being fashionable. But, it was quite the wrong time for Whitlamism and an experiment in centralised social reform. Inflation went beyond 16 per cent during 1974–75 and unemployment reached just under 5 per cent in 1975, figures which disguised the fact that the belated efforts by Labor to adjust were quite impressive.[32]

The second area of difficulty lay in the faulty and inadequate policy, political and personal judgements made by senior ministers—Jim Cairns, Rex Connor, Clyde Cameron, Frank Crean, Lionel Murphy— and, above all, by Whitlam himself. For most of its life the government was addicted to displays of inept, indulgent or incredible behaviour in matters that were only tangential to the central direction of policy.

The first such blunder—which terminated the honeymoon of the Whitlam Government after four months—was Lionel Murphy's spectacular visit to ASIO headquarters, Melbourne, on 16 March 1973. It became a public relations disaster immortalised in the media forever as a 'raid' on ASIO. It sent the Opposition-dominated Senate into overdrive. It inaugurated the schizoid image that beset the Whitlam Government thereafter—dynamic reformism in juxtaposition with administrative and political confusion suggesting a government out of its depth.

However, the worst single blunder came late on the night of 13 December 1974 when four ministers—Whitlam, Connor, Murphy and Cairns—signed an Executive Council minute authorising the raising of a $4000 million overseas loan, an authority designed for a Pakistani 'funny money' operative, Tirath Khemlani. An accurate description of this event came from veteran journalist Alan Reid who said the four ministers 'signed, unknowingly, the death warrant of the Whitlam ALP Government'.[33]

Their decision created an atmosphere and a series of events which led to the resignations of Cairns and Connor and to Whitlam's dismissal by Sir John Kerr. It was the politics of the 'loans affair', as it became known, which, more than any other single event, undermined the legitimacy of the Whitlam Government. It revealed an incompetence that invited an execution. It is a fairly safe proposition that, without the overseas loan authorisation, Malcolm Fraser would not have sought to deny Supply in October 1975 and, therefore, the constitutional crisis would not have arisen.[34]

The 'loans affair' exposed not just a streak of bizarre amateurism which plagued the government. It revealed the defective judgement of Gough Whitlam when assessing individuals and issues. Whitlam was an adventurous leader; but adventure imposes greater demands upon judgement because it increases the stakes. The overseas loan was a misguided foray that would terminate his government. But a more spectacular misjudgement of an individual still lay ahead: Whitlam's conviction before and during the constitutional crisis that Sir John Kerr would act only on his advice—one of the worst misreadings of human nature made by a Prime Minister.

The third major difficulty confronting the Whitlam Government was the sustained campaign of Opposition harassment to which it was subjected. This campaign was comprehensive but its tactical focus was the Senate, the Coalition bridgehead. Australian politics is invariably ruthless; Labor's ineptitude invited the Coalition to marshal its numbers against the government—and the Coalition willingly obliged.

The parliamentary dynamics that shaped the course of the Whitlam Government arose from its minority position in the Senate. The 1972 election was for the House of Representatives only. The 60-strong Senate that Whitlam faced was anti-Labor and unrepresentative of the national mood that elected Whitlam. This Senate was the product of the two previous half Senate polls conducted on 25 November 1967 and 21 November 1970. These were two of the only four half Senate elections since Federation conducted without a House of Representatives election. The Senate numbers were: ALP 26, Liberal–National Parties 26, DLP 5, Independents 3. In the normal course of events the Opposition could expect to have the support of the DLP and one of the Independents, which meant that Labor was likely to be outvoted at least 32–28.

Whitlam refused to give credence to a Senate elected two and five years before. He argued along two lines: that the Senate he faced was electorally obsolete and therefore without legitimacy; and (as he believed in responsible government) that the Senate was institutionally flawed as a representative chamber since it gave equality of representation to States, not people.

But the Senate had a 'life or death' power over Whitlam's program and long before it encountered any substantive ALP legislation the Senate had made its intentions plain. The Coalition rejected Whitlam's view that the Constitution was dominated by the notion of responsible government; the Coalition would use the Senate against Whitlam and it is no surprise that, in turn, it championed the notion of the Senate as a protector of the rights of the people and the States.

The Opposition did three things in the Senate. First, it rejected the legitimacy of Whitlam's mandate, thereby denying his right to enact his program. Second, it defeated a large number of bills in the Senate, thereby demonstrating that Whitlam could not govern as he promised. Third, it blocked Supply, not to reject policy aspects of the Appropriation bills but in order to destroy the government by calling an election at the Senate's behest.

So the Senate was used to cripple the government as a prelude to inviting the voters to bury it.

The irony for Whitlam was that, despite his long preoccupation with how an ALP government would cope with the obstacles to its program provided by the Constitution, the High Court, the States and the Senate, the weight of institutional resistance did prove too great. Many of the centres of power in Australian life—business, media, finance and the States—turned decisively against his government. Labor, it should be remembered, began its rule after 23 years in opposition isolated from and largely ignorant of such power centres. Trying to govern a nation like Australia which has a written Constitution, a High Court, a Governor-General, a strong Federation, a powerful Senate and, above all, a people whose electoral disposition has been flexible but cautious, and trying to govern from the sole power base of the House of Representatives, makes for an unequal contest.

Whitlam, no doubt, felt that he had no choice. But his power base was too narrow and that of his opponents was too broad. Whitlam was an egocentric idealist—he attributed his success to the implementation of his program; in adversity he saw the further advance of that program as the key to his revival. He was, by personality and conviction, incapable of inactivity, of retreat from his program or of a flight to caution. Paul Keating once described Whitlam as a 'jungle fighter, more savage when cornered'.[35]

The Coalition cornered Whitlam by denying Supply in October 1975—and got the fright of its life. A leader under pressure is true to his instincts. Whitlam fought with tenacity—in defence of the mandate theory, the supremacy of the House of Representatives, and for responsible government. He had spent much energy as Opposition leader adjusting to the Coalition's constitutional triumph over Chifley on the issue of Labor's socialism; he would launch as Prime Minister, when threatened, a campaign to secure a constitutional triumph over the Coalition on the issue of the Representatives against the Senate.

When the Senate first challenged and then rejected his bills Whitlam responded as an orthodox constitutionalist—he resubmitted the bills, sought a double dissolution and held a Joint Sitting after the 1974 election. When in 1975 the Senate sought to repeat the process by denying Supply, Whitlam retaliated as a parliamentary radical.

His objective was not just to save his political neck and his government's life, though this was a compelling enough motive. It was—typically Whitlamesque—something greater. He sought to break the Coalition and destroy Fraser's leadership. But beyond this, his ultimate objective, by achieving a victory, was to secure forever an interpretation of the Constitution in favour of Labor, the House of Representatives and responsible government. Whitlam sought to remake the Constitution in Labor's image.

2
Fraser

> *I generally believe that if a Government is elected to power in the lower House and has the numbers and can maintain the numbers in the lower House it is entitled to expect that it will govern for the three year term unless quite extraordinary events intervene.*
>
> Malcolm Fraser, 21 March 1975

MALCOLM FRASER HAD a profound belief in the superiority of the Liberal Party as Australia's governing party. This was the attitude that Labor branded, initially with frustration, later with ridicule, as the 'born to rule' mentality. This outlook was given many labels during the three decades from the early 1950s in which the Liberals saw themselves as the natural party of government. But it was real and it was pervasive. The 1975 political and constitutional crisis can be grasped only in the context of the cultural confidence that the Menzian age had instilled within the Liberal and Country Parties, the non-Labor coalition.

Malcolm Fraser was a product of his era, typified by sustained Liberal electoral success, profound suspicion of the Labor Party as a governing unit, and support for middle ground cautious policies rather than for radical change as the Australian 'way'.

When Fraser, then a senior minister, and his colleagues lost the 1972 federal election, they found the Opposition benches an unfamiliar place. This defeat came only after nine successive federal election victories starting with the triumph of the founder of the Liberal Party, R G Menzies, in 1949. Fraser entered Parliament at the 1955 election and had participated in six of these victories.

Malcolm Fraser had a visceral distrust of the ALP. He did not believe that Labor could govern for long or with success. Like other senior Coalition figures Fraser was hostile towards Labor's proposals for institutional, electoral and constitutional reforms that would alter the established polity and rules of Australian politics. This typified non-Labor thinking after the 1972 election defeat. Then an important development occurred.

As the Whitlam Government advanced it revealed a split personality. Its idealistic reforms were undermined by a penchant for inept administration and ministerial upheavals—and this reinforced the prejudices of the Coalition. Senior coalitionists decided that Labor's occupation of the Treasury benches was an aberration; an eddy in the stream of history. They conveniently forgot their own failures in office in the 1966–72 period after Menzies' retirement.

At the time of Whitlam's victory nobody within the Coalition predicted the intensity of the crisis that would develop in 1975. That situation was driven by forces that emerged and then grew over the three years of the Whitlam Government. The principal elements on the non-Labor side that contributed to the crisis were the election of Malcolm Fraser, a politician of unusual will and genuine authority, to the Liberal leadership; the acceptance as an article of faith within the Coalition that the Whitlam experiment had failed the nation and should be terminated; the alienation of the States, particularly the non-Labor Premiers, from Whitlam, and their participation in Labor's liquidation; and above all, the exploitation by the Coalition of the Senate's rising influence to force Whitlam to the people. The Coalition in the Senate operated on the method outlined by the ALP veteran, Pat Kennelly: 'if you've got the numbers, then you use them'.

The Whitlam Government singularly failed to exploit the weakened condition of the non-Labor side after its December 1972 defeat. The Liberals elected to the leadership an affable plodder, Billy Snedden, inferior to Whitlam in intellect, style and skill. Snedden never enjoyed the respect of his own side, which was plagued by feuds and rivalry. The Country Party under the leadership of Doug Anthony declined to form a Coalition in opposition until 1974 and in the interim relations between the parties deteriorated. Federal President R J Southey was prompted to warn the party to bury the 'personal ambitions and feuds' which, since Harold Holt's death, had been 'deadly and destructive'.

It was a climate ripe for Labor Government mischief-making which, building upon the McMahon legacy, could entrench perceptions of a discredited Opposition. But the Whitlam Government, unlike those of Hawke and Keating in the 1980s and 1990s, proved unable to master the tactics of divide and rule. It possessed neither the drive nor the judgement to demoralise its weakened opponents.

The Fraser factor

In March 1975 Malcolm Fraser staged a successful party room challenge against Snedden, an event that inaugurated the most successful leadership for the Liberals after Menzies. Fraser became a leader of complexity, turbulence and cunning. A product of the Liberal Party, influenced by the Menzian leadership ethic, a professional politician in every sense, possessed of a patrician superiority but burdened by an inability to relate to his fellow man, Fraser, like Whitlam, had a sense of manifest destiny. The chemistry of two such leaders confronting each other was potentially explosive from the start. Unsurprisingly, Fraser saw his destiny as being the restoration of the nation's political fabric and the revival of its economy after the excess of Whitlamism.

The 1975 crisis cannot be understood without an appreciation of the personality and beliefs of Malcolm Fraser. Fraser came from a political family, his grandfather, Simon Fraser, a tough and flamboyant conservative, being a member of the original Commonwealth Parliament. Malcolm spent his first decade on his father's isolated property, periodically afflicted by flood and drought, his temperament shaped by its loneliness, freedom, and conflict with nature.[1] His father, Neville, a World War I veteran with excellent social connections, instilled the values of discipline and self-reliance.

Fraser went to Tudor House near Moss Vale as a young boarder, then to Melbourne Grammar, experiences that confirmed his character as self-sufficient, introspective and determined.[2] But for Fraser, Oxford was the turning point. He absorbed the spiritual values of the British tradition and the lessons of the age. Fraser was profoundly influenced by that generation of intellectuals that had fought in World War II and now preached two ideas—that weakness and self-indulgence had betrayed Britain during the appeasement of the 1930s and that socialism would ruin Britain's postwar opportunity.[3] He returned as a dour dreamer and an Australian nationalist. His career options were limited—the family farm or politics. Fraser's ambition dictated his course.

Politics had flickered across his life. His father had been a friend of Lord Casey. Field Marshal Slim on a visit ruminated that the quest for power had provided the drive for his own career.[4] Oxford had made Malcolm a 'hard options man' but his idealism was fired by youth. He joined the Liberal Party not the Country Party because he thought in national terms; besides, he was aiming for the top. At 25 he became the youngest MP and the first of the postwar generation in the House.

Fraser was isolated in Parliament by youth, shyness and a rich boy label; but he respected his elders, the wartime generation, and he learned.

Fraser's philosophy of government was shaped by his sense of public duty; by his conviction, developed during the post–World War II Keynesian age, that strong governments could steer the direction and secure the fate of their nations; and that the task of leaders was to lead. His early career was undistinguished—eleven years on the backbench. He was neither an intellectual nor an orator and had no inclination to flatter. But his ministerial performance, when the opportunity arrived, was impressive in the three portfolios he held before the 1972 defeat—Army, Education and Science (twice), and Defence.

Fraser was a demanding minister and a prodigious worker, prepared to ring a senior public service adviser at 2 am with demands and then at 6 am for the results.[5] He virtually threatened US Defense Secretary, Mel Laird, when visiting America to renegotiate the F-111 aircraft contract, prompting a US general to call him 'a fierce adversary, a real fighter . . . we certainly felt that we had been taken to the cleaners'.[6] Fraser asked Sir Arthur Tange to become Secretary of the Defence Department partly because he wanted somebody sufficiently experienced and tough to stand up to him. Fraser was an able and aggressive workaholic, prone to pushing issues to a crisis in order to prevail. Tange wrote to Fraser complaining of 'the pressures that you're imposing and the number of crises that are being created . . . to me, entirely unnecessarily'.[7] It was an omen: in a few years Fraser would detonate a crisis on a grand scale.

Fraser, who had inherited a magnificent property, Nareen, which made him very rich, was neither a self-made man nor a battler. The traits that marked him were political toughness, policy grasp and relentless commitment. He was the opponent of the progressive wing of the party in the early 1970s which stereotyped him as a right-wing hardliner. Fraser was a student of politics with a keen grasp of Labor's vulnerability and a penetrating philosophy of leadership.

Before he became leader Fraser repudiated sceptics within the Coalition who feared a return to power during the 1974–75 economic difficulties: 'I do not believe that men and women are governed by inexorable events beyond control. When political leaders say the present situation cannot be helped, it is part of a world situation, they are expressing the futility of their own leadership when, if they were men of real stature, they would be saying "we can overcome"'.[8]

Fraser had no sympathy for Whitlam. He was unyielding in his belief that Labor's economic tribulations reflected an incompetent government and not the rise of difficulties in the international economy which would plague all governments. He saw himself as the leader who could 'overcome' the challenges at which Labor stumbled.

Despite his privileged background Fraser became an apostle of hardship and national peril. Just four years before the 1975 crisis his apocalyptic view of the challenge that faced contemporary politicians was put in stark terms in his Alfred Deakin lecture.

> Through history nations are confronted by a series of challenges and whether they survive or whether they fall to the wayside depends upon the manner and character of their response . . . It involves a conclusion about the past that life has not been easy for people or for nations, and an assumption for the future that the condition will not alter. There is within me some part of the metaphysic and thus I would add that life is not meant to be easy . . . We need a rugged society, but our new generations have seen only affluence. If a man has not known adversity, if in his lifetime his country has not been subject to attack, it is harder for him to understand that there are some things for which we must always struggle. Thus people or leaders can be trapped to take the easy path. This is the high road to national disaster.[9]

Evidence of Fraser's philosophy is replete. In his early statements on Vietnam he said that America, in order to highlight its will, had to be prepared 'to use nuclear weapons should this prove to be necessary'. Fraser was a strong advocate to the Menzies Government of selective national service, including liability for service overseas.[10] His thesis of national sacrifice and challenge was readymade for Australia's security predicament.

It is no surprise that Fraser saw himself as the leader who could 'overcome' and master the challenge that he defined. His interpretation of the rugged society led him to an irresistible conclusion—that neither Snedden nor Whitlam possessed the mettle for the task. Such sentiments lay at the heart of the great contradiction within Fraser—the struggle between order and violence.

As a conservative Fraser was committed to tradition, stability and progress. But during his ascent in the Liberal Party, Fraser over an eight year period had helped to 'kingmake' one leader, and had resorted to the political assassination of two leaders including one whom he had initially backed for the job. Fraser displayed an instinctive grasp of the party's power rituals—the successor staked his claim by recourse to the sword.

It was after the drowning of Harold Holt in December 1967 that Fraser combined with two other relatively junior colleagues to mastermind John Gorton's elevation to the prime ministership which, in turn, led to his own rapid progress. Yet within three years Fraser broke with

Gorton and then destroyed him in a spectacular application of political willpower.

The preliminary battle came when Fraser resisted Gorton's instruction to obtain an order authorising a call-out of troops in the event of the need to quell disturbances on the Gazelle Peninsula in New Britain. Fraser refused; he asked Gorton for a cabinet meeting on the issue. Fraser then contacted the Governor-General, Sir Paul Hasluck—in an effort to prevent Gorton's obtaining Hasluck's signature on the order. He told Hasluck he was opposed and wanted a cabinet meeting. Hasluck, aware that the cabinet was divided, refused Gorton's request for him to sign the order. Fraser said later that, in this situation, the Governor-General was 'a last resort protector of propriety'. The moral was that Fraser had an acute grasp of the relationship between the Governor-General and the executive and was prepared to use this against his own Prime Minister.[11]

The crunch came in March 1971 when Fraser decided to resign as Defence Minister after concluding that Gorton had allowed a damaging story to be published against him. The night before his resignation Fraser misled Gorton over his intentions. Gorton's recollection is that Fraser, whose resignation speech was already written, reassured his leader: 'Don't worry about it, boss—just have a good night's sleep'. Fraser resigned the next day.[12]

Fraser's resignation speech on the floor of Parliament was designed to terminate the prime ministership of Gorton; it was an act of pure ruthlessness. But it was far more. At this point Fraser purported to tell the Liberal Party who was fit to command it and by what standards its Prime Minister should operate.

Fraser declared that Gorton, 'because of his unreasoned drive to get his own way, his obstinacy, impetuous and emotional reactions, has imposed strains upon the Liberal Party, the Government and the Public Service. I do not believe he is fit to hold the great office of Prime Minister, and I cannot serve in his Government'. Gorton fell the next day.

These were the words and actions of a man of pride, passion, and self-assurance; a man prepared to provoke an upheaval and accept the responsibility; a man prepared to strike down others with impunity to validate his own view of party, prime ministership and nation. Fraser created many enemies at this stage. But the message was unmistakable. Four years later Fraser and his backers launched assaults against Snedden, first in November 1974 and then in March 1975 which delivered the Liberal Party into Fraser's hands.

When the Liberal Party changed leaders in 1975 it expected to win the next election; it chose Fraser not to win an election but to validate its leadership ethos. The upheavals Fraser unleashed were justified by his insistence that he was the party's *true* leader. Fraser identified the future of the Liberal Party with his own leadership of the party. The Liberals, by installing Fraser in a coup against Snedden, accepted Fraser's claim to be its *real* leader. It would allow Fraser to determine its future.

These two events—the strike against Gorton and the coup against Snedden—revealed the depth of Fraser's assurance and his willingness to justify political violence to achieve his goals. With each step Fraser became a more sophisticated politician. He grasped that his assault upon Gorton had been too publicly brutal: so in his pursuit of Snedden Fraser cast himself as a man of principle, working in the ultimate interest of the party. Only a leader with Fraser's toughness and self-belief in political combat would have denied Supply for a month in late 1975 thereby forcing a great crisis; only a genuine leader would have kept his own nerve against Whitlam at this time; only a leader of authority could have kept discipline in his own ranks.

It is a reminder that Malcolm Fraser operated in the remnant of the Menzian Liberal Party; since Fraser's retirement Liberal leaders have not been noted for authority and nerve. The hallmark of Fraser's leadership was faith in his ability and his right as leader of the Liberal Party to determine Australia's future course. If that demanded the denial of Supply, then such constitutional audacity was necessary. If it demanded that the Governor-General dismiss the Prime Minister, then such application of the reserve powers was also required. Fraser preached that leadership meant taking the tough option for Australia's sake; it became his text during the 1975 crisis.

The Liberal culture

The 1975 crisis sprang from a coincidence between party cultures. It was the last gasp of the 'born to rule' Liberal Party; it was the final performance of the 'doomed to lose' Labor Party. In a tactical sense Fraser out-thought Whitlam at every point.

Fraser acted from a self-confidence bred into his political blood. It was the fusion between self-interest and national interest—the glue that holds any successful party together. After 23 years of power the non-Labor side detested opposition. It was convinced that the true order of politics would be re-established. This was based upon a faith in the bond between the middle class and the Liberal Party.

After he became leader Fraser praised Menzies as Australia's greatest Prime Minister in terms of this compact:

> A health scheme that worked, a high level of home ownership and stability, a capacity for people to plan ahead, the longest period of full and continuous employment in Australia's history, a very great deal of social progress, a very large number of social welfare programs introduced. There was an aura of predictability and certainty.[13]

The legacy of 23 years of Coalition power from 1949 to 1972 was profound; a period longer than the 1932–52 Democratic Party ascendancy in the United States and still longer than the current post-1979 era of Conservative Party rule in the United Kingdom. The Coalition felt that it possessed a better understanding than Labor of the country in its various dimensions—farm, factory and family. The Liberal elite rationalised its assault through the Senate by invoking its responsibility to lead Australia and insisting that Labor's performance showed that it was unfit to lead. Such sentiments were alive in many power centres—rural, mining, financial and media elites—reinforced by personal networks established during the Coalition's long rule.

Labor's dismal history at the national level explains this sentiment. In the 62 years from the formation of the modern party structure in 1910 to Whitlam's 1972 victory, Labor had governed for 18 years as opposed to non-Labor's 44 years. No ALP Prime Minister had been re-elected. There was a distinct reluctance after Labor's 1972 victory to accept the legitimacy of its credentials as a government. The Coalition parties concluded from history that Whitlam would not last long. But they had another motive—Whitlam was too great a threat if he became established.

Whitlam was feared by the non-Labor side because he was a progressive leader who had tapped a popular wave. Labor's universal health scheme, its education funding policies, its national vision and its pitch to women, immigrants and youth gave Whitlam the potential to consolidate. The Liberal and Country Parties were alarmed at Whitlam's electoral reform program—one vote one value, declaration of campaign fund sources, optional preferential voting, simultaneous elections for the House and Senate. They saw such reforms not as legitimate improvements in the political system but as measures that had to be destroyed because they would disadvantage the non-Labor side.

The Country Party was even more antagonistic to Labor than the Liberals, a result of both fear and confidence. Fear because Labor's electoral reforms would hurt its base by removing the bias towards rural seats. Confidence because it identified Whitlam as a 'cities politician' who would lose in the bush and provincial towns. The Country Party's lethal troika, Doug Anthony, Ian Sinclair and Peter Nixon, worked closely with Fraser.

The Whitlam era induced a paradox—it reinforced the ruling mentality of the Coalition at the precise time that vast social changes were starting to undermine non-Labor's electoral base. Whitlam's failures disguised this trend—but Australia's transformation was proceeding. It was the chemistry of Liberal arrogance and Labor ineptitude that deluded the non-Labor parties into thinking that changes since the Menzian age would not necessarily spill into the party system and eventually alter the balance against them. The Coalition successfully escaped the 1970s despite this delusion; but it proved fatal for the non-Labor side in both the 1980s and 1990s.

In retrospect, Labor's 1972 victory was the harbinger of deep cultural and social revolutions. Economic life was being shaped by unpredictable overseas forces that defied the conventional tools of management. The 'baby boomers', breaking with the 1950s values, were at university or just entering the workplace. The Vietnam legacy had poisoned a political generation against the Coalition. The rise of feminism would change forever female values and encourage women into the workforce, a problem for the Menzian Liberals whose message was pitched to the family home. The waves of postwar European immigrants were starting to make their own demands on the political system. The White Australia policy had just been abolished and multiculturalism was soon to emerge. The advent of Whitlam had fostered a greater sense of Australian nationalism manifested in symbols, foreign policy independence and a flowering of the arts.

The Coalition was aware of these emerging trends in the 1972–75 period. But it was never forced to address them. It declined the opportunity during the Whitlam period to renovate its social philosophy. It was not necessary. Whitlam faltered too soon; the defects of the Whitlam Government became so great that the motivation did not exist for the non-Labor side to reassess itself. Whitlam confirmed the prejudices of the Liberal Party because he alienated the voters. Whitlam's chief defect was his inability to manage an authentic governing party that put real pressure on his opponents.

The Coalition campaign against Whitlam centred on three comprehensive themes. First, that Labor had terminated Australia's postwar economic prosperity; in particular, that it had presided over the demise of full employment and had introduced a high inflation and a big-government economic model that had led to substantial suffering throughout the community.

Second, that Labor was unfit to govern because of its individual and collective impropriety, a phenomenon that reached its zenith in the 1975 loans affair. Fraser and his colleagues convinced themselves that Whitlam no longer possessed any moral claim to govern, as a prelude to trying to convince the public.

Third, that Whitlam's centralist policies were corrupting the federal balance—a theme embraced vigorously by the non-Labor States and exploited by the Federal Opposition, sometimes with more cynicism than conviction. Such rhetoric was handy to buttress the deployment of the Senate against Whitlam.

Fraser's bridgehead—the Senate

The election of the Whitlam Government brought two structural changes to politics. It inaugurated a growing conflict between the Labor controlled House of Representatives and the anti-ALP dominated Senate. And it gave the Coalition Senators a new leverage within their own parties since it was in the Senate, not the House of Representatives, where Labor's program could be terminated.

The watershed in the Senate's evolution had come in 1949 when the Chifley Government's reform of the voting system to proportional representation (PR) came into effect. The new PR system altered the relationship between the two Houses because it was no longer possible for the government to have a comfortable majority in the Senate. PR meant, in practice, that the Senate would always be more evenly divided, with the government struggling to secure a majority and minor parties often holding the balance of power. The change increased the probability that party control of the House would differ from party control in the Senate, thereby creating the conditions that would encourage the Senate to exercise its powers.

The demise of the Whitlam Government was inexorably tied to the rise in the Senate's authority. The Coalition used the Senate to obstruct, deny and then destroy the government. This involved the refusal of Supply to the government—the Senate's ultimate constitutional power, never used before Whitlam's election, and so long unused that some questioned whether such power still existed. The truth is that for most of its history the Senate had declined to act as a co-equal chamber with the House. It was only in the late 1960s that the self-confidence of the Senate was enhanced, thereby creating the climate for the use of its ultimate power.

The main event in this process was the creation in 1970 of the Senate committee system, a cross-party move but heavily guided by ALP Senate leader Lionel Murphy in conjunction with the Clerk of the

Senate, J R Odgers. In his definitive work Odgers declared that the Senate committee system amounted to 'a new era in Australian parliamentary history'.[14] It was a tribute to the ALP's political schizophrenia that while its supposedly binding platform called for the abolition of the Senate its own Senate leader was promoting that chamber's authority against the government.

The proposals for a Senate standing committee system received enthusiastic backing from the national press as a fashionable renovation of a forlorn chamber. The blueprint was prepared by Odgers, the negotiations were conducted by Murphy and the committee system was approved in June 1970. The architect of the Senate's campaign against Whitlam, Reg Withers, later declared: 'The Senate was a very different place when I arrived here in 1966. It was a sleeping beauty. Senator Murphy gave it the kiss of life'.[15]

The rising influence of the Senate was expressed by the ALP Opposition which was willing to use the Senate against the Coalition Government. In June 1970 Labor attacked proposed State tax measures of the Gorton Government. Lionel Murphy set out the position:

> For what we conceive to be simple but adequate reasons, the Opposition will oppose these measures. In doing this the Opposition is pursuing a tradition which is well established, but in view of some doubt recently cast on it in this chamber, perhaps I should restate the position. The Senate is entitled and expected to exercise resolutely but with discretion its power to refuse its concurrence to any financial measure, including a tax bill. There are no limitations on the Senate in the use of its constitutional powers, except the limitations imposed by discretion and reason. The Australian Labor Party has acted consistently in accordance with the tradition that we will oppose in the Senate any tax or money bill or any other financial measure whenever necessary to carry out our principles and policies.[16]

Murphy then incorporated in Hansard a long list of financial or economic measures that had been opposed by the Opposition in the Senate in whole or in part since 1950.

When related measures were contained in the August 1970 budget Whitlam said: 'Let me make it clear at the outset that our opposition to this budget is no mere formality. We intend to press our opposition by all available means on all related measures in both Houses. If the motion is defeated, we will vote against the Bills here and in the Senate. Our purpose is to destroy this Budget and to destroy the Government which has sponsored it'.[17]

It was a remark later used against Whitlam. But Labor had neither a majority in the House nor in the Senate and there was no prospect of the budget being defeated. Whitlam's comments were political rhetoric and he had no power to implement his threat, a fact of which everyone was aware. These comments cannot be used to conclude that Whitlam, if he had enjoyed the numbers, would have defeated the budget to force Gorton to an election.[18] But such remarks from Murphy and Whitlam demonstrate two points.

First, they reveal that the ALP believed that the Senate had the constitutional power to reject money and Appropriation bills. This conflicted with Whitlam's claim during the 1975 crisis that the Senate was acting unconstitutionally. Second, they undermine the claim repeatedly made by Whitlam during the 1975 crisis of a *convention* that the Senate cannot reject Appropriation bills.[19]

Whitlam, in fact, was usually careful not to boost either the Senate's powers or its prestige precisely because he feared that an ambitious Senate might undermine a future ALP government. He worried that the political ambitions of the Senate might expand to deploy its constitutional power.

The atmospherics in which the Senate operated during the Whitlam Government were influenced in part by the new Senate Opposition leader. In December 1972, after the Liberal Party elected Bill Snedden and Phillip Lynch as leader and deputy, an unusual event occurred. The Liberal Senators withdrew to their own party room to elect their own leaders. The practice had been for the party leader to appoint the Senate leader and deputy—but the Senators repudiated this. They wanted to elect their own leader and, in so doing, they chose one of their own. The successful candidate was Reginald Withers, an unknown outside politics and largely unknown outside the Senate, who was initially seen as a rather harmless nonentity. Withers defeated three former Coalition ministers—Kenneth Anderson, Robert Cotton and Ivor Greenwood, the latter being elected as his deputy.

Withers had not even been a minister in the McMahon Government, but as a former Senate Whip he had established a rapport with most, and a trust with many, of his colleagues. Withers could not have won any election by the entire party room; nor would he have been Snedden's own choice. 'I was elected [leader] because I'm such a nice man', he said later with a grin.[20]

Withers had a powerful hand. He spoke not just for himself but for the Liberal Senators who elected him. He would champion the interests of the Senate within the Liberal Party, the Coalition, the Parliament and the country. That was his mandate.

Withers was a Jackie Gleason lookalike, an overweight Bunbury lawyer with a considerable experience of life, a smiling self-deprecating politician who played down his own ability and rose without trace to become Senate Opposition leader. 'I'm just a boy from Bunbury. I'm not a clever man. They're much too smart for me, these Canberra blokes who are supposed to manipulate power', he said in April 1974 after the Senate moved to deny Whitlam Supply.[21]

Withers knew his enemies. His father was an ALP member of the Western Australian Parliament who had been part of the group that put the socialisation plank in the ALP platform in 1921—a father's unknowing gift to his son. The son first met John Curtin when he visited the Withers' household in the early 1940s and in 1946 he met Ben Chifley on the campaign trail. But Withers turned on the issue of bank nationalisation; he joined the ex-servicemen's push against Labor controls and became a dedicated Liberal.[22]

Withers rose from Bunbury politics to become the WA Liberal Party president and, after initial defeats, finally won a Senate place. ALP Senate leader Nick McKenna, who had known his father, told Withers: 'Study the standing orders. Nobody knows them except me'. Withers served his apprenticeship, took points of order and then, as Whip, organised his Senators and responded to their human needs with guile and cheer. If the press gallery ever thought about Withers, which is unlikely, it was probably as an inconsequential timeserver.

But Withers had politics in his blood, cunning in his brain and knew that success was a trade in human relationships. He had little interest in public policy; he specialised instead in that arcane domain of Senate procedures and constitutional powers. Aware that the Senate was a source of power, Withers satirised his lower chamber colleagues: 'I think in some ways the blokes in the Reps have a dog's life, flower shows one day, a fete the next. I deliberately chose to come to the Senate and I like being a Senator. I really do'.[23]

Withers went with the flow; that was his strength. He was never a numbers man. This reputation that he later enjoyed was a media creation. Withers was a shrewd politician but never in the same league as the hard men of politics—a Malcolm Fraser or a Paul Keating. His great skill was his understanding of people.

Reg Withers retained a small town approach to politics and it inspired his cynicism; he dismissed with amusement the reform vision of the ALP and, from his own long contact with Labor, concluded that its ideas were foreign to ordinary Australians and that its internal demons would destroy its electoral appeal. When the Whitlam Government faltered there was a smugness about Withers. The result, after all, was a vindication both of his skill and a lifetime decision to desert his father's path.

The personal and technical abilities of Withers were ideally suited for the political responsibility he now assumed. Neither the government nor the Opposition had a Senate majority in its own right. Skill in Senate procedures and a capacity to fashion a coalition of forces were essential. Withers brought the right ingredients. He was a West Australian who exploited Whitlam's centralism by instinct. He was a pragmatist who kept the Coalition functioning in the Senate with joint Senate party meetings and close ties with the Country Party Senate leader, Tom Drake-Brockman. Withers put a priority on co-operation with the Democratic Labor Party, saying, 'When Vince [Gair] and I have something to decide on tactics he drops in here for a drink or we might have a chat over dinner'.[24] He believed that, put under pressure, Labor would self-destruct.

In mid-1973 Withers declared:

> The Senate however can reject any legislation and this includes appropriation of revenues . . . Rather than the Senate exceeding its powers, it has been more a case of the Senate not using the power that the Constitution bestowed on it . . . It is only over the last few years that the Senate has accepted its responsibilities.[25]

Within the Coalition parties and in the public domain Withers outlined a strategic approach to be followed by the Senate. First, he insisted that the Senate had no intention of usurping the role of the House of Representatives which decided who should govern and took the initiative to raise money. Second, he said that the Senate had a different function from the House which was dominated by the executive, and that it must increasingly function as a proper chamber of review, considering bills in detail and subjecting government action to scrutiny. While the government might find this frustrating, it was 'vital if the Parliament is not to abrogate its duties'.[26]

Third, Withers insisted that Whitlam's situation in which the Senate was not controlled by the government was 'nothing new in this country', pointing out that the Coalition Government had lost control of the Senate at the 1967 Senate election; and that Whitlam, in turn, 'should cease bemoaning the problem as if it was new and unique'.[27] Fourth, Withers lectured his colleagues against 'opposition for the sake of opposition'. Because the Senate could defeat government bills it was imperative for the Opposition tacticians in the House to vote against measures on a selective basis, since such decisions could be carried into effect in the Senate. If the Opposition voted against any measures it disliked then it would reject all bills before the Parliament, an untenable position. The correct approach, Withers argued, was that 'we should not try to unduly hamper the Labor Government, other than in ways which will help in bringing about its ultimate defeat'. Withers knew the difference between tactics and strategy. He wasn't looking for minor victories; he wasn't trigger happy. Withers wanted to save his shots for when they were lethal.[28]

In style Withers resembled a Labor politician. A shrewd judge of popular opinion and political horseflesh, he was unencumbered by false airs. He also did his arm-twisting with a smile. As the Whitlam period advanced, Withers drove ALP politicians to a fury. He pointed out that Whitlam, in his 1972 victory, had failed to gain a majority of seats in Victoria, Queensland or Western Australia. Then he said that the government's problem was that 'they just won't tailor their policies to fit the Senate'.[29] His ALP Senate opponent Jim McClelland declared that Withers 'symbolised for me everything that is second rate in politics'.[30]

History is replete with warnings about the Senate's power. The obstruction that the Whitlam Government faced would become unique in Australian history—but the potential for such a situation to arise had been recognised in the past. The truth was that Labor had not sufficiently studied its parliamentary history. There were distinct parallels between the situation Menzies faced upon winning the 1949 election and that confronting Whitlam in 1972. When Menzies won he faced a Senate with a hostile pro-Labor majority.

The clear priority of Menzies' first term was to strengthen his position in the country to allow a consolidation of his power. Menzies manipulated section 57 of the Constitution in March 1951 in order to secure from the Governor-General a double dissolution election on a Commonwealth Bank bill, while announcing that his campaign would revolve around the issues of communism and defence. The ALP Opposition was taken by surprise by Menzies' speed.[31] Menzies was re-elected and obtained a 32–28 Senate majority, thereby securing his government within the Parliament.

The moral is that Menzies never doubted the importance for a Prime Minister of having a Senate majority.

A further graphic demonstration is contained in his 15 November 1961 policy speech, when Menzies declared:

> The Senate has great powers. It can throw out a budget, or refuse supply; it can refuse to pass any legislation. If, therefore, you re-elect my Government, but after July 1, 1962, when the new Senators come in, the Government does not have a majority in the Senate, the nation's legislation and finances will be at the mercy of the very Opposition which you would have rejected in the House of Representatives! The only way to avoid such an absurdity is to give us a majority in both Houses. If you do not, or if you vote informally for the Senate,

you will find that, instead of electing my own Government for three years, you will have elected it effectively for six months only.

Here Menzies describes the precise problem the Senate caused Whitlam more than a decade later. For a student of history—and Withers knew his Senate history—the Senate was destined to become the tactical focus for the anti-ALP forces. The irony is that the Senate's great powers, created to protect the States against the Lower House, would be manipulated by the Opposition leader in the Representatives for his own party purposes. If Whitlam were to be checked and then broken, such combat would be Senate-based.

Malcolm Fraser knew this; he required no tuition from Withers. Fraser had little love for the Senate but he harnessed Withers and the Senate for his own objectives.

Withers was no match for Fraser as a politician and had the sense never to press him too hard. When the Liberal Party moved from Snedden to Fraser, Withers followed the current. Three years into his own government in 1978 Fraser destroyed the ministerial career of an incredulous Withers by demanding his resignation so as to uphold Fraser's high standards of propriety. At this point a bitter Withers lashed out at Fraser: 'When the man who's carried the biggest knife in this country for the last ten years starts giving you a lecture about propriety, integrity and the need to resign, then he's either making a sick joke or playing you for a mug'.[32] Fraser, as usual, did not respond.

Malcolm Fraser and institutional power

The Whitlam Government recognised Fraser as a formidable adversary but misjudged his political subtlety, a fatal mistake. The mid-1970s caricature of Fraser as a rich grazier with crazy right-wing ideas and tunnel vision was pervasive within Labor and media circles because it had some validity. But Fraser was a man in transition. Elected Liberal leader in March 1975 at the young age of 44, Fraser, aloof and ruthless, was still maturing with a penchant for absorbing the lessons from each political encounter.

Fraser possessed two qualities that guided him both during the 1975 crisis and later—a keen sense of institutional power and an assumption that there was a proper modus operandi that governed personal dealings between elites in public life. These qualities were the essence of a governing mentality; and Fraser enjoyed a governing mentality as a result of his social background and his practical experience of politics. It is these qualities that made Fraser a more subtle adversary than Whitlam realised and, ultimately, they proved to be decisive.

Fraser understood and respected Whitlam as a foe. He feared the oratorical power Whitlam possessed to sway the masses and, aware that this was Whitlam's forte, Fraser looked to other methods to outflank his rival. His first resort was to institutional power.

Fraser knew the prime defect of the Whitlam Government was that it lacked the institutional power to sustain its ambitions. Whitlam controlled the House of Representatives—but he did not control the Senate; Labor governed in only two of the six States; Whitlam had to recognise the limits imposed by the Constitution, the High Court and the Federation since Australia was not a unitary state. Fraser calculated correctly that Whitlam's 'cities strategy', by which he had won the 1972 election, was an insufficient electoral basis to sustain his government and that both rural Australia and the smaller States would reject the ALP's big city orientation.

Against Whitlam's panache, intelligence and flair, Fraser pitted institutional power. He ran a united Liberal Party; he revitalised Coalition co-operation; he deployed the Senate; he called upon the States; he appealed to the rural heartland; he promised the business and financial community a return to sound government and healthy profits; finally, invoking the loans affair and stagflation he moved, in the national interest, to liquidate the Whitlam Government through the available parliamentary institutions, knowing that the decision might reside, ultimately, with the Head of State, the apex of Australia's institutional structure.

This would precipitate a crisis; but Fraser was a politician unafraid of crisis. His career had been marked by a willingness to force a crisis in order to prevail. Indeed, he specialised at putting himself under pressure, so much so that a former manager of his Nareen property once observed that Fraser thrived on 'crises and emergencies . . . when it's quiet in Canberra he will come down here and pick out little things to complain about. When the whole world is against him, he is happiest'.[33]

In office Fraser became adept at making the 'system' work for him—the party, the public service, the cabinet, the office of Governor-General.

In his mobilisation of institutional power Fraser was a leader of authority but not an authoritarian. Fraser, in fact, was a compulsive consulter, a trait that eventually debilitated his own government. All his senior colleagues, his deputy Lynch, Country Party leader Anthony, Senate leader Withers, testified to his obsession for collective action.

As his career lengthened, Fraser's consultations assumed the status of an addiction: endless cabinet meetings, cabinet committee meetings, phone calls to ministers and bureaucrats at any hour of the day or night. Dale Budd, who worked for Fraser in two spells as private secretary when he was Prime Minister, said that 'one of his strengths was his desire to talk out issues with people face to face.'[34]

Fraser, as a leader, secured the maximum united front before combat. He consulted on a methodical basis, and the greatest example of his consultative method as Opposition leader was his decision to block the budget in October 1975. Fraser talked, agonised and tested opinion—repeatedly. In the process he consolidated support for his strike. When he acted Fraser knew that he enjoyed support within the Liberal Party, the Coalition, the States, rural Australia, business, finance and the media and enough backing within the wider community. It was only on this basis that Fraser acted; once he acted he then accepted responsibility.

This explains why Fraser withstood the intense pressure upon him to crack during the four week constitutional crisis. The decision the Coalition parties took to block the budget was collective, firm and unanimous. This meant that if there were to be any change or retreat it would be Fraser's own choice. Fraser, in turn, was psychologically equipped as a man to handle the pressures. The key to the campaign Fraser waged in 1975 was to deny Whitlam's legitimacy. It was normally the ultimate weapon of a governing party, used by Menzies against Labor in the 1950s and 1960s and later by Hawke and Keating against the Liberals. Fraser branded the Whitlam Government the worst since Federation: it was corrupting the Constitution and ruining the economy.

In a psychological sense Fraser understood Whitlam's weakness—that Whitlam would go too far; that his impatience would overwhelm his judgement; that as long as he lived by 'crash through or crash' then, inevitably, he must crash. Fraser was both compelled and repelled by Whitlam's audacity. Fraser could wait, bide his time, until the Whitlam volcano was expended; then government would fall into his lap whenever the next election was due. That would be the risk-free option, the sensible choice of a cautious calculating politician; the decision of a leader who feared that institutional damage might be done by pushing the institutions too far. Fraser was not such a leader.

Fraser was drawn, almost irresistibly, into Whitlam's circle; attracted like a combative moth towards the light, towards a fiery contest. As 1975 advanced, Fraser was gradually intoxicated by Whitlam's electoral weakness. He saw the chance to precipitate the contest and to terminate the Whitlam era. The more Labor faltered the more moralistic Fraser became; the more the success of an early election beckoned the more Fraser focused upon his obligation to the nation to force such an election; the more unpopular Labor became the more Fraser could disguise his act of political violence under the cloak of principle. It was a pattern with which Fraser was familiar.

Malcolm Fraser presented the forcing of the election in only one light—to save the national fabric. It became the duty of a true leader.

This was implicit in the declarations Fraser made from the day he became leader on 21 March 1975. He said that an election would be forced only in 'extraordinary' circumstances or if the government behaved in a 'reprehensible' manner. But Fraser would not eliminate the possibility because he did not trust Labor. In short, if Fraser had to force an election it would be Whitlam's fault; it would arise because the nation could tolerate Whitlam no longer.

This was the context in which Fraser couched his decision and conducted the 1975 crisis. It was the classic case of 'ends justifying the means'. The means were radical but the end, as presented by Fraser, was the restoration of the established order. Fraser schemed, plotted, persuaded—and then declared the issue a question of values.

Fraser assumed that the contest transcended the delivery of a Senate majority to deny the budget. He recognised that, ultimately, it might involve the Governor-General. Fraser, unlike Whitlam, was not a constitutional lawyer; he did not need such a qualification. Fraser knew the institution and he knew Sir John Kerr, although most ALP figures were unaware of this.

Fraser made a conventional assessment of the constitutional position. He reasoned that, provided the flow of funds to the government was terminated by the Parliament, then, sooner or later, an election was inevitable. If Whitlam resisted then, ultimately, any intervention by the Governor-General had to be to encourage or secure an election, one way or another. It was political logic from which Fraser never deviated.

Yarralumla was hardly foreign territory to Fraser; his executive responsibilities had taken him there many times over many years. Fraser had been a personal friend of Lord Casey, the sixteenth Governor-General; he had worked closely with Paul Hasluck, the seventeenth; he also knew John Kerr, the eighteenth.

There was something else that Fraser understood—the Governor-General's final responsibility was to defend the Constitution and uphold the established order. That meant defying a Prime Minister if necessary. Fraser's 'feel' for the office told him this instinctively.

So Fraser concluded that, provided the Coalition was operating within the Constitution, and provided he kept authority over his own party, then he would prevail against Whitlam. It was a judgement based upon his view of how Kerr would operate as Governor-General.

In a deeper sense it was part of Fraser's understanding of how the business of government was conducted at the highest levels in Australia. These ground rules had been largely shaped by the non-Labor side, which had dominated the Treasury benches since Federation and, in particular, during the 1949–72 era. From the onset of the 1975 crisis Fraser was prepared to meet the Governor-General to put the Coalition's case. He was not necessarily assuming that Kerr would sack Whitlam—rather, that Kerr's intervention would be to secure an election.

This was because Fraser operated on the belief that there were established values and processes by which Australia had been run and which its institutional leadership would not forsake. Fraser was convinced that Whitlam—despite his parliamentary brilliance and democratic spirit—had placed himself on the wrong side of those values. It was Whitlam who insisted that the Senate did not have the power to deny Supply; it was Whitlam who insisted that he could govern without the budget; it was Whitlam who maintained that the Senate could not force the House to an election; and it was Whitlam who denied that the Governor-General had an independent discretion or that the reserve powers existed.

Fraser, much to Labor's rage, depicted himself as upholder of the Constitution and defender of the established polity. He judged that Whitlam had strayed outside the acceptable boundaries and institutional values; that Whitlam had offended the governing elites as well as the ordinary people. Fraser depicted himself as the authority figure who was drawing upon powers existing in the Constitution—but which had not previously been used—to remove Australia's worst government.

Fraser was an instinctively aggressive politician. He operated on the premise that power abused was a power forfeited. Convinced that Whitlam was electorally bankrupt and that the Coalition could not lose, Fraser decided to terminate the Labor Government. This was the last fateful decision of the 'born to rule' Menzian age. It worked. The irony is that its success would only help to tarnish, in coming years, the Coalition in whose cause it was taken.

3
1974

We were not defeated.

> Opposition leader Bill Snedden, after Whitlam's 1974 election victory

THE WHITLAM GOVERNMENT encountered a Senate uncontaminated by the popular mood that produced Labor's 1972 election victory. The Senate had not participated in the election. The 'it's time' euphoria never touched its red benches. Whitlam, in fact, was political manna for the non-Labor Senate assertionists—a centralist ALP Government with a legislative reform program certain to antagonise the Opposition and which could be checked only by the Senate.

The Senate assertionists led by Reg Withers now believed that their hour had come. The Coalition needed them; the non-Labor States needed them; and, they believed, the Australian community needed them. The Senate, with rare exceptions, operated as a house of review, with its 'review' decisions overwhelmingly determined by party. Since it was dominated by an anti-ALP majority during the 1972-75 period this gave Snedden and then Fraser the dominant hand in the Upper House. They determined the battle plan; Withers fired the bullets. It was a formidable combination.

The Senate resented Whitlam intuitively. According to Withers: 'Everyone was startled at the speed with which Whitlam and Barnard had run the two man government. Labor behaved like kids let loose in the lolly shop'.[1]

Withers told the Coalition that 'the only group in the Australian community which stands between the present socialist centralist government in Canberra' and its exercise of 'arbitrary power' was a non-Labor Senate. He argued that only the Senate could halt the implementation of ALP policies that would make the Constitution, the Parliament and the social and economic order unrecognisable.[2]

Withers had the numbers to back his words. The ALP had 26 Senators; the Liberal and Country parties had a total of 26 Senators; there were five DLP Senators and three Independents—Senator Michael Townley who almost always voted with the Liberals, Senator Syd Negus who usually backed the government, and Dr 'Spot' Turnbull on whom Labor could usually rely. The government typically could not muster more than 28 votes.

From the start the prospect for conflict between the two houses was considerable. Whitlam had to persuade a hostile Senate to carry his program. The Senate had to ensure that its obstructionism did not provoke a community backlash. However events conspired to turn the Senate against Whitlam within a short time.

On the fifth sitting day of the new Parliament, 7 March 1973, the Senate, on an Opposition motion, disallowed determinations made under the Public Service Arbitration Act on the grounds that public servants might be obliged to join a trade union in order to become eligible for annual leave benefits. The government subsequently adjusted its position to satisfy the Senate majority. 'That stand gave us great heart', Withers says.[3]

On 29 March 1973 the Senate disallowed the Matrimonial Causes Rules proposed by Attorney General Lionel Murphy—for cheaper and simplified divorce—on the grounds that they were inconsistent with the Act and should be implemented by legislation, not regulation.

Whitlam was being put on notice; the Senate's legislative power would be deployed against him.

Sir Paul Hasluck's speech as Governor-General outlining the Whitlam Government's agenda for the twentieth-eighth Parliament conveyed the historic mission envisaged by the Prime Minister: 'The Program which my new Government proposes is designed to achieve basic changes in the administration and structure of Australian society in the lifetime of this parliament'.[4]

But nine days later Withers moved an amendment to the motion for an Address-in-Reply to the Governor-General's speech which was heavily critical of the Whitlam Government. He pointed out that the swing to Labor at the election had been small; that only three States, New South Wales, Victoria and Tasmania, had recorded pro-ALP swings; and that Labor's primary vote was only 49.6 per cent. 'A very large proportion of the electorate did not give the Labor Party a so-called mandate', Withers warned. He said:

> Let us also remember that the Senate was deliberately set up by the founding fathers with its enormous powers to act as a check and a balance to protect the interests of the smaller States from the exercise of the larger. Because of the temporary electoral insanity of the two most populous Australian States, the Senate may well be called upon to protect the national interest by exercising its undoubted constitutional rights and powers.[5]

After some delay the Withers amendment was carried and the Address-in-Reply was presented to the Governor-General in September 1973. The amendment criticised the government for failing to curb inflation, taking decisions that hurt the export sector, undermining defence and foreign policy interests, and advancing the cause of trade unionism at the cost of the economic and social fabric. No Labor Senator attended Government House for the presentation since the Address did not represent the government's position. It was the first time since 1914 that such an amendment had been carried.[6]

The subsequent deadlock between the two houses must be seen against a backdrop of two trends—the campaign by the Coalition Senators led by Withers to increase their own influence, along with that of the Senate, within non-Labor politics; and the acceptance by the Liberal and Country Party leaders in the House of Representatives—Snedden, Lynch and Anthony—that they must combine with the DLP in a Senate majority to deny the Whitlam program.

It was a dramatic move by Attorney General Lionel Murphy that proved to be decisive in shaping the early relations between Labor and the Senate. This was Murphy's visit to ASIO headquarters, the so-called ASIO 'raid'.

Murphy's profound scepticism towards ASIO typified that of a generation of Labor politicians. As Attorney General and minister responsible for ASIO he became convinced, on the basis of evidence,[7] that ASIO was withholding security data on Croatian terrorism. Murphy's urgency was driven by the imminent arrival in Australia of Yugoslav Prime Minister Bijedic who was the target of a number of death threats.

On the night of 15 March 1973 Murphy visited ASIO's Canberra offices where he found files suggesting ASIO's deception and incompetence. Murphy left the Canberra office at about one the next morning and made immediate plans to visit ASIO's Melbourne headquarters. Orders were despatched to seal all safes, cabinets and containers. When Murphy arrived at ASIO headquarters on the morning of 16 March he found, to his surprise, scores of Commonwealth police in attendance, organised by his own advisers. Murphy then spent several hours in talks with ASIO's Director-General, Peter Barbour, and his senior officers. The 'raid' was a public relations debacle for the government and was later criticised by Whitlam as a 'disaster'.[8]

Murphy's ASIO escapade tapped the dark subconscious of Australian politics. It ignited the emotional and ideological fears about a Labor Government, nurtured for a generation past in which elements of the ALP had been depicted as disloyal leftists and enemies of the American alliance.

The 'raid' had three main repercussions. It ended the Whitlam Government's honeymoon and exposed, for the first time, that aspect of its character as an amateurish and unprofessional administration. It helped to unite the anti-ALP forces in the Senate, in particular, it promoted co-operation between the Liberal and Country parties who kept the coalition functioning in the Senate although it had been formally severed, and it was the perfect issue to tie the DLP into the Withers stratagem.

Finally, the ASIO 'raid' confirmed the Senate as the tactical focus for the Opposition offensive. It led to a no-confidence motion being passed against Murphy; the creation against the government's wishes of a Senate select committee to probe the issue; and an eruption of bitterness in the Senate that would endure for three years.

A close media observer of these events, David Solomon, wrote: 'The Opposition hounded Murphy during prolonged Question Times . . . there was almost continuous uproar in the Senate through late March and early April 1973, which appalled [Senate President] Sir Magnus Cormack'.[9]

Murphy, a visionary in his ideas, volatile in his personality, and contemptuous in the face of resistance, was the wrong man for the job of negotiating with the anti-Labor Senate majority. The proof, if it was needed, came when Murphy on 10 May 1973 cancelled a pairs arrangement with the Opposition on the vote to establish the Senate committee following the ASIO 'raid'. It was a futile gesture that enraged his Senate opponents. Withers used his numbers to rescind the vote and declared with finality of Murphy: 'We on this side of the chamber will never trust him again in any matter at all'.[10] Withers had made his judgement on Murphy: 'He was temperamentally incapable of running anything'.[11]

The disposition of the Senate during the early stage of the ASIO debates was described by the Independent, Senator Turnbull:

> What disturbs me is the smell of death in this chamber, of people waiting to kill. One can sort of smell this atmosphere of hate which is per-

vading this chamber and emanating from certain members on the Opposition benches . . . you can see the venom drooling out of their mouths as they wait for the kill. They are waiting and thinking: 'We have got him, we have got the numbers.' It is a numbers game, is it not?[12]

It was only the third month of Senate sittings in the Whitlam era.

Withers, in fact, had made two assessments—that Whitlam would not hold popular support, and that the Senate eventually could finish his government. A year later on 10 April 1974, on the eve of the 1974 double dissolution election, Withers told the Senate: 'We embarked on a course some 12 months ago—I am not trying to be provocative—to bring about a House of Representatives election. That has now been achieved'.[13] The actions of the Senate over the 12 months from April 1973 were consistent with this statement.

By April 1974 the legislative deadlock between the House of Representatives and the Senate had become the greatest and most protracted since Federation. The Senate had twice rejected ten bills. Another nine bills had also been rejected. Six of the bills rejected twice provided the constitutional grounds for the double dissolution. They were the Commonwealth Electoral Bill (No 2) 1973, which enshrined the principle of 'one vote one value' and regular redistributions for the House of Representatives; the Senate (Representation of Territories) Bill 1973 and the Representation Bill 1973, both designed to implement proposals to allow the Northern Territory and the Australian Capital Territory to be represented in the upper chamber with two Senators each; the Health Insurance Commission Bill 1973 and Health Insurance Bill 1973, both designed to implement a system of universal health insurance, Medibank, financed by a tax levy; and the Petroleum and Minerals Authority Bill 1973, which provided for a public authority to assist in the exploration and development of mineral and petroleum resources and to advance Australian ownership.

The electoral reform and health bills were substantial proposals that generated an emotional response.

Whitlam had declared electoral reform his most 'urgent' issue. He was a passionate advocate of 'one vote one value' to guarantee democratic elections. It would be delivered by cutting the permissible variation from the enrolment quota in any electorate from 20 to 10 per cent. However, this bill was seen by the Opposition, not as a remedy for injustice, but as a strike against the system of electorate weighting which had traditionally assisted the Country Party and therefore the Coalition. It was attacked as a measure to corrupt the voting system in favour of Labor against the Coalition. The Coalition's response to the Electoral Bill was driven by an emotional self-interest.

The Electoral Bill was introduced in Parliament by the Minister for Services and Property, Fred Daly, on 13 March 1973. Snedden, in his reply, refused to accept the measures as legitimate reforms and insisted instead that Labor's purpose was 'to perpetuate itself in office'. The response of Country Party leader Doug Anthony was even more hostile. The view of the Coalition, quite simply, was that Labor was not entitled to change the electoral laws: an illustration of the Coalition's alarm about any Labor move to alter the institutional framework and its reluctance to debate such reforms on their merits.[14]

The health reforms introduced by the Social Security Minister, Bill Hayden, were possibly the most widely debated, most discussed and most far-reaching welfare changes on which Whitlam had sought a mandate.

The other four bills rejected twice were referendum bills for constitutional alteration. These changes were designed to introduce simultaneous elections for the House of Representatives and the Senate; to ensure that the House of Representatives and each State House of Parliament had electorates in which the number of people was as nearly as practicable the same; to enable federal funds to be made available directly to local government; and to enable the people of the territories to vote at referendums as well as providing that an alteration to the Constitution required a national majority and a majority in three, as distinct from four, States. The Opposition fought each of these referendum bills. It opposed all four questions when they were put in conjunction with the 1974 election.

The backdrop to the expanding legislative conflict between the House and the Senate during late 1973 was a deterioration in the Whitlam Government's position in the country. This was highlighted by the Parramatta by-election on 22 September 1973 which saw a 5 per cent swing against the ALP; the re-election of State Liberal governments in both New South Wales and Victoria; and the defeat on 8 December 1973 of Labor's dual referendums to give the Federal Government power over prices and incomes.

A report prepared for the ALP Federal Executive on the Parramatta by-election found that 'there was little hostility towards the Government in the Parramatta electorate. The usual response was one of bewilderment: "They're going too quickly" or "They're trying to do too much too soon"'. But the Opposition smelt electoral blood.

The Liberal and Country parties were buoyed by triumphs in the major States. On 19 May 1973 the Victorian Liberal Government under

Rupert (Dick) Hamer was re-elected with a record vote, proof that the Liberals were strong in their heartland State. On 17 November 1973 Sir Robert Askin's New South Wales Liberal Government was re-elected with an increased majority. Then in March 1974 the Liberals under Sir Charles Court narrowly regained power in Western Australia.

The mobilisation of every election result against Whitlam, State or federal, minuscule or major, is captured in a typical remark by Withers: 'He [Whitlam] knows that his much vaunted mandate is today nothing more than a ghost. It was rebutted in the Victorian State election, knocked down in the Balcatta by-election in Western Australia, jumped on in the Greensborough by-election in Victoria, kicked in the head in the Parramatta by-election, and finally buried last Saturday in the NSW election'.[15]

The 8 December 1973 prices and incomes referendum was a fiasco from start to finish. It was initially imposed on Whitlam by the ALP caucus and its campaign saw an open split between the government and the ACTU, with the unions opposing the questions. The referendum defeat gave the Opposition leader, Bill Snedden, a man prone to delusions of grandeur, a false confidence. His first victory against Whitlam on the hustings left Snedden with a mistaken impression of his campaigning prowess. Laurie Oakes and David Solomon concluded that 'Snedden's almost unshakeable confidence in the ability of the Liberal and Country Parties to win an election dated from December 1973'.[16]

Meanwhile Withers had been forced to apply himself to the central question—how the Senate should handle Labor's first budget. In the process Withers had prepared a short note for Snedden which dealt with future tactics:

> We looked at the possibility of using a future financial bill to force an election. I said that we should not oppose a budget. That would be a mistake. Greenwood and I had talked about this. The best approach would be to defer the Appropriation or Budget bills until the government agreed to go to the polls. That is, you don't reject the bills—you use them as a bargaining lever for an election. This became the foundation of what we did in both 1974 and 1975.[17]

Withers and his deputy, Ivor Greenwood, reasoned that if the Senate rejected Supply or a budget then it would hand a powerful weapon to Whitlam. The correct tactic was to defer, not to reject. Withers put this to the Opposition leadership in September or October 1973.[18] His view was that the Opposition should be 'trying to force an election next April/May'.[19]

There were two flashpoints in late 1973 in the intensifying conflict between the government and the Senate. On 16 October a meeting of the federal parliamentary Country Party decided unanimously that the Opposition should block Supply and seek an immediate election. Doug Anthony declared: 'There is an overwhelming feeling in the electorate that the Government had been given long enough and that it should be removed from office immediately'.[20]

The Country Party was undergoing one of its periodic crises of identity. Having refused to enter into a formal coalition with the Liberals after the 1972 election defeat, the Country Party's judgement was so faulty that it was flirting with the idea of amalgamation with the even more crisis-prone DLP. Aware that it would be the major loser from Whitlam's fair-election reform, the Country Party's usually astute leaders were prepared to take desperate action. That is the only description for the party's gamble on an election by blocking Supply only a year after the December 1972 poll.

The evidence suggests that Whitlam would have won. The DLP, sensing its vulnerability, was not interested. The Liberals were half interested, but Snedden was sensibly cautious. He chose to bide his time rather than block Supply to a year-old government that, though vulnerable, still had considerable voter support.

Meanwhile Whitlam's fighting instincts were being aroused by the obstructionism of his opponents. In early December 1973 he came to the brink of calling a general election over a fundamental element of Labor's policy—the Opposition's refusal to accept the philosophy and details of the school funding reforms. This was another emotional issue for the non-Labor side and it came to the verge of a disastrous political miscalculation which could have changed the history of the Whitlam years.

Whitlam declared later that 'the most enduring achievement of my Government was the transformation of education in Australia'.[21]

On the evening of 5 December 1973 he threatened the Opposition with an immediate general election and telegraphed State Premiers asking them to make polling preparations. The threat was in retaliation against the Liberal Party's determination to amend the bills under which a Federal Labor Government was launching a system of recurrent grants to schools worth $694 million over the next two years and based upon a new philosophy—the needs principle—following the detailed recommendations from a committee headed by Professor Peter Karmel.

The bills were designed to terminate, finally, the century-long sectarian debate over state aid by providing a comprehensive approach to all schools, public and private, on a basis of need. In so doing the uniform system of per capita grants to private schools, championed by Malcolm Fraser as a former Education Minister, was being abolished.

The Opposition's response was driven by Fraser in a unilateral display of authority and poor judgement. Fraser sought amendments to be carried in the Senate to prevent the abolition of grants to the most wealthy private schools and insisted upon the principle that every school should attract per capita payments. Whitlam, convinced that the Opposition was fighting on the wrong issue at the wrong time, was determined to call an immediate election on the issue to exploit the Opposition's reluctance to accept his education reforms.

His motive was manifest—to trap the Opposition on the electoral quicksand of school funding elitism—and win a renewed and greater mandate in both Houses.

Fraser kept the Liberals to their position while their leader, Snedden, appeared immobilised. But this time the Country Party, recovering its pragmatism and spearheaded by Peter Nixon, its most realistic politician, defused the crisis. Nixon and acting Education Minister Lionel Bowen, standing in for a sick Kim Beazley (Snr), cut a deal that pacified Whitlam and averted the poll. The upshot was a bizarre vote in the Parliament with ALP and Country Party members voting for the education bills against the Liberals.

Whitlam won a moral victory. He taunted Fraser later with Tawney's dictum: 'It is not sufficient for the conservatives that their children should have a good education. Other children should have a worse one'.[22]

Whitlam retired for Christmas convinced that, when the contest came, he would poleaxe the Opposition. Labor almost certainly would have won any election precipitated by the Senate in late 1973. But such calculations were an admission that the difficulty presented by the Senate was far greater than Whitlam had ever imagined during the long years when he planned for office or during the early months of his government. There was an element of political naivety about Whitlam, disguised because of his apparent sophistication, but prevalent throughout his career. It was during December 1973 that Whitlam recognised the need for, and began preparations for, the next election—it would be a showdown with the Opposition and the Senate.

According to Oakes and Solomon:

> On 10 December, immediately after the unsuccessful prices and incomes referendums, Whitlam discussed the double dissolution possibilities with his cabinet. He told them he was still seriously contemplating having a double dissolution, probably in May [1974] . . . Whitlam made it clear he was getting very annoyed with the obstruction of the

States and of the Senate and that he was prepared, if necessary, to risk the future of his government in order to break the impasse.[23]

The year 1973 had drawn the battlelines. The contest would be joined in 1974, one of the most turbulent years in Australia's political history.

The 1974 election

The problem for Whitlam was that a double dissolution election was most unlikely to give Labor control of the Senate. Its principal benefit would be to enable a re-elected Whitlam Government to pass the bills, on which the double dissolution was granted, at a Joint Sitting as provided under section 57 of the Constitution. But unless Labor had a genuine chance of winning the Senate the benefit of Whitlam's calling a new election was strictly limited.

This was the conundrum facing Whitlam; his solution to it triggered a new upheaval. In early 1974 Labor devised a most unusual tactic—a potential masterstroke—to combat its nemesis, the Senate.

Labor's tactic originated with the most improbable politician, former Queensland ALP Premier and recently removed DLP leader, Senator Vince Gair. Short, fat and colourful, Gair was hated within the ALP as a family hates its renegades. Gair was seen as a Labor rat who had spent his long years with the DLP keeping Labor in opposition and, since Whitlam's election, working to undermine his government. Now Gair was prepared to rat again—this time on the DLP, the party that he had led for eight years until late 1973—a betrayal that would help to bury the DLP itself.

It would become the final epic in a career of betrayal, thus captured: 'Not only did he [Gair] rat and then have the gall to successfully rerat, but in so doing he actually sank the ship [DLP] he was swimming away from—an achievement unequalled in the annals of political rodentry'.[24]

It was ALP stalwart Senator Justin O'Byrne, after falling into a discussion with Gair over their mutual medical problem, Dupruytren's contracture (a complaint in the tendons of the hand), who realised the extent of Gair's alienation from his DLP colleagues. Gair dismissed his colleagues as 'a bunch of drongoes'. Gair was nursed along, until taken to meet Whitlam on 12 March 1974 when he was offered the ambassadorship to Ireland—an irresistible temptation which he accepted the next day.[25]

It was part of an elaborate plan devised by the ALP to win control of the Senate and end its torment. Labor had 26 Senators of whom 12 were retiring at the half Senate election required before mid-1974. That meant that Labor needed to win 17 Senate seats at the election to command a 31–29 majority from 1 July 1974. Labor had some prospects of winning three out of the five Senate seats in four States: New South Wales, Victoria, Tasmania and South Australia. But it was weakest in Queensland and Western Australia where it could only win two seats out of five. Labor needed a circuit-breaker to boost its position in one of these States—and the solution it sought lay in section 15 of the Constitution, a provision central to the crises in both 1974 and 1975.

This provided that when a casual Senate vacancy occurred it was filled for a temporary period by the relevant State Parliament pending the election of a successor at the subsequent election. Gair's term did not expire until 30 June 1977. If he resigned then a sixth vacancy would be created in Queensland at the coming half Senate poll. Competing for six positions, the likely result would be 3–3 between Labor and the Coalition. In short, if Whitlam decided to forgo his double dissolution option and hold instead a half Senate poll, or a House and half Senate poll, with six vacancies in Queensland, then he had a distinct opportunity of winning control of the Senate 31–29. That would eliminate the central difficulty facing his government.

Veteran Liberal backbencher Bill Wentworth delivered a prophetic speech in mid-1973:

> It could be vital if the Labor Party could engineer, before the next Senate election, a casual vacancy for a long-term non-Labor Senator for either Queensland or Western Australia . . . the States where with five vacancies the split would be likely to be three to two against Labor, but with six vacancies the split would be likely to be three all . . . I am not saying that the honourable Senators could be corrupted. In my view they will withstand the offers of corruption that will be made to them.[26]

The Executive Council approved Gair's appointment on 21 March after approval from the Irish Government. Secrecy was very tight. On the same day Whitlam announced that he had advised the Governor-General, Sir Paul Hasluck, to ask State Governors to issue writs for a half Senate election to be held on 18 May. It was an elaborate and clever ALP scheme to win control of the Senate; it could have been a masterstroke.

But news of Gair's appointment was broken by Laurie Oakes in the Melbourne *Sun* on the morning of 2 April. Snedden was incredulous, then outraged. He told his staff that morning: 'If it's right, I'll take the bastard to the country'.[27] The 1974 election was driven by this streak of pure anger. For 17 years the DLP had operated to deny the ALP power. The Liberals who benefited from such retribution could not stomach their betrayal by Gair who was rejoining the ALP for a diplomatic carriage. Such betrayal provoked anger beyond reason within the DLP and the Opposition.

DLP leader Senator Frank McManus, who had replaced Gair in October 1973 and who detested flying, travelled by train that day from Melbourne to Canberra; he had refused to believe the story when he left Melbourne and he still refused to believe the story when a journalist climbed aboard at Albury. In Canberra he called for Whitlam's resignation; then he asked Gair not to accept and was rejected; McManus knew it was a time for martyrs. The DLP was in its death throes.

The same day Whitlam confirmed the appointment in Parliament, which promptly broke into uproar for 30 minutes. The Prime Minister was ebullient in victory. He gloated: 'I hope that Mr and Mrs Gair will be able to welcome me to Dublin next July'. Snedden, red-faced and incensed, declared it 'the most shameful act ever perpetrated by an Australian Government'. Labor felt a surge of success. But the defect that plagued the Whitlam era was lurking—a fatal and amateurish lack of attention to detail.[28]

Gair had not resigned from the Senate. The Whitlam Government had not paid sufficient care to the rules of the Senate—not for the last time. The Queensland Liberal veteran, Senator Ian Wood, took advice from the Clerk of the Senate, J R Odgers, and spoke to Queensland Premier Joh Bjelke-Petersen, Whitlam's arch foe. The legal advice on which they acted was clear—if Bjelke-Petersen issued writs for the half Senate election before Gair resigned then that election would be for five, not six, vacancies. The entire rationale for Whitlam's masterstroke would be negated.

Bjelke-Petersen ordered a special printing of a Queensland Government Gazette that night announcing the issuing of the writs. At midnight the media was informed. A few hours earlier Whitlam had got wind of Bjelke-Petersen's ploy. His press aide, Eric Walsh, had been asked to secure Gair's resignation. Gair, who was enjoying beer and prawns with the Country Party, sent a message to Walsh that 'it's all fixed'—but he never submitted his resignation. The Country Party claimed it had conned Gair—but Gair left the impression that, having got his job, he was now cruelling Whitlam.

The Prime Minister, cocky one day, was a feather duster the next. Whitlam's revised intention was to allow the half Senate poll to proceed with five vacancies in Queensland and, after the election, to resort to the High Court in an effort to win his case on the sixth vacancy and have the third candidate on Labor's Queensland ticket elected. But all this had become academic—Snedden and Anthony were bent on blocking Supply.[29]

The Gair affair transformed the atmospherics of politics. Such an unprecedented event made the unprecedented step of blocking Supply more acceptable. Conveniently, the Appropriation bills were at hand. An angry Snedden allowed his electoral judgement to be affected by the passions aroused by Gair. But those passions, reinforced by the belief that Whitlamism must be anathema to most Australians, led the Liberal Party to support Snedden's decision. Anthony led a party that had advocated this action six months earlier. Snedden had deluded himself since the previous December referendum that he would conquer Whitlam on the hustings. The DLP was drowning; its last instinct was to drown Labor too.

Snedden would be asking Opposition Senators to take action which had never occurred in the 74 years of the Federation. His advice from Withers was that 'some Liberal Senators had doubts about the propriety of using the Upper House to topple a government . . . he could not be absolutely certain that they would go along with the plan. He (Withers) believed, however, that he could "get them onside"'.[30]

At a lunch meeting on 4 April the Liberal and Country parties accepted a recommendation from their joint frontbenches to force an election by blocking Supply. There were only two dissenters, Victorian backbencher David Hamer and prominent Queenslander Jim Killen.[31] Snedden told the meeting: 'I am not prepared to take the responsibility of allowing the country to continue in the direction it is being taken'— depicting his grab for power as an act of high responsibility, a technique Malcolm Fraser would repeat the following year.[32]

The evidence is that Snedden and Anthony, impatient for a contest, instinctively seized their chance. They believed they would win—and they miscalculated.

Snedden told the Parliament on 4 April that the Opposition parties would oppose the two Appropriation bills. He continued:

> If in the Senate all members of the Liberal Party, the Australian Country Party and the Democratic Labor Party oppose the Appropriation bills they will fail to pass. If they fail to pass, it will mean that the Government must go to an election . . . There is a very real fear in Australia today at the direction in which Australia is being forced by this socialist Labor Government.

Snedden signalled that his campaign would be based on the economy, particularly rising inflation, arguing that Labor lacked economic competence. Whitlam, spirited and furious, joined the battle:

It is not just time for the election of a government of Australia but for a Parliament of Australia . . . If the Senate rejects any money bill—the first time that the Senate would have rejected a money bill in the history of our nation—I shall certainly wait upon the Governor-General not merely to dissolve the House of Representatives but to dissolve the Senate as well. For too long the Government elected by the people in December 1972 has been frustrated by Senators elected by the people in December 1967 and December 1970. The way to have a completely contemporary Senate, representing the will of the Australian people, is to dissolve the Senate.

So Whitlam embraced the election Snedden was forcing. His response at this time was the opposite of the stance he adopted in late 1975. There are two reasons. First, Whitlam believed that he could win the election. Second, he believed that May 1974 was the best timing because the economy would deteriorate—a judgement that proved to be correct. The Secretary to the Treasury, Sir Frederick Wheeler, had advised Whitlam that harsh measures would be required to curb mounting inflation.[33]

Whitlam decided on a double dissolution election. He had three options: (1) staying in office to 'crack' the Opposition's nerve—an option he never contemplated; (2) calling a House of Representatives and half Senate poll—an option still possible but superseded by Snedden's decision to block Supply; and (3) a double dissolution—the irresistible choice. Snedden's decision to force a House of Representatives election did not compel a Senate election, but Whitlam had the grounds for a double dissolution.

There were compelling arguments for the double dissolution: since the Senate was forcing the government to the people it was only appropriate that the entire Senate should also face the people; it gave Labor a chance to win control of the Senate in a heavily polarised election battle; and, by maximising the number of bills upon which the double dissolution was obtained, Whitlam could secure passage of these bills in a Joint Sitting if Labor was returned but still lacked a Senate majority. There were six double dissolution bills—three electoral bills, two health bills and a petroleum and minerals bill.

Whitlam's judgement was vindicated by Anthony's speech. The Country Party leader defended the Senate's behaviour over the previous 18 months: 'The only thing that the Australian people gave Mr Whitlam was a mandate to form a new government—nothing else'. That put Whitlam straight: Anthony didn't believe in Whitlam's mandate theory. The message was clear. Only one thing counted—numbers. If you had them, then you used them.[34]

The situation was doubly unusual. For the first time the Senate was forcing a general election; and the Prime Minister was welcoming that contest. But Whitlam still condemned the Senate. He told the nation:

> A group of Senators elected in 1967 and 1970 proposes to deny the Australian government, elected for three years in 1972, the right to govern . . . it strikes at the roots of the Australian democratic system . . . Senators are proposing to sign the death warrant of the Senate. However that may be, they must not be allowed to sign the death warrant of Australian democracy.[35]

The Liberal and Country parties were not ready for an election. They acted more from instinct than hard assessment. It was this miscalculation that probably cost Snedden the prime ministership. Having taken their decision, the Liberal and Country parties were forced to spend hectic days trying to finalise policies on the run. Snedden had taken his decision before telling the DLP. When the worried DLP leaders warned him of the danger that Whitlam might record a 1972 result across both Houses, Snedden merely replied: 'The people will never vote that way again'.[36]

The DLP was trapped—demoralised by the Gair betrayal; it was asked by Snedden to force a general election on an issue that exposed its own bankruptcy. The party would be destroyed by this dilemma. The previous year McManus had held talks with Liberal Senators about a double dissolution election strategy to finish the Whitlam Government. McManus believed that he had an agreement with them that in such an event the non-Labor parties would run a combined Senate ticket in a crusade against Labor. Now Snedden told McManus it was impossible; there would be no joint Senate ticket involving the DLP. The trap was sprung. McManus would later claim that this decision cost Snedden the prime ministership as well as the DLP its life.[37]

If the DLP opposed the blocking of Supply it would be discredited as the party that 'saved' Whitlam; if McManus agreed to force the election the DLP might lose all its places. McManus could not escape the hatreds that perpetuated the ALP–DLP split. He voted for an election; and it was the death warrant of the DLP.

The Parliament had adjourned on 4 April until Monday 8 April—but neither side lost its nerve. There was a fatalism about the main players. From 8 April Whitlam sent more bills to the Senate for a second time in order to maximise the grounds for the double dissolution. The first Appropriation bill was introduced in the Senate at 4.15 pm on 10 April and Withers moved an amendment that 'because of its maladministration the Government should not be granted funds until it agrees to submit itself to the people'.

In the amendment Withers drew partly upon his previous amendment to the Address-in-Reply speech. The reasons offered were: high inflation, social inequities, diminishing the States, harming rural industry, weakening defence and foreign policy, administrative incompetence, and the Gair affair. Withers said:

> Those of us who live in the Senate, who understand why the Senate was created by the Founding Fathers and who know the powers which reside in the Senate, know that we are not doing anything unusual. Let me put it this way: we are doing nothing that is unconstitutional . . . Since the Parliament first met last year we have had a situation in which we have backing and filling, playing cat and mouse with one another, challenging, picking up challenges and refusing them. But nobody has been prepared to bite the bullet. This is the opportunity for the Government to bite the bullet. If it does not there is no more money. It can take its pick.

Withers left no doubt that the Opposition was resolute in forcing an election:

> Whether the Prime Minister jumped or was pushed will be a matter for argument for years to come . . . It has taken some six or seven days to drag these reluctant people opposite to the polls. We have wanted for a long time to go to the polls. We are delighted that we are about to do so . . . We want an election. We have been demanding it, and we have pushed the Government into it.[38]

His deputy, Ivor Greenwood, said that during 23 years of Liberal–Country Party Government Australia had been 'the envy . . . of people in every country' but now, under Labor, Australia was being led 'on the path to ultimate certain disaster'.[39] Virtually every senior Opposition speaker highlighted Australia's escalating inflation rate of 14 per cent as evidence of Whitlam's disregard for people. McManus, riven by the notion of betrayal, damned Whitlam's offer to Gair as 'corrupt' and 'a bribe', declaring him guilty of 'high crime' and 'unfit to be Prime Minister'.[40]

Murphy laid the obvious charge :

> The Australian Country Party, the Liberal Party and the Australian Democratic Labor Party went to an election in 1972 and they were defeated . . . the Opposition parties would not accept the verdict of the people and we have seen during the last 18 months that again and again they have endeavoured to frustrate the government by defeating important parts of the government's legislation, because they simply will not accept the system of government that prevails . . . Some honourable Senators opposite think that they have some divine right to govern.[41]

At the end of his speech Murphy moved the closure of the debate. He foreshadowed that if his gag motion was defeated the government would treat that as a denial of Supply and the Prime Minister would wait upon the Governor-General. Whitlam and Murphy had decided upon this tactic. The Senate divided and the government was defeated 31–26. A caucus meeting was called for 7.15 pm when Whitlam's tactics were endorsed. 'We've got more chance of winning an election now than we would have in eighteen months time', he declared, unconscious of the future irony of this remark.

Whitlam left for Government House at 7.23 pm with a letter that would make history. The double dissolution of 1974 differed from its two predecessors of 1914 and 1951. The earlier dissolutions were given in respect of one bill only. There was a distinct view within the Senate and the Opposition that section 57 did not allow a double dissolution on more than one bill; that it did not permit 'stockpiling' of bills for this purpose.

In 1914 the double dissolution occurred on a bill that was not a vital measure and it was granted despite sustained arguments from the Senate that a genuine deadlock between the houses did not exist. The double dissolution in 1951 was given to Prime Minister Menzies, again on a single measure, a Commonwealth Bank bill. The Governor-General accepted the Prime Minister's advice although Menzies said in his letter that the Governor-General had his own discretion in the matter.

In his letter to Hasluck, Whitlam called the actions of the Senate 'an unprecedented interference in the processes of popular and democratic government'. He advised that six bills met the provisions of section 57 and requested a double dissolution on this basis.[42] Whitlam attached a joint legal opinion from the Attorney General and the Solicitor-General that section 57 was applicable in respect of more than one law. In his letter of reply Hasluck accepted Whitlam's advice and explicitly relied upon the legal opinion he had been given. By this act Hasluck accepted, providing each bill met the conditions for a double dissolution, that governments could 'stockpile' bills in the case of a prolonged dispute with the Senate. This meant a rejection of a narrow interpretation of section 57; its significance was to give the House of Representatives a stronger position vis-a-vis the Senate through the 'stockpiling' mechanism.

Whitlam announced the Governor-General's approval that evening and the House was adjourned amid cries of 'everybody out'. In the Senate a more interesting debate occurred. Withers admitted that the Opposition had 'embarked on a course some 12 months ago to . . . bring about a House of Representatives election'. In other remarks on the same evening Withers made it clear that this was a reference to the Opposition decision a year earlier to reject in the Senate for the first time the 'one vote one value' electoral reform bill. From this moment, just a few months into the life of the Whitlam Government, the Opposition had turned its focus towards another election, driven by its belief that Whitlam was changing the institutional arrangements that had sustained Coalition rule.[43]

After the Senate had voted Supply for the double dissolution Lionel Murphy declared that 'our opponents have sharpened our sense of either justice or injustice'. Withers replied: 'We all this night embark upon the great adventure'. The Senate President, Sir Magnus Cormack, closed the most turbulent Senate sitting since Federation, declaring: 'Farewell, and I shall see you on the fields of Philippi'.[44]

The election was conducted on 18 May 1974 and proved to be one of the closest in Australian history. Whitlam's faith in his campaign prowess was vindicated; he became the first ALP Prime Minister to be re-elected. But securing his government by winning the Senate was elusive; he narrowly failed. Labor was returned with its House of Representatives majority cut from 9 to 5 seats. In the Senate the result was ALP 29, Coalition 29, Liberal Movement 1 (Steele Hall, who would support the ALP on Supply), and one Independent (Michael Townley, who was admitted to the Liberal Party shortly after the election). Queensland was the only State where Labor failed to win five Senators; it failed by a narrow margin which would bring immense consequences. In the Senate the anti-Labor forces were assured of 30 votes, a negative majority.

There was a one per cent swing against the government. But it was worse in rural seats, where the average anti-Labor swing was 3.6 per cent—signs of a looming shakeout. The narrowness of the 1972 victory was now exposed. Labor's new five seat majority was tight. The DLP had been rendered extinct, a joint Whitlam–Gair effort and, for Labor, some compensation. This was the major structural change in the party system during the Whitlam years. It was a tough campaign but a curious result.

In truth, the result was remarkably similar to that of 1972; a mere 17 months was insufficient time for the nation to move decisively for or against Whitlam. But the close vote undermined Labor. It was not until 11 days after the poll, on 29 May, that Whitlam declared victory; in the interim 'the psychological force of a genuine if patchy win bled away'.[45]

Whitlam claimed a fresh mandate: 'In the House of Representatives, the House which decides who shall govern, which alone has the right and power to decide who shall govern, you have given us a solid working majority . . . you have strengthened our position in the Senate'. But the Opposition dismissed Whitlam's claims.[46]

An extraordinary event then occurred; at first it appeared comical but its import was deceptive. The defeated Opposition leader, Bill Snedden, held a press conference in Melbourne and, while conceding that the Opposition did not win the election, refused to concede that it had been defeated. 'We were not defeated', Snedden said, 'but we did not win enough seats to form a government.' He added: 'It has taken ten days even to be sure who has finally won the election. By no stretch of the imagination can this be presented as a clear-cut mandate from the electorate. The message is quite obvious—proceed but with extreme caution.'[47]

Snedden refused to concede that Whitlam was entitled to a full three year term. He expressed satisfaction with his own campaign. He denied that Whitlam had a mandate 'in any significant form'. He announced that the Opposition would use the Senate to try to defeat any bills to which it was opposed. Snedden said that, if the circumstances justified the action, the Opposition would again reject Supply and force an election—but he could not foresee such circumstances at the moment!

It was a denial of the legitimacy of Labor's victory. By refusing to construe the result as a defeat Snedden gave credence to the statements made by the anti-Labor Senate assertionists, Reg Withers and Ivor Greenwood, that Whitlam had not won the election in the Senate. Three days after the election Withers declared: 'You could say that if the Labor Party has a mandate to govern then we have a mandate to oppose'. Greenwood said: 'I would have thought that we have been elected with a mandate every bit as strong as Mr Whitlam's'. In short, the Senate had been given a mandate to oppose of equivalent magnitude to that of the House of Representatives' mandate to propose. The Senate, like the House, had been entirely elected on 18 May. The Senate assertionists had an argument unavailable to them after the 1972 poll. This meant that the conflict between the House of Representatives and the Senate was not just unresolved by the 1974 election; it was, in fact, intensified. The Parliament would continue to be 'unworkable', to borrow Whitlam's phrase. The upshot was the certainty of another early election.[48]

In an article for *The Australian* eight days after the election I wrote: 'The fact that it has brought the government to the very brink of disaster this time means that the obstruction of Supply has been a successful tactic for the Opposition . . . The odds are very short that the country will face another general election within 18 months'.[49]

Snedden was mocked by the media after insisting that he had not been defeated. Events would reveal a validity in his remarks—though the beneficiary would be Fraser, not Snedden. The Opposition was frustrated at failing to win. But it realised that Labor had been weakened, not strengthened. The blocking of Supply was seen as a successful tactic—the mistake had been its timing. Snedden had acted too soon. The Whitlam Government sank into economic difficulty and internal dislocation in July 1974, less than eight weeks after its re-election. Snedden grasped belatedly that he had picked for an election the second last month in which Whitlam would have won; from July 1974 onwards Labor would have lost an election and this situation did not change during the remainder of the government's life.

The six bills on which the double dissolution was granted were passed by the House of Representatives and the Senate again rejected them. The new Governor-General who had assumed office on 11 July 1974, Sir John Kerr, acting on Whitlam's advice, issued a Proclamation to convene a Joint Sitting of both Houses on 6 August 1974 to vote on the bills.

At this point the Senate assertionists went to the High Court to restrain the Joint Sitting on the grounds that under section 57 a double dissolution and Joint Sitting could be held only on one bill. The argument was that if stockpiling of bills were allowed it would lead to 'government by double dissolution'. The gravity surrounding this issue was captured by the Senate's intellectual champion, its Clerk, J R Odgers, who said that any interpretation that unrelated bills could be stockpiled for a double dissolution 'may put in jeopardy the bicameral structure of the Parliament and the powers and independence of the Senate . . .'[50]

Five justices decided in the case *Cormack v Cope*[51] that section 57 *did* operate to cover more than one bill—presumably settling this issue forever. It is a view that strengthens the House of Representatives against the Senate and establishes a basis for 'government by double dissolution'.

The first Joint Sitting occurred over 6 and 7 August and the six bills were passed. Whitlam declared in his speech:

> . . . momentous as the sitting is, the reasons for it are not a matter for pride. It has come about because of the repeated refusal of the Senate to pass legislation which has been approved by the House of Representatives . . . this Joint Sitting is a last resort, a means provided by the Constitution to enable the popular will—the democratic process—ulti-

mately to prevail over the tactics of blind obstruction . . . Even the sitting itself, an event clearly provided for by the Constitution, has been the subject of a desperate last minute, last ditch legal challenge by our opponents.[52]

Snedden began his own speech to the Joint Sitting claiming that it resembled the situation in which 'the parliament of Russia was discussing the colour that the Russian clergy should wear, while Lenin was taking over the country'—a tortuous reference to inflation corrupting Australia.[53] Snedden and Anthony fought to the end on all bills, particularly the electoral bill which they insisted was designed to keep Labor in office. Its principle of a 10 per cent enrolment variance between seats was later accepted by the Fraser Government and applies today.

After the Joint Sitting four non-Labor States—New South Wales, Victoria, Queensland and Western Australia—went to the High Court to challenge four of the six double dissolution Acts, with consequences later for the course of the 1975 crisis.

The 1975 deadlock

Over the next year politics was shaped by three events—a profound alienation between the Whitlam Government and the people as a result of high inflation and unemployment, the loans affair, and a series of internal upheavals; the replacement of Bill Snedden by Malcolm Fraser as Opposition leader in March 1975; and an intensification of the conflict between the House of Representatives and the Senate.

During the 14 months from the mid-1974 election to mid-October 1975 a total of 21 bills meeting the double dissolution provisions under section 57 were stockpiled. This reflected a much graver conflict between the Houses than had existed during the first Whitlam Government. Rejection of government bills became a mundane occurrence as government and Opposition manoeuvred towards another inevitable showdown.

The Whitlam Government's second budget (branded by the media as the 'Cairns budget') was carried in late 1974—with spending estimated to rise a hefty 32 per cent in 1974–75 while monetary conditions meant a credit squeeze. The Opposition bemoaned in the lobbies that it had forced the election six months too early; it also knew that procuring two elections in one year was unacceptable.

When Parliament adjourned in December 1974 there were three double dissolution bills—the Health Insurance Levy Bill 1974, the Health Insurance Levy Assessment Bill 1974 and the Income Tax

(International Agreements) Bill 1974 to help to finance Labor's health scheme. They were followed the next year by the Minerals (Submerged Lands) Bill 1974, the Minerals (Submerged Lands) (Royalty) Bill 1974, the National Health Bill 1974, the Conciliation and Arbitration Bill 1974, the Conciliation and Arbitration Bill (No 2) 1974 and the National Investment Fund Bill (1974)—all negated a second time by March 1975.

By this stage Snedden was campaigning aggressively for another election—waiting for the Supply bills in autumn 1975. Yet the political climate that he fomented took him as its victim. Snedden's tactic had become too transparent—forcing Whitlam to an election to save his leadership from Fraser. Ultimately Snedden succumbed to the dual pressure of a frontal assault by Whitlam and a party room strike by Fraser. On 21 March 1975 the Coalition changed its leader instead of forcing an election—a decision taken in the confidence that its return to power was still certain, merely delayed.

At his inaugural media conference as leader Malcolm Fraser announced that he wanted election talk 'out of the air' and said that governments were entitled to their three year term unless 'quite extraordinary events intervene'. But Fraser did not surrender the option of forcing an early election through the Senate; he was just smarter than Snedden. If he took such an option, Fraser said, then he would ensure that Whitlam 'had been caught with his pants well and truly down'.[54] While Fraser passed Supply, the number of bills stockpiled on the double dissolution list had reached 14 when Parliament broke in June 1975 for the winter recess.

The extra bills were the Electoral Laws Amendment Bill 1974, to introduce among other reforms optional preferential voting, the Superior Court of Australia Bill 1974, the Broadcasting and Television Bill (No 2) 1974, the Television Stations Licence Fees Bill 1974 and the Broadcasting Stations Licence Fees Bill 1974.

By mid-October another seven bills had been added—the Privy Council Appeals Abolition Bill 1975, to make the High Court Australia's final court of appeal; five bills to implement electoral redistributions on the basis of 'one vote one value' in New South Wales, Victoria, Queensland, South Australia and Tasmania; and the Electoral Bill 1975, to limit electoral spending and compel disclosure of campaign fund sources. At this point, with the 'stockpile' at 21 bills, the deadlock between the Houses was the most intense and bitter since Federation.

Both Houses were driven by institutional and party factors. Whitlam was trying to reform the nation from his narrow majority in the House of Representatives. His philosophy was that the pace of reform should not slacken and that Senate obstructionism should be met with only greater pressure. Whitlam would batter the Senate into submission. He took his stand on the principle of responsible government; the faith that under the Westminster system the lower house—the chamber of popular democracy—must ultimately prevail against the upper house.

Fraser was a superior leader to Snedden in every sense. The Opposition was more formidable than in 1974 and its position in the country was stronger. The Senate was emboldened. It had blocked Supply to the first Whitlam Government and emerged stronger; it had subsequently rejected far more bills and witnessed the second Whitlam Government sink into the political mire. The Senate tried to disguise the fact that it was ultimately dominated through the Coalition party room which was manipulated by Fraser and his leadership group in the interests of party advancement—and it fooled nobody.

By late 1975 Labor and the Coalition were heading for their second showdown. It was again a battle conducted between the House of Representatives and the Senate. But there was a fateful difference from the circumstances of 1974. Sir Paul Hasluck had retired; there was a new Governor-General, Sir John Kerr.

4
Kerr

I always remember John saying to me shortly after World War II, 'There is something in me that's got to come out in this country'.

Anne Kerr, June 1995

THE KEY TO the 1975 crisis lies in the complex personal relationship between Gough Whitlam and Sir John Kerr. Whitlam's relations with Kerr were shaped by two factors—his view that the office of Governor-General contained no independent discretion and his personal assessment that Kerr, in the last resort, was a compliant man. Kerr repudiated Whitlam on both counts.

Before the battle was joined in October 1975 Kerr had already decided that Whitlam was a man whom he could not trust. The falling out between Whitlam and Kerr is a story of misunderstanding, then mistrust and, finally, deception. It is their flawed relationship as individuals that created the dismissal.

Whitlam had the opportunity in 1974 to appoint a new Governor-General and Kerr was his choice. The irony for Whitlam in the story of 1975 is that he was sacked not by a Governor-General handpicked by his opponents but by his own appointee. Whitlam made three blunders with Kerr: he picked the wrong man; he alienated that man; and he completely misjudged the man. It is a performance unequalled in the annals of constitutional history.

The relationship between Whitlam and Kerr had two dimensions. It was shaped by the nature of their offices; but, more importantly, it was driven by their responses as individuals in assessing the character and motivations of each other.

In the 15 months between Kerr's assumption of the office of Governor-General in July 1974 and the onset of the constitutional crisis in mid-October 1975, Kerr's confidence in Whitlam had collapsed. When Whitlam launched his heroic campaign to break the Senate and ruin Malcolm Fraser, his entire strategy depended upon a trusting and frank Governor-General. Kerr was not such a man nor such a Governor-General. Whitlam had built his house upon quicksand.

Kerr, as the Queen's representative, based his strategy on the premise that his Prime Minister could not be trusted. He became convinced that Whitlam might try to sack him. It was one thing to harbour such suspicions; it was quite another to act throughout the crisis on this premise. This led Kerr into a trilogy of actions—he refused to talk frankly with Whitlam; then he decided to sack Whitlam; finally he conducted the dismissal as a tactical surprise. No Monarch or Governor-General had behaved in this way before in a constitutional democracy.

The announcement of Sir John Kerr's appointment as Governor-General was made on 27 February 1974 and he was sworn in on 11 July the same year—Whitlam's birthday. Kerr was Whitlam's third choice. His preference was for Sir Paul Hasluck to extend his term as Governor-General until after the House of Representatives elections due at the end of 1975. But Hasluck declined because of his wife's health. It was an illness that would prove politically fatal for Whitlam. The best result for Labor would have been an extension of Hasluck's term. 'I could completely trust him and he believed he could completely trust me', Whitlam says of Hasluck.[1] It is inconceivable that Hasluck would have found himself in a situation of launching a dismissal in Kerr's style.[2]

Whitlam sought Hasluck's advice on other candidates and was given a list of eight names including two of his own ministers, Lance Barnard and Frank Crean. Whitlam offered the position to the youngest man on Hasluck's list who was also his personal choice, Melbourne businessman Ken Myer. When Myer declined for family and business reasons Whitlam then approached Sir John Kerr who was also on Hasluck's list.[3]

Kerr's wife, Peggy, was a friend of Margaret Whitlam from university days in the early 1940s. Whitlam was familiar with Kerr's career and their paths had crossed occasionally over the previous 20 years on political or legal matters. But they were no more than acquaintances. A senior Labor minister, Jim McClelland, one of Kerr's best friends, says that Whitlam 'only knew Kerr casually'.[4] At the time Kerr was Chief Justice of New South Wales and Lieutenant-Governor of the State.

It can be concluded from Whitlam's own extensive explanations that there were three factors in his selection of Kerr—he was a distinguished lawyer and judge; he had been a 'Labor man'; and he was recognised by both sides of politics as an outstanding Australian. Whitlam, not surprisingly, felt that Kerr was 'the best qualified' for the office.[5] Whitlam regarded the appointment as a personal selection by the Prime Minister. He did not seek the advice of his cabinet; the issue was too intimate and too sensitive and the cabinet, in Whitlam's opinion, was presumably too unqualified to judge.[6]

For Whitlam, Kerr seemed almost the perfect appointment. Whitlam, like Menzies, attached great prestige to the post of Chief Justice of New South Wales. He knew that Kerr was not a narrow technician but a man of broad administrative, legal and political experience. Whitlam felt that he understood Kerr: they originated within the same Sydney legal community; they had both experienced the political and industrial struggles of the Labor movement in the 1950s; they were both men of action and intellectuals who had risen to high office; their wives, Margaret and Peggy, were friends of 30 years' standing; they had enjoyed occasional meetings—discussing Labor politics at the beach in January 1955 and jointly drafting a document for the ALP in 1965 advocating a move towards independence for Papua New Guinea. Whitlam noted with approval that Kerr, as a judge on the Commonwealth Industrial Court, had handed down a judgement in *Moore v Doyle* attempting to resolve the wasteful consequences of competing federal and State industrial systems, one of Whitlam's enduring preoccupations. Whitlam felt that Kerr was the ideal candidate to be *his* Governor-General.[7]

Whitlam knew that Kerr, who had made his early reputation at the Bar in the great industrial cases, had been tempted to enter politics. Indeed, one of Kerr's closest friends, James McAuley, recalled that 'so many people over the years had expected John to become Prime Minister one day'.[8]

On 27 December 1974, when Kerr was relaxing over drinks at Kirribilli House with two Whitlam staffers, he recalled that 'as a penniless student he had taken his first wife on ferry trips . . . she liked the look of what was to become the official residence of our Prime Ministers. It was the house she dreamed of living in as they viewed it from the harbour. When he was appointed Governor-General, Sir John said, he had apologised to his wife that the job took him to the wrong house'.[9]

A man such as Whitlam saw Kerr as lacking the strength to commit to politics and prevail. For Whitlam this private comparison between himself and Kerr would have proved irresistible. Whitlam, instinctively, viewed Kerr as a talent without the toughness for political office. Kerr's political timidity was a qualification for the post, in Whitlam's mind. Herein also lay the seeds of his patronising attitude towards Kerr.[10]

But Whitlam had misjudged his man. James McAuley said after the dismissal that 'Whitlam didn't understand Kerr at all.' Whitlam, in fact, saw only what he wanted—and he never looked deeper. To an extent this was understandable.[11]

It did not occur to Whitlam—or to anybody else—that the Governor-General might be called upon to take a life or death decision about his government. Whitlam did not make his choice in this context or apply this criterion. The climate of belief, rather, was that the Governor-General's role was largely ceremonial, a misperception that would be shattered later. Whitlam's view of the constitutional responsibilities was orthodox—that the Governor-General acted on the advice of his ministers just as the Queen acted on the advice of her own ministers.

But there are some issues that Whitlam might have been expected to address. For example, he did not discuss with Kerr his interpretation of the office or its powers. This was important because the appointment of a senior jurist to the office meant that the incumbent would probably have a long-developed intellectual position on the powers of the office. This was precisely the case with Sir John Kerr. Whitlam responds: 'I do not believe any Prime Minister in 1973 would have thought it necessary to do so or to make that a bargaining point about the appointment'.[12]

That was a serious mistake. Whitlam and Kerr began with fundamentally different views of the office and those differences expanded under pressure.

The Kerr career

A brief career resume cannot unlock the secrets within a man's heart—but it does establish some fairly clear points about Kerr. There were decisive clues to his character to be found, if Whitlam had felt such a study worthwhile.

The son of a Balmain boilermaker and offspring of a Labor-committed family, Kerr had decided by the unusually young age of eleven to become a lawyer. Academically gifted, Kerr pursued his ambition with determination and initiative. He looked up H V Evatt's Mosman address and went to his home, a move that saw Evatt help to fund the young man through his law course and Kerr become Evatt's protege for many years. Kerr graduated from Sydney University committed to the ALP and a career as a Labor lawyer. He had a stimulating war, working for Alf Conlon in the Directorate of Research and Civil Affairs, under the overall direction of the Commander-in-Chief, Sir Thomas Blamey. Kerr was promoted under Conlon from private to colonel and then proceeded postwar to the Australian School of Pacific Administration, all of which gave him a taste of military, government and diplomatic life.

It was during this period that Kerr worked closely with a researcher and translator of French, Mrs Anne Robson, who became his second wife in April 1975. They had met initially at a social lunch in Sydney in January 1941, at which time both were married to other people.[13]

On returning to the Bar in 1948 Kerr described himself as a 'fairly orthodox right of centre Labor lawyer, a social democrat, a bit stiffened by experience, a little less idealistic—in fact, quite a lot less idealistic; more pragmatic and more inclined to think that if I went in for politics on the Labor side it would be, without any question, as a kind of liberal-minded administrator of a mixed-economy State'.[14]

Kerr, in fact, was ambitious enough for a political career that as a 36-year-old barrister he sought a seat in the prelude to the 1951 election. Unable to secure a safe seat he reached an agreement with the NSW ALP powerbrokers to contest Lowe, a safe Liberal seat, hoping for a better seat next time. But Kerr subsequently withdrew in favour of Dr John Burton, the former head of the External Affairs Department. He called the venture 'my first and only active step publicly towards a political career . . . I cannot say that I regretted or regret it'.[15]

As an industrial barrister in the early 1950s Kerr accepted briefs from the industrial groups whose aim was to break the communist influence in the trade unions. His greatest victory was to assist right-wing organiser Laurie Short to take control of the Ironworkers Union. During these years the solicitor with whom Kerr worked most closely was Jim McClelland, who became a friend and intellectual companion. It was during these industrial battles that Kerr also became a friend of another union leader, Joe Riordan, later a Whitlam minister. Riordan says of Kerr: 'I regarded him as a friend and he was a guest at my wedding. I had complete trust in his integrity.'[16]

The turning point in Kerr's political life was the ALP split of the 1950s: 'I came to the conclusion that I was neither a supporter of the newly emerging separatist right-wing group—shortly to become the DLP—nor was I any longer interested in being a member of the Labor Party itself, because it was, as I saw it, firmly in the hands of its own left-wing, of which I was an opponent'.[17]

Labor was in decline, perhaps fatally. Kerr's relationship with Evatt died. But he realised that the DLP was doomed to be a minority force. At a decisive meeting Kerr refused the invitation of B A Santamaria and of his friend, James McAuley, to join the DLP. McAuley said later: 'Kerr had a lot to throw away: would any use he could have been really have justified the sacrifice in a perfectly honourable commonsense view?'.[18]

One of the people at this meeting, Jim McClelland, recalls that Kerr spoke against the new party and declared: 'If I wanted to play any future role in politics I would join the Liberal Party'.[19] Of his break with the ALP—and his refusal to embrace the DLP—Kerr said: 'I was free'.[20]

The contours of the Kerr personality were manifest. He was a good mixer, a social being who, according to his own admission, spent a lot of money. He enjoyed life, the pleasures of Sydney, the cultivation of friends and influence. Kerr had physical presence with a mane of hair that had turned white prematurely, which prompted his nickname 'Silver' and would later contribute to vice-regal bearing. With a flair for self-advancement and a penchant for attracting patrons, Kerr was a man of ambition who sought to leave his mark and operate from the epicentre of activity. John Burton criticised Kerr as a man who 'always had an eye for the main chance'.[21] His friends said, rather, that Kerr was a consensus man. His widow, Anne Kerr, says her husband was a man of courage who had 'decided when he was a boy of primary school age in Balmain that he was going to get to the Bar' but whose disposition was 'friendly and affable by nature'—thereby creating the false impression in some minds that he was merely an acquiescent man.[22]

James McAuley made a similar point: 'He [Kerr] could never eat people for breakfast or wield the bloody axe. He is in fact a softhearted person who greatly dislikes taking part in the infliction of hurt on anyone, though in the end he will do what a commonsense practical judgment seems to require as right and necessary'.[23] Critics report that Kerr even used the phrase 'marshmallow centre' to describe his own reluctance to take hard decisions that hurt others.[24]

Yet this reluctance was combined with the faith needed to influence events and an ambition to shape history. Anne Kerr recalls a conversation with Sir John after World War II when she expressed surprise that he had declined overtures for a diplomatic post in horror. 'John said very intensely, "There is something in me that has got to come out in this country." ' Kerr wanted to leave his mark—not just enjoy life.[25]

Jim McClelland describes Kerr as 'a big impressive man who exuded physical and intellectual vitality'. He says Kerr was brilliant but lazy, a 'look mum, no hands' lawyer.[26]

As the 1950s continued Kerr devoted himself to the Bar, the legal profession and an active social life. His practice took him from the steel mills of Newcastle to Northern Territory cattle runs, and through the sweep of city-based manufacturing. He developed a friendship with Sir Garfield Barwick and eventually held the presidency of the NSW Bar Association and the Law Council of Australia as Barwick had done. Kerr was one of the moving forces in establishing the Law Association for Asia and the Western Pacific, known as Lawasia, and was its first president. He was also involved in the Council for New Guinea Affairs, the Industrial Relations Society, the Association for Cultural Freedom and the NSW Marriage Guidance Council.

Kerr sought to work with and through others; he had a superb mind for a brief; he was a pragmatist who had impressive networks. His technique was to mediate and to try to encourage a consensus. He kept an interest, though more distant, in politics—but he had changed sides.

Kerr later recalled:

> In the late fifties and the first half of the sixties, approaches were made to me to consider Liberal candidature in NSW and at the federal level. I thought seriously about these approaches. In summary I should say that on mature reflection I was not interested in NSW politics nor in the Senate. Had I been attracted at all it would have been to candidature for a seat in the House of Representatives . . . The Liberal approaches made to me were always on the basis that top leadership positions could be open to me . . . I had during the sixties been tempted . . . But in 1965 I came to realise that it was not going to be possible for me because of my wife's health.[27]

Jim McClelland recalled that Bill McMahon had told him that at one stage Kerr made an approach to Menzies through McMahon. He was interested in a Liberal seat—and a guaranteed passage into the ministry. It was to be a fast track political career—like that of Evatt and Garfield Barwick. Menzies said 'yes' to the first and 'no' to the second. McMahon reported back and Kerr never followed up.[28]

Kerr went to the Bench in 1966, accepting an offer from Attorney General Snedden of appointment to the Commonwealth Industrial Court and the Supreme Court of the Australian Capital Territory. He also undertook three enquiries for the Federal Government—into administrative law, pay and conditions for the armed forces, and parliamentary salaries. Kerr's most memorable case on the Bench was his decision to gaol unionist Clarrie O'Shea who was defying the penal system of union fines and who, in court, defied the authority of the court. Kerr upheld the law; O'Shea was detained amid uproar; and the penalty system eventually collapsed. Kerr acted as a judge to defend the law, suspecting that his decision would either make or break the penal laws.

In 1972 Kerr accepted appointment by the Askin Liberal Government as Chief Justice of New South Wales, a post for which he had lobbied hard. He also became Lieutenant-Governor and administered the State during the Governor's absence. Jim McClelland recounts meetings with Kerr: 'He would ring me up and ask me to lunch in his chambers . . . he would pour himself a triple whisky and we would share a bottle of wine. The only thing he did not want to talk about was law. He wanted me to tell him what was happening "in the real world".'[29]

As Lieutenant-Governor Kerr came into the close range of the soldier-diplomat Sir Roden Cutler, a long-serving New South Wales Governor whose judgement of people was highly refined. Cutler was unimpressed, and offers a distinctly different insight into Kerr by assessing his ability as a Governor:

> To be frank, I thought his understanding of politics was weak. He would sometimes say to me, 'I think this is going to be a victory for this party or that party' on a certain issue. I often found that his judgement was wrong and that he lacked a real sense of politics.[30]

Cutler's point is significant—it is that Kerr lacked judgement. And judgement is *the* prime requirement for a Governor-General. Whitlam, a colleague of Cutler since university days, did not ask the advice of the Governor before he offered the Lieutenant-Governor the office of Governor-General.

The Kerr appointment

Kerr's position and background made him an obvious candidate for the office of Governor-General. Whitlam put the proposal to Kerr in early September 1973.[31] The only minister in whom Whitlam confided, Lance Barnard, replied revealingly that Kerr was a good candidate since he had once been a party member and was well regarded on both sides.

The Whitlam–Kerr talks covered salary, pension and tenure. In the first of a series of disputes about what transpired during their personal conversations, Kerr says that Whitlam raised these matters.[32] Whitlam, however, insists that Kerr raised them with him when he called on Kerr in his chambers at 4.30 pm on 5 September.[33] The upshot was that Whitlam was happy to make arrangements which he regarded as absolutely appropriate—that legislation be introduced to increase the Governor-General's salary beyond the tax-free $20 000 prescribed in the Constitution to $30 000 and that the Governor-General should receive the same retirement pension as the Chief Justice of Australia.

Kerr, 58, made another request—he would like ten years in the post, a double term. In his present position as NSW Chief Justice Kerr was entitled to remain until age 70. Both Kerr and Whitlam knew that the office of Governor-General was held at the pleasure of the government; but five years was considered a normal term. Whitlam said he could not guarantee a second term but he was prepared as Prime Minister to recommend a second term to the Queen at the appropriate point. He agreed to seek Snedden's approval to a second term at a later time—and Snedden subsequently agreed.[34]

Whitlam says that a few months later, in November and December 1973, he pressed Kerr for an answer to enable him to put a recommendation to the Queen when she visited Australia in February 1974 to open the Parliament. Kerr took his time. He says that he reread H V Evatt's *The King and His Dominion Governors*, spoke with Sir Paul Hasluck and read Hasluck's William Queale Lecture, one of the then most recent and learned statements about the office.

Kerr's wife, Peggy, was initially reluctant. But Kerr says that from the start he was responsive to 'the pull to return to work at the national level and to interest myself in national problems'.[35] Kerr told Whitlam that the office would assist with his wife's illness—'at least at Government House there were servants'. Whitlam was sympathetic.[36]

Kerr's acceptance meant that, finally, he achieved one of the ambitions of his life—a move to the centre of national political power—amid great comfort and grand trappings.

A close friend and supporter, Ken Gee, who had known Kerr throughout his life, says:

> John wanted to be at the centre of power. He knew the Governor-General did more than open bazaars. He realised that he'd be able to talk to Gough and that he'd be an influence in Canberra. He wanted influence and a new challenge. I thought of John as a Confucian. He had a belief in ceremony, ritual and order as an essential element in the stability of a society. He was a magnificent figure and he relished ceremonial functions.[37]

Jim McClelland says that Kerr accepted because he wanted to be 'the number one public figure in Australia'.[38]

Kerr confirms that Whitlam was not interested in seeking his views on constitutional questions or party politics:

> At no stage before my appointment did Mr Whitlam seek to ascertain my views as to the nature of the role and functions of the Governor-General. Nor, very properly, did he ask me anything about my political

views or my attitude to the political parties or their federal policies. He had no reason to believe that I had since 1955 been committed in any way to the Australian Labor Party nor indeed to any party; on the contrary, as a Sydney lawyer he had every reason to know that I had not.[39]

Kerr and his wife Peggy arrived for his swearing-in on 11 July 1974. As Peggy wished Whitlam 'many happy returns' he was surprised to observe Kerr in morning dress and a top hat a size too small. But the Kerrs and the Whitlams enjoyed the luncheon and the dinner on the occasion of the arrival of the Crown's new representative. The mood did not last long. Peggy went into hospital and died in early September. A lonely Kerr took to the bottle more frequently than ever.[40]

Kerr's character as Governor-General

A number of core points emerge from this summary of Kerr's background and Whitlam's offer that are central to the story.

First, Whitlam and Kerr were acquaintances, not friends. They did not know each other well. Whitlam presumed to know Kerr better than he actually did.

Second, Kerr is undoubtedly correct in his argument that it was his achievements in the 20 years from 1954 to 1974 that led to his being invited to become Governor-General—not his active involvement in Labor politics before the Split.

Third, ALP tribalism runs deep and the fact that Kerr had once been an ALP member and was a long-standing personal friend of McClelland and Riordan was considered a bonus by Whitlam and an even bigger bonus by the ALP. This misled the ALP about Kerr. When the crisis came it was assumed within the ALP that Kerr would support Whitlam because he had been a Labor man and had close friends like McClelland in the cabinet—a superficial, a stupid and a false assumption.

This assessment was not just incorrect, it was positively misleading. Kerr's politics had moved towards the Liberal Party. More significantly, his heart had left Labor and his instincts were to pacify the establishment. The woman who saw Kerr socially and professionally at close quarters in early 1975, Whitlam's adviser on women's affairs, Elizabeth Reid, says:

> He had a very strong need to make his mark as Governor-General . . . But he saw himself as quite separate from the Labor Party that appointed him. He talked to me about this a lot. He was different from most other successful Labor people who have a pride in their working-class tradition. Kerr wanted to rise above his roots and

repudiate his origins. It wasn't just a rejection of the Labor Party: he rejected that ethos.[41]

Fourth, Kerr would delight in the ceremony. He enjoyed the post as a social pinnacle. He earned kudos for abolishing the curtsey. But his description of this is illuminating: 'I made the curtsey for myself and my wife optional by saying I preferred to have the head bow by both sexes . . . but ladies if you want to assert your independence by curtseying to the Governor-General and to his wife please feel free to do so and we shall be honoured'.[42] Whitlam says of Kerr that he was 'particularly attracted to my suggestion that the Governor-General should from time to time represent Australia overseas . . . Australia's Head of State cannot do so because when she makes a visit outside Britain she is perceived as Queen of Britain.'[43]

Fifth, Kerr was a formidable man who took himself and his career seriously. Ambition, diligence and the search for advancement were features of his professional life. He was proud of his achievements and aspired to be involved in the power centres of Australian life. He never saw the office of Governor-General as a 'mere ceremonial figurehead'. He overcame initial reluctance about Whitlam's offer when he focused on the access and responsibilities involved and heard Whitlam's plans to enhance the prestige of the office.

Kerr would not be a cypher; he would resent even more bitterly any suggestion that he was a cypher. This was a point that Whitlam did not grasp.

Sixth, Kerr's softhearted nature, enjoyment of social life, caution, reluctance to embrace 'hard options' and desire to find consensus between people offered a lethal trap for the unwary; it sent the wrong signals about his behaviour in a crisis. It concealed his willingness, if pressed, to accept unpalatable responsibilities—notably any responsibility imposed by the law—and, ultimately, to take hard choices. As the O'Shea case showed, he had a sense of duty and would stick by that duty even if the consequences were unpleasant.

Seventh and simultaneously, Kerr sought influence and he wanted to leave his mark upon the country, an unusual mindset for somebody assuming the office of Governor-General. A contrast best illustrates the point. When Bill Hayden or Paul Hasluck left politics after successful careers neither man would have looked upon the office of Governor-General as a chance to exert influence. But Kerr's search for status and desire to leave his mark or influence re-occurs repeatedly in assessments of him. It emerged in interviews with Anne Kerr; his long-term friend Ken Gee; the woman whom he briefly courted in early 1975, Elizabeth Reid; his former friend Jim McClelland; and the former Governor of

New South Wales, Sir Roden Cutler, under whom Kerr functioned. It was a force within Kerr that would almost certainly bring him into conflict and rivalry with Gough Whitlam.

Finally, Whitlam was appointing as Governor-General a man whose views of the office, in one important respect, were diametrically opposed to his own. The matter involved was the reserve powers—the personal discretion of the Governor-General to act without or against the Prime Minister's advice. Unfortunately for Whitlam these powers and their exercise became the central issue in the 1975 crisis. Whitlam's argument at the time was that the Governor-General must always rely upon prime ministerial advice. When I asked him recently whether he believed in the reserve powers, Whitlam emphatically replied: 'No'.[44]

The irony is that Kerr from an early age had been acquainted with the reserve powers of the Crown as a result of his friendship with Evatt and his interest in constitutional law. Kerr says the whole issue 'became a reality for me from my early student days'. He recalls that as a student he discussed with Evatt his thoughts when the latter was actually writing his book on this issue, *The King and His Dominion Governors*, published in 1936. As a result Kerr suggests that his own study of the office of Governor-General was 'embarked at seventeen'. Kerr's background meant that he took the existence of the reserve powers as a given. Any proposition that the powers did not exist or that the Governor-General had no discretion whatsoever would have been inconceivable to him—a point he made in his statement explaining the dismissal.[45]

This conflict of view between Whitlam and Kerr over the reserve powers—which remained completely hidden until 11 November 1975—was a massive crack in the foundations of their relationship.

Evatt was heavily motivated to write his book by a spectacular application of the reserve powers in Sydney on 13 May 1932, when the NSW Governor, Sir Philip Game, dismissed the ALP firebrand Premier, Jack Lang. Evatt wrote as a social democrat concerned about the implications of the powers for ALP governments and as a constitutional scholar. Game's dismissal of Lang had a great impact not just upon Evatt but left a lasting impression upon both Whitlam and Kerr. For Kerr it was proof that such powers existed and evidence that the circumstances of their application were invariably controversial.

The reserve powers derive from the medieval Crown and are deemed to be those discretions that still reside with the Crown after the transfer of most of its powers to the Parliament, the Executive and the Judiciary within a system of constitutional monarchy.

After the 1909–11 constitutional crisis in Britain there was support for the view that the Royal Prerogative had fallen into disuse and no longer existed. Prime Minister Asquith advised George V that 'it is not the function of a Constitutional Sovereign to act as arbiter or mediator between rival parties and policies; still less to take advice from the leaders on both sides, with the view to forming a conclusion of his own'. Evatt says that Asquith 'accurately describes the Whig view of the Constitution'—the very words Attorney General Kep Enderby would use to Kerr during the 1975 crisis, reflecting the view that Whitlam also took.

But Evatt rejected the Whig–Whitlam–Enderby position. Evatt concluded from his study that the reserve powers existed: 'What may fairly be called the extreme Whig view of the Monarchy, whatever validity it is thought to have in point of theory, is not true in point of fact'. Evatt criticised the theory 'as an attempt to reduce the power of the Monarch to a nullity in those very times of great crisis when his intervention alone might save the country from disaster'.[46]

Evatt argued also that there was 'an immense amount of sheer uncertainty and confusion' surrounding the powers. Therefore, he urged their codification in the form of rules of law.

Evatt was an authority but it would be wrong to regard him as authoritative. Evatt feared for constitutional government if the Crown lacked a reserve power to prevent a ministry from attempting a dictatorship. Evatt was a believer in the reserve powers—but he had many opponents. There was a vast range of opinion on whether and to what extent such reserve powers existed. What assurance was there that a Monarch or Governor-General would use such power with wisdom? In 1891 Alfred Deakin declared: 'We cannot afford to have in our constitution any man exercising authority, unless he derives it from the people of Australia.' One of the famous declarations against the Crown's personal discretion came from Lord Esher, close adviser to both Edward VII and George V. In a famous passage he said: 'In the last resort the King has no option. If the constitutional doctrines of ministerial responsibility mean anything at all, the King would have to sign his own death warrant, if it was presented to him for signature by a minister commanding a majority in the Parliament. If there is any tampering with this fundamental principle, the end of the monarchy is in sight.' Yet Esher during the crisis over Home Rule for Ireland did not follow this dictum when advising the King.[47]

Kerr had had 40 years of knowledge of the reserve powers when he became Governor-General. He was deeply familiar with Evatt's arguments and his conclusions. He knew that despite Evatt's arguments no such codification had occurred in Australia. He was familiar with the successive introductions to Evatt's book by Sir Kenneth Bailey and by Sir Zelman Cowen. Kerr had reread all this material when considering whether to accept Whitlam's offer. Out of virtually all the candidates Whitlam could have chosen as Governor-General, he picked a man who by personal experience and intellectual belief was most likely to accept the existence of the reserve powers, and most likely to reject any proposition put to him as Governor-General that attempted to deny their existence or to deny any personal discretion in the office.[48]

This, of course, is the precise position that Whitlam put to Kerr during the 1975 crisis.

It is important not to exaggerate the emphasis placed upon the reserve powers at the time of Kerr's appointment. In fact, they were not at issue at that time at all. It is fair to assume that neither man thought the reserve powers would become a relevant matter during Kerr's period as Governor-General. Kerr always understood that the office was based upon the concept of acceptance of ministerial advice and 'broadly speaking did not involve power or its exercise'.[49] However, by the early 1970s Whitlam and his ministers had long forgotten Evatt's book. McClelland reflected the mood: 'This reserve power thing had been bandied about for years but I don't know anyone who, before 1975, took seriously the notion that the Governor-General would act other than on the advice of his prime minister'.[50]

Kerr was anxious to be Governor-General for a term lasting a decade and all arrangements he made were on that basis. Whitlam and Kerr seemed to have begun their delicate relationship as Prime Minister and Governor-General with sound personal relations. Although there were manifest tensions between the House of Representatives and the Senate by late 1973, when Kerr accepted the office, neither man envisaged the depth of conflict that later developed. However, between the announcement of Kerr's appointment in February 1974 and his swearing-in in July there had been a deadlock between the Houses, a double dissolution election and further evidence that the political and parliamentary conflict was continuing. The omens were that Kerr, who wanted an interesting tenure, would have his hopes fulfilled.

Whitlam's view of the office

Gough Whitlam, too, had an absorbing interest in the ceremony of government; in the forms, symbols and conduct of high office. Whitlam wanted to enhance the status, as distinct from the power, of the office of Governor-General. He realised that he would probably appoint only one Governor-General; his aspirations were vested in Kerr.

At the time Whitlam made the appointment there were, in general terms, two role models that had dominated the position for many years—the political career and the military career.

Whitlam broke these moulds.

There had been four Australian Governors-General by the time of Kerr's appointment as the fifth: Sir Isaac Isaacs, a politician and judge who was Chief Justice at the time of his appointment in 1931 by the Scullin ALP Government; Sir William McKell, an ALP politician and premier, appointed in 1947 by the Chifley Government; Lord Casey, an experienced politician and minister, appointed in 1965 by the Menzies Government; and Sir Paul Hasluck, another experienced politician, appointed in 1969 by the Gorton Government. The emerging Australian tradition was that of an outstanding individual with a long political career; it was the common theme.

The other non-Australian appointments after Isaac Isaacs had been Lord Gowrie, a soldier-statesman; the Duke of Gloucester, son of George V and the first royal Governor-General, who had had a military career; Field Marshal Sir William Slim, a famous soldier; Lord Dunrossil, a British politician of Scottish origin with a war record; and Viscount De Lisle, another soldier-statesman. Lord Gowrie and Viscount De Lisle were Victoria Cross winners. The background of these appointees was military. Each had a military record. Some had an outstanding military record. And the second suit of these Governors-General was politics.

Whitlam set definite parameters for his choice. First, he wanted an Australian; he was determined to cement this principle for all time. Second, he wanted an individual able and vigorous, not at his career twilight. Third, he wanted to avoid a politician—despite his recognition of their previous fine service—in order to ensure that no charge of partisanship could be laid, no claim of 'jobs for the boys'. Of the two politicians on Hasluck's list, Lance Barnard was appointed an ambassador in 1975 and Frank Crean was offered the Commonwealth Bank Board in 1974, which he declined. Whitlam was prepared to appoint these men to posts outside politics—but not as Governor-General. If Whitlam had been prepared to appoint a politician then Barnard, who was respected on both sides, would have been ideal.[51] McClelland says that Whitlam wanted 'a highly respected figure . . . not somebody tarred with the Labor label as McKell was'.[52]

Finally, there is no suggestion that Whitlam even remotely entertained the idea of appointing a military man. He would have considered such a move too old-fashioned; a military man would not have reflected the cultural and intellectual tastes with which Whitlam wanted to decorate Yarralumla. The ALP ethos in the early 1970s after the

Vietnam experience and trouble with the RSL was hardly disposed towards a military appointment. Of course, had Whitlam been prepared to consider a soldier-diplomat then the popular Governor of New South Wales, Sir Roden Cutler, would have been a perfect candidate.

That Whitlam offered the post first to Ken Myer, then John Kerr, is evidence that he was looking for a type of outstanding Australian different from the political–military mould.

In seeking to elevate the office Whitlam wanted an eminent and activist figure. He thought not about his Government's tensions with the Senate but about an enhanced ceremonial leadership for the nation.[53] Kerr later declared: 'I had no reason to think, nor do I now believe, that Mr Whitlam in approaching me about appointment had any expectation of political partisanship or subservience from me in the office'.[54]

The reaction to Kerr's appointment was positive—from the ALP, the Opposition and the media. Sir John was hailed as lawyer, judge, man of achievement. He was accepted across the political spectrum. When Whitlam informed Snedden the latter spontaneously asked if he could make the announcement at his scheduled press conference, an unusual request to which Whitlam agreed. Few appointees to Yarralumla have started with such universal goodwill; none found the chalice turn sour so quickly. The only influential figure who apparently warned against Kerr was ACTU president Bob Hawke: 'I said that Kerr had been sympathetic to the DLP, could not be trusted and was altogether a lousy appointment'.[55]

It is difficult to generalise about the outlook that a politician or a military man might bring to the office. But two such speculations are compelling. Politicians, given their experience of government, parliament and party, will have an advantage in the office of Governor-General as it is 'an essential and integral part of modern national government'.[56] They will be familiar with the issues, procedures and politicians with whom they deal. Having observed the office from the perspective of ministers giving advice, they will be receptive, once appointed to the post, to the need to act upon such advice. But, if a crisis does develop, their experience will fit them to engage in dialogue, mediation and warning to secure the stability of government.

The second conclusion revolves around the philosophy of civilian authority, fundamental to the British military mind. Governors-General from the military can be symbols of unity. A number have shown a subtle ability to combine a ceremonial profile with a veneer of rapport with the common people. A lifetime that has imbued a military man with acceptance of civil authority can deliver a Governor-General receptive to prime ministerial dictates. After the Whitlam dismissal, when the Labor Premier Neville Wran appointed Air Marshal Sir James Rowland as Governor of New South Wales, he quipped, 'I want somebody who knows how to say "yes sir"'.

After Kerr the successive Governors-General were Sir Zelman Cowen and Sir Ninian Stephen, both outstanding lawyers as well as being men of judgement. Bob Hawke then reverted to tradition by appointing Bill Hayden, an experienced ALP politician. In 1995 Paul Keating announced that a High Court judge, Sir William Deane, would become Governor-General to replace Hayden in early 1996. Deane's appointment was seen widely as safe and bipartisan.

The seeds of conflict

Whitlam secured Kerr as Governor-General unaware of the psychological trap he was creating for himself. Kerr was impressed by Whitlam's commitment to enhance the office. Whitlam, in turn, was impressed by Kerr's ability to give the office a more modern complexion. But Whitlam would not tolerate a Governor-General exercising an independent discretion. Kerr would realise this as his term advanced. It was part of the hidden crack in their relationship.

It is the individual who must create his own interpretation of the office, relying upon law, circumstances and his character. This is what Sir John did. There are three elements in Kerr's conception of his office that normally would have remained undetected but, because of the crisis, came to dominate. They are central to the story of 1975.

First, Kerr fell prey to the essential difference between Crown and Governor-General—the absence of the hereditary principle. The Governor-General represents the Crown; but the Governor-General is not a Sovereign and lacks the permanence of a Sovereign. The office of Governor-General is based upon merit not inheritance. It seeks to combine the advantages of a Monarch while minimising the disadvantages; yet it fails. It avoids the monarchical risk that the accident of birth may deliver as King just an ordinary man or even a madman—witness Bagehot's attack upon George III as a 'meddling maniac'. A disadvantage is that the Governor-General is selected by the Prime Minister and holds office while he retains the support of the Prime Minister. So the Crown's representative is hostage to the Prime Minister while simultaneously occupying the supreme place in Australian governance. If the Prime Minister is menacing, then the Governor-General may feel that his position is threatened. This is what happened in 1975. A competitive situation arose between Kerr and Whitlam; between the Crown's representative and the Prime Minister.

Kerr's talks with Whitlam revealed at the start his interest in job security. As Governor-General facing a crisis, Kerr became obsessed that Whitlam might sack him. This fear made him turn inward; a siege mentality developed. It convinced Kerr that he had no ability to influence Whitlam. His concerns about the constitutional consequences of his lack of tenure finally overwhelmed all other conceptions of his office.

Second, Kerr was defective in the classic role of the Crown—dialogue, suasion, mediation, warning—with his Prime Minister. The first and usually the last responsibility of the Governor-General is to maximise the quality of communication and consultation with the Prime Minister. This task is more important during a period of tension; it is imperative during a crisis—and it was Kerr's fate to encounter a crisis. It is a more exacting task if the Prime Minister is imperious or implacable or menacing. Such responsibility has always fallen upon the Crown. It is nothing new. This is manifest from a reading of the great texts.

Walter Bagehot's dictum, which is central to an understanding of 1975, is that 'the sovereign has, under a constitutional monarchy such as ours, three rights—the right to be consulted, the right to encourage, the right to warn. And a king of great sense and sagacity would want no others'.[57] Sir Ivor Jennings put heavy emphasis on the mediating function of the Crown, citing examples spread over three reigns from Queen Victoria to George V: 'The King may also use his prestige to settle political conflict or diminish the virulence of opposition . . . it cannot be doubted that, where opposition has arisen between the two Houses and is likely to lead to a deadlock, the King may . . . act as a mediator between the two sides'.[58] Harold Nicolson in his biography of George V revealed a King whose career was an example of sustained recommendation, conciliation and negotiation towards the goal of stability of government.[59]

The story of 1975 will show that Kerr acted less as a Sovereign or as a Sovereign's representative and more as a judge. In 1975 he chose, ultimately, not to mediate but to gather the facts, write his opinion and announce his decision. Kerr interpreted the office as a jurist and lawyer; he was obsessed with legal opinions; ultimately, his justification was that his actions were constitutional. He called his autobiography *Matters for Judgment*, but judgement is not the primary function of the Crown or the Governor-General. This is a jurist's view of an office that cannot be contained within such a limited dimension. No King or Governor-General can succeed with a perspective dominated by the law, for most of the great issues they confront, as in 1975, are about politics, and the solution required is political. The Governor-General is an integral part of the system of government, not above it.[60]

Finally, it was as a particular type of lawyer that Kerr saw the office—as a believer in the reserve powers. The fact is that Kerr and Whitlam approached the office of Governor-General from different standpoints; this would never have mattered without a crisis to highlight and accentuate the differences. Under pressure Kerr responded according to instinct and training. He fell back upon Evatt. In 1975 he supplemented Evatt's views with an even fuller study of the reserve powers made by the Canadian authority Eugene Forsey.[61]

The application of these powers has been more prevalent by Governors and Governors-General within the Commonwealth than by the Monarch in Britain. The paradox is that the Royal Prerogative is more alive outside Britain than in Britain. Kerr looked to Evatt and Forsey, an Australian and a Canadian. But Evatt exaggerated 'the open-ended quality of the power.'[62] Evatt rejected a body of constitutional theory in Britain that the reserve powers were virtually extinct. He brought the powers out of the shadows into the sunlight; then he argued for the unattainable—that the powers be codified by law. The upshot is that when Kerr passed his judgement he relied upon the reserve powers for its implementation.

It is one thing to believe in the reserve powers. It is another to use them. That takes a certain type of character—and it was Kerr's character. Whitlam had appointed as Governor-General a proud man, preoccupied by his own dignity and ready to leave his imprint on the nation. When such a man with such faith in the reserve powers found himself in the middle of a constitutional crisis, it was an irresistible temptation for him to use that occasion to realise his own destiny.

In summary, Kerr's fear over tenure, his reluctance to mediate and his resort to the Royal Prerogative were his responses to a crisis. They originated within his personality and intellect. But they were also his responses to Whitlam as a man.

Kerr liked Whitlam; but Whitlam failed to cultivate Kerr. This was an art for which Whitlam had no inclination. It was a skill that a Prime Minister required when dealing with a Sovereign. Whitlam had forgotten his Disraeli—a Prime Minister who captured Queen Victoria by flattery, charm and intellect such that she entered 'heart and soul' into the partnership. Whitlam would have used charm on a Queen, but not on a Governor-General.

Whitlam saw Kerr as a Governor-General and as a friend. When Kerr's wife Peggy died in September 1974 Kerr entered a troubled phase of his life where he drank heavily. Whitlam saw more of Kerr;

he was kind and sympathetic. But he never established a bond. This was his opportunity; but Whitlam was not a man to recognise its utility or to provide emotional camaraderie at a late hour for a solitary Kerr in his Yarralumla mansion.

As 1975 advanced a shadow had fallen across their relationship. Kerr still regarded Whitlam with warmth. But he felt that Whitlam took him for granted and patronised him. Kerr was a proud man. He began to wonder if people saw him only as a 'rubber stamp'. That would be an insult to his intellect and his integrity, not just his pride.

5
The loan

I considered whether it was an occasion on which I would have resorted to the 'advise and warn' doctrine . . .

John Kerr

THE LOANS AFFAIR was an unplanned rehearsal for the 1975 constitutional crisis in that Sir John Kerr concluded that his advisers were threatening the law and the Constitution. It was a micro preliminary to the macro spectacular. The Executive Council approval of the $4000 million petrodollar loan on 14 December 1974 was given by the Governor-General. It was John Kerr's signature that launched Rex Connor's dream onto the global financial waters.

After claiming many victims the loan had a final casualty—Kerr's trust in Whitlam. It also had a peculiar legacy—Whitlam's ignorance of Kerr's fears.

The vice-regal conundrum about the loan can be precisely stated. Kerr said that he believed that the Executive Council meeting was invalid, that the legal advice on which the loan authority was based was wrong, and that there was a danger that his office was being treated as a 'rubber stamp'—but he never raised a word of concern with Whitlam on any of these issues at any time. It was this bizarre chemistry of vice-regal concern and silence that would re-occur on a far grander scale during the 1975 crisis.

When the veteran reporter Alan Reid wrote his book on Whitlam, he began by saying that the Executive Council minute authorising the loan was Labor's 'death warrant'. When Whitlam's speechwriter Graham Freudenberg wrote his own book he ventured that the cost of the loan proved 'to be immense—it was government itself'. Few who lived through the events would disagree with such assessments.[1] On reflection Malcolm Fraser says: 'Without the loans affair 1975 would not have occurred—if Whitlam had just accepted a little orthodox advice from the Treasury. The whole thing led to a government in decay, a scandal-ridden rabble'.[2]

The story of the petrodollar loan is without parallel in Australia's political history; a story of events so fantastic they defy belief. It puts the best of Frederick Forsythe to shame. The loans affair burnt anybody who touched it—including Sir John Kerr.

The origins of the loan lay in the strategy of the Minerals and Energy Minister, Rex Connor, for a massive resources and infrastructure program on the one hand, yet maximum Australian ownership and public participation on the other. The loan was designed to reconcile these conflicting aspirations. Labor sought to exploit the change in the international financial system caused by the surge in OPEC oil revenues from 1973, which meant that huge funds were available in the Middle East kingdoms for reinvestment. At the same time 'funny money' middlemen were thriving with promises to locate loan funds under a variety of terms. The idea was to raise funds, not through the normal New York financial channels, long lubricated by the Australian Treasury, but through new channels direct from the Middle East.

Connor, nicknamed 'The Strangler', was a granite-like, old-fashioned Australian nationalist and visionary whose political power rested upon his intimidation of the caucus, his special relationship with Whitlam who admired him deeply, and his ruthless pursuit of his objectives. He was a man possessed by great dreams, dedicated to secrecy, convinced of his business acumen (in contrast to the mining leaders whom he branded 'hillbillies and mugs'), and who, along with most of the senior Labor ministers, was suspicious of the financial orthodoxy of the Treasury. Connor, by a strange and irregular process, was prepared to commission a Pakistani money dealer, Tirath Khemlani—who insisted he could access funds directly with Middle East oil interests—to raise the loan for which Connor had obtained an authorisation. The Treasury, led by its Secretary Sir Frederick Wheeler and his deputy John Stone, and supported by the Attorney General's Department, opposed the undertaking at every point, to the extent of asking Scotland Yard to check on Khemlani.

Stone penned a famous memo dated 10 December 1974 to the Treasurer, Dr Cairns, in which he raised 32 questions about the loan in a devastating critique. Stone queried the wisdom of proceeding through unorthodox channels, the high level of commission, and the legal and financial consequences. The loan proposal caused a level of agitation within senior public service ranks that has rarely been seen before or since.[3]

During the day and night of 13 December senior ministers, along with officials from the Department of Prime Minister and Cabinet, the Treasury, Minerals and Energy, and Attorney-General's, held a long round of talks culminating at the Prime Minister's residence, the Lodge, where a decision was taken. The matter was urgent because Khemlani said the funds were available and Whitlam was leaving for overseas on Saturday 14 December. An Executive Council meeting was required to authorise the loan—and that involved Kerr.

The Australian Constitution (section 61) vests the executive power of the Commonwealth in the Queen and stipulates that it is exercisable by the Governor-General as the Queen's representative. (However, many other powers are vested not in the Queen but directly in the Governor-General.) Section 61 reflects a basic principle of the British Constitution: that the Crown is the source of executive authority and administrative actions must be conducted in the name of the Crown. In practice, however, the Prime Minister and cabinet (neither of whom are mentioned in the Constitution) run the executive by virtue of an election mandate. This principle of responsible government means that the power of the Crown is restricted because it is based upon the advice of ministers who have the support of the House of Representatives. This element is reflected in sections 62 and 63 of the Constitution. They create a Federal Executive Council which is the instrument through which the Governor-General is formally advised on executive recommendations and gives his assent. A person must be sworn in as an Executive Councillor before he or she can become a minister.

The Executive Council meets almost every week, with a quorum required—normally the Governor-General and two ministers; or the Vice-President of the Executive Council (a senior minister) and two ministers; or three ministers, with the most senior taking the chair. Every minute approved by the Council, whether attended by the Governor-General or not, requires the Governor-General's signature. Each minute is accompanied by an Explanatory Memorandum. The Executive Council (EXCO) is serviced by a secretariat within the Prime Minister's Department.

EXCO meetings are an important part of the Governor-General's role in both a formal and an informal sense. Hasluck, Kerr's predecessor, took them very seriously. He was known to question ministers, seek further information, ask whether Cabinet approval was required for a recommendation, and defer his signature, if necessary, until satisfied.

Kerr approves the loan

At about 7 pm on 13 December—Black Friday—Whitlam sought an Executive Council meeting. Kerr was in Sydney staying at Admiralty House. Whitlam rang and found that the Governor-General was at the ballet. He made arrangements to speak to Kerr promptly the next morning. An Executive Council meeting was held at the Lodge late that night or in the early hours of the next day. The ministers present were Whitlam, Cairns, Connor and Murphy. The EXCO minute advised the appointment of Connor as an agent of the Commonwealth to borrow 'for temporary purposes' an amount not exceeding US$4000 million, to determine the conditions of such borrowing, to approve and execute any documents necessary for this purpose, and to authorise some other person to execute such documents. The four ministers signed the minute.

Its content made this an Executive Council minute of great import; its background could only be called extraordinary. This minute would lead over time, it is fair to argue, to the resignations of Cairns and Connor, a community backlash against Labor, a rift between Whitlam and Kerr, a special sitting of Parliament, the calling of senior public servants before the Bar of the Senate, the blocking of the Hayden budget, a campaign to remove Murphy from the High Court, and the resignation later of Bob Ellicott as Fraser's Attorney General.

Fraser charged that the loan authorisation was an effort to subvert the Constitution. It became his strongest single justification for denying the 1975 budget.

But the loan was never raised.

The long meeting at the Lodge on the 13th was conducted in haste and under pressure. Whitlam, Connor and Murphy made their loan preparations in the dining room. In another room of the Lodge the ALP National Executive was meeting, chaired by Bob Hawke. It discussed the electoral fortunes of the ALP unaware that the timebomb to destroy them was being constructed next door. Cairns wandered into the dining room only later in the talks. The Secretary to the Treasury, Sir Frederick Wheeler, fought to the end against authorisation; he urged Cairns not to sign. Wheeler was alarmed about both the policy and the process.[4]

It was late, too late, when they began to prepare for the actual Executive Council meeting. The Secretary of the Prime Minister's Department, John Menadue, started the process. Then Whitlam tried unsuccessfully to ring Kerr direct. An officer of the Prime Minister's Department tried to contact Kerr's Official Secretary, David Smith, also in Sydney with Kerr. Smith returned the call from Admiralty House but it was not until 2 am that they eventually communicated. The officer told Smith that an Executive Council minute would be transmitted in the morning for Kerr's signature after the night's meeting. A puzzled Smith replied: 'How could there be an Executive Council meeting? There couldn't be an EXCO meeting unless the Governor-General was informed that there was to be a meeting'. Smith concluded that perhaps Whitlam had contacted Kerr directly. Early the next morning Smith went to Kerr's bedroom. Kerr was still in his dressing gown; he told Kerr of the 2 am call. Kerr was disturbed; he knew nothing about a meeting.[5]

Whitlam told Kerr by phone about 8 am on 14 December that an Executive Council meeting had taken place the night before. According to Kerr: 'The Prime Minister said that the circumstances were most exceptional and as it was the middle of the night it was decided not to wake me up for advance approval of the holding of a meeting in my absence but to call me in the morning to get my approval, after the event, of what had been done. He advised that I should give this approval by signing the minute'.[6] Whitlam had despatched a special messenger to Sydney with the minute and Explanatory Memorandum.

Kerr's first complaint is clear: 'The purported [Executive Council] meeting of 13 December 1974 was in my view invalid'.[7] Kerr says his view was that only the Governor-General or the Vice-President of EXCO could validly call a meeting. The meeting of 13 December did not meet this test. The Vice-President was a minister, Frank Stewart—and he did not call the meeting. In a review of these events Professor Geoffrey Sawer also raises the possibility that the meeting was invalid. However, he argues that, even so, this would not necessarily invalidate the authorisation of Connor since the meeting of ministers still had legal authority to advise the Governor-General to issue the authority that he did issue.[8]

Kerr's concerns deepened when he was told that, during the Friday, officials had discussed a possible meeting. Normal practice was for Government House to be notified when it was apparent that a meeting might be necessary—but this practice had not been followed.[9] Neither before nor since has an EXCO meeting been called without the Governor-General's prior approval.[10] Government House saw a conspiracy—that the need for a meeting was known before Kerr left Canberra and he was deliberately not told.

Kerr said later:

> It was a complete departure from established practice not to inform Government House that a meeting might be necessary . . . I can imagine that in a moment of great crisis a sudden meeting might be

needed in the middle of the night without the possibility being anticipated. If this were the situation the Governor-General should be awakened and his approval obtained. But on 13 December the facts were such that I could have been told in Canberra or later in Sydney . . . If I had been told of the possibility I could and would have either stayed in Canberra or come back from Sydney in time for a late 'middle of the night' meeting. I once flew down during the night from Katherine in the Northern Territory—about some 3000 kilometres—for what was expected to be an important Executive Council meeting.[11]

There is no doubt that Whitlam had made a mistake—but there is no reason to think that Kerr was excluded deliberately. Whitlam denied any intention to exclude Kerr. The Secretary of the Attorney General's Department who was at the Lodge meeting, Sir Clarence Harders, says: 'There was a delay in contacting the Governor-General to inform him that an EXCO meeting would be required. But this was merely a product of the pressures and haste at the time. There was no intention of deliberately excluding Kerr'.[12]

Had Kerr been present at the meeting he would have approved the minute. Because he was not present his prior approval for the meeting should have been obtained. This failure of procedure only invited Kerr and Smith to conclude that the Governor-General had been bypassed either deliberately or because he was not taken seriously. Smith, after checking with his own public service colleagues, reached this view and advised Kerr of his opinion.

The loan and the law

There was, however, a more substantial problem with the Executive Council minute—an issue that would be debated over the next several years. The authority was to raise a loan for 'temporary purposes', which meant that Loan Council approval under the Financial Agreement was not required. In any other circumstances Loan Council approval *was* needed, which meant that the State premiers would be involved. By describing the loan as being for 'temporary purposes' the legal obligation to involve State governments was avoided.

But the real purposes of the loan were manifestly not temporary.

Connor later told the Parliament how he envisaged the monies would be used:

> Apart from the completion of the natural gas pipeline from Cooper Basin–Palm Valley–Dampier–Perth, provision was made for the 84 miles submarine pipeline from Dampier to the North Rankin production platform. Provision was made for participation in the necessary petrochemical plant at Dampier, to extract the natural gas liquids for conversion

into motor spirit and other derivatives. The cost of three uranium mining and milling plants in the Northern Territory and assistance to the Cooper Basin natural gas consortium, in which the Australian Government is now a partner, was included, and also the cost of the plans to economise in diesel fuel consumption, by electrification of the heavy freight rail areas in New South Wales and Victoria. Initial expenditure on coal conversion and solar energy research was also provided.[13]

The loan was Connor's brain-child: it was to maximise local ownership and massively boost resource developments; its successful negotiation would have been presented as a great political coup for Labor. Its purposes were not temporary: the most likely definition of a 'temporary purpose' loan is a loan that is to be repaid within a year.[14]

The Explanatory Memorandum attached to the EXCO minute that Kerr read sometime after 9 am on 14 December at Admiralty House listed none of these projects. It was deliberately vague. It said that the Australian Government 'needs immediate access to substantial sums of non-equity capital from abroad for temporary purposes'. The purposes it mentioned were 'exigencies arising out of the current world situation and the international energy crisis' and the need to strengthen Australia's external position, to protect Australia in terms of minerals and energy, and to deal with unemployment.

No written legal advice was provided to Kerr; even more extraordinary, it appears there was no written legal advice before the ministers. Whitlam later told Parliament: 'The former Attorney General [Murphy] advised *orally* that, in the exceptional circumstances I have outlined, the borrowing could *probably* be regarded as a borrowing for temporary purposes within the meaning of the Financial Agreement'.[15]

Murphy's then departmental head, Sir Clarence Harders, says: 'The minister conferred with the department at the time. We did not support his argument regarding temporary purposes'.[16] At an earlier meeting the Solicitor-General, Maurice Byers, had advised that the Murphy opinion was 'an arguable view but it was a long bow'.[17]

Acting on the advice of his Prime Minister, Kerr signed the Executive Council minute at Admiralty House on 14 December 1974. When the funds failed to materialise, Connor's authority was revoked by Executive Council minute on 7 January 1975. A fresh authority in the same terms but with a limit of US$2000 million was given in a minute authorised at a properly constituted Executive Council meeting on 28 January 1975, again signed by Kerr. The authority was revoked, finally, on 20 May 1975.

A subsequent Attorney General's Department memo tried to explain Murphy's opinion:

The Attorney General's reasoning began with the proposition that Australia was facing a major economic crisis . . . he said that, in order to deal with these acute problems, the Australian Government needed money for the 'temporary purpose' of averting this economic disaster otherwise likely to occur by April/May 1975 . . . He recognised that the expenditures would involve long-term programmes but said the borrowing would nevertheless be for the 'temporary purpose' of meeting the immediate crisis.[18]

Graham Freudenberg offered a rationalisation: 'The hostility of the States precluded a formal approach to the Loan Council. The hostility of the Senate precluded an approach which would have required prior legislation'.[19]

But it was the unorthodoxy of the proposal that drove ministers towards such secrecy. Any secrecy could only be temporary; the loan had to stand or fall on its political merits. Whitlam said in mid-year that, if the loan had been raised, it would have been brought before the Loan Council. The puzzle, therefore, is why ministers had sought to avoid the Loan Council in the first place through the 'temporary purposes' provision. Whitlam had a narrow majority at Loan Council with three Federal Government votes and the ALP States of South Australia and Tasmania. No doubt there would have been a political row at Loan Council. But there would have been a political row sooner or later anyway—even if Loan Council approval had not been sought—since the source, size and purpose of the loan had to be made public eventually.[20] The real explanation is surely that Connor advised that the funds were available immediately and that speed was of the essence.

When the issue did become public Whitlam's principal defence was that the loan had not been raised. He explained that legal efforts had been made to ensure that Khemlani would have no claim against the government. Whitlam declared: 'Not a cent has been paid to the gentleman. Not a cent has to be paid to the gentleman. Not a cent will be paid to the gentleman'.

Khemlani broke Rex Connor's heart, then his career. In early 1975 Connor was a man possessed, consumed by his dream. He would wait up all night in his Parliament House office, sitting next to the telex, waiting on the confirmation that he believed would be Australia's triumph, his vindication and Labor's masterstroke. After the tribulations caused by the failed loan search it is easy to overlook the soaring political hopes that Connor and his colleagues vested in this endeavour.

It was the national interest that drove Rex Connor. He can be criticised for his naivety and poor judgement. But there is no charge against Connor's integrity, nor that of the other ministers. The

Opposition implied in the lobbies that ministers were chasing personal gain. There is no evidence for this.

As 1975 unfolded, the news of this confidential loan authority—and a subsequent loan authority provided personally by Cairns to another intermediary—increasingly dominated the political agenda and the media. When the EXCO minute and Explanatory Memorandum were released, the Governor-General was criticised, publicly and privately, for signing the minute and for failing to question the government's actions.

During the special sitting held to discuss the loans affair on 9 July 1975 the former Solicitor-General, future Attorney General and senior Liberal, Bob Ellicott, declared:

> This debate raises a question which man has constantly had to face. It is simply this: Do the ends justify the means? . . . I cannot believe that any honest man could advise the Governor-General to approve of that minute if he knew that the borrowings were for 20 years and were to meet the long-term energy purposes of the Government. I do not believe an honest man could do it. I believe it was an illegal and an unconstitutional act . . . although this minute bears the seeds of its own destruction I cannot imagine that His Excellency, a lawyer of great eminence, would have approved this minute unless he had received assurances and advice that satisfied him that this was indeed a borrowing for temporary purposes. To satisfy him that it was, was to deceive him . . . If the Governor-General was deceived it is the grossest deception which any person in government could practise . . . I believe there is a prima facie case against the Government . . . The question that is constantly asked is: where is the charge? That is the charge. The action was unconstitutional, unlawful and based on deception . . . It can be answered only before a Royal Commission or before the people.[21]

The Opposition leader, Malcolm Fraser, accused Labor of 'an illegal conspiracy to evade the Constitution'.

Kerr declines to warn

There can be no doubt that Kerr would have read this Hansard carefully, just as he would have read the hundreds of newspaper articles about the loan. The loans affair dominated politics for several weeks during the middle of 1975. The more it was discussed the more the focus returned to one issue—the EXCO minute, its origins, ethics and legality. Kerr was at the heart of this debate. In the lobbies the question repeatedly asked was whether Kerr had been compliant, deceived or overruled.

Bob Ellicott says: 'It was bound to create tension between Whitlam and Kerr. It made Kerr troubled about the government and the bona fides of its conduct . . . I'd say it was the greatest blunder Whitlam committed, perhaps in his lifetime'.[22]

In his autobiography, published in 1978, Kerr explains his approach to the EXCO minute in detail. He maintains that it prejudiced his attitude towards the government, made him wary of Whitlam and encouraged him, as the constitutional crisis approached, to guard against any exposure to the 'rubber stamp' criticism.

In the account given below of Kerr's response to the EXCO minute there is a fascinating conflict between Kerr and Whitlam about timing. Kerr says that all his doubts were held at the very time he signed the minute, while Whitlam says this is nonsense and that Kerr only constructed these doubts later, in mid-1975, when the loan became discredited and Kerr was being criticised for his own role.

But it is important to remember that, regardless of whether Kerr formed these attitudes on 14 December 1974 or only in mid-1975, such attitudes *were* formed and they were substantial in shaping Kerr's outlook towards Whitlam in the constitutional crisis.

Referring to his 8 am phone call with Whitlam on 14 December, Kerr says:

> My view, even before looking at the constitutional provisions, was that the purposes mentioned by the Prime Minister did not seem to be temporary and that the Attorney General's advice was probably wrong. I said to the Prime Minister that the purposes did not seem to be temporary to me. He replied that the Attorney General believed that the point was arguable.[23]

Before the documents arrived, Kerr says that he checked the Constitution and confirmed his view. He contacted the Solicitor-General by phone who confirmed the basis of the legal advice from Murphy. According to Byers he told Kerr what he had told Whitlam—Murphy's opinion was arguable but a long shot.[24] According to Kerr, Byers 'said that he thought the Attorney General's view was an arguable or tenable one'. Referring to the minute, Kerr says that his 'personal opinion' was to 'doubt its validity'.[25]

Nevertheless, Kerr did three things: (1) he signed the minute; (2) he raised no queries with Whitlam nor conveyed to Whitlam his fears that the EXCO meeting was invalid nor that the EXCO minute was invalid; and (3) at the end of January he signed another minute in the same terms, only for half the amount.

Whitlam drew the obvious conclusion, indeed the only conclusion available to him on the facts. He assumed that once the situation had been explained to Kerr the Governor-General accepted it without misgiving. Whitlam says:

> Except in a telephone call to Mr Byers, Sir John Kerr never raised the matter of the loan minute with any Minister, departmental head or legal adviser before a public controversy arose in June and July. In July and August he told me that he was being embarrassed in the clubs by snide questions whether he had been approving any billion dollar loans recently. He was apprehensive that people might regard him as slack in not having presided over a meeting of the Executive Council instead of merely signing the documents when they were sent to him. It is as simple as that; and all Sir John's thousands of words cannot change it. He became concerned about his complicity in the events of 13–14 December 1974 only when they became a matter of political controversy, and when the people with whom he wished to ingratiate himself starting ribbing him about it. Legality or propriety had nothing to do with it.[26]

Kerr's justification for signing the minute was that the legal doubts he harboured should be resolved by the courts, not by the Governor-General. He says: 'My personal opinion was to doubt its validity but pursuant to the doctrine that justiciable legal questions should be left to the courts for decision I did not act upon any legal opinion of my own'. Kerr felt, too, that he must act on ministerial advice. In relation to the EXCO meeting he was satisfied, on reflection, that if rung in the middle of the night and asked his approval for a meeting he would have given it. In relation to the minute, he was faced with a decision made by four senior ministers who had decided that the issue should not go to cabinet. He was aware that his signature was not a personal approval but an approval as Governor-General based on advice.[27]

According to Kerr the next issue was whether he should raise his concerns with Whitlam:

> I considered whether it was an occasion on which I would have resorted to the 'advise and warn' doctrine on the policy and politics of the matter . . . I concluded that, even if present, I would not have resorted to this doctrine, faced by political unanimity and no known controversy. At the meeting an absolutely firm political decision had been taken and any attempt to change it would have been fruitless. There was no value in my volunteering political advice which had no chance of being accepted . . . My judgment was quite clear in this case—on the Saturday morning I considered but at once rejected it.[28]

Kerr went further to argue that, had he known about the political and administrative differences behind the scenes at the time, this would only have confirmed his decision 'that I should not intrude into the policy and politics of the matter'.[29]

The Governor-General presided at an EXCO meeting on 7 January 1975 at which the loan authority was rescinded. He said nothing, although after the withdrawal of the authority there was obviously an opportunity to reflect upon his earlier concerns with either the Prime Minister or the acting Prime Minister. Then, on 28 January at an EXCO meeting presided over by Kerr the authority was reinstated for half the amount. At this meeting, Kerr says, he asked Murphy's opinion and the Attorney General advised that the loan was legally justified despite the Financial Agreement regarding Loan Council.

Kerr reports: 'I came to the conclusion that in this situation it would be useless for me to try to discuss policy and of no relevance what my own legal opinion might be'. He declined to ask Murphy for written advice. He felt there was no point because he would 'run violently into a brick wall'. Kerr concluded that there was 'nothing I could do about it'.[30]

There are two interpretations of what really happened. First, Sir John, contrary to what he said later, was not fundamentally concerned at the time about the loan—not until it became such a controversy six months later. That is why he signed the minute without expressing his fears to Whitlam; why he never expressed them even after the authority was terminated three weeks later; and why he signed a second authority without expressing any such concerns about either of them. This is the Whitlam theory—that Kerr's fears were constructed in mid-1975, strictly in hindsight.

Whitlam says that Kerr, far from having concerns, was swept up in the loan enthusiasm. He reports that five days after he signed the minute Kerr presided at an EXCO meeting with Rex Connor and Kep Enderby as ministers and that Sir John was eager 'to discuss the progress of the talks about overseas loans and the immense potential of the projects which they would finance'.[31]

The alternative interpretation is that Kerr's account is accurate—that he was seriously worried from the start but decided to say nothing.

The difficulty with this version is in attempting to reconcile Kerr's worries with his silence. Kerr depicts himself as a Governor-General who was simultaneously alarmed about the loan authority but fully justified in refusing to raise his concerns with Whitlam. This is strange behaviour at any level of human endeavour. One could be forgiven for concluding that Kerr wants the best of both worlds.

If it is assumed that Kerr's version, not Whitlam's, is the truth—and nobody will ever know—then it appears that the Governor-General acted with little judgement or commonsense. The real point, though, is the insight it offers into Kerr's understanding of his office.

Kerr and the office

Kerr has two justifications for not raising his concerns at the time with Whitlam. First, that it was not his task to raise a legal or constitutional issue since that was, ultimately, a matter for the courts. Second, that he could not have influenced Whitlam so any discussion would have been futile.

Taking the first point, there was, of course, no certainty that the matter would ever go to the courts. In the event the courts never expressed a view on its legality. However, the responsibility of the Governor-General is to query, counsel and warn if he feels that the government is making a serious error of legislative or executive action. That is the role of the Sovereign; it is the role of the Governor-General.

Sir Paul Hasluck in his William Queale Lecture—the document Kerr read before taking office—makes this point with force and at length:

> A decision in Executive Council is the final executive action . . . One of the main responsibilities of the Governor-General as President of the Executive Council is to make sure that all actions of the Government are constitutionally correct and lawful . . . a Governor-General is both a watch-dog over the Constitution and laws for the nation as a whole and a watch-dog for the Government considered as a whole. He does not reject advice outright but seeks to ensure that advice is well-founded . . . Various steps are open to him. He can ask questions. He can seek full information. He can call for additional advice on any doubtful issue. In a matter of major importance he may suggest to the Prime Minister that an augmented meeting of Executive Council be held to consider all aspects of a question . . . With the Prime Minister the Governor-General can be expected to talk with frankness and friendliness, to question, discuss, suggest and counsel. The role of the Crown in the Executive is to ensure that decisions are made with care and in accordance with the law. This is ensured, not by the exercise of a veto, but by the influence on Ministers and public servants of the fact that the final scrutiny of a proposal for executive action will be a thorough scrutiny maintaining both law and principle.[32]

Hasluck's statement was a general proposition; but he could have been writing about the loan authorisation.

Kerr did not follow Hasluck's prescription because, he argued, the courts could decide the issue. At this point Kerr's judicial view of the office of Governor-General collapses completely.

The reason for having a Governor-General is to try to correct any problem at source—at the executive level. The executive power of the Commonwealth is vested in the Queen and 'is exercisable by the Governor-General as the Queen's representative'. A Governor-General fulfilling his responsibility under the Constitution and following the conventions outlined from Bagehot through to Hasluck would raise these concerns with his Prime Minister. That is the traditional task of both Crown and Governor-General; it is consistent with the doctrine that the Crown acts only on the advice of his ministers. Indeed, by allowing that advice to be tested the doctrine grows stronger.

The Governor-General or the Monarch must press the matter when it is serious. On every count and on Kerr's own admission the loan authority was a serious issue. A diligent and active Governor-General would have pressed the matter.

The then Attorney General's Department chief, Sir Clarence Harders, concludes: 'I think a Governor-General who had the concerns about the EXCO minute and its legality along the lines expressed by Kerr in his book should have raised these concerns at the time with the Prime Minister'.[33]

Kerr understood these arguments. As early as February 1975 he was making speeches endorsing Hasluck's interpretation of the office and vice-regal responsibilities, even using the same words as Hasluck.[34] But he refused to apply them to the loan.

Kerr's second justification for his silence was the belief that he would have no impact; that he was, in effect, a Governor-General without influence. The first reply to this, of course, is that nobody will ever know because he didn't try. The second reply is that his construct, classically, is a contradiction in terms.

A King has influence; the only Kings without influence are dead or deposed. The Crown does not possess the power it once did, but it does possess influence. Such influence if pressed can be enormous. The history of twentieth century Britain is that of influential Monarchs—George V, George VI, Elizabeth II. It is easier for a King or Queen of Britain to exercise influence than it is for a Governor-General. The Crown of Britain can trace itself back to Egbert in 809; it has twelve centuries of weight; a King has no need to justify his influence since it exists as a natural right while his Crown exists.

A Governor-General lacks a King's advantages of tradition, hereditary continuity, religious sanction and royal ceremony. In egalitarian Australia a Governor-General is under pressure to earn his influence. However, since the unbroken line of Australian Governors-General was established at the time of Lord Casey, followed by Hasluck, a distinct effort was made to lift the profile and influence of the office within the process of government. Hasluck was not just a theoretician; he was a practitioner. He queried, counselled and warned in dealing with ministers. He certainly had influence. Indeed, once the office has no influence then it should be abolished. But influence does not come easily.

Whitlam could be an intimidating Prime Minister, particularly when told what he didn't want to hear. Prime Ministers tend to be overbearing. Yet the influence available to a Governor-General as the Crown's representative is unique. It was not a case of Kerr exercising a veto; it was a case of Kerr ensuring that Whitlam knew he had concerns and persuading Whitlam to address them. Nobody should underestimate the pressure on a government to respond to such concerns put in a firm way by the Governor-General.

Given the complaints that he raised about the loan process in his memoirs, there are several things that Kerr should have done at some stage. He should have told Whitlam that the calling of the 13 December EXCO meeting was a serious breach of procedure; he should have sought assurances that it would not re-occur; he should have asked the Attorney General to put his advice in writing; he should have asked for a far more detailed Explanatory Memorandum from his ministers; he could have written to Whitlam setting out all his doubts in a way that required a considered response; he could have asked Whitlam if he was really satisfied with the departure from normal loan channels and usual commission and whether he would be embarrassed to have the details made public. In Hasluck's words, he should have spoken to Whitlam in a frank and friendly manner about his concerns. By such action Whitlam would have been alerted to the fact that the Governor-General had serious worries. But Kerr did none of this.

Why?

Kerr was still inexperienced in office; he was finding his way; he would have disliked such a tough call; perhaps he was emotionally debilitated because of his wife's death only three months earlier; he was facing in Whitlam a man of formidable dimensions and intimidating presence; he could have feared that his relationship with Whitlam would be damaged at the start of his term. Kerr had no stomach for 'advising and warning' at this time on this issue. It was not his style.

An official close to Kerr at the time—and a supporter—says:

> There was no point. It would not have achieved anything. To let Whitlam know that Kerr was unhappy would only have run the risk of hurting their relationship. Kerr concluded it was best to regard the event as 'water under the bridge'. He was a forgiving man. He hoped

it would not re-occur. Kerr, after all, never assumed there would be a future constitutional crisis.[35]

That is about the best explanation we are likely to get.

It is salutary to recall the description given of Kerr by his friend and supporter, James McAuley, who said that Kerr wasn't ruthless enough to become Prime Minister, that 'he could never eat people for breakfast . . . he is in fact a soft-hearted person who greatly dislikes taking part in the affliction of hurt on anyone'.[36] Kerr knew that he was dependent upon Whitlam for access to information in the discharge of his duties and for the conditions of his life—budgets, staff, overseas travel. Kerr was anticipating a ten year term—and it was early days yet.

The other explanation for Kerr's behaviour during the loans affair is Whitlam's. In effect, it is an accusation: that Kerr manufactured his concerns only well after the event.

Whitlam's reply to Kerr is sharp. Referring to the EXCO minute, he says:

> To suggest that the very fact that its validity might become a matter for the courts—'justiciable', Sir John's word—was itself the excuse and the reason for not raising it with me is monstrous. Elsewhere, he asserts that the central role of the Governor-General is to prevent illegal conduct by Ministers; that assertion forms part of his defence for his conduct on 11 November 1975 . . . His real concern had nothing to do with the validity or otherwise of the Executive Council minute of 13 December 1974; it arose only when that cancelled minute became a matter of political controversy. If that is not so, if Sir John Kerr's professed concern antedated the events of June and July 1975, then he is all the more blameworthy . . . if he had doubts, it was his duty as Governor-General to 'advise and warn' his Prime Minister of them . . . it was the obligation of any man of honour to speak man to man about them.[37]

Kerr and Whitlam—the loan's legacy

It was an evil wind on land and water in the summer of 1974-75. Cyclone Tracy took Darwin; a bulk carrier broke the Tasman Bridge, splitting Hobart in two. Whitlam returned from Europe for the first disaster; for the second he lost his composure over in The Hague. Kerr spent a lonely summer at Admiralty House in Sydney, next door to Whitlam's often empty Kirribilli House. But there was some joy—and Whitlam's conclusion was that the social activity on the harbourside mocked Kerr's later claims of grave misgiving.

On the evening of Saturday 28 December Kerr tapped on the window at Kirribilli House when two of Whitlam's advisers, Elizabeth Reid and Patti Warn, were working. Warn wrote:

> With a muttered 'Don't leave me with him' Liz went and greeted him with a gracious 'Oh Sir John! Do come in.' (I had known from Liz that Sir John was paying a certain amount of attention to her around this time: she had certainly had a meal at Yarralumla and had been rung by him on a number of occasions.) Sir John explained that he had been walking in the gardens of Admiralty House when he saw the lights on at Kirribilli and, knowing that the Prime Minister was due to return from Darwin that evening, he felt he should come over in case he could do anything.[38]

They had a rambling two hour discussion over Scotch which included a discussion of Kerr's courting days and the government's fears that Cairns intended to reappoint the attractive but unqualified Junie Morosi to his staff. Warn continued:

> Liz and I said we thought her appointment . . . would be disastrous and Sir John said he would see if anything could be done to block it. He contacted his aide-de-camp and told him to ring Alan Cooley of the Public Service Board with an instruction to him to provide advice on Junie Morosi's terms of employment as approved and the extent to which they departed from the norm.

It grew late and the women were going to a nearby party. Kerr seemed to have settled in, so they invited him to attend if he wanted. Kerr went on 'at some length about how restrictive the life of the Governor-General was, particularly as far as a personal life was concerned. He was especially unhappy that he was unable to just drive off into the night . . . Liz accompanied him back into the garden on his way back to Admiralty House to keep him company. When she returned she was a little dishevelled and professed great relief that she had got away'. But Sir John took up their invitation and arrived at the party about midnight, where, fortified by more Scotch, he finished by telling the guests that 'he was the only person in Australia who could get in touch with Her Majesty'.[39]

Over the coming weeks Kerr saw Whitlam, Cairns and many ministers at functions—at lunches, dinners, breakfasts—particularly during late January and early February. All reports were of a favourable disposition and a very social Governor-General. He saw Liz Reid— Whitlam's adviser—on a number of occasions in a brief courtship. Whitlam, on reflection, did not believe that Kerr was a troubled man at the time over the loan authorisation, which was still secret. Whitlam felt there was an incongruity between Kerr's relaxed behaviour and his later claims that he had been agitated over the loan to such an extent that it could not be raised with the Prime Minister.[40]

To be successful the relationship between a Governor-General and a Prime Minister depends, above all, on trust. If trust is missing then so is frankness; and that sows the seeds of misunderstanding and suspicion. That is the legacy of the loans affair between Whitlam and Kerr.

Whitlam paid the political price for his loan blunder as 1975 unfolded. It was a heavy price; but so was the folly. He also mishandled the Executive Council processes—and this, in turn, deeply upset Kerr. But Kerr, given his own version of events, mishandled Whitlam. He was not frank with his Prime Minister; he kept his doubts to himself; he did not use his discretion. By staying silent he left Whitlam with a false impression. He would repeat the same behaviour during the constitutional crisis.

Kerr, whether his doubts existed at the time or only in mid-1975, was left suspicious of Whitlam. His fear was of being seen as a 'rubber stamp' Viceroy. In truth, if Kerr was seen as a 'rubber stamp' then it was his own fault—not Whitlam's. It was quite easy for a Governor-General to despatch such impressions—but Kerr missed the opportunity to do this over the loan approval. The irony is that Kerr then resented Whitlam for treating him as a 'rubber stamp' and for belittling him. It was the worst mistake Whitlam could have made with his Governor-General. Kerr said:

> I had learned some lessons from the loan affair . . . I knew that I should need to keep a very watchful eye on events. The warning I had received left me somewhat changed in my attitude as to the vigilance that might be necessary to my office and its duties. I did not intend to deal with any crisis which might involve exercise of the reserve powers acting automatically as a rubber stamp for whatever the Prime Minister might advise; and I stiffened myself against the need to be ready to make an informed and neutral assessment should critical discretionary matters arise for my decision.[41]

Whitlam was in trouble. His political edifice during the coming crisis would depend upon one foundation—that Kerr would do only what he, Whitlam, advised and nothing that he did not advise. Whitlam did not know that this foundation had a deep flaw. The loan approval had undermined Kerr's trust in Whitlam.

6
The deadlock

> *The House of Representatives—the people's house—alone determines who shall govern Australia.*
>
> Gough Whitlam, 15 October 1975

ON FRIDAY 12 SEPTEMBER 1975 Gough Whitlam delivered a speech in Goulburn which foreshadowed his plan to defy any deferral of the budget by the Senate—the strategy that ended two months later in his dismissal. His decision was driven by survival. Whitlam agreed with Fraser's calculation—Labor was certain to lose a late 1975 election. In the final resort, that is why Fraser wanted an election and why Whitlam was determined to avoid one.

The political mood was different from that of autumn 1974 when Whitlam embraced an election showdown after Snedden announced that he would block Supply. In September 1975 Whitlam, a perpetual optimist, still believed that his government would recover from the loans affair and the current stagflation—but it needed time. 'We were emerging from the winter of our discontent', he said later.[1] The mid-1975 reshuffle that put Bill Hayden into Treasury and Jim McClelland into Labour and Immigration offered Labor an outside chance for recovery down the track. So Whitlam decided that a late 1975 election was not to be tolerated.

In his speech the Prime Minister said:

> There are no laws applying to a situation where supply is refused by an Upper House, no laws at all. There is no precedent in the Federal Parliament and the last State precedent was in Victoria in 1947. And there is, in fact, no convention because people never used to think it could

happen, so it's never been discussed. And accordingly one can only say that there is no obligation by law, by rule, by precedent or by convention for a Prime Minister in those circumstances which are threatened, to advise the Governor-General to dissolve the House of Representatives and have an election for it . . . and the Governor-General can get advice from the Prime Minister alone. I think that this is the law and this is the propriety.[2]

Whitlam argued that in Australia and in other Westminster democracies the Prime Minister was entitled to remain in office while he commanded a majority in the Lower House.

Whitlam had two motives. First, to dissuade the Opposition from trying to force an election on the 1975 budget, by making this option too hazardous for Fraser. But Whitlam's declaration was not just a threat. Anyone familiar with his penchant for 'crash through or crash' tactics would have realised that Whitlam meant what he said. So the second motive was to declare his hand: if the Opposition tried to force an election the Prime Minister would not resign but would remain in office to wage a political battle against the Senate. Whitlam's statement meant that the blocking of the budget could precipitate a political and constitutional struggle.

The position Whitlam outlined was based upon the notion of responsible government implicit in the Constitution—a Prime Minister was commissioned because he had the support of the House of Representatives, the government was responsible to the House of Representatives, and while a Prime Minister enjoyed the confidence of the House of Representatives he was entitled to govern.

However, this view was qualified by the existence of the federalism principle reflected in the powers of the Senate and, in particular, section 53 which gave the Senate the power to reject or to defer an Appropriation bill. The Senate was vested with such powers on the assumption that it would operate as a States House. But the Senate was run as a party chamber and was now contemplating the use of its financial powers to despatch the House to the people.

The significance of Whitlam's stand is that he was attempting to resolve the compromise in the Constitution between responsible government and federalism by securing a victory for the former. If Whitlam could stare down a Senate that was trying to blackmail the House into an election then, in effect, he would crush this power by practical politics. Whitlam's position was tantamount to changing the Constitution—by practice, not by referendum.

So Whitlam put the nation—but notably Fraser and also Kerr—on notice of his intentions. If Fraser tried to destroy his government then Whitlam, in turn, would defy Fraser's Senate in order to achieve both a political victory over the Opposition and a constitutional victory by altering the power balance in favour of the House against the Senate.

The position Whitlam adopted had one assumption as its linchpin: that the Governor-General would act only on the advice of the Prime Minister and not without his advice. It is significant that in his speech Whitlam argued that the Governor-General could obtain advice only from the Prime Minister.

From the start Whitlam understood that in order to defy Fraser he needed the support of Kerr. His speech was not just a warning to Fraser; it was a public declaration to Kerr that, in this situation, Kerr had to follow Whitlam's advice.

The next House of Representatives election was not due until the middle of 1977. However, a half Senate election was required before mid-1976, as the three year terms of the short-term Senators elected at the May 1974 double dissolution would expire at 30 June 1976. In technical terms Whitlam had a range of election options if Fraser blocked the budget—a double dissolution election; advising a half Senate election which was due before mid-1976; advising a House of Representatives election with half the Senate; or calling a House of Representatives election alone. The option of remaining in office and defying the Senate was tagged by the media as the 'tough it out' strategy, a phrase that Whitlam disliked.

The electoral weakness of the Whitlam Government had been documented by the Bass by-election on 28 June—caused by Barnard's acceptance of an ambassadorship—which recorded a swing of 15 per cent against the ALP. Bass proved Labor's electoral rot. Withers says: 'There would have been no election in 1975 without the Bass by-election and Khemlani. I can't understand why Gough got rid of Lance. Why would you do it?'[3]

From this time Fraser faced internal pressure to force a late 1975 election. However the August 1975 budget—the only budget of Bill Hayden—had been received well. Its strategy was to lay the basis for growth while winding back inflation over a two year period. Labor's credibility began to rise from an apparently hopeless trough. Fraser declared on 21 August, two days after the budget, that 'at this stage it's our intention to allow the budget passage through the Senate'.[4]

But within days Fraser was openly canvassing support for an early election. Doug Anthony was a public and private advocate of forcing Labor to the polls. One of Fraser's concerns was to ensure that any blocking of the budget was seen not as a cynical grab for power but as a principled act for the national benefit.

The change in Senate numbers

Three days before Whitlam's Goulburn speech an event occurred that became pivotal to the subsequent constitutional crisis. The Queensland Premier, Joh Bjelke-Petersen, procured the nomination to the Senate of an obscure French-polisher, Albert Patrick Field, to replace Bert Milliner, a Queensland ALP Senator who had recently died. Bjelke-Petersen (who had played a decisive hand against Whitlam before the 1974 poll) would deliver a majority to the Opposition in the Senate before the 1975 poll.

The Coalition's votes in October–November 1975 to defer the budget were carried only because of the change in the composition of the Senate from that which had been elected by the people in the May 1974 double dissolution. In May 1974 the Senate result was Labor 29, Coalition 29 and two Independents—Michael Townley (Tas), a Coalition backer, and Steele Hall (SA), a renegade Liberal who backed Whitlam on Supply. So the numbers were split 30–30 on the main question.

But in early 1975 Whitlam appointed Lionel Murphy from the Senate to the High Court. The NSW Liberal Premier, Tom Lewis, exploited the then casual-vacancy provision of the Constitution (section 15) to appoint an Independent, Cleaver Bunton, instead of an ALP Senator to the vacancy. (Section 15 stipulates that a Senate vacancy is filled by the respective State Parliament choosing a successor pending an election.) This was the first startling example of a series of events in 1975 in which the non-Labor side, at State and federal level, used the provisions of the Constitution in a way that breached hitherto followed conventions in order to weaken and then destroy the Whitlam Government. Bunton's appointment reduced Labor's Senate numbers from 29 to 28. But on the budget Bunton would vote with Labor. So the overall strengths of Labor versus Coalition remained equal on the vital question.

However, Labor's position became perilous with the death on 30 June 1975 of Bert Milliner. This reduced Labor to 27 Senators. It meant that on the Supply question the numbers would become 30–29 in favour of the Coalition (with Hall and Bunton backing Whitlam). Bjelke-Petersen, in effect, would determine the final vote through the operation of section 15 in filling the casual Senate vacancy. If Milliner, a dead ALP Senator, were replaced by a new ALP Senator the Supply vote would divide 30–30. This would give the Opposition a negative majority; that is, it could defeat measures and it could defeat the budget. But it would lack a positive majority; that is, the numbers to control the Senate. It would not be able to carry motions in the Senate and it would not be able to defer the budget—which was the tactic that Reg Withers had devised.

Fate was cruel to Whitlam in delivering this ace into the hands of his principal enemy. Bjelke-Petersen taunted and then tortured the Labor Government. He began by saying that after a death it was logical to appoint a man from the same party. Then he wrote to the leader of the State ALP parliamentary party, Tom Burns, asking for the submission of three names. Labor refused to submit a panel of names. It believed that, by right, by convention, by morality, the ALP should choose the replacement. It nominated a left-winger, Dr Malcolm Colston. Bjelke-Petersen said 'no' and the Queensland Parliament voted Colston down once, then twice.

The veteran analyst Alan Reid criticised Labor's tactics:

> I could never understand this intransigence on the part of the ALP. To have submitted a panel would have undoubtedly been a blow to ALP pride. But if the ALP had submitted a panel the ALP would get an ALP successor to Bert Milliner. And, in politics, pride is less important than strength . . . in this case strength essential for the survival of the Federal ALP Government.[5]

Reid is right to argue that Labor should have submitted a panel. Whitlam should have persuaded the Queensland ALP to this course. That would have maximised the chance of getting an ALP replacement, despite weakening the principle involved. Bjelke-Petersen relied upon a 1962 precedent when a State Coalition Government required the ALP to submit two names and then voted for its preferred ALP replacement. In 1975 Labor displayed a reckless disregard for its own self-preservation by declining to give the Premier a candidate other than Colston, who as a strong left-winger was an obvious target for Bjelke-Petersen's antagonism. Labor took a stand on principle—and this is understandable. But Labor's interests involved doing whatever was required to secure an ALP replacement. It should have been guided by power not principle; it should have put the survival of the Whitlam Government before its own dignity.[6]

Given Bjelke-Petersen's animosity towards the Whitlam Government it is very doubtful that he would have found any of the three ALP nominees satisfactory, even if Labor had submitted a list. But the Premier did ask for a list rather than begin the process by rejecting an ALP nominee, and Labor should have pursued this option.

In a bizarre circumstance Bjelke-Petersen appointed Albert Field, who had contacted his office volunteering to stand as a 'true' Labor man. Field was elected by a vote in the Queensland Parliament in which the Liberal ministers voted against Bjelke-Petersen. En route to

Canberra Field declared that 'Mr Whitlam will never get a vote from me'; then he said that he would support any moves to force an early election. He was sworn in amid a walkout of government Senators except for the ALP leader, Ken Wriedt, who sat stiffly with his back to Field as he was administered the oath. Field's appointment took the rancour within federal politics to a new intensity.

Labor challenged Field's eligibility to sit and, eventually, Field was given a month's leave from the Senate on 1 October. That meant that the Senate would be 59-strong during the critical month of October. Bjelke-Petersen's refusal to appoint an ALP Senator meant that on the Supply issue the vote was 30–29 in favour of the Opposition. Bjelke-Petersen had delivered a majority to the Opposition; it had the numbers to pass a deferral motion, not just to deny the bills a passage. It could now execute the tactics that Withers had designed.

It was the action of the Queensland Government that enabled Fraser to block the budget and secure the dismissal of Whitlam.

Whitlam declared that the Senate had been 'corrupted' since the May 1974 election. The manipulation of these numbers by Bjelke-Petersen, in a constitutional way, gave the Opposition a majority that it did not win through the ballot box. This was the origin of the 'tainted Senate' accusation that Whitlam used mercilessly during the crisis. It was a moral case against any decision by Fraser to defer the budget; but it was also the means by which Fraser got the numbers to defer the budget. Fraser merely used the numbers that fell to him. Former Whitlam minister, John Wheeldon says: 'The Liberals claimed to be concerned about the Field appointment but they were hypocrites. They passed a motion criticising it and upholding the convention, but if they were serious they should have instructed one of their Senators not to participate in subsequent divisions. But they wouldn't do that.'[7]

Fraser blocks the budget

The next pivotal event was the High Court's ruling on 10 October that the Whitlam Government's legislation to allow the Australian Capital Territory and Northern Territory to be represented in the Senate was valid. This law meant that at the next Senate election two Senators would be elected from each of the Territories. Under the Constitution the new Senate would not be constituted until 1 July 1976—but the four new Territory Senators would take their seats immediately after the election. So would another two Senators—those elected in New South Wales and Queensland as replacements for Bunton and Field. So if the half Senate poll were held in late 1975 a 64-strong interim Senate would be constituted for a few months, until 1 July 1976, that would comprise the existing Senate plus the elected replacements for Bunton and Field plus the four Territory Senators. A strange situation indeed.

Labor had an outside chance of winning control of the Senate during the interim period. This was because Labor expected to win one of the two Senate places in each of the ACT and the Northern Territory. In addition it hoped that the second ACT place would fall to the anti-Fraser zealot, former Liberal Prime Minister, John Gorton, running as an Independent and a supporter of the ALP on the Supply question. Labor believed that it had prospects of securing the replacement Senate places in New South Wales and Queensland. In any such election Labor's aim was to win control of the interim Senate with the support of Hall and Gorton. The Coalition was horrified at the prospect, though it was a remote one.

In this situation Labor would be able to pass all its bills, its electoral reforms including optional preferential voting, and its redistribution based on the one vote one value law. Whitlam had only an outside chance of controlling the interim Senate; but to the Coalition an outside chance was too great.

This prospect encouraged the Coalition to follow two mutually reinforcing paths: (1) deciding to block the budget and force a general election; and (2) acting to ensure that any half Senate election called by Whitlam would be effectively aborted by having the four non-Labor Premiers advise their State Governors not to issue the writs for such a poll.

Fraser knew that a necessary condition for forcing an election was unity within his own ranks. It was the Coalition Senators who had to vote down the budget, endure the attack that they were abusing the system of parliamentary government, and handle any community backlash.

In an effort to influence the Liberal Senators, Steele Hall wrote a dramatic open letter to Fraser:

> I believe Labor will be defeated whenever a general election is held. In this event it is very important that the manner in which you assume office should have the long-term approval of most Australians. We ought not to underestimate the ability of the electorate to recognise shabby behaviour . . . I hope you will at least consider my prediction that if you take, or attempt to take, the Prime Minister's office by the device of a vote in the Senate, your leadership capacity will automatically degenerate to the disadvantage of the Liberal Party. If you 'assemble' your members in the Senate to reject supply you will consciously destroy the stability of Australian politics which we as Liberals have grown to expect under our administrations since 1949 . . .[8]

A number of Senators had reservations about blocking the budget. The strongest resistance came from a party veteran, Alan Missen (Vic), who opposed such action on principle. There were other opponents, sceptics and worriers, notably Don Jessop (SA), Eric Bessell (Tas), Neville Bonner (Qld) and Condor Laucke (SA). Withers felt that the former Senate leader, Kenneth Anderson, found the notion particularly unpalatable. In the House of Representatives there was one known opponent—Ian Macphee.[9]

Outside Canberra the most senior Liberal opposed was the Victorian Premier, Sir Rupert 'Dick' Hamer. 'I didn't think it was the role of upper houses to prevent governments from operating and I doubted its wisdom', Hamer says.[10] The South Australian division was the other major point of resistance that Fraser would have to combat, in particular the powerful former Premier, Sir Thomas Playford.

Malcolm Fraser prepared his ground thoroughly. He conducted several talks on a one-on-one basis with Missen and a couple with Macphee. According to Withers, 'Missen knew that without Fraser's goodwill he wouldn't get re-endorsement'.[11]

In his speech to the Liberal Party Federal Council on Sunday 12 October, Fraser's direction was not hard to identify. He argued that the decision was not between expediency and principle but between 'two heavy and conflicting principles'. They were the right of a government to a three year term and the responsibility of an Opposition to terminate 'the incompetence, the damage, the failures of the worst government in our history'.

On 13 October the Liberal Federal Council passed a motion in support of denying Whitlam the option of calling a half Senate election. It was, in effect, an appeal to the four non-Labor Premiers to advise their Governors, if the situation arose, not to issue writs for a half Senate election. The Queensland Premier, Sir Joh Bjelke-Petersen, and the NSW Premier, Tom Lewis, had agreed; Western Australia's Sir Charles Court was expected to agree; only Victoria's Sir Rupert Hamer appeared to be equivocal.

Just two days before the Coalition voted to defer the budget Alan Missen wrote that 'there were some ten Senators who were, in differing degrees, hostile to the idea of using the Senate as a means of throwing out the Government and requiring an election'.[12] This is similar to the assessment of Don Jessop that 'before the budget was blocked I think there were about eight or nine Senators who shared my feeling that we shouldn't do this'.[13]

But Missen was not a martyr; he would not sabotage his party's position unilaterally. He had made a private decision recorded in his diary: 'I had long since determined that it was not a matter where one person could thwart the whole of the Party and, in fact, there would be a need for a reasonably sized group of Senators before they could take such a traumatic step.'[14] Missen and Fraser had a discussion on 14 October in which Missen felt that Fraser was moving to block the budget.

That same day the debate on the budget took its final twist in the bizarre brand of politics in which the Whitlam Government specialised. The loans affair claimed its next victim—R F X Connor, the architect and mastermind of the search for overseas funds. Further revelations from the loans intermediary, Tirath Khemlani, sealed Connor's fate. A new document from Khemlani revealed that Connor had given misleading answers in denying his ongoing contact with the loan middleman after the EXCO loan authority was terminated on 20 May 1975, and that Whitlam, relying upon Connor, had also given Parliament misleading assurances that there were no further loan negotiations after this date.

Khemlani's revelation doomed Connor, Whitlam and the ALP Government. Whitlam advised Connor that he would have to resign, not because of his conduct but because he had misled the Prime Minister. Connor resigned on 14 October, with the ALP caucus voting 55–24 to accept his resignation offer. Ken Wriedt became Minerals and Energy Minister and Paul Keating was elected to the ministerial vacancy. Whitlam declared that 'a great minister and a close friend and colleague has fallen'. When the House sat Fraser and Lynch launched the final stage of their campaign—to implicate Whitlam in the loans affair and to force the Prime Minister's resignation.

Connor's departure closed Fraser's mind. It made the blocking of the budget in the Senate in order to force a general election an inevitability. The folly of the Whitlam Government had made it difficult to argue a principled position within the non-Labor side. Fraser was handed an embarrassment of weapons. Labor's level of incompetence merely invited execution. Connor's resignation was equal testimony to Whitlam's sense of honour and to his failure as an effective leader.

Such was the Whitlam Government.

Any remaining Coalition opponents of blocking the budget had their case destroyed. Malcolm Fraser who said in March 1975, upon becoming leader of the Opposition, that he would only block Supply if there were 'extraordinary' or 'reprehensible' events had this definition satisfied on virtually the exact day that his leadership group was to make its final decision.

Bill Hayden says: 'The risk for Fraser was that Labor was improving. I think from the 1975 budget that Labor was pulling itself together.

Fraser was only able to get away with it because of the loans affair. Otherwise his action would have been seen as destructively opportunistic.'[15] Withers claims that 'the loan and Khemlani offended the country's sense of public morality'.[16]

On 15 October the Coalition leadership group decided to block the budget in order to force Whitlam to the polls. It took this decision only after the toughminded Country Party shadow minister Peter Nixon asked what would happen if the budget was blocked and Whitlam stayed in office, as he had threatened. Wouldn't that situation be left to Kerr to resolve and wasn't Kerr favourably disposed to Labor, Nixon asked.

Fraser had already analysed the risk identified by Nixon. The conclusion that Fraser had reached was quite simple: provided that the Senate blocked the budget and kept blocking the budget then, one way or another, there had to be an election. Fraser felt confident that he had the authority within the Coalition and the support of his colleagues to withstand Whitlam's campaign of retaliation. But Fraser had also made a further calculation—that if the deadlock over Supply continued and Sir John Kerr was forced to intervene then any such intervention, provided the Senate remained firm, would be to secure the election that the Senate was seeking. Fraser felt that Kerr's response would be dictated by his obligations as Governor-General, not by his past association with the Labor Party. History was to vindicate Fraser's logic.[17]

Missen knew the cause was lost. After attending a meeting of Opposition Senators he wrote: 'It was very clear to me that I would have nobody who would stand up to the ultimate question of crossing the floor if the proposal was made'.[18] Missen was by himself—and he had decided that a solo effort would be futile.

The Opposition shadow ministry met and endorsed unanimously the recommendation from the leadership group. The same recommendation was put to a meeting of the Liberal and National parliamentary parties. This was a crucial meeting. Fraser expected that the looming confrontation would be protracted. He needed a unanimous decision and he told the parties he wanted a unanimous decision. Whitlam would be looking for cracks in the Opposition's unity to break its nerve.

Many Liberals spoke in favour, including Jim Killen who had opposed the move to block Supply in 1974. There were only two speakers with reservations—Alan Missen and Don Jessop. The latter spoke only briefly and said he would adhere to the party room decision. Missen delivered a cogent speech against the recommendation:

> I said that, while there was a constitutional right to do so, it was a right which only should be used in the most extreme circumstances. I

drew to the attention of House of Representatives members that they were the most democratically elected House, and that they would be betraying the actions of their forefathers, who fought for the supremacy of the democratically elected House of Parliament over many years. I felt this would be a betrayal of them. I made a second point, that the reaction to this would be a long and bitter campaign. I saw no reason to think that the Prime Minister would give way at all to the demand for an election and that he would fight it out over a long period . . . I felt that it was most likely that the Opposition parties would win an election . . . but it would leave great scars which would affect the Constitution of this country for many many years . . . I urged the Party not to agree to the course proposed, which I felt was, both in principle and practice, to be deplored . . . I finished by stating that it was, of course, a matter on the conscience of each individual Senator, and I would have to make my decision as to how I would vote in respect to such a matter and I reserved my right to do so.[19]

Missen said that governments had a right to remain in office for their three year term. He warned that the contemplated action might turn the blocking of Supply into a regular political tactic.

Before the meeting finished Lynch had a private chat with Missen who pledged that he would not repudiate the party or 'go against it in a unilateral revolt'. This was a vital assurance in which Fraser put great store. So Fraser got his unanimous decision.[20]

That afternoon, 15 October, Fraser announced the Opposition's decision at a hostile press conference, thereby confirming the phenomenon of the Whitlam era in which the conservative parties operated as constitutional radicals. At 4.35 pm Withers rose in the Senate to announce the Opposition's intention and moved an amendment to the Loan Bill to the effect that it not be proceeded with until Whitlam agreed to an election. Withers said that the government no longer had 'the trust and confidence of the Australian people' because of:

(a) the continuing incompetence, evasion, deceit and duplicity of the Prime Minister and his Ministers as exemplified in the overseas loan scandal which was an attempt by the Government to subvert the Constitution, to by-pass Parliament and to evade its responsibilities to the States and the Loan Council;

(b) the Prime Minister's failure to maintain proper control over the activities of his Ministers and Government to the detriment of the Australian nation and people; and

(c) the continuing mismanagement of the Australian economy by the Prime Minister and this Government with policies which have caused a lack of confidence in this nation's potential and created inflation and unemployment not experienced for 40 years.

The amendment was carried 29–28 (a pair granted on each side) and a similar amendment was carried the next day in relation to the Appropriation Bills. The die was cast.

Withers said that once Whitlam agreed to the election the Senate would pass the bills immediately. He declared that Whitlam 'has lost the confidence of the people and he has lost the confidence of the Parliament'. He attacked Whitlam's claim that the Senate could not force an election as 'incorrect' and 'unconstitutional'. He said the Parliament was in a state of 'total deadlock', with a deadlock over 21 double dissolution bills and now the budget. The only recourse was an election. Withers declared that 'any government of any persuasion, if it had any decency in this situation, would resign . . . Mr Whitlam is not a president, he is not a dictator and he is not a king. He is a Prime Minister who had duties and obligations to the Parliament . . . He has lost the confidence of the Parliament'. Withers dismissed any notion that a half Senate election called by Whitlam would suffice.[21]

Behind the Opposition's stance was a subtle and critical tactic. The Senate did not reject the budget. Withers hammered this theme. Indeed at one point he said: 'We are not cutting off the flow of money to the people. We are merely adopting the constitutional method of giving the people a choice.' To reject the bills meant that the Opposition would lose control of them. The bills could be reintroduced only by the government. The Withers tactic, accepted by the Opposition leadership group, was to defer the budget pending Whitlam's decision to call an election. It was the tactic Withers had first advocated in late 1973. To pass such a motion the Opposition required a majority in the Senate. It had the required numbers (30–29) in an effective total of 59, given that Senator Field was on extended leave of absence. Steele Hall (Liberal Movement) and Cleaver Bunton (Ind.) voted with Labor. The numbers remained the same throughout the crisis.

One of the younger ALP Senators, John Button, summed up the position: 'The attitude of the Opposition is simply this: we can do anything we like which is not prohibited by the Constitution'. Steele Hall, attacking the Coalition, delivered his lethal line: 'Let it be remembered that the Opposition succeeded only because a Labor Senator died. They did it over a dead man's corpse'.[22]

In his statement Fraser said:

> The Opposition now has no choice. We will use the power vested in us by the Constitution . . . The Labor Government 1972–75 has been the most incompetent and disastrous government in the history of Australia. Although Australia has basically one of the strongest and healthiest economies in the world, in three years this has been brought to

the brink of disaster by incompetence of the worst kind ... We are
dealing with a chain of improprieties which constitutes one of the most
extraordinary and reprehensible episodes in Australia's political history.
... I now call upon the Prime Minister, if he has a shred of decency
left, to put an end to this whole sorry episode and place himself and
his government before the ultimate tribunal of the people.

Whitlam defies Fraser

It was a fateful decision for the Parliament and the Constitution. The majority view of jurists is that Fraser had the constitutional power in the Senate. Fraser's aim was to achieve political power—regardless of the lofty rationale offered. But the consequences would transcend party politics.

The founding fathers had envisaged that the Senate might reject tax and financial bills on grounds of policy. Fraser's proposal was different—he intended to block the bills appropriating funds for the ordinary annual services of government in order to force the House of Representatives to the people. Fraser's argument, in effect, was that the Senate, as well as the Representatives, could declare no-confidence in the government. While governments could not be made and unmade on the floor of the Senate, the grant of Supply offered the Senate a biannual chance to terminate a government. In justifying his subsequent intervention on the side of the Senate, Sir John Kerr and his adviser, Sir Garfield Barwick, enunciated the political theory that a government was responsible not just to the Representatives but to both Houses.

There is no doubt that Fraser's action, if successful, would elevate the Senate against the House of Representatives. There was no provision in the Constitution to the effect that if the Senate blocked Supply a government was obliged to resign or advise an election. Consequently, if Fraser succeeded he would move the practice and theory of the Constitution and Parliament into new and uncharted waters.

At various times his predecessors had expressed a different opinion. In 1968 Sir Robert Menzies had urged that a Senate not thwart the Representatives on Supply since this would be 'a falsification of democracy'. In 1967 Harold Holt as Prime Minister declared that it was an established principle that the Senate should not reject the financial measures of the Representatives. No precedent existed for Fraser's stance from the time of Federation until the Senate sought to block Supply in 1974. The political difference in 1975 was that the Prime Minister had decided to exercise his rights under responsible government and remain in office despite the Senate's action. Whitlam was under no constitutional obligation to resign or advise a general election when the budget was blocked. Few authorities outside the Opposition argued such a position at that time.[23]

Both Fraser and Whitlam resorted to the Constitution and convention to sustain their respective positions. There was an argument that a convention existed that the Senate not block Supply to force the Representatives to an election. Whether or not such a convention did exist is debatable; at various stages both Labor and Liberal leaders had made comments favouring each view. But 1975 was the point at which the convention would be either entrenched or discredited. Fraser voted, in effect, against any such convention; but he recognised the argument *for* a convention and justified his action only on the grounds of a government guilty of 'extraordinary and reprehensible' action.[24]

Fraser's audacity was met by Whitlam's. At this point the logic of Fraser's stance soon became apparent—it required Kerr to dismiss Whitlam to validate the Senate. The parliamentary institutions would face their greatest strain since Federation, because the quest for electoral power was accorded a supreme and exclusive priority.

Sir Garfield Barwick was visiting Menzies when news was relayed of Fraser's decision. According to Barwick, Menzies was 'somewhat angered by the decision'. He said: 'The young fools are too impatient. If they give this fellow [Whitlam] enough rope he will hang himself.' Menzies asked Barwick what he thought. Barwick replied that 'assuming a proper occasion I would not be troubled by a refusal of Supply by the Senate'. But Barwick argued that on political grounds it should only be done if the winning majority was sufficient to ensure two terms—and he was dubious of that.[25]

The ALP caucus met at 7 pm, about two hours after Withers delivered his speech in the Senate. Whitlam moved instinctively; he would 'tough it out' and defy the Senate. Whitlam said he wanted the Senate to vote either to accept or to reject the budget, not just to defer the budget. He would continue to refer the bills to the Senate until it took such a vote. (Whitlam believed that Fraser would have much more difficulty trying to persuade the Senate to reject the budget outright.) In the meantime the government would remain in office. Whitlam did not rule out the option of calling a half Senate election at some stage. He received the strong endorsement of the parliamentary party. There were only two dissenters—Senate leader Ken Wriedt and Senator John Wheeldon, who argued that the right course for Whitlam was to call a double dissolution election.[26]

Wheeldon says: 'The Liberals behaved disgracefully. But we shouldn't have contributed by trying to stay in office. They broke one convention and we broke another.' He thought that about a quarter of the caucus favoured going to an election.[27] Ken Wriedt echoes these sentiments: 'The parliamentary system was being put under great strain by the Opposition. I wanted to protect the system. I asked myself, "What was more important—to preserve our democracy or to preserve Labor in power?"'[28]

That night Whitlam delivered an address to the nation which signalled that a great struggle had been joined:

> The House of Representatives—the people's house—alone determines who shall govern Australia. That principle has been upheld since Federation. It has never been broken or challenged except during this Government's life . . . It is this unrepresentative Senate, this tainted Senate, which Mr Fraser intends to use as a weapon to strike down the democratically elected government . . . The Government will not yield to pressure. We will not yield to blackmail. We will not be panicked. We will not turn over the government of this country to vested interests, pressure groups and newspaper proprietors whose tactics would destroy the standards and traditions of parliamentary government.[29]

Whitlam's unprecedented stance had the backing of his principal advisers—the Secretary of the Prime Minister's Department, John Menadue; his deputy, Geoffrey Yeend; the Secretary of the Attorney General's Department, Clarence Harders; and the Solicitor-General, Maurice Byers. Byers recalls: 'It was either before the budget was blocked or immediately afterwards that I had a discussion with Whitlam. He said the Senate was blocking Supply and asked if the government was obliged to resign, and I said "no".'[30] Harders says: 'I believed that Whitlam's decision to "tough it out" was a legitimate tactic and within the law. I think he was entitled to test the strength of the Senate since Senators themselves were expressing concerns at the Opposition's approach. I did not try to discourage Whitlam from this tactic which was obviously designed to achieve a political solution.'[31] Yeend believed that it was a political crisis that would have a political solution and that Whitlam was entitled to bring pressure upon the Senate in that cause.[32]

The government would not run out of funds immediately. It had provision for about six weeks. But from the moment Whitlam announced that he would defy the Senate and would not seek a general election, the Prime Minister was dependent upon the Governor-General's acquiescence. Whitlam felt confident about Kerr; he was sure his edifice was built upon rock.

Kerr on the eve

But Whitlam had made a great miscalculation about his Governor-General—already. Kerr, previously worried about the loans affair, had soured towards Whitlam much more during September and early October. On the eve of the great crisis Kerr, far from being on Whitlam's side, was deeply resentful of the Prime Minister. Their personal relationship was flawed—though Whitlam did not understand this—and that meant that their official relationship was compromised. Kerr, in addition, had extra reason to be on his constitutional guard. Kerr's heart and mind had moved a long way during 1975.

The early months of 1975 had been difficult for Kerr—he was lonely, isolated and worried about his status. Kerr was drinking heavily and anxious to remarry. He was interested in Elizabeth Reid, Whitlam's high profile adviser. They had appeared on television together promoting 1975 as International Women's Year, and had also cooperated on assistance to Darwin after the cyclone. However, their relationship had become social as well as professional. At one point in early 1975, Kerr had floated the idea of marriage to Reid, an invitation she did not pursue. She recalls his precise words: 'Why should you be working for the second most important man in the land, when you could be married to the most important?' Reid continues: 'There was no doubt in Kerr's mind that he saw himself as the most important person in the nation.' Reid saw more of Kerr during this period than anyone else in the government, including Whitlam.[33]

Jim McClelland also saw his old friend around this time. He recalls:

> It was after Kerr had been appointed Governor-General, and after his first wife's death. He was lonely and wanted a chat, and was at my place at Point Piper. We told him at the end that he couldn't drive home to Kirribilli because he might get pinched. So we rang Admiralty House, who sent out a car with a spare driver to take Kerr's own car back. I was going down the path with Kerr so he wouldn't fall arse over head. He stopped halfway down and said, 'Give us a kiss'. I gave him a peck on the cheek. But it wasn't enough. He puckered up and said, 'No, give us a real kiss'. That's one of the reasons he was so distraught about my reaction to the dismissal. I think he loved me.[34]

It was a love that would turn to alienation, even hate. After the dismissal McClelland made the most bitter attacks on Kerr, and when Kerr wrote his memoirs, he made McClelland a non-person; his name did not appear in the book.

One of Kerr's greatest supporters, Ken Gee, once a Trotskyite fellow-traveller with McClelland, suggests in defence of Kerr that McClelland honed his wit and intelligence to elevate 'venom to an art form'. Gee describes McClelland as 'a man of great talent . . . but he is also a self-confessed great hater . . . Is it significant that the most concentrated vitriol is poured over those who were closest, Kerr and Wran?'[35]

Early in 1975 Kerr, on an evening stroll at Kirribilli, bumped into an old friend, Anne Robson, in the street and asked her to dinner some time later. They drove to Jonah's at Whale Beach, a restaurant whose spectacular clifftop setting must have reminded his Francophile companion of the Cote d'Azur. They sat alongside the picture window beneath an easter moon. 'What do you want to go to Paris for?' Kerr asked. 'Why don't you stay here . . . and marry me?' So she did.[36]

On 21 April Kerr told Whitlam, who was about to depart for the Commonwealth meeting in Jamaica, that he would be marrying a friend of 30 years standing on 29 April, during Whitlam's absence. She was divorcing her husband, Hugh Robson, a District Court judge. Whitlam congratulated Kerr on marrying such an accomplished woman, a former French interpreter whom Whitlam had met at conferences years earlier. He reminisced that Hugh Robson had organised the bachelor dinner for him before his own marriage to Margaret.[37]

A week later, in Kingston, the message was given to the entire Australian party—officials, advisers and media—that Whitlam wanted to see them to make an announcement. There was speculation among the journalists about the subject since such a gathering was unusual. I recollect an ebullient Whitlam's short speech announcing that the Governor-General had remarried. The Kerrs were toasted in their absence by Australians in the West Indies. Whitlam's delight was manifest, a delight that puzzled many of us who were far less impressed by a vice-regal marriage. Whitlam was happy for Kerr; he wanted his fellow Australians to share the occasion. Clearly Whitlam felt his relations with Kerr were warm and constructive.

This event would have an unhappy sequel. Whitlam would later blame Anne Kerr for his dismissal. In Whitlam's eyes she became a Lady Macbeth.

The subsequent tension should not disguise the warmth that did exist between Yarralumla and the Lodge. It flickered according to the moods and events. The most startling example offered by Whitlam of Kerr's discursive and speculative style was the Governor-General's exploration with Whitlam, early in his term, of the notion that if the Senate could not amend money bills then perhaps it could not reject them. It was a theme that a Labor minister and old colleague of Kerr's, Joe Riordan would later pursue with him.[38]

However the Secretary of the Prime Minister's Department, John Menadue, who used to brief Kerr regularly, had an even more startling example closer to the blocking of the budget. Menadue recalls:

> It was before the crisis began, when I went to Yarralumla to see the Governor-General. He said to me when discussing the political climate that he would regard any blocking of the budget by Fraser as improper. He also said with approval that his information was that Menzies thought that Fraser was 'wet behind the ears' to try this tactic.[39]

This was one of the first examples of a technique that Kerr would perfect—the reassuring word or opinion, invariably interpreted as significant by his government interlocutors at the time but that would ultimately prove to be misleading as a guide to his actions.

Kerr had his political opinions. But his constitutional responsibilities were another issue—and they were now alerted by the High Court. Its judgement in the *Petroleum and Minerals Case* was delivered in June 1975 with the reasons handed down on 30 September. The Court decided that section 57—the double dissolution provision—did raise justiciable questions and a majority found that the bill in question had not properly met the double dissolution conditions.

That is, Whitlam gave wrong advice to Hasluck on this bill and Hasluck was at fault in granting the 1974 double dissolution on the bill. By implication the Joint Sitting that Kerr convened should not have passed the bill. But the court had opened a Pandora's box, which prompted Professor Geoffrey Sawer to venture that it would have been better if the court had never intervened in the operation of section 57 which, after all, was about allowing the people to decide through an election.[40]

In an obvious reference to the Court's decision Whitlam on 2 July declared: 'I hate to think that, if the double dissolution had been granted on the sole Bill which has been the subject of judicial interpretation, instead of six Bills, we might have to resuscitate a defunct parliament of 15 months ago'. The majority of the bench, however, baulked at any conclusion that the High Court might find a dissolution or election itself invalid.[41]

To Kerr, the judgement was sobering. He saw a High Court making decisions about the legality of what Hasluck had done. Whitlam claimed later that Kerr was 'shattered' at the judgement and that he became extremely 'wary of doing anything that the High Court might judge him on'.[42]

Kerr's legal faculties now became more focused. On 25 August in a significant speech he pointed out 'that advice given to my predecessor,

Sir Paul Hasluck . . . was held to be legally wrong. I, too, had accepted advice to the effect that the proposed law could be dealt with at a Joint Sitting, but the resulting legislation as passed by the Joint Sitting was held to be invalid.'

Kerr argued that the best course for a Governor-General faced with having to approve a matter of some legal doubt was to accept the advice of his ministers and to allow the High Court to exercise its function as ultimate guardian of the Constitution. But he did not stop there. Three times in his speech Kerr mentioned Hasluck on the question of the Governor-General's final discretion:

> In abnormal times or in the case of any attempt to disregard the Constitution . . . it would be the Governor-General who could present the crisis to Parliament and, if necessary, to the nation for determination . . . [In] the ultimate he can check the elected representatives in any extreme attempt by them to disregard the rule of law or the customary usages of Australian government and he could do so by forcing a crisis.

A reading of this speech leaves the unmistakable impression that Kerr was ruminating on the Governor-General's obligations and discretions—in particular on his role in a crisis.[43] Kerr said this speech showed that 'at the end of August my mind was engaged on the question of the reserve powers'.[44]

There is no evidence that anybody in government took notice of this speech.

There was another issue on Kerr's mind that he raised in the speech—the possibility that a Governor-General might go beyond the Attorney General and Solicitor-General for legal advice.

Whitlam's 'Goulburn Declaration' was delivered a little more than a fortnight after Kerr's speech.[45] From this point Kerr knew the odds for a Supply crisis had firmed dramatically. He then moved with some despatch.

Just eight days later, on the night of 20 September, Kerr spoke to the Chief Justice of the High Court, Sir Garfield Barwick, to enlist his help. It was at the annual dinner of members of the Order of St Michael and St George. Barwick presided as chairman with Kerr sitting on his right and the Governor of New South Wales, Sir Roden Cutler, on his left. During a lull in proceedings Kerr spoke confidentially to Barwick, saying that he was 'very worried' about events in Canberra. According to Barwick, Kerr felt 'that neither of the protagonists was disposed to give way and that if each maintained his stand serious difficulties were likely to arise'. Barwick later told the former Whitlam minister, Clyde Cameron, that Kerr's words were that 'these two bulls are at one another's throats and neither wants to give in'.[46]

Kerr asked Barwick if he could see 'any way in which the High Court could be called upon to resolve the situation should it develop'—Barwick assumed that Kerr meant a deadlock between the chambers over Supply. Barwick says he was unwilling to be drawn. But he said 'that the matter appeared to be one for the Parliament itself and not for the Court to resolve. I added that, in the long run, the matter might land on his, the Governor-General's, table.'

Barwick continues:

> The Governor-General then asked me if I would be prepared to advise him as to his own position if need arose . . . I said that that would depend upon what I was asked and the circumstances in which I was asked. There the matter rested . . . I am bound on reflection to say that I had left the door open for the Governor-General to approach me.[47]

The reaction of Gough Whitlam to this exchange—had he known about it—would have been one of anger and dismay. Obviously, it would have destroyed his faith in Kerr.

Several conclusions arise from this discussion. Kerr believed that as Governor-General he might become involved in a parliamentary deadlock; to this end he was seeking to enlist the Chief Justice as an adviser in such a situation; his thinking would have been confirmed by Barwick who warned him that as Governor-General he might have to address—or by implication resolve—any deadlock; finally, Kerr wanted to ensure that he knew where the Court was standing in that event.

Kerr knew Barwick as a man and as a judge. Jim McClelland reports: 'Kerr, throughout his career, always sought Barwick's esteem and approval'.[48] Joe Riordan says: 'I heard Kerr speak of him when they were both barristers. Kerr was in awe of Barwick. Once Barwick gave Kerr advice about his powers or duty there was no way it would not be followed.'[49] There should be no illusions about this approach—nor of Kerr's follow-up to Barwick on the eve of the dismissal. Maurice Byers says flatly: 'Kerr must have known what sort of advice Barwick would give'.[50]

Barwick and Whitlam had been rivals for years. More recently, there had been an issue between them—the appointment of Lionel Murphy to the High Court. Barwick, as Chief Justice, was proprietorial about 'his' Court. According to Barwick he had discussed with Whitlam some possible candidates. In February 1975 Whitlam rang him one evening to say: 'Murphy has agreed to accept the appointment'. Barwick's reply was unforgiving: 'But he is neither competent nor suitable for the position'. Barwick was concerned that Labor saw Murphy as a future Chief Justice. It is a coincidence, of course, that after Murphy's appointment in early 1975 the Commonwealth rarely secured a favourable judgement from Barwick.[51]

It is noteworthy that before the crisis erupted Kerr was talking to Barwick about his concerns, not to Whitlam, to seek advice from the Law Officers, Attorney General Enderby and Solicitor-General Byers.

Anne Kerr says: 'John could see what was going to happen. I remember him saying to me, some time before Supply was blocked, "I've got a feeling there is a constitutional crunch coming and I'll be in the middle of it."'[52]

Just twelve days later, on 2 October, there was a change in Whitlam's office when Liz Reid, his adviser on Women's Affairs, resigned. Reid had seen Kerr socially in the period between his first wife's death and his second marriage. Indeed, she had had far more contact with Kerr than had anybody else on Whitlam's staff. An upset Reid, when talking to her friend Patti Warn, another Whitlam aide, about Labor's prospects, told her: 'Everyone thinks the GG's on our side. He's not, he's not.'[53]

On the day she resigned, Reid warned Whitlam about the Governor-General:

> I wanted to get through to Gough the point that Kerr had no loyalty to him simply because Gough had appointed him as Governor-General. There was no feeling of loyalty to Gough or sense of support for his government. Gough had this quaint logic—'I appointed him, so he's going to be loyal to me'. He was quite wrong. I spoke to Clifton Pugh about this. Clif and I knew what the Governor-General thought and the way he was talking about himself and Whitlam. There was a powerful sense of self-aggrandisement in the way Kerr saw his role. But I think that Gough did not believe that I was in a position to know these things about Kerr. He was the master politician, not me. I suspect if I had been a male member of his staff, then he would have listened.[54]

Whitlam and Kerr were moving within different constellations. Whitlam was preparing for an epic battle in the cause of Responsible Government. But Kerr was lining up Barwick as his principal adviser—and that meant Kerr felt he might have to exercise his vice-regal discretion. This was the only situation in which he would need Barwick's advice. Byers was right—Kerr knew his Barwick. He would have known instinctively if not explicitly that Barwick was a believer in the reserve powers. And the reserve powers were on Kerr's mind.

At this time or shortly afterwards during the deadlock Kerr was reading Dr Eugene Forsey's text *The Royal Power of Dissolution of Parliament in the British Commonwealth*. Forsey would have helped to shape the direction of Kerr's thinking on the crisis and injected intellectual steel into his existing belief in the reserve powers. In his final chapter, from which Kerr quoted in his memoirs, Forsey described the reserve powers in a triumphal fashion:

> The danger of royal absolutism is past; but the danger of Cabinet absolutism, even of Prime Ministerial absolutism, is present and growing. Against that danger the reserve power of the Crown, and especially the power to force or refuse dissolution, is in some instances the only constitutional safeguard. The Crown is more than a quaint survival, a social ornament, a symbol, 'an automation with no public will of its own'. In certain circumstances, the Crown alone can preserve the Constitution . . .

Forsey, after discussing Evatt's writing, claims that the reserve powers may 'be one of the few safeguards against dictatorship by "the leader of the junta wielding for the moment the power of the office"'.[55]

What on earth would Whitlam have thought if he had known that this was Kerr's intellectual preparation for the crisis?

The breach

At this point one of the extraordinary and decisive features of the crisis was sealed—Kerr's loss of confidence in Whitlam. Kerr made the momentous decision that Whitlam had forfeited the prime ministerial expectation of a frank outline of the Governor-General's thinking. He cut Whitlam off from an honest dialogue because of discussions that occurred before the crisis was joined.

Shortly before the resignation of Rex Connor from the ministry on 14 October, Kerr claimed that in a discussion with Whitlam, the Prime Minister 'told me that if Supply were denied he would carry on without Supply'. This is not surprising, as Whitlam had declared this position on 12 September. According to Kerr, Whitlam 'said he intended to destroy forever the power of the Senate to refuse Supply'. Again this is not surprising, as Whitlam was to use similar words to these in public.[56] It was in this conversation—which took place before the budget was deferred—that Kerr made what he regarded as his only effort to 'advise and warn':

> In the course of the conversation I said to him on the subject of governing without supply, 'Do you think that this is the wisest course? Wouldn't it be better to go for an election even if you lose? Your opponents will have a difficult time next year if they win, and provided we do not have chaos over supply you would have a very good chance of coming back as Wilson did in England. You are still young and,

even if you lose now, if you play your cards right you could easily have a second term as Prime Minister.[57]

(Given the magnitude of Labor's election defeat in December 1975, which guaranteed Fraser two terms, Kerr's political advice can hardly be called prescient.)

According to Kerr, Whitlam 'rejected this approach out of hand. He said he would never be forced into an election by the Senate denying supply'. Kerr says that this was one of the first conversations in which 'an implacable element' began to appear in Whitlam's approach to the potential crisis. He says that Whitlam 'made it clear that my suggestion was not discussable and never would be'.[58]

Kerr gives no date and no location for this apparently decisive discussion. He says that his impressions were confirmed on 14 October, on the eve of the storm, when they had a further talk during Whitlam's attendance at Government House for the swearing-in of Ken Wriedt as the new Minerals and Energy Minister.[59] Kerr says that in this discussion Whitlam rejected the urgings of a senior minister (later confirmed by Anne Kerr as Wriedt) to hold an election. But Kerr gives no details of this discussion.[60]

Kerr says that his abovementioned comments went 'as far, as Governor-General, as I could prudently go in the exercise of my right to "advise and warn"'.[61]

If Whitlam was as vehement as Kerr says about governing without Supply, then Kerr's response does not constitute the exercise of the Crown's 'advise and warn' prerogative. Kerr's remarks about former British Prime Minister Harold Wilson and Whitlam's future election prospects are redolent of the speculation of political journalists at a late night party. If Kerr was trying to moderate Whitlam's position, then inviting Whitlam to consider his defeat at an election and then a political resurrection akin to that of Harold Wilson (scarcely Whitlam's favourite politician) would have had no impact whatsoever. It is hard to understand how Kerr could interpret his comments as being an exercise of his 'advise and warn' discretion. The comments—speculative, and bad speculation too—are nothing of the sort. If Kerr was serious at this point in exercising his 'advise and warn' prerogative, then he should have spoken along the following lines:

> Prime Minister, you can, of course, govern for some time without the passage of the Appropriation bills, by relying upon existing appropriations. That tactic may succeed by frightening the Opposition parties into changing their mind and passing the Appropriation bills. But you and I both know that this tactic has a limited shelf life. As we approach the point when funds required for the normal services of gov-

ernment are imperilled then you have a duty as Prime Minister to give me advice that resolves the deadlock short of that crisis, and I have a duty as Governor-General to ensure that I receive such advice.

This was Kerr's position, but he declined to articulate it. Such signals would have been given by a wise Governor-General or a wise Monarch. They would have constituted genuine advice and warning. In order to grasp the tone and nature of this process it is salutary to refer to Walter Bagehot's classic account:

> To state the matter shortly, the sovereign has, under a constitutional monarchy such as ours, three rights—the right to be consulted, the right to encourage, the right to warn. And a king of great sense and sagacity would want no others. He would find that his having no others would enable him to use these with singular effect. He would say to his ministers: 'The responsibility for these measures is upon you. Whatever you think best must be done. Whatever you think best shall have my full and effective support. But you will observe that for this reason and that reason what you propose to do is bad; for this reason and that reason what you do not propose is better . . . Supposing the king to be right, and to have what kings often have, the gift of effectual expression, he could not help moving his minister.[62]

I believe, on the basis of the account provided by Kerr himself, that the fair and balanced judgement is that Kerr did not seriously exercise the 'advise and warn' prerogative. It should be remembered, again on Kerr's own account, that the above conversations were the only occasions on which he claims to have tried to exercise this prerogative. It should be further noted that both conversations were conducted *before* the deferral of Supply by the Opposition on 15 October. My conclusion is that Kerr, unlike Bagehot's sagacious king, was not prepared to speak firmly to his Prime Minister, thereby passing up the opportunity to influence him.

That these talks occurred before the deadlock is important. It gave Kerr an opportunity to outline his thinking to Whitlam before the battle was joined and before emotions threatened reason.

In summarising his position after the two conversations Kerr says of Whitlam:

> On both occasions my suggestion was rejected out of hand and very forcibly—the manner in which it was done was one of the circumstances which led me to foresee there would be no compromise on his part. From that time forward [14 October] my opinion was that he was beyond the reach of any argument of mine, or even discussion. Everything he said publicly, or privately to me, thereafter strengthened me in that view.[63]

So Kerr had decided there was no point in his trying to counsel or persuade Whitlam; that there was no purpose in his having frank talks with Whitlam. He had reached this position on the day before the Opposition deferred Supply.

Kerr's justification in taking this attitude was Whitlam's intransigence. People who saw and spoke with Whitlam at this time will understand the point. There was a directed fury in Whitlam's manner when he set about cracking Fraser and his Senate numbers. There had to be, given the task. Whitlam believed he would prevail and that the pressure would become too great on the Senate. So did many other people, including Liberals. But politics is always the art of the possible. Events and circumstances change. For Kerr to declare that there would be no compromise on Whitlam's part ignores the fact that Whitlam, as a politician, would have to adjust his position to whatever events occurred during the crisis—and he did, seeking on 11 November a Senate election.

The position Kerr took was identical with his stance on the loans affair—he internalised his concerns and became more watchful. After a halfhearted effort he forsook further attempts to talk seriously to Whitlam because he could exert no influence over him. Again, this appears to be a contradiction in terms. It is difficult to understand how, during a Supply crisis, the views of the Governor-General could not influence his Prime Minister. Kerr knew he had great powers in this situation; by definition he had great influence—whether through words, acts or silence.

Kerr always had an alternative—to have an honest, serious and frank dialogue with Whitlam. That, of course, is merely what would be expected of the Crown or the Crown's representative.

By declining to do this Kerr only encouraged Whitlam to conclude that Kerr acquiesced in his tactics. What other conclusion could Whitlam draw? This is the conundrum in the personal relations between them.

Ultimately, the judgement Kerr made involved a personal assessment of Whitlam. He concluded that Whitlam was not to be trusted and he proceeded on this assumption throughout the entire crisis. Kerr's apparent justification for not trying to use his influence with Whitlam is impotence—and here the contradiction in his position is manifest. Kerr sacked Whitlam without warning on 11 November, but then insisted in his memoirs that he could never have influenced the Prime Minister's behaviour that provoked his decision to sack!

Kerr was a 'king' who eschewed persuasion, the kind of king who is an object of Bagehot's contempt. He was a Governor-General equipped with an array of defined and undefined constitutional powers, operating within an Australian milieu whose recent practice, as outlined by Hasluck, was that of vice-regal influence when required, now absolving himself of his 'advise and warn' prerogative merely because of Whitlam's intransigence. Kerr was not in an easy position; but that is the nature of the office. Occasionally kings or Governors-General face a parliamentary deadlock which requires all their personal and official skills. Governors-General are selected precisely because they are considered to be people of wisdom and experience. Most successful Australian Prime Ministers are invariably intransigent, never more so than when trying to defy a Senate blocking a budget. That does not absolve a Governor-General of his responsibility.

However, an outstanding issue remains—how accurate is Kerr's account of these two meetings with Whitlam at which he decided that the Prime Minister's attitude was implacable?

Gough Whitlam says that neither discussion took place. He points out that the last time he spoke to Kerr before 14 October was when Whitlam and Fred Daly attended an Executive Council meeting on 7 October. Referring to Kerr's claim that he could return to office after an election defeat in a fashion similar to that of Harold Wilson, Whitlam says: 'I would have certainly remembered such a remark; I would certainly have responded to it. It was never made, as Mr Daly confirms. Sir John is imagining that he put to me the argument he was to put to Mr Hayden on 6 November and to the Speaker Gordon Scholes on 11 November.'[64]

Whitlam is equally adamant that no discussion was conducted on 14 October at the time of Wriedt's swearing-in: 'It was a very short meeting because Senator Wriedt and I had come from our party meeting in the morning and had to return for Question Time in our respective Houses. Supply was not discussed.'[65] Wriedt says he has no recollection of any such discussion but cannot say it did not occur.[66]

Perhaps it is not surprising that Whitlam and Kerr have different recollections of these meetings. From Kerr's own account there is no suggestion that they were other than passing and probably brief conversations—not formal discussions.

The fact that Whitlam says he cannot remember what Kerr describes as the only occasions on which he exercised his 'advise and warn' prerogative merely underlines the argument I have been advancing—that Kerr did not seriously and formally attempt to exercise this prerogative, if he attempted to exercise it at all.

There must, of course, be more to the story.

There is: Kerr's job security.

Kerr had always put a premium on job security. This issue, previously dormant, was now emerging. Soon it would dominate. Kerr would conclude within a few hours that his 'implacable' Prime Minister was prepared to sack him in order to break Fraser and the Senate.

7
The battle

It could be a question of whether I get to the Queen first for your recall or you get in first with my dismissal.

Gough Whitlam to Sir John Kerr, 16 October 1975

ON THE NIGHT of 16 October 1975 the Governor-General hosted a state banquet at Yarralumla in honour of the Prime Minister of Malaysia, Tun Abdul Razak. In Kerr's study—the room in which he dismissed Whitlam twenty-six days later—there was a gathering that included the guest of honour and his wife, Gough and Margaret Whitlam, and Sir John and Lady Kerr. Kerr recalls that Whitlam, referring to the Supply crisis, 'said to me with a brilliant smile, "It could be a question of whether I get to the Queen first for your recall or you get in first with my dismissal." We all laughed.'[1]

This exchange had a lasting impact on Kerr. Here was Whitlam on the night the Senate had deferred the Appropriation bills for the first time joking that he might have to dismiss Kerr if the Governor-General planned to dismiss him. Whitlam later confirmed the conversation but dismissed its significance. Pointing out that he knew Tun Razak well, Whitlam described his remark as 'flippant' and designed to move the conversation to another subject.[2]

Only an innocent could accept Whitlam's disclaimer at face value. Whitlam had a vast knowledge of constitutional history. It is fatuous to believe that his comment was not delivered with a purpose. Anyone familiar with Whitlam's personality knew that he deployed humour (along with irony and sarcasm) as a political weapon.

Kerr said later that he regarded this 'supposed joke as carrying a very real threat'.[3] Anne Kerr confirms the impact of Whitlam's remark at the time.[4] Sir John said the remark 'quite devastated me. It shattered me to think that he could say such a thing. Oh yes, we all laughed. But I didn't feel like laughing. I felt it represented just one more piece of his psychological warfare.'[5] Alan Reid reported that Tun Abdul Razak had been 'mildly astonished' at the remark. He also claimed that Tun Razak's impression was that while Whitlam's comment 'might on the surface be intended as humour there was an undertone of real threat'.[6]

An official close to Kerr says: 'This incident was grossly offensive. The Governor-General felt humiliated in front of others. He had no doubt that it was a brand of intimidation.'[7]

Whitlam's response has been to reject any suggestion that he might have dismissed Kerr or even contemplated this action. He says:

> At no time during the crisis had the possibility of replacing Sir John Kerr been a significant element in my thinking. I never bothered even to inquire into the legal or practical procedures for so drastic and unprecedented an action. I have not to this day. As to thinking it could be done by a telephone call, had I not, within that very month, had the experience of revoking Sir Colin Hannah's dormant commission as Administrator? That process took ten days . . . From the time of my remarks to Tun Razak to the hour I was dismissed, I never gave the possibility of dismissing him [Kerr] before he dismissed me a second's thought or a second thought.[8]

The day before the dinner for Tun Razak the Queensland Governor, Sir Colin Hannah, flouting his obligation to remain politically impartial, had launched a public attack on the Whitlam Government. His comments were widely condemned; they were seen as an example of the decline of conventions in the climate of the times. As a senior State Governor Hannah held a dormant commission to act as Administrator of the Commonwealth in the absence or incapacity of the Governor-General. Whitlam briefed Kerr that Hannah's dormant commission must be removed. Kerr agreed. Whitlam prepared the documents which, he says, 'we sent by courier to London to the Queen's Secretary'. The Queen followed the advice and revoked Hannah's commission in late October. Whitlam later observed that it was not reinstated by the Fraser Government.[9] He says: 'It took a week for my submission to be delivered by courier to the Queen and for her to cable her consent'.[10]

The significance, as Whitlam points out, is that 'Kerr knew the process for the Queen to sack a Governor-General'.[11] He had seen the procedure at close quarters in relation to Hannah. There was a formal procedure involved—and it took time.

Kerr nominates two other discussions before the deadlock in which Whitlam 'made it clear he knew I might dismiss him'. They were held on 15 September and 29 September.[12]

The first was in Port Moresby on Independence Day when, Kerr says, Whitlam told him that if the Senate rejected the Appropriation bills he might still present them to the Governor-General for assent. Kerr says he parried the issue, though remarking that it would cause uproar. Kerr claims that Whitlam also said that if, during a crisis, he was contemplating the termination of Whitlam's commission then Whitlam would have to point out that Fraser could not obtain Supply either—because new legislation would be necessary. Kerr says this exchange was significant because it revealed that Whitlam had already in mind 'the possibility of my contemplating his dismissal'.[13]

Whitlam says of this Port Moresby conversation that it 'did not take place'. He says that, during the day, he and Kerr attended three functions and 'were never seated or standing together and there was always a great number of others speaking to each of us'.[14]

Kerr reports that on 29 September he had a discussion with Whitlam over the problem of advising a Senate election as a response to a parliamentary deadlock if the Opposition refused interim Supply. Kerr reports that Whitlam recognised there would be a 'profound constitutional crisis' when the money first started to run out. Whitlam finished by telling Kerr that in a crisis he 'would certainly not recommend a double dissolution'. According to Kerr's version Whitlam said that he 'would argue to me that he was entitled to retain his commission for as long as he held the confidence of the House of Representatives despite his failure to obtain Supply'.[15]

In his own book, Whitlam confirmed a 29 September discussion and did not dispute Kerr's account.[16]

The 1975 deadlock was conducted in the shadow of the New South Wales Game–Lang crisis of 1932—the history of which was familiar to both Whitlam and Kerr. On 15 October Whitlam told Parliament that he had been 'carrying out some research into the general question of dismissals of governments or rejections of Supply and the like'. He alluded to the dismissal of the New South Wales Premier, Jack Lang, by the Governor, Sir Phillip Game. Whitlam's purpose was to quote from a letter written by Robert Menzies to Game supporting his decision.[17]

Menzies had said:

Under the Australian system of universal suffrage and triennial Parliaments, with a legally recognised and responsible Cabinet it must, in my opinion, follow that so long as a Premier commands a majority in the Lower House, and so long as he is guilty of no illegal conduct which would invoke the exercise of the Royal Prerogative he must be regarded as the competent and continuing adviser of the representative of the Crown.[18]

Whitlam used Menzies' comments to bolster his own argument. (Kerr later claimed that Menzies' remarks were not relevant in the 1975 context where Supply had been blocked.[19])

In fact, Game's dismissal of Lang, while controversial in its own right, offers a contrast with Kerr's dismissal of Whitlam. Game relied on the illegality of actions taken by his ministers to justify Lang's dismissal. He gave Lang ample warning in person and by letter—unlike Kerr in 1975—saying that 'my position is that if my Ministers are unable to carry on essential services without breaking the law, my plain duty is to endeavour to obtain Ministers who feel able to do so'. Lang replied by letter: 'if . . . you are requesting the resignation of Ministers you are hereby informed that your request is refused'. Whereupon Lang was dismissed on 13 May 1932.[20]

But Kerr had thought more deeply about this Game–Lang precedent than had Whitlam. In his memoirs Kerr, who had studied the crisis as a student, observed: 'It is something of a mystery why *Lang did not try to get rid of Game* before he was himself dismissed'.[21]

So Kerr, in his consideration of the 1932 crisis, was alive to the possibility of Premier Lang's removing the Governor before Game could act. It is a further insight into Kerr's sense of vulnerability.

It is clear that Kerr—given Whitlam's remark at the Tun Abdul Razak function, his reflections on the Game–Lang crisis and his September talks with Whitlam—had the possibility of prime ministerial action against the Governor-General as a factor in his mind from the start of the 1975 crisis.

This is confirmed by Sir Roden Cutler who visited Admiralty House with his wife for dinner with the Kerrs at which the crisis was canvassed. The dinner arose because Kerr had long planned an official overseas trip in November 1975 to Canada, the United States and Ireland. This meant that Cutler, as the senior State Governor, would stand in for Kerr during his absence. If Kerr's trip had proceeded as planned, then the resolution of the crisis would have fallen to Cutler. (In his memoirs, Kerr related that after Fraser's statement on 15 October, he decided that his responsibility was to remain in Australia, and subsequently he put a recommendation to Whitlam that his trip be cancelled.[22]) When Cutler attended the dinner, he still believed that he would be assuming responsibility during Kerr's absence.

Cutler's recollection of the dinner reveals the different outlooks of the two men. Cutler says:

> I told Kerr at dinner that I was happy to take over from him during his trip. When we spoke of the crisis I said that I thought that he should talk to the Prime Minister. I said I thought that the matter was one for the Parliament to solve and told him that as far as I could see, that some Opposition Senators might waver or be ready to cross the floor. I didn't think it was a sound principle for the Senate to hold up Supply when there was a majority government, although I recognised that, legally, the Senate could do this. Kerr played his cards very close to his chest. He gave me little indication about his own thinking and no hint that he would dismiss the government. However, he left me with the clear impression that he felt it was pointless for him to talk to Whitlam about the situation and that he wanted to avoid such discussions. At one stage I said to Kerr that there was, of course, the possibility that the Prime Minister might move to dismiss him. He became very activated at this point, saying, 'Yes, I know, I know'. It was obvious that he had given some thought to this possibility. At this point he said to me that he felt that he should remain in Australia and that it was his duty to accept the responsibility that fell to him in the situation.[23]

Cutler, unlike Kerr, felt sure that the correct Vice-regal response to any potential threat from Whitlam was to engage the Prime Minister directly. For him, this was a responsibility and common sense. But Cutler was a man already enshrined in the hall of distinguished Australians, at ease with his reputation and confident of his ability to handle difficult men, including politicians.

Kerr had been appointed by Whitlam and could be removed by a Whitlam request to the Palace. The Queen would not refuse to follow any such advice from her Australian Prime Minister. There is no question that this sense of vulnerability based on his lack of job security shaped Kerr's attitude towards Whitlam. Kerr believed that Whitlam would not tolerate dissent or disagreement from his position and that, ultimately, Whitlam would not stop at trying to remove him. Kerr was not a king; he held office at Whitlam's pleasure and, technically, could be removed at his displeasure.

Malcolm Fraser sees this as the key to the crisis: 'The Queen has tenure and she couldn't be sacked. But a Governor-General holds office at pleasure and if he ceases to please then he can be removed by a Prime Minister'.[24]

There is a psychological paradox at the heart of the 1975 crisis—Whitlam never seriously contemplated that Kerr might dismiss him, yet Kerr was obsessed with the notion that an alarmed Whitlam might contact the Palace to dismiss his Governor-General. Whitlam was overconfident; Kerr was overly suspicious. As a consequence Whitlam was too cavalier in his handling of Kerr; Kerr was extremely calculating in his conduct towards Whitlam. These moods prevailed throughout the period.

Would Whitlam have been prepared, ultimately, to recommend Kerr's removal? I asked him in May 1995:

> KELLY: If earlier in the crisis Kerr had indicated to you his concerns about your strategy, would you have put in train an approach to the Palace to have him removed?
>
> WHITLAM: No. I would, I believe, have said, 'Will you write down what your fears are. Let me think over it and write back'. Or, if he'd expressed a threat, I would have reported it to the House of Representatives . . . and got a vote of confidence.
>
> KELLY: It was still possible for you to go through the process—it would take time as it did with Hannah—but you could have still gone through the process to remove Kerr?
>
> WHITLAM: Oh yes, yes, yes you could.
>
> KELLY: Do you think it would have been viable politically at the time?
>
> WHITLAM: I don't. I don't think it would have suited me to look as if I was sacking the Governor-General.
>
> KELLY: Does that mean you wouldn't have done it?
>
> WHITLAM: I don't think I would have.
>
> KELLY: You would have had a problem if Kerr had been frank with you and indicated what his thinking was?
>
> WHITLAM: Yes. But I would have told the Parliament. I would have exposed him.
>
> KELLY: But if you had made this public, what Kerr said to you, if Kerr indicated he was thinking of sacking you, presumably Fraser would have then gone public and said, 'Well, Kerr ought to sack him'.
>
> WHITLAM: Yes. But if I just moved to sack Kerr, and the first thing that the public knew was that I advised the Queen and she'd sacked him, I think I might have been as popular with the public as Kerr is now.

It is wrong to see Whitlam in this crisis as a Prime Minister brooding about Kerr's loyalty; on the contrary his blunder was to take Kerr's loyalty for granted.

The cardinal misjudgement Whitlam made was personal—far from devising plans to remove Kerr, he was deluded into thinking that Kerr was his man. This led directly to his dismissal.

Anne Kerr recalls: 'John told me that Gough once told him, "You couldn't be PM John. You're not ruthless enough"'.[25] Whitlam didn't think Kerr was ruthless enough to dismiss him. He never planned for a dismissal contingency. John Menadue, the then head of the Prime Minister's Department, says: 'I don't believe the idea of dismissal seriously entered Gough's head during the period of the crisis'.[26] Graham Freudenberg says: 'To the last hour, Whitlam had complete confidence in Sir John Kerr and had every reason to believe that he had Kerr's confidence'.[27]

Whitlam's senior aide, John Mant, reflects: 'I think he saw Kerr as someone who had failed to achieve his potential and had become a rather weak man who would act on ministerial advice and do his bidding. The impression that Kerr was drinking and had had an interest in women who were ALP staffers contributed to Gough's attitude towards Kerr'.[28] Reflecting on his appointment of Kerr, Whitlam says: 'At the time, of course, I didn't know about his drinking problem'. It is an easy shot; but Whitlam's puritan outlook must have reinforced his patronising view of Kerr.[29]

It is clear that Whitlam was influenced by Kerr's past associations with two of his ministers, Jim McClelland and Joe Riordan. Kerr described McClelland as 'an old and close friend' and Riordan as a 'good friend'. It was natural for Whitlam to think such personal bonds would further underwrite Kerr's loyalty.[30] The friendship factor is crucial. Whitlam was fortified because some of his ministers were old and close friends of Kerr.

Whitlam had convinced himself that the reserve powers were an arcane and irrelevant constitutional relic. Whitlam was a contemporary constitutionalist. He believed in the convention that the Governor-General acted only on ministerial advice. His obsession over decades with the House of Representatives as the forum of popular democracy cannot be overestimated. He could not accept, emotionally, the application of a vice-regal power against the Representatives. John Menadue says: 'Gough could not really believe that Kerr would dismiss him because it would be a negation of what he believed in'.[31]

Denial of the reserve powers was orthodoxy among the senior ministers. It was certainly the view of Attorney General Enderby who says, 'I never ever had a discussion with Gough about the reserve powers. The idea of dismissal was not an option in our thinking.'[32] Jim McClelland, the minister whom Whitlam was most likely to heed in relation to Kerr, says: 'It was as unthinkable that a Governor-General would act against the advice of his Prime Minister as it was that the Queen of England would do that. I thought Kerr accepted that'. So even the minister closest to Kerr did not grasp his belief in the reserve powers.[33]

Whitlam publicised his view of the Governor-General's role and on 17 October, when interviewed on *This Day Tonight* by the ABC's Richard Carleton, the following exchange took place:

> CARLETON: Sir, must Sir John Kerr accept your advice whatever advice you give him?
>
> WHITLAM: Unquestionably. The Governor-General takes the advice from his Prime Minister and from no one else.
>
> CARLETON: And must act on that advice?
>
> WHITLAM: Unquestionably. The Governor-General must act on the advice of his Prime Minister.
>
> CARLETON: There is not tolerance here, he must do . . .
>
> WHITLAM: None whatever.
>
> CARLETON: Fine. Well obviously there is a dispute in the community, but your view is quite plain.[34]

Whitlam was not trying to humiliate Kerr; quite the reverse. Whitlam felt that he was helping Kerr in the teeth of outrageous Opposition demands that the Governor-General intervene against his Prime Minister. The message he was trying to send, ironically, was that he believed in Kerr. Menadue says: 'Gough had strong views on Kerr's loyalty. He believed everything would be alright'.[35]

But the combination of Whitlam's patronising personal attitude towards Kerr and his inability seriously to contemplate the reserve powers proved deadly.

One of Whitlam's ministers, Clyde Cameron, reports that the artist Clifton Pugh, who was painting Kerr's portrait at the time, recalled the Governor-General's resentment towards Whitlam. Cameron says: 'Pugh told me that he was working on the portrait when the details of what Whitlam said on television were confirmed to Kerr. He was furious. Kerr's face, according to Pugh, went a deep red. But he made no comment.'[36]

It is tempting to contrast Menzies and Whitlam as vice-regal managers. In 1951 Menzies sought a double dissolution from Sir William McKell, a former ALP politician, with Evatt assuring Opposition leader, Ben Chifley, that it would be denied. Menzies, far from instructing McKell, told the Governor-General that he was 'not bound to follow my advice' but had to be satisfied himself. Menzies got his election—and never looked back. Menzies put the onus on McKell; he told McKell that the decision was one for his own discretion. He elevated McKell and such deference paid dividends.

Maurice Byers, the Solicitor-General in 1975, says: 'The pressures on Whitlam were so continuous and so strong. He failed sufficiently, I think, to realise that, strictly speaking, there was only one important person and that was Kerr. Therefore, Kerr should have been cherished and he wasn't.'[37]

Kerr was offended in a personal sense at Whitlam's insistence that the Governor-General had no choice but to follow his advice. Kerr was a proud and ambitious man; but he felt humiliated and belittled. He felt that Whitlam's tactic was to intimidate and patronise him. It is not surprising that Kerr reached this conclusion since Whitlam was an intimidating man who was giving advice in a fashion that was designed to eliminate any alternative.

Whitlam and Kerr were friendly with each other—but not mates. Anne Kerr describes the relationship:

> John and Gough Whitlam were not friends as such. Not the way one usually talks about friendship. They weren't heart to heart associates. It would be correct to say that they were friendly with each other. But Gough Whitlam almost never came out to Yarralumla just to have lunch with John or to have a chat . . . Whitlam completely misjudged John. Perhaps this was because John, as a man, was friendly and affable by nature. He never lost his temper. I can never remember his voice being raised. He wanted to work with people, not against them. Whitlam misinterpreted this as acquiescence. He was extraordinarily misguided in thinking that my husband would fall in with his plan and would not have the integrity to live up to his responsibilities as Governor-General.[38]

Of course, in an intellectual sense Kerr could not be intimidated by Whitlam on this issue; Kerr was never in doubt about the existence of the reserve powers. It was a given in his intellectual life.

It is true, as recounted earlier, that Kerr had decided not to speak frankly to Whitlam about the crisis. But it is equally true that Whitlam was not enthusiastic about any such serious discussion. 'I think his attitude was that there was nothing to discuss', says Menadue.[39]

That was a grave blunder.

It was Whitlam's job to persuade Kerr to accept his position, a point that Whitlam never comprehended. He failed to think the situation through from Kerr's perspective. This was Whitlam's usual defect in management of people. Mant says: 'I think it was consistent with

Gough's character for him not to have had a proper discussion with the Governor-General during the crisis'.[40]

Clyde Cameron confirms this assessment:

> Before the 1951 double dissolution Menzies obtained an opinion from Garfield Barwick that the Governor-General had a discretion whether or not to accept a Prime Minister's advice to dissolve the Parliament. Kerr raised this issue with Whitlam when Whitlam and I were at Government House on 6 June 1975 for my swearing in as Science Minister. He said to Whitlam: 'You know Gough, in 1951 McKell was told that as Governor-General he didn't have to follow the Prime Minister's advice'. But Gough immediately changed the subject. He didn't want to talk with Kerr about the Governor-General's powers.[41]

Asked whether he deliberately sat down with Kerr during the crisis to review the situation, Whitlam says: 'I'd always stay with him as long as he wanted to talk. But I didn't look as if I wanted to talk on more and more things than he was wanting to talk on.' Clearly, this was not the attitude of a Prime Minister who felt any need to persuade his Governor-General. Asked whether he made it easy for Kerr to be frank with him, Whitlam replies: 'I would have thought so . . . I was always quite good-humoured with him and friendly with him. There was never any asperity between us. I think he didn't have the guts to raise any of these things with me because he knew that I would know the constitutional and political proprieties.'[42]

In truth, Whitlam had no interest in talks with Kerr that canvassed any option other than his own victory.

So Whitlam never tackled Kerr to determine how long the Governor-General would support his approach—an extraordinary and probably fatal omission. Kerr, in turn, decided that if Whitlam did not wish to confide in him then he would not confide in Whitlam. If Whitlam offered no confidences then Kerr would not take Whitlam into his own confidence.

McClelland also spoke to Kerr during the crisis—on three occasions according to Kerr. He adopted the same approach as Whitlam. McClelland explains: 'I never discussed with him the way he saw the Governor-General's role . . . I made no attempt to influence him. I just discussed what was happening . . . I thought, "No, he's got to make up his own mind and I shouldn't tell him what he's got to do." The second reason is that I didn't think it was necessary.'[43] Obviously this second reason is the dominant. McClelland, like Whitlam, assumed that Kerr was 'on side'. That meant he didn't require persuasion. Whitlam did not grasp that he had to persuade Kerr to his position and consequently he did not try.

Whitlam's tactics

In the first of the great parliamentary debates conducted on the floor of the House of Representatives there was no mention of the Governor-General in the speeches given by Whitlam and Fraser. This is because the Governor-General's role, at this stage, was given only marginal consideration in the public debate. While there was manoeuvring over Kerr's role, it was largely submerged by the drama over the parliamentary deadlock.

On 16 October Whitlam moved a motion which noted Labor's election victory in December 1972 and again in May 1974 and then asserted:

1. This House declares that it has full confidence in the Australian Labor Party Government.
2. This House affirms that the Constitution and the conventions of the Constitution vest in this House the control of the supply of moneys to the elected Government and that the threatened action of the Senate constitutes a gross violation of the roles of the respective Houses of the Parliament in relation to the appropriation of moneys.
3. This House asserts the basic principle that a Government that continues to have a majority in the House of Representatives has a right to expect that it will be able to govern.
4. This House condemns the threatened action of the Leader of the Opposition and of the non-government parties in the Senate as being reprehensible and as constituting a grave threat to the principles of responsible government and of parliamentary democracy in Australia.
5. This House calls upon the Senate to pass without delay the Loan Bill 1975, the Appropriation Bill (No. 1) 1975–76 and the Appropriation Bill (No. 2) 1975–76.

In speaking to his motion, which was carried by Labor's majority, Whitlam said:

> This House must expose the political opportunism of the Opposition in the Senate for what it is. And what it means is constitutional revolution—the proposition that governments can be unmade by the Senate and not by the House of Representatives—the people's House . . . the Senate cannot, does not, and must never determine who the Government shall be . . .
>
> The Leader of the Opposition announces with some pride that departments are running or will run short of funds. Of course they will run short of funds. The Leader of the Opposition is refusing to pass the Appropriation Bills in the Senate which provide for the ordinary annual services of the Government. He will be responsible for

bills not being paid, for salaries not being paid, for utter financial chaos, and this will continue as long as the Leader of the Opposition refuses to allow the Senate to pass the Supply already authorised by this House, the people's House. And now, like a pyromaniac, he dances around the fire. He will get burnt.

Whitlam said that in the 75 years since Federation there had been 20 occasions on which the annual Appropriation bills had come before a Senate in which the government did not have a majority. No such bill had ever been rejected. Whitlam said that the Senate vote on the previous day was a 'complete distortion of what the people decided about the Senate in May last year'. This was because of the Queensland Premier's dishonourable behaviour in refusing to appoint an ALP Senator to replace the late Senator Milliner. Whitlam also referred to 'the grossly improper incitement' of non-Labor State governments to prevent their Governors from issuing writs for any half Senate election.

He concluded in these terms:

> It is because this Government has attempted to make this Parliament the instrument for reform, for long overdue change, for progress, for the redistribution of wealth, for the uplifting of the underprivileged, for the reduction of the privileges of great wealth and deeply entrenched vested interests, an instrument towards equality of opportunity for all Australians, that our opponents and those vested interests have from the very beginning, as Senator Withers revealed, embarked on a course to destroy this Government at the earliest opportunity. But what they are really doing is destroying the very basis of parliamentary democracy in our country . . .
>
> The issue is the unconstitutional and undemocratic conduct of a chance majority in the Senate . . . It is the Senate which is on trial . . . it is the Senate, the Liberal Party and the Liberal leader which, by the course they are now attempting, have sown the seeds of their own destruction.[44]

In his reply Malcolm Fraser declared that there was 'a universal call' around Australia for the Whitlam Government to face an election. He dismissed Whitlam's motion as an effort by the government 'to use its synthetic temporary majority in this House to try to claim that it has the confidence of the Australian people'.

Fraser accused Whitlam of being a hypocrite, pointing to Whitlam's attack on the Coalition Government's 1970–71 Budget. He recalled that Whitlam had told the House: 'We will vote against the Bills here and in the Senate. Our purpose is to destroy this Budget and to destroy the Government which has sponsored it'. Fraser continued: 'This eminent legal authority was asserting the power and right of the Senate.

What humbug have we had from this eminent legal authority today? . . . He changes his principles as he changes his jobs.'

Fraser said there were two charges against the Whitlam Government—its gross mismanagement of the economy and its impropriety, the latter dating from the loan authority. Fraser then mocked Whitlam:

> He has brought down his colleagues. He has brought down his party to the lowest depths at which it has ever been . . . They will be right behind him as he walks over the cliff and takes them all to doom and destruction like lemmings falling into the sea. The Prime Minister cannot long delay the serious judgement of the Australian people.[45]

During the debate one of the few references to the Governor-General came from Liberal frontbencher Jim Killen, who referred to Evatt's work *The King and His Dominion Governors* and said, 'It is wrong to assume that the Governor-General is a mere tool in the hands of the dominant political party. I trust that the Prime Minister will reflect well upon these words.'[46]

Whitlam's tactic was to demand that the Senate either pass or reject the budget—not merely defer it. This reflected his belief that Fraser could not muster Senate support for a rejection.

From the start there were two tactical difficulties facing Whitlam in relation to the Senate that afflicted him throughout the crisis. The first was that he was attempting to deny the constitutional power of the Senate. The second was that he deluded himself about the viability of his half Senate election option.

Whitlam claimed that in deferring Supply the Senate was both breaking convention and the Constitution. This was a powerful moral argument. But the overwhelming view of jurists was that section 53 gave the Senate the power to block Supply. It said that the Senate could not originate or amend money bills. The orthodox view was that the Senate could reject or defer such bills. Whitlam was trying to use political and moral pressure to force the Senate to retreat; to snap its nerve. But the Senate had the force of law behind it. Whitlam was trying to change the law by assertion and by politics. If the Senate declined to crack then Whitlam would have to face the consequences of his failed strategy. He could not just remain in office once Supply began to expire in late November.

Whitlam's second problem was his failure to think through the half Senate election option. He did not grasp the fact that his two preferred options—'toughing it out' or calling a half Senate election—were likely to be mutually exclusive if not exercised almost simultaneously at the start of the crisis. The 'toughing it out' option meant staying in office and trying to crack the Senate's will. The half Senate option meant seeking a poll, in the context of the deferral of Supply, to both pressure the Opposition into passing the budget and to win control of the Senate. The options were mutually exclusive because the Governor-General could hardly accept a half Senate election if Supply were to expire before the declaration of the results. If a Prime Minister insisted on advising a Senate election in this situation then a responsible Governor-General could only agree by pointing out that if Supply expired during the campaign due to the Senate's persistence in blocking the budget, then, at this point, the onus would rest upon the Prime Minister to provide further advice in order to prevent severe hardship in the country.

If Whitlam's initial response on 15 October had been to seek a half Senate election then the Governor-General would presumably have agreed to such a poll. Fraser disputes this assessment saying it is 'ludicrous' to think a Senate poll would have been sufficient.[47] But it is difficult to see how Kerr could have refused.[48] The poll could have been completed by the end of November, just before the deadline for the exhaustion of Supply.

But the longer Whitlam pursued his 'tough it out' tactic without a Senate election, the more likely a Governor-General would query prime ministerial advice for such an election when it was finally offered. This is because a Senate election called when Supply was close to being exhausted would not be conducted until after the Supply crunch came and because, given the Senate numbers, the election would be unlikely to deliver a pro-ALP Senate majority and therefore provide any solution. In addition, a Governor-General would realise that the calling of such an election would reflect the lack of success, to that stage, of the 'tough it out' tactic. This problem for Whitlam was really his lack of a fallback position. Whitlam assumed that if neither Fraser nor the Senate cracked then he could intensify the pressure by calling a half Senate election whenever he wanted. Of course, he never raised this with Kerr to test whether his assumption was sound. The longer the crisis continued, the greater became the probability of the Governor-General's querying rather than accepting such advice.

All this amounted to a serious oversight by Whitlam and his advisers; a failure to analyse their position. It suggests that Whitlam's dogmatic style during the crisis reflected not just a tactical disposition but his true condition. Whitlam's determination to confront the Senate was not matched by a cool assessment of his fallback options. In short, Whitlam did not cover himself in case his 'tough it out' tactic failed—an elementary blunder.

The truth is that in this situation there was only one fallback option—calling a general election. Whitlam's real options on 15 October to implement his strategy of defying the Senate were that he could (1) 'tough it out' or (2) 'tough it out' *and* keep the pressure on Fraser by recommending a half Senate election to Kerr. But if either option failed in its purpose then his only substantial recourse was a general election.[49]

In retrospect, option (2) seems the superior choice. It is fascinating to speculate on whether it would have succeeded. Its advantages were: that Whitlam would have met the Senate head-on by calling an election for the chamber that blocked the budget; that the election would have been dominated by the Supply issue which heavily favoured Whitlam; that Whitlam's actions would have tested whether the Coalition was in fact prepared to implement its threat to deny election writs in the four non-Labor States, an action that would have been widely condemned; and finally that Whitlam would have kept both Houses sitting and campaigned from the floor of Parliament by returning the budget to the Senate for approval. Such tactics would have imposed greater pressure on the Senate to pass the budget than the 'tough it out' tactic by itself—the course he chose.

The problem was that Whitlam kept changing his mind about the half Senate option. On 15 October he held out a half Senate election as a possibility. On 17 October he said he would call a half Senate election only if the Senate rejected the budget. On 21 October he said he would tender no advice to the Governor-General for either a House or a Senate election until the crisis was over and the budget passed. Finally, on 11 November, he told Kerr that he would be seeking a half Senate election. Whitlam was merely deluding himself; he did not have the weapon of a half Senate poll to deploy at a time of his own choosing when his 'tough it out' tactic faltered.

The Ellicott opinion

The first substantial argument for the Governor-General to intervene in the crisis was mounted on 16 October by the Opposition frontbencher R J Ellicott QC. The shadow cabinet had wanted a legal opinion issued and nominated Ellicott for this task. He was the most sophisticated lawyer within the Opposition, a former Solicitor-General, a prominent barrister, an acquaintance of Kerr and a relative of Sir Garfield Barwick. Ellicott says of the opinion: 'It was my point of view, nobody else's. It was drawn to influence constitutional thinking and the Governor-General.'[50] It became known as the Ellicott thesis; its conclusion was broadly similar to the opinion Barwick gave Kerr 24 days later. Labor's response was to reject Ellicott's opinion out of hand, but history suggests that this was a miscalculation.[51]

Ellicott said:

> The Prime Minister is treating the Governor-General as a mere automaton with no public will of his own, sitting at Yarralumla waiting to do his bidding. Nothing could be further from the truth . . . A Government without supply cannot govern. The refusal by Parliament of Supply, whether through the House or Senate, is a clear signal to the Governor-General that his chosen Ministers may not be able to carry on. In the proper performance of his role, he would inevitably want to have from the Prime Minister an explanation of how he proposed to overcome the situation. If the Prime Minister proposed and insisted upon means which were unlawful or which did not solve the problems of the disagreement between the Houses and left the Government without funds to carry on, it would be within the Governor-General's power and his duty to dismiss his Ministers and appoint others.
>
> In the current situation now facing us, the Governor-General, in the performance of his role, would need to know *immediately* what steps the Government proposes to take in order to avert the problem of it being without Supply in the near future . . . He is not powerless and the proper exercise of his powers demands that he be informed immediately on this matter.[52]

Ellicott identified the matters on which the Governor-General was entitled to information from the Prime Minister. Depending upon such advice, the Governor-General:

> . . . should ask the Prime Minister if the Government is prepared to advise him to dissolve the House of Representatives and the Senate or the House of Representatives alone as a means of ensuring that the disagreement between the two Houses is resolved. If the Prime Minister refuses to do either it is then open to the Governor-General to dismiss his present Ministers and seek others who are prepared to give him the only proper advice open. This he should proceed to do.

There are three salient points to make about this opinion: (1) it said that Kerr had a duty to act immediately by seeking advice from Whitlam; (2) that such advice should concern how Whitlam intended to overcome the denial of Supply; and (3) that if this advice involved unlawful or inadequate means then Sir John had a power and a duty to dismiss the government.

It is a matter of record that Kerr rejected points (1) and (2). He declined to act immediately by seeking such advice from Whitlam. (Indeed, as confirmed by Kerr, at no stage of the crisis did he follow Ellicott's opinion and seek advice from his Prime Minister on how Whitlam intended to resolve the deadlock.) Moreover, while Kerr agreed with the fundamental point (3), that he had the power to dismiss the government, he rejected the immediacy of the timing conveyed in the Ellicott opinion.

Kerr read the newspaper reports of the opinion. His secretary, David Smith, rang Ellicott to obtain a copy.[53] Kerr says: 'On the question of timing I found myself in disagreement with Mr Ellicott . . . Much could happen in the weeks after 16 October and I disagreed with Mr Ellicott as to what I or Mr Whitlam should do at the time when Mr Ellicott's document came forward.'[54]

In his memoirs Sir John quotes with approval Professor D P O'Connell, Professor of Public International Law at Oxford University, who referred in a January 1976 article to the view that Whitlam should have been given the opportunity to test the Opposition and try to break its nerve. Professor O'Connell says that this is a judgement that 'only the Governor-General was in the position to make'. Kerr's point, of course, is that he did make such a judgement. He gave Whitlam such an opportunity spanning 27 days. By not acting immediately Kerr rejected one element in Ellicott's argument—and he made his rejection clear to Whitlam himself when the opinion was released.[55]

Whitlam recalls that he left a caucus meeting on 21 October to take a call from Kerr. He says that Kerr asked: 'This Ellicott thing . . . it's all bullshit isn't it?' This is the same version that Whitlam gave me as background when I interviewed him in February 1976, and the remark is published in my book.[56] Whitlam took heart from Kerr's apparent rejection of the Ellicott opinion—but this was a false hope. It is now clear that, while Kerr rejected Ellicott's view that he had a duty to ask Whitlam immediately to resolve the crisis, he still agreed with Ellicott's essential proposition: that if Whitlam was unable either to produce a solution or to advise an election then he did have an obligation, eventually, to dismiss the Prime Minister.

The irony of the Ellicott opinion is that Kerr, in fact, refused to take even the first—and important—step recommended by Ellicott. It was a prudent and appropriate step for a Governor-General in Kerr's position. This was, in Ellicott's words, the need for the Governor-General 'to have from the Prime Minister an explanation of how he proposed to overcome the situation'. Once Supply was deferred it was sensible for a Governor-General to inquire of his chief minister how he planned to resolve things. Ellicott says: 'I made that point according to the book—it is consistent with Bagehot.'[57] It would have been better for all concerned if Kerr had taken Ellicott's advice on this point. It is also the approach advocated by Sir Paul Hasluck, who said that the Governor-General in dealing with his Prime Minister 'can be expected to talk with frankness and friendliness, to question, discuss, suggest and counsel'.⁵⁸ But Kerr had decided not to ask Whitlam; he took Whitlam's declared stance as being beyond influence.

Kerr suspected that if he did question, suggest and counsel Whitlam that Whitlam might only grow suspicious—and that Kerr's own position might be in danger.

Ellicott knew Kerr as a constitutional lawyer and as a man. He was convinced that Kerr would be receptive to his argument. The morning after Supply was blocked another friend of Kerr, Jim McClelland, strode into the same breakfast room as Ellicott. McClelland couldn't restrain himself. He walked up to Ellicott's table and said, 'You won't get away with this, Bob. The mob won't wear this.' According to McClelland, 'Ellicott looked up at me and fixed me with what I can only describe as a patronising stare. "Oh yes we will", he replied. "In the end this will all depend on Old Silver and he'll do the right thing."' McClelland was not suggesting that Ellicott had spoken to Kerr. In fact, he had not. The point is that Ellicott knew his man—better than Whitlam or McClelland did.⁵⁹

Ellicott provides his own appreciation of Kerr:

> He wasn't a weak man. He was a person who liked to get a consensus. He was liberal in his views, not dogmatic, yet on the other hand he was a traditionalist who emerged from the Labor Party of the '30s and '40s. He was always prepared to express strong views about matters . . . as a counsel he was resolute . . . he was a man you might think was weak or soft but underneath he was strong.⁶⁰

The significance of the Ellicott opinion is that it became Malcolm Fraser's text. Within a few days Fraser would tell Kerr to his face that the Opposition believed that the opinion would have to be heeded by the Governor-General. Ellicott says: 'I think the opinion did influence him. Kerr told me, when it was all over at a later stage, that Fraser owed a lot to the opinion.'⁶¹

Kerr took Ellicott's thesis sufficiently seriously to ask Whitlam for an opinion on it from the government's Law Officers—the Attorney General and the Solicitor-General. He conveyed this request during their phone discussion of 21 October. Kerr recalls that Whitlam 'agreed to get such an opinion on his own behalf and said he would probably pass it on to me'. On returning to the party room Whitlam asked the Attorney General, Kep Enderby, to prepare an opinion for Kerr from himself and the Solicitor-General.⁶²

During the crisis Whitlam ran Labor's tactics, politically and legally. His office chief, John Mant, says: 'One of the mistakes was the absence of an appropriate co-ordinating group responsible for strategy and assessing contingencies'.⁶³ The Senate leader, Ken Wriedt, was scarcely involved in any tactical talks, a terrible blunder. Kep Enderby played little part. Maurice Byers says that in his view 'it was catastrophic to have Enderby in the job; the real Attorney General was Gough'.[64]

In their advice Byers and Clarence Harders, the Attorney General's departmental head, emphasised the Senate's breach of convention, and Whitlam drew heavily on their advice. But Byers and Harders had insights into the crisis that Whitlam did not fully appreciate. Byers says:

> The advice I gave from the start was that the Senate was refusing to exercise its law-making powers with the intention of procuring a dismissal. That was not, in my view, a valid pursuit by them of their powers to make laws. The Senate was holding the appropriation in its grasp, the purpose being that if the ministry was dismissed and a new ministry appointed then the Appropriation Bills, having been passed by the Representatives, could then be passed by the Senate. That was the purpose of it. It seemed to me to be obvious.[65]

Asked if Whitlam and his advisers saw a dismissal strategy in this same context, Byers replied:

> I don't think this point was as clear in Whitlam's mind as it was in my mind. The reason was because he was so immersed in the political battle that was going on. I wasn't.
> What I told them was that the actor could be and only could be the Governor-General. He was the person who could change the situation if otherwise it remained static. Therefore the logic of the situation was to remove the likelihood of an intervention by him. You did that by explaining in your speeches that this was a contest between the two houses of parliament—the Representatives wanting Supply and representing the people of the Commonwealth of Australia and the Senate which only represented the people of the States . . . [The] traditional view was that the Crown should not intervene because by intervening the Crown would be brought down to the same level of a contestant . . . I told them this. I told them more than once. But they didn't appreciate it. They thought I was just having a fight with Bob Ellicott.[66]

Graham Freudenberg, who wrote Whitlam's speeches during the crisis, later lamented the 'invincible blindness' that caused them to discard the Byers drafts which dealt with Ellicott's argument about dismissal and the reserve powers.[67] Whitlam's office didn't think this was the issue.

Byers, unlike Whitlam, believed that the reserve powers existed. He felt that Whitlam's task was to ensure they were not used against him: 'Kerr was a lawyer. He had profound views about the Governor-General's powers. Knowing he was a lawyer, he should have been buttered up . . . but Gough was putting Kerr under psychological pressure and that was unwise.'[68]

On 20 October Harders advised in a note sent to Whitlam through Menadue:

> It would not be wise for the Prime Minister to simply assert that the Governor-General must at all times and in all circumstances act on his advice . . . The vital issue has been stated again and again by the Prime Minister . . . It is not the short-term interest of any of the political parties that is important. What is important and what must be maintained in the interest of parliamentary government in Australia is the maintenance of the convention. The convention must prevail. So long as, in the end, the Governor-General is thoroughly seized of what is at stake, and acts accordingly, it does not really matter whether, in point of fine analysis, he has acted on the Prime Minister's advice or in the exercise of a discretion reposed in the Queen's representative.[69]

The primary task, according to Byers and Harders, was to convince Kerr that Whitlam's position was right. Yet almost no effort was directed to this. Byers was correct in warning of the risk of a dismissal; Harders was correct in advising against derailing the issue onto whether Kerr must accept Whitlam's advice. These blunders involved, ultimately, failure to understand Kerr's character and motivation.

There were, however, missed constitutional opportunities. The most significant involved including a provision in the Appropriation bills that they return to the Representatives after being carried by the Senate, before receiving the Royal Assent. It was a precautionary recommendation and, as events proved, a farsighted one. Menadue and Harders involved their departments of Prime Minister and Attorney General's in assessing this option. Clarrie Harders says: 'This was a significant proposal. It meant that the lower house would retain an ultimate control over the bills. It would have made it necessary for Fraser to secure the bills through the House of Representatives as caretaker PM in order to secure Supply. This means that Fraser could not have given a guarantee to Kerr that he could secure Supply.'[70]

The tactic would have prevented Kerr from commissioning Fraser on 11 November on the condition that he secure Supply. But it was rejected as too provocative; a decisive omission. 'We were so naive', Menadue laments.[71]

Another proposal, which Whitlam sensibly rejected, was for the government to ask Kerr to address the Senate. In a memorandum Harders raised the possibility of the Governor-General 'addressing both Houses of the Parliament'. Menadue discussed with Whitlam a proposal to ask Kerr to speak to the Senate. Whitlam's response was, 'it won't be necessary'. This would have been a dubious tactic and anyway Kerr did not believe that it was the Governor-General's task to tell the Senate how to exercise its powers.[72] With typical misplaced confidence, Whitlam told Freudenberg of this proposal: 'It is not the function of the Crown to bail out the Opposition'.[73] It is obvious that Whitlam's rejection of all these options was because he had such confidence in Kerr remaining supportive that he believed they were unnecessary. This theme occurs repeatedly. When Menadue asked whether 'Jack Bunting or myself should go to London to brief the Palace' Whitlam again replied that such action 'won't be necessary'.[74]

Kerr hardens against Whitlam

Meanwhile, the Opposition seized the Ellicott opinion and began to market it. On Sunday 19 October Malcolm Fraser told a 12 000-strong Melbourne rally that Kerr might have to intervene to resolve the crisis. Fraser said that he expected the Governor-General would act 'quite soon' to break the deadlock. The same weekend Ellicott appeared on the television program *Federal File*, saying that if Whitlam maintained his position then Kerr would have no option but to withdraw his commission. This Opposition line received extensive media coverage. *The Australian* carried a banner headline declaring: 'Fraser says Kerr must sack Whitlam'.[75]

On 19 October Kerr rang Whitlam at Kirribilli House and raised two issues. First, Kerr said he was embarrassed by the newspaper reports. He said they appeared to be designed to intimidate him and to influence his actions on the Supply issue. Whitlam says that Kerr expressed concern about the cover story in *The Australian* on the previous day under the headline: 'Will Sir John Kerr act?'. Second, Kerr asked Whitlam whether he should consult with the Chief Justice, Sir Garfield Barwick, on the crisis.[76]

Whitlam told Kerr not to consult with Barwick. He pointed out that only one Governor-General, Sir Ronald Munro Ferguson, had consulted with a Chief Justice. That was in 1914 over the first double dissolution—at an earlier stage of Australia's constitutional development—with the Chief Justice being Sir Samuel Griffith, one of the founding fathers. Whitlam pointed out that the Australian High Court had no advisory role; indeed, in 1921 the Court had said it would not give advisory opinions. Whitlam also pointed to the danger of a Chief Justice advising a Governor-General on any matter that could subsequently come before the High Court itself.

Whitlam believed that he was acquainted with history and precedent on this issue. There was an obvious point which he did not make to Kerr—in politics Barwick had been Whitlam's rival; on the Bench he had been a conservative. Whitlam would not want Kerr talking to Barwick.[77]

Kerr disputes Whitlam's account of this discussion. He says that he did not ask Whitlam whether he could consult with Barwick. Kerr claims that before the crisis he and Whitlam discussed the principle involved—since Hasluck had supported the right of the Governor-General to consult the Chief Justice—and that Whitlam did not share Hasluck's view.[78]

The point, however, is that Kerr wanted advice and Whitlam failed to provide it efficiently and promptly. This oversight betrays a complacency and misjudgement. Human nature should have instructed Whitlam that, having told Kerr he couldn't see Barwick, he needed to offer a substitute.

Byers says: 'I think it was unwise not to give John Kerr the chance to talk to people such as myself if he had wanted. Gough was definitely opposed to that.' Byers recalled an occasion—before the crisis—when this issue of his direct access to Kerr arose and Whitlam vetoed it.[79]

The Opposition had left Whitlam behind. Kerr received Ellicott's opinion—in effect, the Opposition's legal opinion—about 17 October. On 19 October Kerr asked Whitlam if he could consult with Barwick; on 21 October he asked Whitlam for an opinion from the Law Officers on the Ellicott thesis—but he had to wait until 6 November when Enderby delivered this advice. Kerr went through most of the crisis without any written advice or opinion from the government! And he was a Governor-General with a legal mind and a penchant for written opinions!

Whitlam should have driven to Yarralumla to see Kerr on either 15 or 16 October, at the start, with a legal opinion explaining his position and, in particular, his support for Responsible Government as embodied in the Constitution. There should have been a covering note from Whitlam which constituted formal advice to the Governor-General. Whitlam should have explained his stance to Kerr over a Scotch. He should have offered at this time to make the Solicitor-General, Maurice Byers, available to Kerr for direct consultation and advice during the crisis. He should have explored directly with Kerr his views on Whitlam's strategy. He should have insisted that the detailed opinion from the Law Officers replying to Ellicott be given to Kerr just a few days after his 21 October request.

None of this happened.

Whitlam did not handle Kerr with attention or prudence or advice; instead he was making public declarations that Kerr had no discretion and privately instructing him not to see Barwick. The Governor-General felt that he was not getting access to the advice that he requested.[80] Whitlam was not heeding the elementary point made by Byers and Harders—it was necessary to persuade Kerr to a belief in the Prime Minister's position.

The immediate voter reaction to the crisis was to sympathise with Whitlam and to be apprehensive about Fraser's action. This was documented in public opinion polls throughout the crisis. The polls gave Labor great heart and put the Coalition and the Senate under intense pressure. But such voter sentiment on the Supply issue was separate from how people would vote at an election. Fraser's dilemma was that he had sufficient support to win an election but the voters did not support the tactics he was using to procure an election. On the other hand, Whitlam needed to translate this surge of voter sympathy based on the idea of a 'fair go' into an Opposition retreat on Supply, in order to avert the election that he would still lose.

Labor's electoral tactics during the deadlock were revealed by the Treasurer Bill Hayden in Parliament on 16 October when he explained the consequences of deferring the budget:

> It is no exaggeration to assert firmly and with a great deal of concern that the economy of this country, if the present course of action which the Opposition has set in train is pursued, will get out of hand, that there will be a major economic collapse, that a substantial number of enterprises in the corporate sector will fail, that there will be an upsurge in unemployment and generally that there will be the worst deepening of the recession that we have seen at any time since the great Depression of the 1930s . . .
>
> Let me give some illustrations of the effects of delaying the budget . . . Aged persons hostels, aged and disabled persons homes, organisations for assistance to the handicapped—to give just a few examples—will not obtain money necessary to pay the people who provide the services. I mention the construction contractors who have built the buildings to accommodate the aged and those people who supply the goods and services necessary to allow those contractors to build those buildings.
>
> Hospital services will grind down. Much medical research will have to be stopped. The Council for the Aged, the Council for Social Services and the Red Cross Organisation, to mention 3 agencies in the community, will find that their funds will have dried up. They will not be able to function for long. Education in the States will be short of some $360m at least. I cannot see how the Defence forces will operate at all because included in those Appropriation Bills which are being

delayed—or rejected—by the action of the Senate is $1,710m for that purpose . . .

People throughout the country will find that they will not be able to obtain their Medibank medical benefits. The State hospitals will find that the allocations of finance on the 50/50 cost sharing arrangement for operating costs under Medibank will not be available.[81]

On the same day, in the Senate, Steele Hall told the Opposition that the public reaction against its move made a retreat inevitable. He said: 'I forecast that within three weeks this budget will be passed completely in the Senate because public pressure will be overwhelming in one week's time . . . The Opposition is not standing on principle; it is standing simply on the numbers, and the numbers are not with them.'[82]

The question of 'who's to blame' was the core issue in the electoral politics of the crisis. The atmosphere was filled with emotion and bitterness. Thousands of people demonstrated in Melbourne against Fraser in the opening days. On 16 October several thousand demonstrators took to the lawns opposite Parliament House. The worst incidents occurred in Hobart on 17 October when Fraser was howled down by a hostile crowd of 4000 people in the city's Franklin Square. Punches were traded and Liberal parliamentarians and supporters scuffled with demonstrators. On the same day in Brisbane 5000 people attended a Labor rally in King George Square to hear Hayden tell them that the government would not surrender.

Whitlam grew more determined and dogmatic as the mood on the Supply issue ran in his favour. There was euphoria within Labor ranks, a fevered confidence fed on emotion. But there was a danger that Whitlam would become too convinced that the Senate would crack—a risky stance for a Prime Minister who had no fallback position. Voter sympathy towards Labor became a trap—a factor in undermining Whitlam's judgement.[83]

At this point, on 18 October, Kerr says that he conducted an important discussion with Whitlam—three days after the budget was blocked. He does not say where it was held—but his description of Whitlam's mood is vivid and his claim is that Whitlam had hardened on the Supply question.

Kerr continues:

> He said he would advise no election of any kind whatsoever . . . The Prime Minister said again that he was determined to break the Senate's power, which enabled it at its whim to force an election of the House of Representatives by denying Supply. He had reached the conclusion in October that we had come to a great moment of history

such as happened in the United Kingdom in 1909–10. He had, he
said, finally and irrevocably decided never to take the House of Representatives to the people because the Senate denied it power to govern
by cutting off money.

    Mr Whitlam seemed to me to be in an exuberant, even a
euphoric, mood on 18 October. In the same conversation he said to
me, 'You are in the position of George V'. My riposte was, 'But you are
not in the position of Asquith. You cannot pack the Senate.'

There is nothing surprising about these remarkable comments—
they are consistent with Whitlam's public comments.

But Kerr says:

> Already that day the Prime Minister was talking of finding a way of getting the banks to lend to everyone to whom the Commonwealth owed money—public servants, troops, police, contractors and so on—the amount owed . . . The crisis would, he argued, be no real constitutional crisis, because despite denial of Supply he would still be able to govern, and there would be no excuse for me to demand evidence from him that he could get Supply, *and no excuse for removing him and sending for someone willing to advise an election.*[84]

The notion that Whitlam was telling Kerr on 18 October that there
would be no grounds on which to dismiss him—thereby confronting
the dismissal issue directly with the Governor-General—is extraordinary.
Whitlam did not canvass this in public; he denies that he canvassed it
in private.

    In his own memoirs Whitlam addresses this conversation of which
Kerr gives such a long account: 'Sir John, however, does not say where
this discussion took place, and for good reason; it did not take place.
He was in Canberra on the day and I was in Sydney (I opened the
Gymea Lily Festival, which was given extensive cover on television).'
Whitlam brands Kerr's account as 'imaginary'.[85]

    Kerr, however, draws his familiar conclusion from Whitlam's dogmatism in this alleged exchange:

> I clearly felt that no comment or suggestion from me would be welcome; and this was the climate, from the second week of October onward, of all my conversations with Mr Whitlam regarding his intention to govern without Supply. I was being *told* what the Prime Minister intended to do . . . I never again felt I could *talk* to the Prime Minister about his policy on Supply.[86] [Kerr's emphasis]

    The principals dispute the conversation but its significance for Kerr
is predictable. He used this alleged exchange to confirm the decision,
which he had already taken, based on a discussion before 14 October,
that there was no point in talking to Whitlam about Supply. He

concluded, further, that Whitlam regarded dismissal as an option in the crisis.[87] The Governor-General, on his own admission, confirmed his decision of 'silence'—not to canvass the Supply issue with his Prime Minister.

I believe that Kerr had decided, not so much that he could not influence Whitlam, but that he did not want to influence Whitlam. It is obvious that if Kerr had possessed the will to speak firmly to Whitlam about his chosen course then he would have influenced Whitlam. Kerr's real decision was that Whitlam had forfeited the right to a frank dialogue. Kerr developed a victim mentality. He convinced himself that Whitlam was being intimidatory and disrespectful of him personally and of the office of Governor-General constitutionally. So Kerr cut Whitlam off. He dealt with Whitlam in a spirit of friendly propriety, but he denied Whitlam access to his thinking about the crisis, notably what would happen if Whitlam's tactics failed. Kerr decided that Whitlam would live with the consequences of his own dogmatism.

A worried shadow cabinet met in Melbourne on Sunday 19 October—a special meeting called to assess its position just four days after blocking Supply. Fraser opened the meeting and, carefully and deliberately, listed a series of options:

> One: we can sit tight. Two: we actually reject bills in the Senate, thus fulfilling Whitlam's condition for an election of some kind. Three: we withdraw as gracefully as possible. Four: we give him Supply until February—invite the government to accumulate as many bills as it likes for a double dissolution, on the basis that there will be a double dissolution in February. We could say we'd guarantee that if we failed to get a majority in the Reps, we would pass all the double dissolution bills even if we had a Senate majority. Five: agree to a full half-Senate, if that is what Whitlam asks for. Six: I publicly seek an audience with the Governor-General—to explain our actions and seek advice. Seven: I see the Governor-General privately.[88]

After shadow cabinet members had expressed their views it was agreed that urgent steps were needed to explain the Opposition's position at branch level. There was a feeling that if support eroded at grassroots level within the Liberal Party then the strategy would collapse. There was even discussion about an indirect approach to the Queen, perhaps through a friend of Fraser, Lord Carrington, then leader of the Opposition in the House of Lords—but it was not taken up.

There were two lessons from the meeting—that Fraser would consult his colleagues at length and that he was flexible and calculating in assessing his best course.[89] A contrast to Whitlam. The key to Fraser's success was that the senior ranks were committed to the Supply decision. He could marshal their backing to hold the waverers.

The following day, Monday 20 October, Fraser faced a potential loss of nerve in his South Australian division. The former Liberal Premier Sir Thomas Playford—Australia's longest serving Liberal Premier—was expressing his opposition to deferral of Supply to South Australian Liberals. Liberal Federal Director Tony Eggleton reported to Fraser that the South Australian Liberal leader David Tonkin had told him that Adelaide Liberals and prominent businessmen were extremely uneasy. Tonkin's view was that 'we have not convinced our own people'. In addition, South Australian Senator Don Jessop had written to Fraser, saying that he had received many messages 'from Liberals of equal integrity and importance as Sir Thomas Playford' also expressing concern. Jessop rang Fraser to convey directly his worries.[90]

Jessop had been an original critic of the decision. He says:

> I had discussed this issue with Tom Playford, whose concerns had been expressed in his telegrams. At one party meeting in this period I used one of Tom's phrases to oppose our action. He had said that 'if you have an election before Christmas then you'll win but you will be greeted as an invading army by a hostile citizenry; if you have an election after Christmas then you'll also win but you will be greeted as a rescuing army by a grateful citizenry.[91]

Malcolm Fraser was 'alarmed'. He promptly organised a campaign centred on Jessop to ensure that he got extensive party feedback supporting the decision, a technique that apparently worked.[92] 'Jessop was alright once he learned there was solid South Australian opinion for our action', Fraser recalls with a smile.[93]

The next step required great delicacy—the intervention of the father and founder of the Liberal Party. Fraser desperately needed Menzies to endorse his decision. Even a silent Menzies would have been damaging; a critical Menzies would have destroyed Fraser's position. But Fraser, unlike Whitlam, had addressed his political requirements with a methodical efficiency.

Fraser says: 'I knew that Menzies didn't like the Senate being used in this way any more than I did. I wouldn't have been surprised if he'd been critical of it. So I did a bit of research and found that he had issued a statement in 1947 that supported the Victorian upper house blocking Supply. I had a photocopy of this when I went to see him . . . but I didn't have to persuade him. He said as much as he hated it there was no option.'[94]

The upshot was a statement that had the ring of Menzian clarity:

> If we desire to know what are the powers of the Senate over money Bills, we find them expressly set out in the Constitution. The draftsmen of the Constitution included these provisions because they knew that the smaller States, i.e. smaller in population, would not vote for Federation unless they had some protection given to them in the Senate and they got it. And they still have it . . . While the Senate may not itself amend what we call 'money Bills', it can pass them, or reject them, because these are the powers of the House of Representatives in respect of the same measures . . . It would be absurd to suppose that the draftsmen of the Constitution conferred these powers on the Senate with a mental reservation that they should never be exercised . . .
>
> Everything depends on the circumstances. For a Government, fresh from the people with a victory, to be challenged in the Senate under section 53, would be, in my opinion, wrong. Not illegal, no, but politically wrong.
>
> But these are not the circumstances today. The Government has, in the last 12 months, itself put up a record of unconstitutionality and, if it is not too strong a word, misconduct on a variety of occasions . . . This, if there ever was an occasion, was one when the Senate ought to have exercised its undisputed right to defer or reject financial measures involved in the Budget.[95]

On the same day as this statement, 21 October, there was a shadow cabinet and then a joint parties meeting. Several speakers in the party room complained about the impression being created in the media that many of them were wavering. Fraser criticised false press reports. Even Don Jessop appeared more relaxed. Only Tasmanian Senator Eric Bessell took the other tack—he was worried about the enormous number of complaints. Bill Snedden told the party to stand firm. South Australian Senator Condor Laucke agreed. He said that he had reservations before the decision; now it had to be supported. Overall, Fraser took heart.[96]

At the shadow cabinet Fraser canvassed the possibility of moving from a 'defer' to a 'reject' position. He himself thought there was no certainty that Whitlam would call an election if the budget were rejected. It was agreed that 'defer' remained the best tactic. The meeting also discussed whether Fraser should ask to see Kerr—and decided to wait a while longer.[97]

There was, though, no doubt that Fraser would soon have approached Kerr directly: 'I would have regarded it as part of my job to ensure that the Governor-General was aware of our position'.[98]

Kerr consults Fraser

Kerr was now prompted by the force of public opinion to intervene in the crisis. His passivity was no longer sustainable. It is almost as though Kerr was shocked by the calls for his involvement to help procure a solution. Professor Colin Howard of Melbourne University declared that 'the Governor-General is the only person left with sufficiently high office, and who is not identified with either party, to resolve the situation'.[99] There was strong media backing, too, for Kerr's engagement.

Kerr, however, was quite reluctant. He described his subsequent dialogue with the leaders as being 'forced' upon him by the public mood. Indeed, he refers to 'the need to give the public some evidence of my very deep concern'.[100] It is a fact that even when Kerr was involved in this subsequent dialogue with both leaders that he was reluctant to commit his office to the role of mediator in a genuine sense.

In his memoirs Kerr argued the case for a limited role for the Crown or the Crown's representative in a situation of deadlock. He does this by referring to the British precedent of 1910 when George V desired to see the Opposition leaders. Prime Minister Asquith objected with his famous quotation: 'It is not the function of a Constitutional Sovereign to act as arbiter or mediator between rival parties and policies, still less to take advice from the leaders on both sides, with a view to forming a conclusion of his own.'[101] Kerr quoted Asquith to support his own view of a limited role for the Crown in this situation. But he declined to point out that George V overruled Asquith and insisted that he needed to obtain firsthand knowledge by conferring with the political leaders.

Sir Ivor Jennings argues that in a case of deadlock 'it cannot be doubted' that a sovereign can mediate. The task is to get the timing right; too late 'will be ineffectual', too early may be too partisan.[102] Former Governor-General Sir William McKell said: 'I would have called both Mr Whitlam and Mr Fraser to Yarralumla and warned them I would have to intervene unless the crisis was resolved by a specific date'.[103] Maurice Byers says: 'I think he should have called both leaders to him and pointed out the chaos which their behaviour was threatening . . . It is a position commensurate with the Crown . . . to warn ministers and Opposition as to the consequences of their actions'.[104]

It is true that Kerr did become involved in a dialogue with Whitlam and Fraser to see if a political settlement was possible. But he was hesitant. His performance during this subsequent dialogue suggests that he saw the role of Governor-General more in terms of imposing a constitutional solution rather than in negotiating a political settlement.

This point has not been properly appreciated, primarily because Kerr did meet and discuss the situation with Whitlam and Fraser.

A Governor-General is advised by his ministers. His office exists not as a constitutional umpire but rather a constitutional guardian. It is this latter responsibility that allows a King or a Governor-General to intervene and deal with both sides during a crisis. It is because such mediation represents a departure from a King's normal functions that its conduct is so grave and delicate. The central responsibility of the Crown or the Crown's representative *during those rare occasions of crisis* is to become involved in order to ensure a political solution to a political problem. This averts the need for a constitutional solution with its danger of accusations against the Crown or the Crown's representative. The challenge facing a King or a King's representative in such a situation is to secure a solution yet keep the Crown impartial.

Acting on the degree of public disquiet, Kerr took advantage of a discussion with Whitlam on 21 October after an Executive Council meeting and the swearing in of Paul Keating and Rex Patterson. He asked for Whitlam's consent to his having talks with Fraser on the crisis. Kerr said he merely wished to assess Fraser's intentions directly. Kerr told Whitlam he believed that the crisis, though serious, was still a political crisis—'it had not yet crossed the threshold into a true constitutional crisis'. The money had not started to run out. Whitlam 'readily agreed' to Kerr's seeing Fraser.[105]

It was a fateful move.

It altered Kerr's role and it changed the chemistry of the crisis. It meant, inevitably, that Kerr would become involved in a dialogue with Fraser on the crisis as part of the search for a solution.[106] A Governor-General is not an 'honest broker' between Government and Opposition. He acts on the advice of his ministers. He exists not as a constitutional umpire but as a constitutional guardian. It is this latter responsibility that allows a King or a Governor-General to intervene with both sides during a crisis. It is because such mediation represents a departure from a King's normal functions that its conduct is so grave and delicate. The challenge facing a King or a King's representative in such a situation is to secure a solution yet keep the Crown impartial.

Whitlam let Kerr see Fraser because he trusted Kerr. Whitlam recognised the pressure on Kerr to become involved; he hoped this process might assist him. (Anything that might encourage Fraser to retreat!) There was misleading media speculation at the time that Kerr might ask or encourage Fraser to change his mind and let the budget pass. Whitlam agreed 'readily'; he probably acted on instinct and in hope.

In this decision Whitlam misjudged both Fraser and Kerr.

First, he was probably too arrogant to believe that Fraser might exercise a greater influence on Kerr than he did. Yet that was the risk. Whitlam misjudged this risk because he underestimated Fraser and trusted Kerr. Fraser says: 'Whitlam couldn't stop our talks. You can't deny the Governor-General access to the leader of the Opposition any more than you can deny him access to the Chief Justice'.[107]

Second, Whitlam did not realise that Kerr distrusted him. Kerr, according to his own admission, had decided already that he would not talk frankly to Whitlam because the Prime Minister was 'beyond the reach' of argument. So Kerr, distrusting Whitlam and concerned that Whitlam might even move against him, now sought Whitlam's permission to begin talking to Fraser.

This gave Fraser a chance to succeed where Whitlam had failed—to shape Kerr's response and, above all, to convince Kerr to trust him.

On that same afternoon the second parliamentary debate occurred over Supply, with Whitlam moving successfully that the Senate's vote 'is not contemplated within the terms of the Constitution' and asking the Senate to pass the bills. In his speech Whitlam said it was a matter of 'establishing the principle beyond all doubt for the future, for all time . . . for all future Prime Ministers'. He said that Fraser's action, if successful, would divide Australia 'and leave a legacy of bitterness unequalled since 1916 . . .'[108]

Remembering Kerr's complaint to him about Fraser just two days before, Whitlam accused the Opposition—notably Fraser and Ellicott—of trying to intimidate the Governor-General.[109] He said the Opposition was 'seeking to bring reprehensible pressure to bear' on Kerr to persuade him into 'dismissing me as Prime Minister'. But Whitlam then moved from defending Kerr to instructing Kerr. Echoing Asquith he continued:

> Nor is it the function of the constitutional monarch or the viceroy to act as arbiter between rival parties, still less to take advice from leaders of both sides with a view to forming a conclusion of his own . . . If the Governor-General were to intervene by dismissing ministers, he would be expected to do the same on another occasion . . . The Crown would become the football of contending factions.

Growing in confidence Whitlam now ruled out any half Senate poll: 'I shall not advise the Governor-General to hold an election for the House of Representatives at the behest of the Senate. I shall tender no advice for an election for either House or both Houses until this constitutional issue is settled.'

He concluded:

> The message from the Senate constitutes an act of constitutional aggression by the Senate . . . Not for the first time is government of the people for the people by the people—and in our case, by the people's House—at stake. In the words of Lincoln when he was trying to avert the greatest constitutional convulsion in the history of democracy, let me say to the Leader of the Opposition and his followers: In your hands and not in mine rests this momentous issue. You can have no conflict without yourself being the aggressor. You have registered no oath to destroy the Constitution, while I have the most solemn one to preserve and defend it.
>
> The Leader of the Opposition maintains that all that is required for Australia to avoid the evil consequences of his own actions is for us—the elected government—to cave in. Of course, if Britain had caved in in 1940 a great deal of inconvenience would have been avoided. But the destruction of British parliamentary democracy would only have been postponed. We will stand up for the rights of this House and the rights of the Australian people. We will not surrender.

Malcolm Fraser rose with disdain and referred to 'the oddness—one might almost say the madness—of the analogies which the Prime Minister seeks to draw'. He reminded the House that Lincoln lived in a land where the Senate and the House 'have concurrent powers in relation to financial matters'. Fraser continued: 'The Prime Minister is asking this House to carry a resolution in defiance of the Constitution itself because the motion says that the purposes of the resolution are not contemplated in the terms of the Constitution'. In order to sustain this point Fraser quoted Quick and Garran on the Constitution: 'The Senate has co-ordinate powers with the House of Representatives to pass all Bills or to reject all Bills. Its right of veto is as unqualified as its right of assent . . .' Fraser quoted an eminent High Court judge, Lionel Murphy, who had declared that 'there are no limitations on the Senate on the use of its constitutional powers'. Then he quoted Whitlam and Menzies to reinforce the same point.

In his conclusion Fraser declared:

> This is the first time that a democratically elected Prime Minister has sought to continue in government when the Parliament has denied him money. Then he makes a charge against us. This is his own charge—a charge against himself of trying to bully the Governor-General. What more outrageous proposal could the Prime Minister have made? Everything he said on *This Day Tonight* and in this Parliament was as a direction to the Governor-General. That is not something that ought to occur . . . The Constitution is not only for a

Prime Minister. Once he has lost the capacity to govern because money is cut off he has then lost the capacity to stay in his present place.[110]

But the powerful speech from the Opposition was that of Bob Ellicott. He admitted that he had resolved from the time of the 9 July special sitting on the loans affair—'the most rotten thing that has happened in this country since Federation'—to throw out the government.

He continued:

> The Prime Minister said in Question Time that I was not born in 1911. He thought that I might not have heard of Asquith. But I had heard of Asquith when I was a little boy. What I learned about Asquith was that Asquith had the courage to face the people . . . Do not imagine that any man behind me or any man in the other place is going to let our side down, because he is not . . . The longer you delay and the longer you allow the demagogue to control you, the worse it will be for the Labor Party, and have no doubt about it . . .
>
> There is no constitutional crisis. The fact quite clearly is that the Prime Minister has a role to perform now . . . The Constitution provides a process that can be followed . . . There is only one piece of proper advice for him to give the Governor-General, and that is to dissolve this House or to have a double dissolution . . . I have little doubt that he will not do it. We know that by the way he has been going on here and on television—the irrational stance, those eyes that flash in defiance of the Australian Constitution . . . Nothing that has been done so far on our side is not proper, is not right. The Governor-General clearly has a power to dismiss his ministers. The Prime Minister says, 'The Governor-General has to do what I say'. If I wanted I could quote 10 or 15 leading constitutional authorities. They are all quoted in Dr Evatt's book. They are all there. The Prime Minister knows they are there. They all say that the Governor-General has a Reserve Power in these circumstances.[111]

The hyperbole in Whitlam's speech inspired his supporters. But its substance would prove more important. In his speech Whitlam: (1) declared that he would not call an election under pressure from the Senate—which Kerr later said 'confirmed my belief in an irreversible attitude by Mr Whitlam against an election'; and (2) while defending Kerr also appeared to be publicly instructing Kerr.

Malcolm Fraser saw Kerr at Yarralumla on the same evening for their first talk. Fraser met not a stranger but a man whom he felt he knew well. As Defence Minister, Fraser had chosen Kerr to conduct the complex report on defence force pay. Fraser said: 'Even after I had resigned from Defence I used to go along and talk to John Kerr and he'd bounce some of his solutions off me. That was all unofficial, and nobody really knew it was happening. But he wanted to—so I made myself available. And I got to know him.'[112]

During the crisis Fraser privately told his colleagues that he knew Kerr as well as Whitlam did—but probably few believed him. 'Whitlam wasn't aware of my associations with Kerr. I had a knowledge of this man', Fraser says.[113]

Fraser was given a drink and told by Kerr that the meeting was to assess 'where we were heading'. The conversation lasted more than an hour. Had Whitlam spent a full hour discussing the crisis with Kerr? It is by no means certain.

In his memoirs Kerr provides a fascinating summary of the discussion with Fraser:

> Mr Fraser said that a firm decision had been taken to deny Supply, that this would be persisted in to the end, that whatever the press said or predicted the Bills would be deferred as often as they were presented and the Prime Minister would have to face the country. I asked him about the solidarity of the Coalition attitude and the likelihood of defection. His answer was that the Senate and the Coalition would be firm and constant on deferral of Supply.
>
> In view of the current discussion on the difference between deferral and rejection of Supply, I asked him why deferral had been chosen. He said that Supply had been deferred so that, *should it come to a dissolution, he would be able to guarantee Supply by passing the Appropriation Bills immediately*. I told him not to assume that I accepted the Ellicott thesis but he responded to this by saying that, if the Prime Minister tried to govern without Supply—and he certainly would be forced into that position—he (Mr Fraser) would need to be in the position of being able to guarantee Supply although the Prime Minister could not.
>
> I had in my mind at that time, though I did not mention it to Mr Fraser, the discussion between the Prime Minister and myself in Port Moresby when Mr Whitlam said to me, 'Fraser would be no more able to guarantee Supply than I would because new legislation would be necessary and it wouldn't pass the House'. He had recognised, however, that it might be possible for the Senate to revive the Bills which had already passed the House and pass them in the Senate.
>
> Mr Fraser's attitude in this first talk with me and until the end was that deferral was not a sign of weakness due to internal problems with some Senators, but a deliberate and unanimous tactic designed to leave him flexibility of action. Mr Fraser did not at any time attempt to give me any advice. He simply told me that he and his supporters were firmly determined to deny Supply by deferral, to keep their options open, to operate on the broad basis of the Ellicott thesis and to await events. I gave Mr Fraser no indication whatsoever of my reaction to all of this except when I said he should not assume that I would act on the Ellicott thesis . . . Mr Fraser believed at that time that there

already was a serious constitutional crisis. The attitude of the two parties in his view made such a crisis inevitable and he considered that we were now in the presence of that crisis.[114]

If Whitlam had heard this Kerr–Fraser exchange, which he had sanctioned earlier the same day, he would have felt sick to his core. On Kerr's own account Fraser had played a beautiful hand. In sixty minutes he had changed the atmospherics of the crisis. Fraser had (1) informed Kerr that the Opposition would not retreat; (2) explained that the 'deferral' strategy had a calculated purpose, namely to enable Kerr to commission Fraser as Prime Minister because he could deliver Supply—an invitation to the Governor-General to dismiss Whitlam; and (3) told Kerr that there was already a constitutional crisis since the parties were deadlocked—which implied that a stage had already been reached where Whitlam's dismissal was justified.

Fraser, like Whitlam, had a formidable presence. There is no reason to suppose that Kerr did not take his remarks at face value. For the Governor-General who called this meeting to assess 'where we were heading' it was a sobering encounter. It is true that Fraser did not give Kerr advice. But he did everything short of this. He explained to Kerr that the foundation of the Opposition position was that unless Whitlam relented Kerr would be forced to replace him as Prime Minister. Fraser said later that his talks with Kerr 'were designed to get the right result'.[115]

From the time Fraser left this meeting he never wavered in his belief that Kerr would intervene, finally, on the Opposition's behalf if Whitlam refused to call a general election. Reflecting later on whether he felt that Kerr would act on the Ellicott thesis, which involved dismissal, Fraser said: 'I was convinced that he should, and I believed he would. I also believed that he would do it at the last possible moment.'[116] Fraser made his own judgement of Kerr as a man—and the conclusion he reached was the exact opposite of Whitlam's.

The solidarity of the Opposition during the crisis was, to a considerable extent, a function of Fraser's determination, and that determination was founded upon a judgement of Kerr.

Fraser's meeting with Kerr was surrounded by a fracas. Before the meeting the Official Secretary, David Smith, told some journalists that Kerr was upset about the Opposition declarations, so prominently reported, that the Governor-General would have to intervene.[117] After the meeting there was speculation—probably leaked by Labor—that Kerr had reprimanded Fraser. Hurried denials, provided in background briefings to journalists, were issued by Fraser's office and by Smith.

Did the possibility of Whitlam's dismissal arise at this discussion? Kerr says that he was only seeking information from Fraser. But the senior Country Party politician Ian Sinclair later said: 'Malcolm reported back on the conversations he had with the Governor-General . . . and while it's true that at an early stage he'd indicated that Sir John had suggested that a possibility was the sacking of the government, it wasn't one which either Malcolm or we rated as a probable outcome . . . at least initially'.[118] In response Fraser says: 'There might have been a theoretical discussion saying: these are the options available. But John Kerr never for one minute gave me an indication of what was in his mind or what he was going to do.'[119]

Clearly, if Kerr and Fraser discussed theoretical options—and dismissal was one—then that would have been extremely significant. It would have told Fraser that Kerr saw dismissal as a possibility.

The head of the Prime Minister's Department under Whitlam and then Fraser, John Menadue, gives his own startling account of this initial Kerr–Fraser exchange—a version Menadue says was given him by Fraser. According to Menadue, in this meeting Kerr 'had indicated to Mr Fraser that he [Kerr] had the threat of dismissal hanging over him and that if he showed his hand to Mr Whitlam that he would be dismissed'. Menadue identifies the significance of such a comment: 'I think that was sufficient indication that anyone would need that the Governor-General's decision or action would be unacceptable to Mr Whitlam.' If this remark was made it could have only encouraged Fraser to hold firm and Menadue says: 'He [Fraser] was given encouragement to continue on the course that he was on.' Such a remark would allow only one interpretation—that Kerr didn't trust Whitlam; if made, it was a betrayal of Whitlam. Pressed on this issue in an interview with me on October 10 1995 Menadue said that Fraser gave him this account on 28 January 1976 when Fraser raised the dismissal in conversation. Menadue made two notes for file; one went into the Prime Minister's Department records and the other, sighted by me, is among his personal papers.

When I asked Fraser about Menadue's account and his note, he insisted that Menadue was wrong. Fraser says that during the crisis he was aware that Kerr felt his position was at risk from Whitlam but Fraser is adamant that Kerr did not act improperly by saying this to him during their talks.

The next day, Fraser changed his public stance towards Kerr—he became deferential. The contrast with Whitlam was sharp. It was manifest that Fraser had reappraised his public relationship with Kerr. After conferring with his leadership group on Wednesday 22 October

Fraser declared on television that evening that the Opposition would abide by any decision reached by the Governor-General. He said: 'We would obviously look very closely at any request from the Governor-General because I have a very high regard for the office. Any decision made by the Governor-General would obviously be a decision we would follow.' In a separate interview Fraser repeated the message: 'If he gives a decision we would respect and accept it absolutely. If he gives advice we would give the greatest possible weight to it because of the respect we have for the office and the man.'[120]

This statement was widely misinterpreted by the media and the Labor Party as a backdown by Fraser—the first of several such misreadings. It was not; it was purely tactical. If the Governor-General moved in any way against the Opposition then Fraser had prepared his retreat. But Fraser was also offering a public encouragement to Kerr to intervene; he was signalling that the Opposition believed Kerr had a role to play; he was saying that the Opposition would defer to Kerr's judgement, that the Coalition trusted Kerr.

Fraser was flattering Kerr. Whitlam, of course, was patronising Kerr.

Henceforth Fraser never made any public comment telling Kerr what to do. Whitlam, by contrast, had told Kerr publicly what to do—to act only on Whitlam's advice. Kerr felt belittled by Whitlam; by contrast Fraser sought to elevate Kerr. Fraser was now challenging Whitlam to show the same respect for Kerr's office that Fraser himself had displayed.[121]

By 22 October, a week into the crisis, there was a public mirage and a private reality. The mirage was that Whitlam appeared to be winning. The voters disliked deferral of Supply. Whitlam dominated Fraser in the House. Kerr was now involved and the upshot was a softening in Fraser's approach. This was the public mirage, a distortion of the true picture.

The private reality was that Kerr had decided not to question or confide in Whitlam—a decision of which Whitlam was in ignorance. Even worse, Kerr feared that Whitlam, if compelled, might try to sack him. Fraser, for his part, had contained the doubters within his own ranks. He was now in a dialogue with Kerr. He had told Kerr not just that the Opposition would hold, but that its tactics assumed the Governor-General would have to dismiss Whitlam if he refused to advise a general election—and at that point Kerr could be assured that Fraser would obtain Supply as Prime Minister.

Whitlam, blind to his alienation from Kerr, was being outmanoeuvred by Fraser.

8

Failed compromises

> *If they were deceived, they deceived themselves.*
>
> Sir John Kerr on Gough Whitlam and his ministers

> *To state the matter shortly, the sovereign has, under a constitutional monarchy such as ours, three rights—the right to be consulted, the right to encourage, the right to warn. And a king of great sense and sagacity would want no others.*
>
> Walter Bagehot, *The English Constitution*

THE MID-STAGE OF the 1975 crisis was dominated by the search for a political solution based upon two compromises—but the opportunity was lost. Whitlam and Fraser had the chance to strike a bargain, defuse the deadlock and walk away with each leader protected by a facesaving formula. Sir John Kerr acted as an intermediary but not as a mediator. He sat at the table but refused to play his hand.

Whitlam and Fraser rejected a settlement because each believed that he would prevail—which meant that one had made a fatal miscalculation. The paradox of the crisis is that by 3 November Whitlam had persuaded Fraser to offer him a compromise that averted an immediate general election on the budget. It was a vital concession. But this was not sufficient for Whitlam—he wanted a lot more. Whitlam refused this compromise and chose to keep the crisis going to achieve his real aim, a total victory over Fraser and the Senate and the breaking, in effect, of the Senate's power over Supply forever.

In this period the Whitlam Government intensified its dual attack on the Opposition—that deferring the budget was constitutional vandalism and that it threatened people with an economic and social collapse. By these appeals to moral force and financial fear Whitlam sought to break the will of the Opposition and the Senate. As the crisis continued, demands for a settlement grew—from the public, the media and from many politicians in whispered tones behind closed doors.

Fraser, under intense pressure to retreat or compromise, kept his nerve in public, despite some private agonising. His tactic was to maintain internal discipline by orchestrating a national display of support from the non-Labor side, State and federal.

This mid-phase of the crisis was conducted at two levels—in public as an epic confrontation, and within the confines of Government Houses around the nation as Whitlam, Fraser and Kerr conferred about a compromise.

Whitlam won the public contest—the people overwhelmingly opposed the blocking of the budget. But Whitlam, instead of negotiating, pressed ahead. By holding out for a total victory Whitlam was to lose everything.

Labor launched a sustained assault upon the Coalition in the House of Representatives on 23 October. The Treasurer, Bill Hayden, declared: 'So long as the Appropriation Bills (Nos 1 and 2) are not passed there will be a shortfall in budget outlays of $700 million to $800 million a month. It will be more in December because of a bunching of planned outlays in that month. Gross domestic product in Australia is currently running at less than $6000 million a month; so we are talking about cutting off a flow of funds equivalent to around one-eighth of GDP each month'.[1]

Hayden said that the services sector had already been subjected to severe contraction; seasonal unemployment during summer would now be far worse than usual. The Minister for Services, Fred Daly, said that travel entitlements of parliamentarians would have to be restricted. Education Minister Kim Beazley said that pay for Northern Territory school teachers, allowances for Aboriginal children and also for tertiary students across the nation would cease in three weeks. The Minister for Northern Australia, Paul Keating, said that Darwin reconstruction work would soon cease, a devastating blow for the Territory. Agriculture Minister Rex Patterson explained that meat export would halt because the government could not pay meat inspectors.

Ministers focused on the Northern Territory and the ACT—crucial areas in any half Senate poll. It was a parliamentary blitz that left the

Opposition benches worried about the politics of blocking Supply and speculating over a compromise.

Later the same day Fraser held a press conference which captured the ongoing tensions between himself and the media:

QUESTION: Are you surprised at the backlash against your decision to block the budget?

FRASER: I've not had great evidence of a public opinion backlash.

QUESTION: What did you think of a public opinion poll which showed that 55 per cent of people don't want an election?

FRASER: That same opinion poll shows that a great number of people don't want this present government to continue . . .

QUESTION: In your last press conference you talked about universal support for an election. Where does that universal support come from?

FRASER: There is a good deal of support for an election all around the country.

QUESTION: You said universal, Mr Fraser. Would you say universal business? Universal trade unions? Universal from the populace? What is your source?

FRASER: There is a great deal of support from many different sections of the Australian community for an election.

QUESTION: Have you requested the government's permission to speak to the Treasurer or the Reserve Bank about how seriously the economy is going to be damaged? I heard your shadow Treasurer this morning and he dismissed this as unimportant . . . I ask you how seriously have you addressed yourself to this problem? What do you think is going to happen? How much are you going to put us through and for how long?

FRASER: We are not putting the economy through the wringer . . .

QUESTION: Mr Fraser, sorry, I don't want to interrupt this, but would you answer the first question: how seriously have you addressed yourself to this problem and have you sought any official advice?

FRASER: The question of whether or not the economy is being hurt rests entirely in the hands of the government, because in the proper course of events the Prime Minister ought to have ordered an election before this. If anyone is hurt it is because he has refused to do so.

QUESTION: Do you have any conscionable problems about the actions you have taken and the consequences for Australia?

FRASER: The action we have taken is right to remove from Australia the worst government since the beginning of Australia.

FAILED COMPROMISES

Whitlam's tactic throughout the crisis was to insist that the Senate vote to accept or reject the budget. He said:

> Mr Fraser stuck to the tactic of deferral because he was stuck with it. He knew that the Senate would not vote to reject Supply; the numbers were not there to do so . . . While Liberal Senators had been prepared to go along with the tactic of deferring a vote on the budget, it was common talk that many of them would never vote against this or any other budget because they would regard that as a usurpation by the Senate.[2]

Evidence of such fears came from Tasmanian Liberal Senator Eric Bessell, interviewed on the ABC on 25 October:

> INTERVIEWER: And if it came to a pure rejection of Supply you wouldn't vote?
>
> BESSELL: I would not vote for a rejection.
>
> INTERVIEWER: Well, in point of fact, you could be a very important Senator if it came to that crunch situation?
>
> BESSELL: I would think that there would be a good many others who would feel the same as I do on that particular item, on that particular matter, on the question of rejection.[3]

Whitlam exploited Bessell's concession to great effect. He repeatedly called upon Fraser to pass or reject the budget, declaring that the Opposition would not command the numbers for rejection. Whitlam was encouraged by information from one of his ministers, Joe Riordan, who was close to another Tasmanian Liberal, Senator John Marriott. Riordan says:

> The clear and unmistakable impression I gained was that Marriott and several others would not refuse Supply. In other words, when the budget had been delayed for as long as possible and the stage had been reached where it was a case of passing or rejecting it, the budget would have passed the Senate.[4]

South Australian Liberal Senator Don Jessop had put his opposition to rejection on the public record some weeks earlier. In a letter to the Adelaide *Advertiser* Jessop said, 'it is my view that the appropriation should be allowed to pass and only in extreme circumstances would I agree with the rejection of a future supply bill'.[5] Whitlam, in recent times, has named four Senators whom he believes would not have rejected the budget—Bessell, Marriott, Tom Drake-Brockman and Condor Laucke.[6]

Whitlam's argument contained moral and constitutional force. His problem, though, was that Fraser, relying upon the Withers stratagem, did not want to reject the budget. Fraser's preferred tactic was deferral. On 28 October Fraser told Parliament: 'While the measures are deferred it is within our power to resurrect the measures once it is known there is to be a House of Representatives election'. Whitlam may be right; the Senate may not have voted to reject the budget. Ultimately, the point didn't matter; deferral was enough and sufficient for Fraser's purpose.[7]

Labor's sense of unreality over this issue even extended to the Governor-General. According to Riordan he had a discussion with Kerr 'in the early stages' of the crisis, in which he put to the Governor-General that if the Senate could not amend a money bill then it was illogical to suppose that it could reject such a bill. 'Whilst he [Kerr] did not specifically endorse this view, he did not demur either', Riordan says. 'My impression was that he agreed based on the advice he had given me in a totally different setting 20 years earlier . . . There was not the slightest hint or any intimation that he felt the Senate enjoyed the power to block Supply.'[8]

These remarks are symptomatic of the disposition of the three senior ministers who knew Kerr—McClelland, Whitlam and Riordan—to interpret Kerr's thinking to suit their own position.

The full extent of Labor's strength on the Supply issue was revealed in an *Age–Herald* poll, published on 30 October, showing that 70 per cent of people in capital cities believed the budget should be passed and only 25 per cent said it should be blocked. More people blamed the Opposition for the crisis than blamed the government. A total of 44 per cent said that Labor should call a general election, compared with 55 per cent who said that it should govern. This was matched by several leading newspapers who now cautioned an Opposition retreat.

Such polls created euphoria within the ALP which was reinforced by Whitlam's Napoleonic performances. But Labor's polling adviser, ANOP's Rod Cameron, told ALP national secretary David Combe that Labor should not confuse its support on Supply with its standing in terms of an election. They were quite separate. Despite the Supply issue cutting Labor's way, the government would still be defeated at an election.[9]

Alternative financial arrangements

Whitlam had two tactics to reinforce his campaign to collapse the Senate's will. They were a scheme involving alternative financial arrangements to Supply, and a half Senate election option. Both had substantial difficulties associated with them which the Prime Minister seemed unable or unwilling to confront.

The alternative financial arrangements were intended to enable the government to meet some of its obligations without parliamentary appropriation. The idea was without precedent—but so was Whitlam's predicament. His purpose was to 'buy' time. The scheme worried the private banks, alarmed the Opposition, concerned the public servants involved and troubled the Governor-General. But it seemed to be legal and the government was fortified by opinions to this effect. Beyond that, the politics of the alternative arrangements never made any sense.

In tactical terms the scheme was a blunder. It is testimony to Whitlam's faulty judgement during the crisis and his failure to insist upon proper planning and co-ordination in relation to Labor's objectives. The scheme gave a worried Malcolm Fraser his most effective political weapon—the claim that Whitlam intended to spend money without parliamentary approval.

Soon after the budget was blocked in the Senate a special cabinet committee was established to study how the government could keep paying its employees and contractors. A task force of officials from Treasury, Prime Minister's and Attorney General's departments was established to examine how the government could meet its obligations after 30 November. During the process the membership was enlarged to include both the Reserve Bank and the Commonwealth Bank.

According to the Governor-General, Whitlam mentioned the scheme to him in exuberant tones, just three days after Supply was blocked.[10] Whitlam denied this conversation but it is clear that at some stage Whitlam briefed Kerr on the scheme.[11]

On 31 October Whitlam said in an interview: 'If it comes to the crunch it is probable that the government can govern without the budget . . . It's a messy business, it's inconvenient to a lot of people, but nevertheless the Australian Government's obligations will be met'.[12]

The essence of the scheme was simple—to replace government expenditure by bank credit. But its execution was incredibly complicated.

The proposal was that all federal departments would give their employees documents stating the amount due to them for the preceding pay period. This would be called a Certificate of Indebtedness. A similar document would be issued to suppliers of government goods and employees in statutory authorities.

The system was further explained in a joint Enderby–Byers legal opinion:

> The Certificate will contain an endorsement to the effect, as is the case in law, that it is neither a cheque nor a negotiable instrument . . . The employee will present his certificate to a bank (whether government or

private) and will enter into a contract of loan with that bank for an advance equal to his nett salary . . . The Government will announce the introduction of legislation to enable it to pay interest to the bankers and to give an undertaking, subject to legislation being passed, to pay interest at a rate to be struck. When the Appropriation Bills have been passed the banks will be paid direct sums equalling in total what they have advanced the various employees and suppliers. These payments will discharge the employees' obligations to repay their various loans except for interest, which latter obligation will also be discharged by the Government should its interest legislation pass the Parliament. Under the proposal no money is withdrawn from the Treasury either directly or indirectly . . . The proposal and its effectuation are, in our opinion, clearly constitutional.[13]

On 31 October the task force produced a submission for the ministers which began boldly: 'The scheme is considered by officers of Attorney General's Department to have every prospect of withstanding legal and constitutional challenge; it is regarded as a technically feasible scheme'.[14] But the submission then raised a series of worries:

(a) The participation of banks would be an essential element of the scheme and they would need to be consulted before detailed planning was commenced . . .
(b) The Government administration machinery would be subject to very heavy additional work loads. A minimum period of three weeks would apparently be needed for relevant Government printing and distribution requirements . . .
(c) Unforeseen legal complications, which would need to be solved, could arise in the administration of the scheme.
(d) Parliamentary approval of legislation to authorise the payment of interest would be required; this could raise questions of parliamentary proprieties and tactics.
(e) The co-operation of the States would be desirable, particularly in the area of handling stamp duty problems.

These considerations point up very large administrative, political and legal difficulties—even assuming a firm constitutional foundation.[15]

At this point the absurdity of the venture is manifest. There was never any prospect that the scheme would become operational. That was guaranteed as a result of its reliance for success upon the private banks and the States. Both institutions were deeply antagonistic towards Labor. No private bank was likely to be a genuine participant. The Bank of New South Wales obtained advice from William Deane QC, who had given the Opposition an opinion on the overseas loan—and he cast serious doubt on the scheme's legality.[16] The federal treasurer of the Liberal Party, Sir Robert Crichton-Browne, was a member of the

Commercial Banking Company board and, Fraser says, 'we knew all about it through his sources'.[17] The CBC obtained its own legal advice on the scheme which was critical of its proposed operation and its legal basis. Why Labor believed the private banks would help to bail out an unpopular ALP government in the process of being forced to the ballot box by Fraser defies the imagination.

Professor Geoffrey Sawer said: 'The banks were being asked to accept a business risk. If the Ministers were correct and the Senate likely soon to cave in, this risk would be small, but what if the Ministers were wrong? . . . I would have advised the non-government banks not to agree.'[18]

Much effort was expended on these alternative arrangements—yet Labor's assumptions were naive and confused.

The arrangements were not integrated into an overall political strategy for Labor; indeed, they seemed to undermine Whitlam's efforts to crack the Opposition's nerve. Whitlam wanted it both ways. He sought to intimidate the Senate into passing the budget by holding the Coalition responsible for the threatening financial crunch—yet he sought to avoid the crunch by meeting government obligations through a credit arrangement that bypassed the Parliament.

At the very time that Whitlam was depicting Fraser as damaging the Constitution, Fraser was able to argue that Whitlam planned the ultimate breach—to govern without Parliament. The scheme had a final significance. It gave Kerr further confirmation that Whitlam had moved beyond acceptable limits. Whitlam repeated his usual mistake with Kerr—he assumed that the Governor-General would have no difficulty with the scheme.

On his own initiative Kerr saw Treasurer Hayden on 30 October for a briefing. He told Hayden that he would need to be informed in future of how any such scheme would work, along with its legality and practicality.[19]

On 4 November in Parliament Hayden was blunt about the situation:

> It is quite obvious that the funds appropriated under Supply will run out. If no alternative arrangements were made quite a cataclysmic situation would develop in this country. To the extent that alternative arrangements can be made, they would be made lawfully and constitutionally under existing parliamentary approval and the position could at least be moderated; but it would be wrong to expect that alternative arrangements can be made in a way which is as efficient and comfortable in its functioning as the present system or to cover all contingencies.[20]

Hayden was open about the magnitudes involved for any alternative scheme. He said that the denial of Supply meant that funds between $8000 million and $9000 million were being delayed, which represented a contraction equal to about one-eighth of the monthly formation of the gross domestic product.[21]

On the same day, Whitlam told Parliament that 'the Government expects that all banks will co-operate in relieving hardship to persons who would ordinarily be paid by the Australian Government . . .'[22]

This statement was a fantasy. It is true that senior management within the banks were co-operating with the government's initial planning. That did not mean, ultimately, that the banks would proceed.

That night Fraser appeared on the ABC's *This Day Tonight* declaring that Whitlam 'has posed the greatest threat to parliamentary democracy since the beginning of Federation by saying that he will govern without the Parliament'. Fraser was outraged by the scheme. Even years later he says: 'This scheme tells us more about the character of the Whitlam Government than anything else in this whole issue. If Whitlam had been able to govern and spend money without the approval of Parliament then that's it. It was a giant step towards a dictatorship. It was one of the most serious actions by a government since Federation.'[23]

Whitlam replied the next day, outlining his bedrock stance on the alternative scheme: 'There is no possibility of this Government doing anything which the law officers of the Crown do not certify is within the statutes and the Constitution of this country'.[24] The trouble for Labor was that its alternative measures were unprecedented, subject to conflicting legal opinion and would be depicted by its opponents as governing without approval of funds by Parliament.

The measures were also the cause of inevitable friction within the cabinet. The concerns of Hayden and Ken Wriedt were known at the time.[25] Wriedt says:

> It seemed to me that we were being manipulated in the cause of survival. I believed that you played the game straight or you didn't play at all. Of course, Fraser was manipulating the system. But I couldn't accept that we should get in the gutter with him. I felt that most Australians were so angry with Fraser that if public servants didn't get paid the backlash against him would be ferocious. I felt the politics worked best for us without the scheme.[26]

Hayden explains his own position:

> I made it clear I'd go along with [the measures] for a period which I believed was justified. After that I wouldn't. We had a legal opinion supporting them. I saw them as a stopgap measure that would work briefly

but messily. I recognised that Whitlam was playing bluff poker for high stakes and was happy to go along on that basis. But Ken Wriedt and I had made it clear in cabinet that if it went beyond a reasonable period—which was pretty short—then our disenchantment would be expressed.[27]

This raises the question whether it was Whitlam's intention to implement the scheme or not. Riordan says: 'Nobody could imagine any of the banks lending money for such a purpose'. He insists that the scheme must be seen in the context of 'the tactical game of bluff and counterbluff that was occurring at the time'.[28]

Twenty years later, the scheme has almost been relegated to a non-issue by former Labor ministers. The philosophy they apply is 'out of sight, out of mind'. The Labor Party does not wish to be reminded of the alternative financial arrangements. In fact, these arrangements were real and were pursued vigorously with the banks. Any claim that the scheme was a bluff to intimidate the Opposition will come as a surprise to the bank executives who were involved in talks about its implementation. There were three arguments against the scheme. First, its constitutional foundation was in dispute. Despite the advice from the Law Officers, the Opposition and the banks had their own legal advice to the contrary. Second, the implementation difficulties confronting such a scheme were daunting in scope and administration. The resistance from the banks would have been immense. Finally, the scheme would have been a symbol of Labor's determination to step beyond the boundaries of financial and political orthodoxy; it would have turned the business establishment against Labor with an even greater fury and it would have surely alarmed the public.

These proposals left Kerr more suspicious of Whitlam, worried that Whitlam might resort to illegal methods and, above all, alarmed about Whitlam's judgement and his ruthless will to prevail.

Kerr's intervention on 11 November meant that the scheme never reached implementation. In summary, the scheme's only rationale was as a political tactic. Yet judged by this criterion it was a complete failure.

Whitlam's other tactic—a Senate election—received more attention as the crisis advanced. Despite his rhetoric Whitlam kept this option open. On other occasions he speculated about a Senate poll if the Senate rejected the budget outright. Whitlam saw the poll as a further 'turn of the screw' on Fraser. A judgement in retrospect is that Whitlam should have called a Senate election on 15 October, kept referring the budget to the Senate and conducted, in effect, a referendum on Fraser's blocking of the budget, an issue that favoured Labor.

It is unfair, however, to blame Whitlam for not calling a Senate poll at the start. The full extent of its political value in mid-October is obvious only with the benefit of hindsight—the Senate proved more resolute than Whitlam had imagined. The reason why Whitlam declined to call a Senate election in mid-October, at the start of the crisis, is because Labor's electoral fortunes were at rock bottom. Whitlam's argument at that time against a Senate election was the same as his argument against a Representatives election—Labor's electoral standing was too weak.

On 30 October the ALP National Executive met in Canberra with a majority keen to see a half Senate election. Its champion was the ACTU and ALP national president, Bob Hawke, who believed that a Senate poll would maximise the pressure. Whitlam and ALP National Secretary David Combe still opposed the election for tactical reasons. Whitlam's first preference was to crack the Senate within the Parliament—short of any poll. Combe, relying upon ANOP advice, was worried about Labor's vote. Election analyst David Butler concluded that this option 'was not very likely to give Labor a complaisant Senate'.[29]

Whitlam was hesitant; Fraser had served notice that the Coalition would sabotage this poll in the four non-Labor States. Graham Freudenberg reports that Whitlam explained his position in a note: 'Am not going to allow the present Governor-General to be the first in our history to be rebuffed by a State Governor not only wrongly advised but instinctively willing to break an unfailing and unchallenged tradition of three-quarters of a century'.[30]

Labor seemed unaware that, as the crisis advanced, its option of a Senate election was being extinguished—because the deadline for the exhaustion of Supply was approaching. Kerr would insist upon a solution by the time this deadline was reached. It would be difficult, though not impossible, for the Governor-General to approve a Senate election if the result would not be available until after Supply had been exhausted. Moreover there was a danger that both the Governor-General and Opposition would interpret any Senate poll called late in the crisis as a last resort and a sign of Labor's weakness.

The Kerr compromise

On 30 October Kerr put a compromise to Whitlam and McClelland who were attending an Executive Council meeting and whom Kerr invited to lunch.[31] Kerr's proposal was his only initiative to find a solution during the crisis. It showed a Governor-General a fortnight into the deadlock prepared to explore a very limited opportunity for a settlement.

The compromise involved Fraser making the concessions. The plan was that the Opposition would pass Supply and Whitlam, in turn, would pledge not to hold the half Senate election until close to mid-1976. This meant the new Senate would not meet before 1 July 1976—that is, that Labor would forfeit any opportunity to constitute the 'interim Senate' before 1 July in which it had a chance, though only a slim chance, of gaining a majority. According to Whitlam, Kerr had first raised this possibility with him three weekends previously in Sydney.[32]

Kerr's intention was to offer Fraser an honourable retreat—if that was Fraser's need.

The Governor-General explained his motives: 'I knew Mr Whitlam believed that the Senate would break; and a compromise proposal about the timing of a half Senate election might be so designed, if there were a movement towards breaking, as to make this in public terms a little easier for the Opposition'. In short, it was a means of getting Fraser off the hook. It would also test whether Fraser had any interest in being let off the hook.[33] Kerr was not pressing Fraser; he was offering an opportunity if Fraser was interested.

This lunch left a lasting impression on Whitlam and McClelland. Their memory was of three men chatting as friends, with Kerr freely discussing the crisis over food and wine; not for an instant did Kerr say or imply that he had any concern with Whitlam's approach although he was, in fact, deeply concerned about it. Kerr's compromise confirmed the view of Whitlam and McClelland that Kerr was trying to be helpful.[34]

Whitlam recalled the reassuring context in which Kerr described his idea: 'He said that Mr Fraser had to have an escape or he would be ousted like Mr Snedden and that it would be bad for the parliamentary system to have three Leaders of the Opposition in one year'.[35] Whitlam felt that Kerr was trying to do him a favour. Kerr, in fact, was only doing his job by testing whether this compromise was available.

McClelland said of the lunch: 'The only deduction which could not be drawn from what he said to us was that he contemplated in any way exercising the option which he ultimately exercised. In fact he led us to believe that that was not on his mind and would never be on his mind.'[36]

This lunch offers a bizarre retrospective into the relationship between Whitlam and Kerr during the crisis. Whitlam formed the impression from Kerr's remarks that he was 'on side'. But McClelland offered this subsequent observation:

> Kerr invited us to stay for lunch. I had a glass of wine with him. Whitlam didn't. He was a very abstemious fellow, Gough. This was during the crisis and on an occasion like that you might have expected Whitlam to have been a bit ingratiating. After all, he was in the presence of the man in whose hands his fate lay, even if he did not believe he would axe him. But he was quite the opposite. He was almost dismissive in his manner. He was not rude but certainly in a hurry to get the meal over and get back to the important business of governing the country. He certainly made no attempt to stroke the Governor-General's ego. He was obviously taking Kerr for granted.[37]

McClelland concludes from this lunch 'that not a suspicion had entered Whitlam's mind that Kerr would act the way he did. Everything he said and did indicated that he regarded Kerr as the purely decorative figure who did what the Prime Minister told him to.'[38]

It was a strictly social event with sufficient small talk and enough wry humour to delude Whitlam and McClelland further. At one stage Kerr looked at Whitlam and, nodding towards McClelland, asked, 'Well, how's he going?'. Whitlam paused and then replied, 'Good, bloody good, but he gets a bit histrionic at times'. Presumably they all grinned.[39] There was flattery—from Kerr of McClelland. As they were leaving Kerr said to his old friend (referring to McClelland's ministerial job): 'Of course all this . . . is just gloss on your career'.[40]

McClelland has given this remark great psychological weight. He says:

> Kerr's comment I believe, in retrospect, was a preparatory apology for dismissing me as a minister. That Kerr should think I would just accept dismissal is a terrible reflection on his values. His idea—you'll take this in your stride—reveals the nature of the man. I would never accept a reconciliation with him after this. As far as I was concerned he could get fucked.[41]

This lunch invites a dual assessment—Whitlam's insensitivity towards Kerr was matched only by Kerr's determination to conceal his hand from Whitlam.

After the dismissal Whitlam and his ministers were to accuse Kerr of deception—a lethal accusation against the Crown or its representative. Kerr's reply was that Whitlam and his accusers misread his character, and that 'if they were deceived, they deceived themselves'.[42] He continued: 'Mr Whitlam knew of the danger that I might dismiss him. He recognised it and several times referred to it.' More recently Anne Kerr says: 'Whitlam knew what he was risking. He knew that dismissal was a possibility.'[43]

McClelland says: 'There was no question of warning him, of saying, "Well look, aren't you taking a little bit too much for granted? How is this stalemate going to be resolved?" He [Kerr] didn't say anything like that. He could have given Whitlam hints that he didn't have the game completely sewn up and that Kerr was not his stooge. Kerr certainly did not do that in my presence.'[44]

But McClelland's lasting antagonism towards Kerr originated in another conversation he held with the Governor-General at about the same time. Kerr and McClelland were friends who had kept their personal links after Kerr became Governor-General.[45] On this occasion Kerr rang McClelland at home in Sydney about 7 pm; McClelland thinks it may have been the evening of 4 November, though the sequence of events points to an earlier date.[46] The subject was the Kerr compromise.

McClelland has described this discussion several times over the last 20 years. His first outline in February 1976 was given to the Senate:

> The Governor-General spoke to me about Mr Fraser having painted himself into a corner and how we could get him off the hook, how he and I and the Labor Government could collaborate to solve the problem by finding a solution for Mr Fraser which would not involve a total loss of face . . . The Governor-General said to me, 'I believe that what is primarily on their mind is a worry that if you get a majority for a short period you will introduce electoral reform that will put the Country Party out of business.' He said: 'I believe that the best contribution that I could make in this crisis would be to call up Mr Fraser and suggest to him that he could save face by agreeing to a suggestion such as that.' . . . Why did he [Kerr] talk to me? . . . The reason the Governor-General rang me was to lull me and my party into a false sense of security.[47]

In his memoirs McClelland says:

> My wife answered the phone and she summoned me in rather wounded tones. 'It's John Kerr,' she said. 'He didn't even greet me, though he must have known it was me.' . . . That surprised me too, since Kerr had always treated Freda with great courtesy and affection. Kerr asked me if I had made any headway with Whitlam on the half-Senate proposition. I said, truthfully, that I felt confident that Gough would buy the idea . . .' 'Well,' said Kerr. 'That might solve the problem.' I was certain then and am certain now that the tenor of Kerr's remarks was to the effect that the dismissal of the government was not an option he had considered.[48]

In an interview for the tenth anniversary of the dismissal McClelland offered a version of what Kerr had said—not 'his exact words' but 'the tenor of the conversation'. According to McClelland: 'I said, "Well, does that mean we're not going to have to pack our bags?" He said, "Oh no, nothing like that's going to happen".'[49]

McClelland said he then spoke to his wife—who had always had doubts about Kerr. 'I said to her, "Look, all your fears are groundless. I've just had a conversation with him [Kerr] and there's no question of him doing the dirty on us". I have the clearest recollection of that conversation with my wife which indicates to me that the conversation I'd had with Kerr had totally satisfied me that dismissal was not up for consideration at all.'[50]

Kerr rejected any view that he misled McClelland: 'Neither the purpose nor the effect of my conversations with Mr McClelland during the crisis was to lull him or anyone else into a false sense of security ... At no stage did I ever say to anyone anything that ruled out the use of the reserve powers. At no stage did I say or agree that there was no crisis until the money had finally run out.'[51]

Whitlam was not enthusiastic about the compromise—but he gave Kerr the approval he sought to put the idea to Fraser.

The Governor-General saw Fraser the same afternoon of 30 October after he lunched with Whitlam and McClelland. It was his second meeting with Fraser during the crisis. He floated the compromise but Fraser was unimpressed. He felt that there was little chance of Labor winning a temporary Senate majority anyway—so there was no bonus for him in the deal. Fraser told Kerr that he was not interested; he was standing firm. However Fraser did not tell Kerr that his real fear about a Senate election was the extra pressure it would impose on the Opposition to pass the budget.[52]

Fraser, according to his biographer Philip Ayres, felt that 'if Whitlam advised an immediate half Senate election and Sir John accepted this, the pressure on the Opposition to back down would probably be irresistible'.[53]

There are several points to make about Kerr's compromise. First, it revealed a Governor-General becoming further involved in the crisis. Second, Kerr cleared his initiative with Whitlam. Third, Kerr now had further confirmation that Fraser would not retreat. Finally, Kerr left Whitlam and McClelland with the impression—either by accident or by design—that he felt Fraser was in political difficulty and that this compromise might ease his retreat; not that he felt that Labor was in difficulty and that this compromise would test whether there was any hope for Whitlam by persuading Fraser to back off. This, however, was the real position. Whitlam and McClelland did not comprehend the full picture.

The significance of the Kerr compromise is that it further deceived Whitlam into believing that Kerr was sympathetic to his position—when, in fact, its rejection by Fraser only further convinced Kerr that Whitlam's position was untenable.

While Kerr says he spoke to McClelland only three times during the crisis—once being the 30 October lunch with Whitlam—McClelland confirms that he advised Whitlam at this time that Kerr was loyal.[54]

In McClelland's 1985 interview with Bruce Stannard the following exchange occurred:

STANNARD: Did you tell Gough?

MCCLELLAND: Yes, sure I did, I told him there was no danger from Kerr.

STANNARD: What was his reaction?

MCCLELLAND: Well, it coincided with what he believed.

STANNARD: Can you remember exactly what happened?

MCCLELLAND: Well, Gough was almost contemptuous of Kerr. 'Well, comrade,' he'd say to me, 'What's in old Silver's mind?' Then I'd tell him whatever Kerr had told me. It was never on any more serious note than that. It was never a matter of sitting down in any strategic sense and saying, 'Now, do we have to take this, this and this into consideration?' It was a fleeting almost jesting consideration to Gough. It's almost laughable in retrospect . . . the almost total lack of communication between these two men. It's unbelievable in retrospect isn't it? I've often thought that when Kerr writes things like, 'If Whitlam's men were deceived, they deceived themselves,' . . . the sort of remark was directed at me . . . that he may not even himself have been very clear in his own mind about the way he was talking to people in those days. After all, the conversation with me occurred at 7 pm. That's fairly late in the day for a man of Kerr's habits.[55]

I spoke to Whitlam about Kerr in early November 1975. He said he was convinced that Kerr would 'do the right thing'. At one point Whitlam told me: 'I'm as certain about Kerr as I am about any other issue in my career.' He also put a strong emphasis on the fact that McClelland was equally convinced. The question that arises is whether Whitlam was really trying to convince himself![56]

Bill Hayden acknowledges that the responsibility for the misjudgement of Kerr lay with Whitlam, but says: 'I think that Jim McClelland has a lot to answer for. Right through this process McClelland wasn't reading the man [Kerr]. I think that Gough was very influenced by McClelland. We are used to seeing Gough as his own man, strong and determined. But he was extraordinarily susceptible to those few people who became his confidants. McClelland used that relationship quite a deal.'⁵⁷

There was, however, another effect flowing from Kerr's initiative—it helped to spur Fraser towards his own compromise proposal. This was altogether more substantial.

The Fraser compromise is the pivotal point in the crisis. It is at this stage that the crisis could have been settled. It is the stage at which Whitlam made an error of judgement that led to his downfall. It is also the point at which Kerr was further obliged to speak frankly to Whitlam but declined to do so.

The Fraser compromise

On 2 November a beleaguered Malcolm Fraser chaired a summit of non-Labor leaders in Melbourne in order to produce a show of federal–state unity. Fraser was under intense pressure to retreat—and he was feeling the strain. Facing an ebullient Whitlam, a critical public, a worried Coalition party room and a Governor-General who was inquiring about a political compromise, Fraser desperately needed a show of strength. But he got more—a tactical twist that helped to turn the tide.

During the three hour meeting that began at 2 pm at Treasury Place, Fraser asked his colleagues a series of questions which drew some to the false conclusion that he was retreating. In fact, he was testing their support. The Premiers of Queensland and New South Wales, Bjelke-Petersen and Lewis, were aggressively supportive. So was Western Australia's Premier Court who kept in touch by phone. But Victoria's Premier Hamer was anxious to defuse the confrontation. Bjelke-Petersen later claimed that Fraser had been about to surrender at this meeting, an unsubstantiated claim dismissed by Fraser as 'absolute arrant nonsense'.[58] Reg Withers says that 'Fraser wasn't looking for a way out'.[59]

The upshot was a communique reflecting the united stand of the non-Labor side. It was designed to intimidate any waverers, to kill the prospect of a Senate election and to impress Kerr. Subsequent events revealed that it succeeded brilliantly. The communique said that the leaders:

> ... agreed unanimously that the Federal Opposition should maintain its current stand designed to give the people the opportunity to pass judgement on the Whitlam Government. The meeting condemned the threats by the Prime Minister to attempt to govern without a budget ... The meeting today expressed absolute determination to let the people be the judges through a general election. They agreed that any attempt to bypass the proper parliamentary processes should be

opposed in every possible way. The meeting agreed that the Leader of the Opposition, Mr Fraser, should seek to call on the Governor-General as early as practicable to report on the outcome of the Melbourne discussions.

The leaders threatened that non-Labor Premiers would advise their Governors not to issue writs for any half Senate election sought by Whitlam—an assault upon conventions essential to a successful democracy. After the meeting Fraser declared that Whitlam's alternative arrangement for Supply was 'the way to establish a dictatorship'.

However there was another tactic in play.

Concern was expressed during the meeting that the Coalition might appear too dogmatic and resistant to any settlement. After all, Kerr had just proposed a compromise and Fraser had rejected his offer. It is hardly surprising that at this point Fraser felt a tactical imperative to appear conciliatory as well as strong. Hamer floated a compromise which was accepted—the Opposition would pass Supply provided Whitlam advised a Representatives election to be held in conjunction with the Senate poll before mid-1976. Fraser was stripping off his mailed glove to reveal a velvet fist.

'I wanted to avoid a head-on collision', Hamer says. 'I always doubted whether the Senate would reject the budget.'[60]

No other event has received such an undeserved lack of attention as this compromise. It offers an insight into the true nature of the crisis.

As a tactic it was designed to depict Fraser as a reasonable man, anxious for a solution—not the wrecker that Whitlam had painted him for a fortnight. But there was a downside that Fraser realised—the concession would make him look weak. Some Liberals would think that it was the halfway house to surrender. That might weaken their own resolve. Fraser suspected that Whitlam would interpret his offer as evidence that he was beginning to crumble; as the sign for which Labor had waited so desperately for so long. The risk for Fraser was that the tactic might become self-fulfilling in this sense.

But the concession must be assessed as strategy—a task so far ignored. When one examines this proposal from all angles there is one overwhelming conclusion—it was a substantial retreat.

Fraser's offer meant the budget would be passed immediately. There would be no general election. The nation would repair to its summer season and forget the high drama. Whitlam would stay in office. He would spend Christmas at Kirribilli relaxing and plotting his electoral revival. Whitlam could depict himself as the winner in the epic deadlock between the two Houses.

There was one concession required of Whitlam—that he advise a general election to be held by early June 1976 at the latest, seven months away.

How much of a concession was this?

Whitlam would lose his option of having a separate Senate election before mid-1976 and then running the Representatives for a full three year term with an election in the first part of 1977. On the other hand, if there had been no 1975 crisis, Whitlam would have seriously considered holding a double dissolution in autumn 1976 anyway—given that a Senate poll was due.

In his book Whitlam says that his intention, if there had been no crisis, was to hold the half Senate election in 1976 and, if still faced with a hostile Senate, a double dissolution election in late 1976. This meant a term only six months longer than Fraser offered him in the compromise. Asked recently whether he would have conducted a double dissolution or a half Senate election before mid-1976, Whitlam said: 'I hadn't made up my mind. I would have kept [open] that option'.[61]

The terms of the short-term Senators elected at the 18 May 1974 double dissolution expired on 30 June 1976 (because they were backdated to 1 July 1973), which meant that a half Senate poll was needed before mid-1976; only four such polls have been held since Federation. It would have been a normal thing to conduct a double dissolution instead since Whitlam already had 21 double dissolution bills—and probably more in another six months. Whitlam would have time before the election to overhaul Labor's image using Hayden and McClelland to market a new profile.

The Fraser offer was a serious compromise from his remorseless insistence on an immediate election. Fraser's situation was that 'he knew that a number of his colleagues were by now extremely worried and there were times when he doubted whether he was going to get the result he wanted'.[62] Fraser says: 'It was our effort to help to resolve the crisis . . . but Whitlam probably concluded that our mob was cracking'.[63] Withers repudiates any suggestions that Fraser was losing his nerve: 'The Melbourne meeting was not about compromise. Fraser was being tactical. He certainly wasn't looking for a way out and he wasn't about to back down.'[64]

Fraser took the proposal to the Governor-General on Monday 3 November, having cleared it through the shadow cabinet. Fraser told Kerr that federal and State Liberals had met at the weekend and had endorsed the stance on Supply. It was binding and they would hold firm. Fraser explained that they were prepared to offer a concession and he briefed Kerr on the proposal before making the offer public.

Kerr recalls: 'Mr Fraser said that this was as far as the Opposition parties were prepared to go and that if it were rejected they would unfailingly stand firm on the refusal to pass Supply'.[65]

The two men then discussed Whitlam's alternative financial arrangements. Fraser repeated to Kerr the Opposition's deep concerns about the plan to bypass the Parliament via the banks. According to Fraser's official biographer, Kerr then made a significant comment. 'Sir John indicated to Fraser that he thought the Government might have real legal difficulties with that, and quoted chapter and verse of a particular Act. It was just a small observation in passing, but it seemed a token of sympathy and support and it gave comfort at a time when comfort was sorely needed.'[66]

This is a very significant incident. It reveals the great value to Fraser of his dialogue with Kerr. In these talks Fraser would have been searching for signs of Kerr's sympathies. It may have been only a 'small observation' but it was important to Fraser. It was improper for the Governor-General to be telling the leader of the Opposition his worries about the government's alternative financial arrangements, only necessitated in the first place because the Opposition had blocked Supply.

Malcolm Fraser's career was in the balance; it would be determined by his reading of Kerr's mood. Kerr had not conveyed these concerns to the Prime Minister; now he was hinting at them to Fraser. The message was that Kerr was worried about Whitlam's alternative financial arrangements, that he was sceptical about whether they would work. The remark could only have encouraged Fraser to hold firm. Its symbolism cannot be ignored; to Fraser it was 'a token of sympathy'.

This account—when considered with the versions provided by Labor ministers of their discussions with Kerr—suggests that the Governor-General's style was to sympathise with the politician to whom he was talking. During the crisis both Whitlam and Fraser were left with the impression of a supportive Governor-General. Were they both wrong? Probably not. But Kerr, if he did intervene, could only support one side against the other.

In his press statement after briefing Kerr, Fraser said:

> I make this proposal because I believe that commonsense, reason and a concern for the people of Australia must prevail. By their actions, the ALP has eroded our way or life and our institutions. Now Mr Whitlam proposes to govern without the Parliament. Mr Whitlam must now decide whether he will continue to defy the Constitution or allow the people to vote. We are prepared to put the nation first. Is Mr Whitlam?[67]

Kerr saw Whitlam at Government House, Melbourne, 30 minutes after Fraser left. It is a meeting that has received little attention in the analysis of the great crisis, yet it is decisive. It is the moment at which Whitlam snatched defeat from the jaws of an acceptable compromise.

Whitlam rejected the Fraser concession out of hand. According to Kerr:

> He indicated that he had already heard the substance of Mr Fraser's press statement but that he would have nothing whatsoever to do with any election for the House of Representatives. He said he would never advise an election for the House of Representatives until he himself was ready to do so, and certainly not at the behest of Mr Fraser or the Senate.[68]

This accords with Whitlam's own account to the Parliament. We can assume he spoke forcefully to Kerr since Whitlam was filled by an intellectual passion on this issue.

Why didn't Whitlam say 'yes', have his budget passed, proclaim a victory, declare a triumph for the People's House over the Senate, announce that the election would be held in six months which was the usual time to bring both Houses into synchronisation, and use Fraser's retreat and the Hayden budget as the foundations for his government's revival?

Whitlam says an 'overriding' reason for rejecting Fraser's offer was that it meant 'a six month long election campaign'. This point is true. But it hardly constitutes a reason for rejection. The same could be said for many, probably most, federal elections since the parliamentary cycle typically means that the last several months before the election are dominated by campaigning.[69]

The real reason is that Whitlam, during the crisis, had developed other objectives in addition to avoiding an immediate election. They were set out in his speeches, a reading of which suggests that Whitlam had three other objectives: (1) to break the Senate's power over Supply for all time and ensure that no Opposition and no Senate would ever contemplate such an action again—that is, to achieve an alteration in the existing power balance between the Houses and ensure that Whitlam's own interpretation of the Constitution was carried into the future; (2) to destroy Malcolm Fraser in political terms just as *he* had already destroyed, or helped to destroy, Harold Holt, John Gorton, Billy McMahon and Billy Snedden—the four previous leaders of the Liberal Party—thereby ensuring that Fraser, even though he would probably remain leader, would be irreparably damaged by virtue of his decision to ignite this confrontation; and (3) to ensure that in terms of both appearance and reality there could be no suggestion that the Senate or Fraser had determined the timing of the next House of Representatives election.

Acceptance of the Fraser compromise did not satisfy these three tests.

Yet Whitlam could achieve these great goals only with Kerr's support.

Whitlam, in fact, had become a victim of his own tactics and their apparent success. There was a remorseless logic to his position. Having decided to defy the Senate and remain in office, Whitlam had no option but to justify his unprecedented action by reference to the unprecedented nature of the struggle. His action could be justified only if Australian democracy were at stake—the right of a government to govern, the right of the People's House against the Senate—and indeed Whitlam said that this was the issue. It began as an effort to deny Fraser an immediate poll that Labor was certain to lose; but it quickly became a test of the Parliament and the Constitution. Not only did Whitlam assert this; he believed it. Whitlam's objective was to break forever the Senate's power over Supply and destroy the Opposition that tried to use it.

As early as 20 October Whitlam had declared: 'I've never been so certain in anything in my life as I am, that the Senate's money power will be broken as a result of this crisis. No future Australian government will ever be threatened by the Senate again, with a rejection of its budget, or a refusal of Supply. Never again.'[70]

Fraser was right in thinking that Whitlam would interpret the offer as weakness. Whitlam was not interested in a settlement based upon compromise. Whitlam was not interested in a deal that allowed Fraser and the Senate to keep face. They had started the war; but Whitlam would finish it.

Whitlam would not compromise because he believed that he would win—absolutely. Whitlam's career had been devoted to the long struggle between Labor and the Constitution. He understood the issue. Whitlam was convinced that he was on the verge of the greatest parliamentary and constitutional victory for the ALP since the time of Federation. It would involve a resolution of the contradiction between responsible government and federalism inherent in the Constitution since its inception—a resolution in favour of responsible government, the House of Representatives and the ALP's view of Australian democracy. Whitlam felt that Fraser, not himself, was embattled. Whitlam's instinct told him to avoid a partial victory when a total victory was near.

Why did Whitlam think a total victory was near? Because he

believed that Kerr was with him. Provided Kerr stayed firm, then Whitlam could smash Fraser and the Senate.

At this point the scale of Whitlam's misjudgement, already serious, became monumental.

He was in 'crash through or crash' mode. Whitlam's career experience told him to press ahead. Whitlam grasped that once you maximise the stakes then the gains are also maximised. He was chasing a pure and complete victory. The risk, in this frame of mind, is that a politician fails to make the cool and calculating judgement of men and events that is required.

Whitlam did not have the contingency plans needed to sustain his strategy. What would he do if Fraser held firm until Supply ran out? At this point he couldn't just stay in office. His alternative financial arrangements and Senate election option, either separately or jointly, were not a viable solution.

It was 3 November—the day before the Melbourne Cup—and Whitlam became the greatest gambler of all. A Prime Minister with an accurate or acute reading of his Governor-General and of his situation would have accepted the compromise offer.

Reg Withers says: 'Of course, Whitlam should have taken the deal. He would have bought time with a better looking government, Hayden as Treasurer and time to forget Khemlani. The Senate would have thankfully given up.'[71]

Bob Ellicott says: 'In retrospect, it is a very reasonable proposal. The only reason Whitlam rejected it was because of his "smash the Senate" attitude. This is perhaps a fresh insight into the crisis. It would have given him an honourable way out and allowed him to take advantage of the voting trend and a more responsible hand through Hayden as Treasurer.'[72]

During their discussion Whitlam and Kerr both made serious errors of judgement without which the crisis would have been resolved.

Whitlam's mistake was elementary. This was the point at which he had to satisfy himself that Kerr would tolerate his 'tough it out' tactics. To this stage of the crisis Whitlam had not tried to engage Kerr and ventilate his thinking. He assumed that Kerr would act on his advice and he interpreted Kerr's sympathetic utterances as confirmation of this. But if Whitlam was rejecting the offer then he should have taken out insurance. Whitlam should have asked Kerr how he saw the crisis evolving, how Kerr saw his own role and his options and whether he had any worries with Whitlam's approach. Whitlam could have used Fraser's offer as the basis for such a discussion. This was the time for Whitlam to take Kerr seriously and bring a tactical appreciation to his talks with Kerr. Yet Whitlam didn't; he may in fact have done the exact opposite.

Kerr's account of this discussion continues:

> Mr Whitlam told me that the only way an election for the House could occur would be if I dismissed him. The expression he used was: if I were willing 'to do a Philip Game'. This revealed him to be taking into account the possibility that I might exercise the reserve power. Being, I suspect, of the opinion that I would probably not be strong enough to do it, Mr Whitlam was using an expression which, as both of us I am sure recognised, carried the implication of the unpleasant consequences to myself in controversy and obloquy if I did. I made no comment.[73]

When I put this to Whitlam he replied: 'I never spoke about Game to him'.[74] In his book Whitlam did not deny the comment outright, merely using the word 'allegedly' in relation to the Philip Game line. It is a fact that the phrase 'do a Game' was one used by Whitlam in conversation during the crisis. My discussions with former Labor ministers left the impression that they would not be surprised if Whitlam did use this phrase to Kerr. Anne Kerr reports: 'I can remember John telling me that Whitlam had said to him that he might have to "do a Game".'[75]

(In my interview Whitlam had an emotional reaction to the reference to Game. He says that Game, unlike Kerr, acted 'completely honourably' and put the issue in writing to Lang. He continued: 'Game was a decent man. One of the difficulties—I have never said it before—is that his [Kerr's] second wife is as much to blame as Kerr . . . This [dismissal] would never have happened if his first wife had retained her health'.[76] It is an accusation that Anne Kerr rejects as 'complete rubbish' arguing that she sought to 'support' her husband, not to 'influence' him.[77])

If Sir John's version of Whitlam's remark to him about Game is accurate, then the conversation is remarkable. It amounts to a foolhardy provocation of Kerr based upon a judgement that Kerr could be intimidated. It would be evidence of Whitlam's confrontational mindset. It means that Whitlam himself was raising the dismissal option with Kerr as a prelude to burying it. If true, it means that Whitlam, having rejected a compromise that would have saved an immediate election, instead of using this discussion with Kerr to test that his assumptions were firm, indulged in a statement of bravado that could only have alienated Kerr further. If true, it is almost incomprehensible behaviour.

Clearly, Whitlam would never have made this comment if he felt that dismissal was a likely option. He didn't. If he made it, then he did so only to reinforce to Kerr his determination to break the Senate.

The Governor-General—given the discussion he outlined—would only have concluded that Whitlam was dictating to him; that Whitlam was trying to intimidate him; that Whitlam felt Kerr lacked the stomach or nerve to dismiss him.

It is equally true that if Whitlam made this statement then Kerr should not have ignored it. If Whitlam was telling Kerr that the only way an election could be obtained was by his own dismissal, then that was an extremely serious matter that Kerr should have taken up with his Prime Minister. The idea that a Governor-General would seal this comment away, not respond directly, but rely upon it to shape a response of sudden dismissal without proper warning is extraordinary behaviour and alien to the Crown or the Crown's representative. Yet this is precisely what Kerr did.

At this point in the crisis Kerr should have spoken directly to Whitlam about his concerns. Kerr was only a few days away from an intellectual embrace of the dismissal option.[78] Yet in this discussion he allowed Whitlam to reject a reasonable compromise only because Whitlam wrongly believed that Kerr was supporting him.

It is tempting to conclude that Kerr knew exactly what he was doing—he was letting Whitlam hang himself. And Kerr would not stop the execution. He had previously decided there was no purpose in trying to acquaint Whitlam with his own thinking. By refusing to deal frankly with Whitlam, Kerr was, of course, only encouraging Whitlam to reject the offer and stay firm. Kerr did this in full knowledge that the potential consequence was Whitlam's dismissal. Kerr's silence was consistent with a mindset that was going to allow Whitlam to bear the consequences of his own position.

When defending himself later against charges of deceiving his ministers Kerr says:

> At no time did I say anything that could be taken as ruling out that possibility [dismissal]. Whenever the issue arose, I simply kept my own counsel. It appears that Mr Whitlam and others read into my deliberate and obvious silence whatever they wanted to ... Mr Whitlam and others wanted to believe that there was no risk of my acting. But the risk was always there ... Mr Whitlam and his colleagues clearly made the judgment that I would not have the courage to do what they knew I was entitled to do and, as many were arguing, should do. This was their judgment: I can hardly be blamed for the fact that they misread my character. If they were deceived, they deceived themselves.[79]

Whitlam did deceive himself. He did misread Kerr's character. But it is equally true that Kerr sought to fool Whitlam. Kerr's silence was an elaborate deception. Its entire purpose was to lull Whitlam into a false sense of security lest he become alarmed and possibly move against Kerr.

On this point Bob Ellicott offers a startling analysis:

> My view of Whitlam's psychology, and here perhaps I disagree with Kerr, is that I think the shock of learning that Kerr was seriously considering the situation would have made him [Whitlam] act much more responsibly. He might say with bravado 'I'd have rung up the Queen immediately', but I don't believe he would have done that. That may be too optimistic a view of Whitlam. But I have a degree of faith in the man and his ultimate integrity. I sensed a messianic attitude on Whitlam's part. He was riding this white charger called 'Smash the Senate' and nothing was going to take him off unless Kerr did something.[80]

But Kerr had decided to do nothing. It is fascinating that Ellicott disputes that Whitlam would have moved against Kerr. He believes that Kerr could have influenced Whitlam. Yet Kerr had chosen to abandon any such effort.

This was a serious misunderstanding of Kerr's responsibility as the Crown's representative. It was again a reflection of Kerr's judicial view of his office and his reluctance to commit to a political solution. Kerr had defined the limits to his office: 'I had no desire, or intention, to give political advice to either side.'[81] The point is that Kerr's first responsibility was to promote a political solution. The danger was that by keeping his silence with Whitlam, Kerr would only allow the crisis to intensify with an eventual resolution through the Reserve Powers with all the risks this involved for the office.

Whitlam's tactics in public and in private rested upon a determination to 'tough it out' until the Opposition's nerve cracked and Supply was passed. But why didn't Kerr follow the Hasluck philosophy? Why didn't Kerr simply ask Whitlam what advice he would tender if the Opposition didn't crack? This would signal to Whitlam that other advice—such as an election—would be required by Kerr.

At this point, on 3 November, Kerr should have exercised his 'advise and warn' discretion in order to ensure that he did not have to exercise more drastic powers some days later. He failed completely to understand the onus upon him to help to secure a political solution to a political crisis before the situation demanded an intervention from the Crown's representative.

A prudent Governor-General would have spoken to Whitlam along these lines:

Prime Minister, since you have rejected Fraser's compromise can I ask how you intend to resolve the crisis if the Senate continues in its action. You will be aware that in a few weeks Supply will start to run out. A solution will be required before then. You should be aware that at this point I will need to have fresh advice from you since I cannot allow a government to remain in office without Supply from the Parliament.

It was not too hard to say. It was the responsibility of a Monarch or a Governor-General in the interests of a settlement. But Kerr, as he revealed, had a different perception of the office:

There is a parallel in legal affairs which Mr Whitlam, a lawyer, should have understood. Sometimes judges encourage parties to settle judicial issues by agreement among themselves. If such attempts fail, the judge has no alternative but to return with the parties to court and decide the matter. Then he must decide the issue on its merits; often total victory for one party or the other is the only possible outcome. So it is with the Governor-General in considering the exercise of the reserve powers.[82]

This passage reveals a flawed view of the office. It compares the routine of judicial decision-making with the Governor-General's exercise of the reserve powers. The point is that judges must pass judgement. That is their essential task and it is a fact that their judgements will be for or against one side. The task of the Crown's representative is to avoid to the utmost such judgements which, by definition, threaten the impartiality of the Crown. A Monarch who thinks or acts as a judge will alienate his subjects. Any comparison of the Reserve Power of dismissal with judicial activity invests such power with a mundane familiarity that mocks both the extreme rarity of its implementation and the politically explosive nature of its execution. The task of the Crown or the Governor-General is to wield influence to achieve solutions that avert the need for any resort to the Reserve Powers. A dismissal should only occur when all other options have been exhausted.

Jim McClelland offers an acute critique of Kerr: 'He knew throughout the crisis that he might finally decide to dismiss the government . . . at no point does he explain why, apart from his fear that it would ensure his own sacking, he did not simply say to Whitlam: If you can't get Supply by a certain date I might have to dismiss you.'[83]

If Whitlam did raise the dismissal option in their talk on 3 November by using the phrase 'do a Philip Game', then there was no better time for Kerr to discuss this option with his Prime Minister. Instead,

Kerr took the remark at face value and it helped to inspire a surprise dismissal a week later.

So why didn't Kerr talk frankly with Whitlam?

Kerr has explained—because he thought Whitlam might sack him.

As Melbourne Cup Day dawned on 4 November 1975 the crisis had taken a fateful twist—but not all three players grasped its import. Fraser, with his olive branch rebuffed, was determined to stand firm. Whitlam, having decided to pursue total victory in order to break both the Senate's power and Fraser's leadership, had made a fatal blunder. He did not realise that Kerr would give him only another week. Kerr, having listened with sympathy to both leaders, now felt that time was running out; that Whitlam and Fraser had both dug in; that neither retreat nor compromise was likely; that this situation—which Kerr had encouraged through his silence—would soon force him to resolve the crisis by his own hand.

9
The solution

> *I now told the Governor-General that if Australia did not get an election the Opposition would have no choice but to be highly critical of him.*
>
> Malcolm Fraser, recalling his words to Sir John Kerr on 6 November 1975

MALCOLM FRASER'S PUBLIC offer of a compromise only intensified the belief within the Opposition backbench that the crisis would be resolved through some form of Coalition concession. This was also the advice that the founder of the Liberal Party, Sir Robert Menzies, gave Fraser about ten days before 11 November. Menzies, along with a growing number of Liberals, believed that Fraser lacked the support to impose an election upon Whitlam.

Aware of the need to keep Menzies' backing, Fraser paid him another visit, only to find that Menzies was dubious about the Coalition's predicament. Fraser recalls: 'He just said, "I don't think you are going to get an election from this man, Malcolm. You might have to retreat." I said, "I am going to get an election from this man, sir. I don't know how to retreat on this issue". That was the discussion.'[1]

On Sunday 2 November, the day the compromise was decided—but before its announcement—the prominent Liberal backbencher, Ian Macphee, wrote a letter to Fraser which would have reflected a growing body of party opinion.

Macphee said:

> For a variety of reasons we are seen to be wrong. The PM has convinced many that, however disappointed they may be with his Government, we are attacking the Constitution and democracy . . . The

public—or that section of the public whose goodwill we require—is not impressed favourably by our arguments. (Evidence is plentiful.) People do not want Labor but they do not want us in this way. We are seen to be grabbing for power to win by default . . . If we win an election stemming from the present crisis we will have the outright hostility of nearly 50 per cent of the electorate . . . adherence to our present course (if the GG does not appear to respond as we believe appropriate) would be most unwise. Indeed, given the PM's intransigence, I believe it would be irresponsible.

Macphee argued that Fraser should back down: 'Such an act would do much to restore your credibility and would be seen not as capitulation but as courageous statesmanship.' The letter was signed 'with best wishes and complete support'.[2]

Macphee, like Menzies and many other Liberals, believed that Fraser would have to organise a retreat.

The Coalition parties' meeting on Tuesday 4 November saw a series of complaints about Fraser's compromise. Reg Withers explains: 'The Senate was furious about Fraser's offer. The offer had been made without the Senate's approval. This meant that Senators who had to implement the blocking of the budget and wear the odium just hadn't been told what was happening.'[3]

New South Wales Senator Sir Kenneth Anderson was upset, given the determination to stand firm the previous week. Senator Peter Baume agreed, saying he had learnt about the offer from a taxi driver! Fraser replied that he had felt the need to put some proposal before the Governor-General and, once done, had to announce it immediately—otherwise Whitlam's office would have distorted the proposal. Bill McMahon backed Fraser saying that the leader must have such authority. There was talk about leaks to the media and how to combat Labor's scare tactics which focused on the dire consequences once the funds expired.[4]

Victorian backbencher Alan Jarman reported that there had been a survey in his electorate of public attitudes to the blocking of Supply with an encouraging result for the Coalition. Fraser told Jarman he was not too interested in opinion on the Opposition's tactic; the polls that counted were those on voting intentions. This was the Opposition's strength. Fraser told the meeting the parties should concentrate their attack on Whitlam's efforts to circumvent Supply.[5]

But Fraser knew that he had to secure an election soon—otherwise the pressure on the Coalition would become too great.

The assumption within the government—though not universally embraced—was that the Opposition would crack. This could occur in one of two ways—defections on the floor of the Senate or a change of mind by Fraser induced by party pressures.

During Melbourne Cup festivities Sir John Kerr and the Governor of New South Wales, Sir Roden Cutler, were guests of the Governor of Victoria, Sir Henry Winneke, at Government House in Melbourne and they attended the Cup Eve reception on Monday 3 November. Kerr was able to consult the other two vice-regal representatives about the crisis. He reviewed the course of events if Whitlam advised a Senate election and the non-Labor premiers adhered to their November 2 summit proposals and advised their Governors not to issue the writs. According to Gough Whitlam, Cutler and Winneke said they would have to accept the advice of their Premiers. So Kerr could be confident there would be no Senate election in the four States with non-Labor premiers.

Whitlam remarked: 'It would have been an outrage for Premier Lewis and Premier Bjelke-Petersen to prevent the people of their States from choosing successors to Senators Field and Bunton. Each would have been capable of such an outrage. Premier Hamer was at least reluctant but had nevertheless told his Governor that there were occasions when one had to go along with one's party'.[6]

Hamer denies this: 'I did not inform the Governor of any such intention. If Whitlam called a Senate election then an election would be held in Victoria.'[7] But Kerr's Melbourne Cup discussions would have probably confirmed his thinking that a Senate election would offer little prospect of resolving the crisis.

Cutler, however, offers a different perspective on the Senate election from that provided by Whitlam. Interviewed for this book, Cutler says the New South Wales Government had not foreshadowed with him any possibility of advice not to issue Senate election writs. Cutler then offers these comments:

> If I had got such advice from the New South Wales Government then I think I would have argued against the Government's advice on that matter . . . If the Government had given me this sort of advice in 1975 then I think I would have had to question that advice. I would have to either accept the advice or disagree and when I disagreed I would have advised the Queen of my position and accompanied that with my letter of resignation. There would always be a step before this. It was always my practice to stay in close touch with events in Parliament and with my premier and so I would have had a long discussion about this matter first with my premier, Tom Lewis.[8]

This stunning revelation suggests that the Opposition's efforts to thwart a Senate election might have backfired. If Cutler had acted along these lines the embarrassment for Fraser would have been severe. Any suggestion of Cutler querying his premier's advice or resigning because he refused to accept such advice would have brought the Supply crisis to a head. It suggests that if Whitlam had sought a Senate election at an early stage then Fraser's move against the writs would have backfired.

Sources have confirmed that Kerr, while at Government House, Melbourne, took the opportunity to raise the crisis with Winneke, a former Chief Justice of the Victorian Supreme Court. It was sensible for Kerr to talk with Winneke—the surprise is that in his memoirs he says nothing of these discussions. Winneke offered Kerr his opinion—but it seems that Kerr was not responsive.[9] A source very close to the late Governor has confirmed Winneke's views—he believed that any intervention by the Governor-General had to be based upon the 'advise and warn' doctrine. Rupert 'Dick' Hamer, the then Victorian Premier, reports that after the dismissal he discussed the matter with Winneke, whom he describes as 'a fine lawyer and a practical man'. Hamer says: 'He was very critical of Kerr. He thought that the dismissal was conducted ineptly and that its execution was not proper. He believed that it was wrong for the Governor-General not to warn Whitlam first.'[10]

Sir Roden Cutler provides his own recollection of after dinner talks at Government House, Melbourne, conducted between Kerr, Winneke, himself and the British High Commissioner. He says:

> Kerr did not signal his hand. He did not say that he intended to dismiss Whitlam . . . Winneke spoke at length giving his view on the situation. I think that Winneke and myself felt that the wise course was to call Whitlam in and explain the situation pointing out the consequences if Supply was not granted. The Governor-General, having covered the ground and explained the situation to the Prime Minister could then ask Whitlam to consider his position and tender advice on the matter. Eventually Kerr said, 'It's time to go to bed'. As we were going up the stairs he said to me, 'Winneke doesn't understand the position and it's pointless to keep up the discussion'. I was aware at the time that Kerr was conscious of the possibility that Whitlam might try to move against him first and I was aware that he was not discussing the situation with Whitlam. I think my view would have come through this night that he should talk to the Prime Minister.[11]

On 4 November—the day after rejecting Fraser's compromise—Whitlam's mood in Parliament was almost triumphant. He anticipated the Coalition collapse; he mocked his opponents. He dismissed the Fraser compromise with ridicule and taunted the Opposition with the threat of a Senate election. Whitlam's flamboyance disguised the defects of his own position. He said:

> When there will be an election for the Senate depends upon various factors. I notice that honourable gentlemen opposite have become quite distraught at the prospect that there might be an election for the Senate at the usual time in November or December before the new Senators take their places on July 1 ... [It] would be in accordance with precedent for me to advise the Governor-General to request State Governors to issue writs for a Senate election in this year. I am not persuaded that I should do so ... My ordinary view is that elections should take place closer to the expiry time of the shorter term Senators. Nevertheless I am influenced by the advice of editorials in the *Age* and the *Australian Financial Review* to consider an earlier Senate election ... But I want to assure honourable gentlemen and right honourable gentlemen that I am still thinking the matter over. I am not over-euphoric because of the overwhelming results of the opinion polls.[12]

The government benches roared with delight.

But Whitlam was changing position. Having declared for the previous two and a half weeks that he would not advise an election for either the House or the Senate until the budget was passed, he was now flirting with the half Senate option. Whitlam said on 4 November that he was 'not persuaded' to this option. But just two days later he told Kerr that he would probably advise this course.

A request to Kerr for a half Senate election would be a turning point. The compelling defect in such an election was the absence of Supply. Whitlam's problem by early November was that he would be asking Kerr for a half Senate election without having Supply for the duration of the campaign, let alone until a declaration of the result. A Governor-General would be reluctant to agree unless there was provision for Supply. Alternatively Kerr could act on advice, grant the Senate election but inform Whitlam that a solution to the crisis would still be needed when Supply began to expire, which would occur before the Senate election was held. If Kerr refused a Senate election then he would surely precipitate a crisis with Whitlam. If Kerr agreed, then Whitlam, in effect, would have enlisted the Governor-General in his cause. In this situation Fraser would face extreme pressures to buckle and pass the Appropriation bills.

Whitlam did not evaluate the critical question—would Kerr authorise a Senate poll without Supply? He just assumed it—but this assumption was a terrible risk. It reveals, again, that he should have discussed options with Kerr much earlier.

Whitlam was falling victim to the conundrum involved in the Senate election option. He could not call the Senate election when the budget was blocked because Labor's electoral support was too weak. It was the

Gough and Margaret Whitlam with Sir John Kerr on 22 October 1975, a few weeks before the Dismissal. (News Limited)

Sir John Kerr at the Melbourne Cup on 4 November 1975. During the Cup festivities he consulted the Governor of Victoria. (News Limited)

Malcolm Fraser leaves Parliament House to meet the Governor-General on 6 November 1975. This meeting was the most important Malcolm Fraser had with Sir John Kerr. (News Limited)

Malcolm Fraser, surrounded by angry demonstrators, leaves Parliament House shortly after the House of Representatives was suspended to advise Sir John Kerr of the double dissolution. (News Limited)

The Governor-General's secretary, David Smith, on the steps of Parliament House reads Sir John Kerr's proclamation dissolving the two Houses of Parliament. (News Limited)

Gough Whitlam delivers his dramatic response to the Governor-General's proclamation. 'Well may we say "God Save the Queen" because nothing will save the Governor-General.' (News Limited)

The caretaker prime minister, Malcolm Fraser, with Doug Anthony and Sir John Kerr. (News Limited)

A smiling Malcolm Fraser at the press conference shortly after his appointment as caretaker prime minister. (News Limited)

Gough Whitlam speaks to the crowd outside Parliament House the day after being sacked as prime minister. (News Limited, Duncan)

politics of the rejection of the budget that lifted Labor's standing over the next three weeks. Yet as time advanced Kerr was less likely to approve a Senate election because Supply would expire before it was held.

By this stage Whitlam was in total 'crash through or crash' mode. The only concession he offered was a signal that he would accept the Kerr compromise on the timing of the half Senate election—but Fraser had rejected this anyway.

In Parliament on 5 November Whitlam gave the clearest insight into his reasons for rejecting the more substantial Fraser compromise:

> I believe the people have made it quite plain and I believe before very long the Senate itself will accept that the Senate is not entitled to usurp the money powers of this Parliament. Section 53 of the Constitution lays down the Senate's power as regards money bills. It says that it cannot initiate them. It says it cannot amend them. It says that it can request the House of Representatives to amend them and that the House of Representatives may accede to that request or may reject it. Section 53 of the Constitution, it will be noted, does not expressly say that the Senate can reject money bills.[13]

The motion Whitlam kept moving and carrying in the House of Representatives declared that the Senate's action 'is not contemplated within the terms of the Constitution'. Later the same day, when moving this motion yet again, he said the Senate's action was 'unconstitutional'.[14]

Whitlam referred to a letter published in the *Age* on 27 October by Sir Richard Eggleston, a former judge of the Commonwealth Industrial Court, and one of the rare jurists who argued that the Senate was exceeding its powers. Building upon Eggleston's arguments, Whitlam declared: 'There is therefore nothing in the Constitution that warrants the view that the Senate may hold up an Appropriation Bill until the duly elected Government formed in this House capitulates to the Senate's demand for a general election of members of this House.'[15]

Having enunciated his belief that the Senate was defying the Constitution, Whitlam then explained just why he would not accept Fraser's compromise: 'The blackmail, of course, is still there. The only difference is that the time for the payment of the ransom has been generously extended . . .' Noting that the Opposition had shifted ground with its compromise, Whitlam continued:

> I repeat that they are still making the same unacceptable demand, namely, for a general election for this House . . . To give in to this blackmail would be to abandon these constitutional principles. The Government is duty bound to reject the demand and to oppose the course

the Senate is attempting to take: that is to say, to determine the timing of a general election for the House of Representatives . . . To accept the Senate's claims now would be to accept the right of the Senate to have the House of Representatives dissolved without itself having to go to the people.

Behind the present constitutional struggle is the wider political question of the way in which Australia's whole political future will develop. The question is not just whether this particular Government will be allowed to govern for the term for which it was elected; the question is whether any duly elected government will be allowed to govern in the future if in its own right it does not also command a majority in the Senate.[16]

This is the clearest statement of Whitlam's intent to achieve a total victory amounting to a destruction of the Senate's belief in its power to block Supply and, for practical purposes, the triumph of his own interpretation of the Constitution.

But by early November the 'tough it out' approach had been applied for three weeks. Fraser had been its equal. Whitlam now began preparations for a riskier measure—calling the half Senate election poll—in order to intensify the pressure. Fraser was also prepared to raise the stakes. In public he warned that Whitlam was threatening to assume dictatorial powers; in private he was preparing to tell Kerr to dismiss Whitlam.

Replying to Whitlam's motion on 5 November, Fraser said:

The Prime Minister seems to believe that the Constitution is Mr Whitlam . . . The Prime Minister forgets that the Parliament is composed of the Queen—in this case the Governor-General—the Senate and the House of Representatives. The attempts of the Prime Minister to take to himself total and dictatorial powers will not succeed. They cannot be allowed to succeed. It is the Parliament that must prevail . . . not this Prime Minister, this greatest of all politicians!

The Government now says that it will govern without Supply. How? Why? The Parliament is not entitled to know. The country is not entitled to know . . . The one threat to democracy is when one gets a Prime Minister of this kind who is terrified to face the electors of Australia, terrified to face his masters, because he knows that he would be banished.[17]

Kerr's final consultations

The next day, 6 November, Kerr saw Fraser with Whitlam's approval in a final effort to test whether the crisis could be settled short of his intervention. The Governor-General was not hopeful. Kerr again asked Fraser whether he would accept the compromise that Kerr had pro-

THE SOLUTION

posed on 30 October—that the Opposition pass the budget on the condition that Whitlam hold a late Senate poll just before mid-1976. The Governor-General raised this because Whitlam had already rejected Fraser's own compromise. But Kerr had to add two conditions required by Whitlam—that the Senate election be held in all States on the same day and that the voting system be Labor's proposed preferential system.

Fraser's reaction was predictable.

Kerr reports: 'Mr Fraser was not interested at all. He said the terms he had already announced were final. He said that the Senate had shown its firmness and would continue to do so.' Sir John was not surprised.[18]

A decisive stage in the dialogue between Kerr and Fraser had now been reached. Malcolm Fraser, a master of pressure politics, turned his sights on Kerr; Fraser went on the offensive.

'This was the most important meeting I had with the Governor-General', Fraser explains. 'The background was that my earlier couple of meetings with him had been very low key, they were really responding to his questions and how I thought the issues had to be resolved.'[19]

The two men were alone in the study at Yarralumla. Their talk became frank and direct. Fraser says:

> I had been thinking of making this point at the second last meeting. But I had waited, wanting it to have more effect. My feelings on this were very firm. I now told the Governor-General that if Australia did not get an election the Opposition would have no choice but to be highly critical of him. We would have to say that he had failed his duty as Governor-General to the nation. I made it clear that the Opposition would have to defend itself and its actions to the people. John Kerr, you see, was in the invidious position of being highly criticised for doing the right thing and highly criticised for doing the wrong thing.[20]

Fraser knew that the only way a pre-Christmas election could be obtained—the timetable on which he was relying—was if Kerr intervened by early the following week. So Fraser assumed that this discussion might be his last chance to influence Kerr. He did not miss the opportunity. According to Fraser: 'I said . . . that there ought to be an election—and that if there wasn't an election the Opposition would need to explain itself . . . I told him we'd be saying he had failed in his office because he had not given the people an election, which it was in his power to do'.[21]

Fraser also advised Kerr that the Coalition was sure that it would win an election; that once the crisis was resolved public opinion would move decisively in favour of the Opposition; and, therefore, that any action by the Governor-General would be massively endorsed by the people.[22] This was to reassure Kerr about taking a momentous step.

Kerr's own account of this meeting provides a revelation of Fraser's skill:

> He [Fraser] realised that he could not advise me but felt he should say that if I failed to act in the situation which existed I would be imperiling the reserve powers of the Crown forever; he accepted that the discretion was mine but inaction on my part, with Supply running out, the Senate firm on deferral, and the Government asserting a right to govern without Supply, would destroy the reserve powers.[23]

Asked about Kerr's reference to the reserve powers, Fraser replies: 'I don't think I said that'. But he confirms that this was the sense of his position.[24] There is no doubt of the force of Fraser's stance:

> KELLY: When you gave Kerr this warning did you indicate then that you believed the issue should be resolved through a general election before Christmas?
>
> FRASER: Oh, he knew that was my view. Very clearly, yes. The Government was running out of Supply . . .
>
> KELLY: Well, what would you have done if the crisis had gone the other way and Kerr hadn't intervened the way he did?
>
> FRASER: Then there would be a different kind of crisis. You would certainly have to say that the Governor-General was betraying his trust to the people of Australia. That would come out, in political terms, as a very sharp criticism of him and you would be stating the reasons for it pretty succinctly.[25]

For all practical purposes, Fraser *was* advising Kerr. The implications of this advice were sensational—that the Governor-General had a duty to secure an election and that both men knew that this was code for the dismissal of Whitlam. Fraser was telling Kerr to accept his responsibility as Governor-General. If he refused he would be attacked publicly by Fraser. Presumably Fraser would blame Kerr for denying Australians the opportunity for an election; the chance to remove Whitlam and to secure a new future. Fraser explains:

> I said something like, 'Sir, in many ways, you and your office are the last protector of the Australian people.' . . . I repeated that the only thing the Opposition was asking for was an election. . . . I told him frankly that this was a wretched government, that Australians want to vote, they want to be able to make a judgement about it . . . there needed to be an election and . . . he should do everything he could to achieve it.[26]

THE SOLUTION

In this meeting—the fourth between the two men to discuss the deadlock—Fraser exploited to the hilt the great benefit he enjoyed from having access to Kerr during the crisis.

The issue was now pressing upon the principals. Their careers were in the balance. Fraser's confidant from those times, Tony Staley, says: 'I'll never forget talking to Malcolm about a failure. It happened in the last few days before the dismissal. Malcolm indicated to me that if he lost the struggle he would certainly consider an immediate resignation as leader. However, he would renominate. The purpose would be to give the party an option to select another leader if it was so inclined'.[27]

There were, in technical terms, two ways in which Kerr could procure an election. He could persuade Whitlam to advise an election by speaking frankly to him and indicating that the alternative was dismissal; or he could just dismiss Whitlam and commission Fraser on the basis that he advise an election. But Kerr had already decided not to advise and warn Whitlam because he believed that Whitlam could not be influenced and might try to sack him. Hence, by Kerr's logic, his only election option was dismissal.

Fraser left Kerr with the same confidence he had felt about the Governor-General throughout the crisis—that Kerr would intervene and that he would wait until the last possible moment. Fraser, like Whitlam, knew the timetable from the Electoral Office. If there were to be a general election before Christmas the last viable date was 13 December and in order to stage such an election the Parliament would need to be dissolved around 11, 12 or 13 November. So Kerr had to act within five or six days.

This pre-Christmas election timetable became the deadline around which all three men worked—Fraser, Whitlam and Kerr.

Fraser says: 'I left Kerr confident. I was confident because of my judgement about John Kerr's character. By this stage it was getting close to the deadline.'[28]

On the evening of 6 November, at about 7 pm, I saw Fraser in his office, having requested a meeting with him on a non-attributable background basis. I had spoken earlier in the day to Whitlam who assured me that Kerr was 'rock solid' and would only act on his advice. Sitting across the table from Fraser I was surprised by the depth of confidence he displayed and, even more, by how explicit he was in predicting Kerr's actions. Fraser stressed that Kerr would 'do the right thing'. He said that he believed that the crisis would be resolved by Christmas and that the resolution would be procured by the Governor-General's intervening to secure a general election by this time. He was quite firm on the Christmas deadline. When I asked how Kerr would secure an election Fraser told me that he believed 'the Governor-General . . . will sack the Prime Minister'. This, he felt, was the logic of the situation.[29] This discussion occurred five days before the dismissal and on the evening after his last meeting with Kerr on the deadlock.

Asked about this conversation twenty years later Fraser says:

> If I was seeing anyone associated with the media I was going to be extremely confident and you will understand that . . . However, I was confident because of my assessment of John Kerr's character. I also believed, once it got into a waiting game, that Kerr wouldn't act until the last moment. He would hope that other events would resolve the matter. I believed he would wait pretty much until 11 or 12 November and get the issue all wrapped up before Christmas with an election. Obviously it was getting close to the deadline . . . I don't know how close John Kerr had been to Whitlam in earlier days, but I think I had a better basis for making a judgement about the decision John Kerr would make in the end.[30]

Reflecting on another occasion on his view of Kerr, Fraser said: 'The most important elements in my mind would have been my reading of the Constitution, my knowledge of him as a lawyer, and my belief that he had to do what was right in the end.'[31] Fraser believed he had a better psychological understanding of Kerr than did Whitlam.

Neither Fraser nor Kerr describe the chemistry of this discussion—but it was conducted at a time when Kerr was close to deciding that he must dismiss Whitlam.

A fundamental question arises—did Fraser receive any sign or hint from Kerr's remarks or body language that he intended to dismiss Whitlam? Kerr kept this secret from Whitlam, but was he equally successful at keeping it from Fraser? It is an extraordinary fact that by the evening of 6 November Whitlam was supremely confident that Kerr would 'do the right thing' and Fraser was extremely confident that Whitlam would be sacked. After the dismissal Whitlam propagated an unsubstantiated conspiracy theory that there was some backchannel communication between Kerr and Fraser through the Barwick–Ellicott connection. This appears far too elaborate; it ignored the obvious. Fraser was talking to Kerr at their regular meetings and it was Fraser who made the judgements about Kerr's intentions based upon these talks. Was Fraser's deep confidence after this meeting based not just on his assessment of Kerr but on indications that Kerr had given him?

Kerr says that he did not give Fraser any indication of his own thinking in this discussion.[32] Fraser confirms this: 'There was nothing by word or deed given me that suggested he was going one way or another . . . Kerr never raised the dismissal option with me. He was quite scrupulous. Of course, I raised the dismissal option with him.'[33]

However, John Menadue, a senior official says: 'Some time after the election, when I was discussing things with Malcolm Fraser, he told me that during his talks with Kerr before the dismissal Kerr had told him [Fraser] that he couldn't discuss options with Whitlam because if he had then Whitlam would be on to the Palace to have him removed.'[34]

Malcolm Fraser denies that Kerr made any such remark.[35]

Clearly, this was how Kerr felt; if he had told Fraser then it was tantamount to Kerr's declaring his mistrust of Whitlam and a decisive signal to Fraser that he would prevail. It serves as a reminder that Kerr could have said a variety of things to Fraser which had nothing to do with sacking Whitlam but which would have encouraged the Opposition leader.

Whitlam had two important discussions on the same day, 6 November. He conferred with the Chief Electoral Officer, Frank Ley, about election deadlines. Ley's advice was that if Whitlam wanted to conduct a half Senate election before Christmas then that poll would have to be called, at the latest, on Tuesday 11 November. Ley said that the last practicable pre-Christmas election date was 13 December. Whitlam decided to further intensify the pressure—he all but settled on a Senate election.[36]

The Prime Minister saw Kerr the same day. The Governor-General reported that Fraser had no interest in the compromise proposal that Whitlam hold a late Senate poll just before mid-1976 and that the Opposition, in return, pass the budget.

Whitlam told Kerr that he would probably advise a half Senate election to be held on 13 December. Whitlam said nothing about provision for Supply, an omission that Kerr noted.[37] Kerr observed later: 'If the Prime Minister so advised and I acquiesced, and if the Senate held firm . . . the election would be held after money had run out, as it would by 30 November.'[38] Kerr, aware that Whitlam would want a Senate election the next week, knew it was decision time for him.

Kerr had a busy day on 6 November—he also saw Treasurer Hayden and Attorney General Enderby.

The Governor-General sought a meeting with Hayden, ostensibly to review the alternative arrangements and to discuss Supply. Hayden outlined the situation—Supply would begin to run out from the end of November. He gave Kerr a document explaining the alternative financial arrangements through the banks.

This is a significant meeting for two reasons. The account provided by Hayden offers the fullest picture of the style with which Kerr conducted his dialogue with politicians during the crisis. Second, as a result of this discussion Hayden concluded that Kerr would probably sack the Whitlam Government.

Hayden recalls:

> I had been told by Kep Enderby that Kerr was okay, that he was one of us, and I should tell him everything, warts and all, about the 'gap' financing process. I accepted that and came out and spoke to him. I explained that on the advice of the Attorney General's Department the scheme was quite legal. But I said frankly that there would be problems in its functioning—since I had been told to be absolutely candid with him.[39]

> But to my surprise Kerr didn't seem to be terribly interested anyway. He was relaxed, quite genial, he asked me if I wanted a drink and he had a tumbler of Scotch, brought in by James Heenan (the butler). I told Kerr that we had about a few weeks reserve of cash. I advised Sir John that, although somewhat messy, the scheme was workable and furthermore it was legal on the advice of the Attorney General's Department . . . I was taken by surprise to find Sir John apparently little, if at all, interested in much of what I said.[40]

Kerr, after praising Whitlam's campaign ability, asked Hayden how he thought that Labor would go in an election. 'If there's an election any time soon, we'll be devastated, we'll be done like a dinner', Hayden replied emphatically. But Hayden, a suspicious man by nature, was immediately alerted that something was wrong.[41]

Continuing his account of the discussion, Hayden said:

> He [Kerr] unexpectedly embarked on a discursive commentary about how highly he regarded Gough Whitlam's magnificent fighting ability, especially with his back against the wall. He said that Gough Whitlam fought like a lion, but even if he were defeated next time he would certainly fight his way back the time after that. I recall observing rather wryly that it was easier to get out than to get back in. Sir John dismissed, graciously, but quickly, discussion about diffident Senators retreating from the brink as too uncertain.

Hayden recalled Kerr's saying to him that Whitlam could 'do a Wilson'—a point Whitlam later raised to reveal Kerr's faulty memory since Kerr claimed to have said this to Whitlam.[42]

Hayden acted instinctively. His intuition told him that Kerr was moving against the government. Hayden, interviewed in June 1995 in his Governor-General's study at Yarralumla, takes up this remarkable story:

I left here [Government House] with a sense of agitation. I went
straight to Whitlam's office instead of going out to catch a plane to
return home. Whitlam was in a meeting so he came out of his office
to see me. He was wearing a blue and white striped shirt. He was standing against the wall, even more larger than life. I said to Gough, 'My
copper instincts tell me that Kerr is thinking of sacking us and calling
an election'—or words to that effect. Gough looked at me. He was fid-
dling his spectacles around in his hand. He said to me, 'No comrade.
He wouldn't have the guts for that.'

There are many things in my life that are now just a blur. But a
few stand out like a great promontory with a lighthouse on it and
that's one of them. You don't forget it. Gough, incidentally, denies that
this conversation ever took place. But it certainly did.

You see, Kerr just wasn't interested in what I was saying. Nor in
the papers I had brought. My first instinct was to think this was
strange, that it was extraordinary given the situation. I thought if he's
interested in sorting out options that this didn't seem to be the right
behaviour. Then there was this speculation, this thinking aloud—if
there's an election, that Gough can get back. It was also his [Kerr's]
mood. It didn't seem right for a man sorting a problem out. It was
more appropriate for a man who had *already* sorted out the problem.
This was a giveaway for me. After being a cop for eight years there are
things you look for, that are ingrained in you. It's your instinct.[43]

Whitlam's mindset had blinded him to all signs of trouble. Hayden
left Parliament House trying to console himself that Whitlam was closer
to Kerr than he was and therefore Whitlam should know. When I asked
Whitlam if he had said to any ministers that Kerr wouldn't 'have the
guts' to dismiss them, he replied: 'No. I don't think I did.'[44]

And 6 November was the very day that Kerr all but decided to
dismiss Whitlam.[45]

It is salutary to reflect upon Hayden's description of Kerr's mood
and his style. Kerr conducted these talks over a drink; he was relaxed
and his conversation was speculative. Is this the way Kerr spoke to Fraser
the same day? If Hayden concluded from his talks that Kerr was likely
to dismiss Whitlam, then was Fraser able to draw a similar deduction?
Hayden hardly knew Kerr; but Fraser had enjoyed the benefit of four
discussions with the Governor-General during the crisis.

The fact remains that there were two politicians who felt after their
talks with Kerr on 6 November that he was likely to dismiss the
government—Fraser and Hayden.

The Governor-General's scepticism about the alternative arrangements seems to have been profound. In his memoirs he says:

> I did not discuss the legal and constitutional issues with Mr Hayden
> but I had serious doubts as to the legality of the scheme; I believed

the banks would have very grave doubts and would certainly seek legal advice. The clear impression I formed, apart from the great administrative burdens and cost of the scheme and its failure to cover the whole field, was of its inadequate, inappropriate and, from the point of view of the law as it governed the banks' activity at least, probably illegal nature. It hardly seemed possible to me that the banks could reach a decision to accept the scheme, if they ever did, without long delays. They would need time to consider their policies and to study administrative problems. Their depositors, customers and shareholders would be very nervous and the scheme might be challenged legally. My belief was that the private banks would not feel able to participate and would not. I had no knowledge, however, before 11 November of their actual attitudes or of the legal advice they were getting.[46]

Kerr was not sufficiently worried about the alternative arrangements to spend much time asking the Treasurer about them on 6 November. Alternatively, Kerr may have adopted with Hayden the same procedure that he adopted with Whitlam—a refusal to discuss his concerns frankly with his ministers.

The government, however, was pressing ahead with its alternative to Supply. The same day, there was a meeting in Canberra between officials from Treasury, Attorney General's, the Prime Minister's Department, the Reserve Bank and bank officials to hammer out the basis of the scheme. There was profound concern within the senior management of all the banks. Legal opinions sought by the banks were being finalised over the next few days. There was very little prospect that the banks would have co-operated with the government if the issue had continued. After the dismissal, on the afternoon of 11 November, the chairman of the Bankers' Association, Tom Bell, made a public statement saying that the banks, after considering the scheme, were not able to accept it in totality. There can be little doubt that Whitlam's dismissal brought relief and celebration to bank managements across Australia.

The truth is that the alternative arrangements did not shape Kerr's final decision. There was never any suggestion from Kerr, at the time or later, that if there had been no alternative arrangements then he would have acted in a different way. But the financial proposals were influential. Their role seems to have been one of reinforcing Kerr's dismissal decision. Once again, his own legal opinion was in conflict with those of the Law Officers. Kerr interpreted the alternative arrangements as evidence that Whitlam's 'tough it out' tactic was faltering. He said they were evidence that Whitlam no longer believed that 'denunciation' would deter Fraser and that Whitlam had to confront the real risk that 'the Senate would stand firm'.[47] Finally, Kerr interpreted these plans as evidence that Whitlam was prepared to resort to likely unconstitutional measures to avoid an election; that the Government would not be constrained by the legal orthodoxy; and that these actions would not be tolerated by the Australian public.

On the same day, 6 November, Kerr saw the Attorney General, Kep Enderby, who handed him two documents. The first, headed 'joint opinion', was an unsigned legal advice on the alternative arrangements. According to Kerr, Enderby at the time he handed over the document wrote the word 'draft' on the top in his own pen. It was an unsigned draft from the two senior Law Officers, Enderby and Maurice Byers. It is inexplicable that the government did not provide Kerr with formal written and signed advice earlier. The opinion said: 'The constitutional provisions relating to Parliament's control over expenditure by the Executive are observed in letter and in spirit. Nor does the proposal contemplate nor allow the doing by indirection of what may not be done directly. The proposal and its effectuation are, in our opinion, clearly constitutional.'[48]

Kerr was unimpressed.

He said later: 'It seemed to me to be quite likely that the banks would receive different legal advice. Further, it seemed likely to me that they would require an agreement with binding legal force . . . Constitutional uncertainties might easily lead the banks not to agree to join in the scheme, their legal advisers so advising them.'[49]

The second document was the more important. Enderby gave Kerr a 28 page opinion with Byers' signature—but not Enderby's as Attorney General—which replied to the Ellicott opinion of 16 October. This followed Kerr's request to Whitlam on 22 October for advice from the Law Officers on the Ellicott opinion. Enderby said that he was giving Kerr the document, with Whitlam's approval, as 'background'. He said it contained Byers' views—but indicated that there were sections of the opinion with which he disagreed. Enderby had intended to get Byers to refine his argument and shorten the document. The Attorney struck out Byers' signature with his pen and added the word 'draft' to the top.[50]

Enderby recalls: 'Kerr asked me whether I had an opinion on the matter and I said to him, "I am a Whig. I believe in the Whig view of history on these matters", which obviously meant I didn't believe in the reserve powers. Kerr said nothing. I left never thinking for one moment that he might sack us.'[51] Before leaving Enderby volunteered that the Liberal Senators were looking for an excuse to abstain and that they would go to water. 'That's certainly not what Fraser tells me', Kerr replied—having spoken to Fraser earlier that day. The Governor-General seemed quite convinced on this point; Enderby made a mental note at the time. When Enderby crossed out Byers' signature he told Kerr there were sections of the document with which he disagreed. Kerr asked Enderby about the status of the document. He was told that it was a guide to the formal advice he would receive.[52]

Not surprisingly, Kerr was even more unimpressed. He had requested advice from the Law Officers more than a fortnight earlier. The document he received used the term 'we' and was clearly written as a draft for both Byers and Enderby to sign. But Enderby deleted Byers' signature, said he disagreed with parts of the opinion and foreshadowed formal advice at a later time. Such advice was never delivered before 11 November. The crisis lasted 27 days but neither the Prime Minister nor the Attorney General ever gave Kerr formal written advice from the Law Officers. This was an incomprehensible failure.

As argued earlier, written advice should have been given to Kerr immediately upon the deferral of the budget in mid-October. It should have been followed up later with more detailed written advice. Kerr, after all, was actively seeking such advice. As a lawyer he would have expected it. Kerr's irritation was understandable. It could have only left the impression of a government that took him for granted. Byers was angry with Enderby—whom he brands as a 'silly fellow'—for crossing out his signature.[53] After the dismissal Kerr had the opportunity to confirm with Byers that the document had represented his opinion.[54]

Enderby should perhaps have been alerted by Kerr's comments to the effect that the Senate would not crack. If Enderby, like Hayden, had reported to Whitlam, then two warnings might have had some effect. More likely, Enderby, like Hayden, would have been told there was no reason to worry.

A close reading of the Byers opinion—on which Kerr was not obliged to set much weight, given Enderby's remarks—reveals the folly of not providing formal advice along these lines.[55]

The first point to make about Byers' opinion is his statement of the issue: 'whether the deferring of Supply by the Senate solely to procure the resignation or, failing that, the dismissal of the Ministry as a step in a forced dissolution of the Representatives compels His Excellency to dissolve that House.' So Byers was addressing the dismissal question. For him—if not for Whitlam—it was a central issue.

Byers said that the principles of responsible government 'permeate the Constitution' and noted that 'this particular power of the Senate has never before been exercised'—a fact suggesting that the convention claimed by the House of Representatives exists. Byers said the Senate's resolution sought to secure either the ministry's resignation or the

Governor-General's dissolution of Parliament after dismissing the ministry and taking advice from a minority ministry. He continued:

> The Ministry has not resigned and will not do so. That leaves only a forced dissolution. Dr Jennings (*Cabinet Government*) . . . observes that 'No Government has been dismissed by the Sovereign since 1783' . . . Dr Forsey (*The Royal Power of Dissolution of Parliament*, 1943) says that, 'In the overseas Empire there appears to have been only one instance of this: New Brunswick in 1853.' . . . We have referred to forced dissolutions only to indicate that their rarity and the long years since their exercise cast the gravest doubt upon the present existence of that prerogative.

Byers reviewed sections 61, 62 and 64 of the Constitution—which incorporate the cabinet system into the Constitution via the Executive Council—concluding that the executive power of the Commonwealth was exercisable by the Governor-General on advice of a ministry with the confidence of the House of Representatives. He argued that the Governor-General's powers to dissolve the Parliament before the expiry of its term (sections 28 and 5):

> . . . do not, considered alone, afford any guide as to the circumstances when the extreme and abnormal reserve powers of dismissal of a Ministry and consequent dissolution of the Representatives should or may be exercised or even that they still exist. This is the field of convention and discretion. But it is, we think, not correct to treat the exercise of those powers as demanded when refusal of Supply is threatened or when it occurs. To do so is to deny, for example, a vice-regal authority to offer suggestions where the circumstances have reached a stage sufficiently grave to warrant His Excellency's adoption of that course . . . the mere threat or indeed the actual rejection of Supply neither calls for the Ministry to resign nor compels the Crown's representative thereupon to intervene.

The next stage of Byers' argument was to point out that section 57 provided a constitutional solution to deadlocks between the two houses and it was obvious that this section applied to money bills as well. The opinion continued:

> If such be the section's purpose and intended operation, how is it possible consistently with the Constitution that a reserve power of uncertain existence and unknowable constituents must be exercised in a way necessarily denying effect to the one constitutional provision expressly directed to the solution of deadlock between the Houses? We do not find it possible ourselves to accept that view and to the extent that Mr Ellicott does so he is, we think, clearly wrong. That neither or either House intends to compromise is not to the point, should it be the fact.

> The section exists to permit that opportunity and to allow a joint sitting to be held whose decision finally resolves the difference.

Finally, Byers referred to Quick and Garran's discussion of the conflict, recognised by the founding fathers, between responsible government and federalism—between the authority of the House of Representatives and the States' House. The federalists who had sought by specific constitutional provision to ensure that 'the State House could, as effectively as the primary chamber, enforce its want of confidence by refusing to provide the necessary supplies' had had their recommendations rejected. It was misleading to treat the Senate's power to reject Supply as 'untrammelled by convention or practice'. The Ellicott view, that the Senate could reject or defer Supply and force the Governor-General's action against his ministers, implied a process that 'may be indefinitely repeated and may involve deleterious consequences to the working of the constitutional provisions'. A view which 'looking only to the existence of the legal power disregards or ignores constitutional practice hitherto apparently governing the exercise of those powers, requires, we venture to think, the gravest consideration before its adoption could even be contemplated'. Therefore, the Ellicott opinion was 'wrong'.

It is unlikely that the Byers opinion had much influence upon Kerr. It was delivered too late; it was not formal advice; it was not accompanied or followed by oral support from Whitlam; and it represented a view that Kerr had already rejected. In his book Kerr provided a detailed critique of Byers.[56]

Kerr identified 6 November as 'a decisive point in my approach to the crisis . . . it was not until the end of that day of 6 November that I knew I must make up my mind as to any action to be taken by me, and follow that decision through'.[57]

On the same evening Whitlam and a small group of family friends dined at Zorba's Restaurant in Canberra:

> Whitlam's mood was of supreme confidence . . . he was relaxed and expansive, reflecting on the crisis, the inevitable backdown which he believed Fraser now faced and his own plans for the future. Whitlam and Freudenberg discussed at length the consequences of such a backdown for Fraser. They both believed he would retain the Liberal leadership but they were certain that he would be permanently handicapped, that the electorate would never forgive his costly grab for power, and that henceforth Whitlam would hold a major advantage over his rival . . . Freudenberg put his beer on the table and said, 'Kerr is still the best appointment we've made'. Whitlam smiled. 'Too right', he replied . . . He toasted the man who was about to sack him.[58]

Kerr's final deliberations

Kerr now formed the following conclusions: that Fraser would not compromise; that the Opposition would not crack in the Senate despite Labor's claims to this effect; that Whitlam had no intention of calling a general election although he would probably seek to reinforce his 'tough it out' tactic with a half Senate election which he would request from Kerr in the coming days; that the alternative arrangements would probably not work and raised severe legal problems; that if the crisis were to be resolved through a general election before Christmas then the Parliament had to be dissolved on 11 November at the latest—in five days time.

Kerr now turned his mind to the dismissal; it moved from being an option to being his choice.

Kerr operated on the basis of a number of political judgements and legal beliefs. First, the Senate had the power to block Supply (section 53) and no convention stood in the way of this action. He said: 'My opinion, that the Senate has untrammelled power to refuse or withhold Supply, was I believe the accepted view until the propaganda and argument of October–November 1975'.[59] In his legal opinion Byers argued that other sections of the Constitution offset section 53. Kerr did not believe that any 'offsetting' factor existed. He also rejected the view that any unwritten convention could develop to overrule the Constitution itself. Kerr agreed with Ellicott that the power existed and that it could be used solely to determine the term of the House of Representatives. Kerr concluded that since the power existed political motives for its use were legally irrelevant.[60]

Having taken this position, however, Kerr was forced to acknowledge its consequences: 'There is a sense in which a Government must retain the "confidence" of the Senate to be able to continue in government. It must have the confidence of the Senate expressed by the passing of Supply by the Senate.'[61] Accordingly there are no grounds for arguing Whitlam's position—that the House of Representatives is entitled to assert its legislative will over the Senate.

The Governor-General's position on the Senate's power was reinforced by a High Court judgement given on 30 September 1975 in the *Petroleum and Minerals Authority Case*. Sections of the judgement were incorporated into Hansard on 30 October by Malcolm Fraser. In these, four judges, Barwick, Gibbs, Mason and Stephen—the Chief Justice and next two Chief Justices and a future Governor-General—made it clear that they believed the Senate had the power over Supply.[62] The significance of this is that if the question of the Senate's power over Supply had come before the High Court then it would have ruled for the Senate and against the government.

The second assumption on which Kerr acted was that a government had a responsibility to obtain Supply for the funding of government services. It was through the Parliament that these funds had to be obtained and the Parliament consisted of two houses. Kerr felt that 'the primary duty of a government is to ensure the provision of Supply to the Crown'.[63] Section 61 of the Constitution made it clear that the executive power of the Commonwealth was vested 'in the Queen and is exercisable by the Governor-General as the Queen's representative . . .' Whitlam was attempting to secure Supply in two ways—by forcing the Senate to 'crack' and by his alternative arrangements. But the Senate had not been 'cracked' and Kerr concluded that the alternative arrangements were never going to satisfy the requirement for Supply.

Kerr's third assumption was that if a government could not secure Supply then it had to advise an election or resign. Whitlam was refusing to do either.

Kerr's fourth assumption was that the Queen had no role in the crisis and that any intervention had to come from the Governor-General. He believed the Constitution (Section 61) gave all the reserve powers to the Governor-General. This was the principle adopted by the Queen herself, as later correspondence from the Palace proved.[64]

During the crisis Kerr wrote regularly to the Palace in a series of letters that outlined the nature of the crisis and his own approach. He felt an obligation to keep the Queen informed of developments and possible options for settlement. But Kerr saw a sharp distinction between such 'briefings' and his own decision to use the reserve powers. Kerr believed he should not inform the Queen of his intention. In his memoirs he said:

> I did not tell the Queen in advance that I intended to exercise these powers on 11 November. I did not ask her approval. The decisions I took were without the Queen's advance knowledge. The reason for this was that I believed, if dismissal action were to be taken, that it could be taken only by me and that it must be done on my sole responsibility. My view was that to inform Her Majesty in advance of what I intended to do, and when, would be to risk involving her in an Australian political and constitutional crisis in relation to which she had no legal powers; and I must not take such a risk.[65]

Kerr argued that had the Queen been told and then offered advice to him the Crown would have become embroiled in the crisis. If the Crown, having been told, did nothing, then the Queen would also have courted criticism for her refusal to become involved.

The Governor-General decided that he had to accept 'full accountability' for the dismissal: 'In this way I could hope to protect the Crown in Australia from any serious risk of being weakened by events.'[66]

However, Kerr took this argument to the next stage. There was another way the Queen could become involved—if Whitlam, upon finding of Kerr's intention, advised the Crown to remove Kerr and appoint another Governor-General. Kerr argued that he must act to avert this possibility.

So Kerr's fifth assumption was the need for secrecy as he began planning to dismiss Whitlam.

In his memoirs Kerr offered this justification: 'I believed, quite starkly, that if I had said anything to Mr Whitlam about the possibility that I might take away his commission I would no longer have been there. I conceived it to be my proper behaviour in the circumstances to stay at my post and not invite dismissal.'[67]

In power terms, Kerr had decided to dismiss Whitlam before Whitlam had a chance to dismiss him. It was that elemental, that primitive. But Kerr sought a loftier motive than merely saving his own job. His justification was to preserve the reputation and impartiality of the Crown.

If Whitlam advised the Queen to remove Kerr then the Queen would be obliged to take his advice. Kerr rejected the possibility that the Queen might exercise some kind of reserve power and ignore such advice.[68] Depending upon the manner in which such advice was given there might have been a delay—but Kerr feared that if this was truly a 'competitive dismissal' contest then Whitlam would seek to minimise the delay.

Kerr's concern that Whitlam would try to remove him had become an obsession.

During the crisis Kerr and his official secretary, David Smith, had discussed this prospect. As a result Smith had rung the Queen's private secretary, Sir Martin Charteris, to inquire about the procedures for a Prime Minister to remove a Governor-General. The advice from Charteris was that a communication by phone would not suffice; the Palace would require formal advice through a signed letter. This was before fax machines so that meant, at the very least, a 24 hour delay while a letter was couriered to the Queen. In practice, it would mean a far longer delay.

Charteris explains the position: 'You couldn't just pick up the telephone and fix it up that way. I am sure that written notification would have been required.'[69]

One Yarralumla source says: 'The message from Sir Martin was that the Queen would have to accept any advice from the Prime Minister but in the process there could be to-ing and fro-ing.'[70]

Drawing upon his own experience as Governor-General, Bill Hayden says: 'If Whitlam had tried to sack Kerr then Buckingham Palace would have taken an inordinately long time to get back to him by which time the issues here would have been sorted out one way or other.'[71]

From the message that Charteris gave Smith—along with Kerr's knowledge of the time it took Whitlam to remove Sir Colin Hannah's dormant commission—it is clear that the Governor-General knew that Whitlam could not procure his rapid dismissal.[72] Hayden's assessment is convincing. The Palace would stall over process and procedure in order to ensure it was not involved.

So Kerr's decision was that his obligation to protect the Monarchy required him to refrain from informing the Queen and to keep his intentions secret from his Prime Minister.

It is an irony. In the cause of protecting the Crown's impartiality Kerr was taking action that would prejudice the Governor-General's impartiality. This was the argument against his decision. Nowhere does Kerr address this obvious objection to his action.

Kerr's original conclusion was to secure an election. The normal action of the Crown, having taken this decision, would be to 'advise and warn' the Prime Minister along these lines. The Prime Minister could then advise an election himself—or he could risk dismissal and a forced dissolution and election. Most Prime Ministers, given the choice, would keep their jobs and go to the polls. The advantage and importance of the 'advise and warn' process is that it enables a political solution to be obtained without any resort to the reserve powers.

By deciding not to warn Whitlam, Kerr made a dismissal certain. He eliminated the 'advise and warn' mechanism because, he claims, Whitlam had said that he would never advise a general election at the behest of the Senate. By not giving Whitlam a choice Kerr committed the Crown's representative, first, to a dismissal and, second, to a dismissal by stealth. The emotional import of this type of dismissal is explosive. It was one thing for the Crown to give a Prime Minister a choice under threat of dismissal; it was another to plan a dismissal by ambush. Such an act would undermine any claim by the Crown's representative to have acted with justice or impartiality.

By declining to exercise his 'advise and warn' discretion Kerr left unanswered the question of whether Whitlam's threats to move against him were the normal bluff and bravado of politics—the brand of pressure tactic practised by the professionals on issues from the mundane to the decisive—or whether Whitlam was serious.

Kerr didn't *know* that Whitlam would seek his removal. But Kerr, with help from Whitlam, convinced himself. The ultimate judgement on Kerr is that he put a higher premium on the Crown's reputation than he did on the Governor-General's. He chose a course that was certain to prejudice the office of Governor-General; on the other hand, he could not be certain that resort to the 'advise and warn' process would plunge the Queen into the crisis.

Kerr professed his knowledge of previous crises. But there was no precedent for the manner in which he intended to exercise the reserve powers. He was not following the pattern of 1932 when Game dismissed Lang; on that occasion Lang received warning in writing and had time to change his course. Game based his dismissal on illegality of the government. On these two counts Kerr was not 'doing a Game'.[73] There seems, in fact, to be no other occasion on record where a Governor or Governor-General dismissed by surprise a ministry retaining the confidence of the Lower House, using as a defence of his method the need to protect the Crown lest his ministers try to dismiss him.

Whitlam observed that Kerr 'was plainly obsessed by the fear that I would procure his own dismissal by the Queen; and he believed that to prevent this he was justified in practising any deception.'[74]

Kerr's distrust of Whitlam drove his behaviour during the crisis. It crippled him as a mediator; it denied him the chance to pursue a political solution by putting Whitlam under pressure; finally, it drove his solution.

Whitlam and the Palace

So, would Whitlam have dismissed Kerr?

Fraser, like Kerr, had no doubts: 'John Kerr was between a rock and a hard place. The Queen has tenure. But a Governor-General holds office at pleasure and if he ceases to please a Prime Minister can pick up the phone and neutralise him. John Kerr knew that if he had the sort of conversation which the Queen would have in Britain then he would be sacked.'[75]

Asked how certain he was about this, Fraser replied: 'I'm certain. Whitlam's whole demeanour indicated that Kerr had to do what he wanted. The Queen would have immediately become the centre of the problem. John Kerr did the only thing he could do to keep her out of it. He hasn't been given adequate credit for that.' Pressed further on the issue of certainty, Fraser said: 'It's a judgement of men and people in circumstances . . . You can't prove it mathematically as two plus two equals four. But you can't prove a murder case on that basis either. It's a question of your judgement in the situation and the known facts.'[76]

Asked if he intimidated Kerr during the crisis, Whitlam replies: 'I don't know. Admittedly he was a gutless fellow. But I never threatened Kerr. I believe that Fraser did. Fraser told Kerr that if he didn't sack me the Coalition would attack Kerr in the Parliament and outside it.'[77]

Asked if he would have put in train an approach to the Palace to remove Kerr, Whitlam said no—that he would have asked Kerr instead to put his concerns in writing. 'I was always quite frank with him. He was not frank with me', Whitlam says. 'I don't think it would have suited me to look as if I was sacking the Governor-General.'[78]

Opinions on this issue—and they can only be opinions—differ. Byers, asked if Whitlam would have been prepared to dismiss Kerr, ventured: 'I think so'. John Menadue says: 'I think Gough would have done it'. Whitlam's private secretary John Mant says: 'Occasionally Gough made a joke about removing Kerr, but I don't really believe he would have done this. It's not realistic to think that Gough would contact the Palace during the crisis and recommend that the Governor-General be replaced.'[79]

Bill Hayden says he has 'no idea' what Whitlam would have done—but insists that if he had moved against Kerr 'the public would have reacted strongly against such an action'.[80] Jim McClelland, asked if he thinks Whitlam would have moved against Kerr, says: 'No, I do not . . . I can't see Gough on the phone to the Queen saying, "Sack this bloke". Gough was a great constitutionalist . . . I don't think it was in his nature to do that.'[81] Pressed further McClelland says: 'If Gough was prepared to be this tough then why didn't he just "tough out" the dismissal when it came? Just defy Kerr and reject his letter? Kerr would have gone to water. But Gough was steeped in the niceties of Westminster and he wasn't a revolutionary.'[82]

Asked if Whitlam would have dismissed Kerr, Sir Roden Cutler says: 'I thought it was a possibility and that's why I raised it with Kerr. But my judgement is that he would not do it. I must say that in all my dealings with him I found that Whitlam was honest and direct with me.'[83]

Bob Ellicott, who made a close psychological study of Whitlam as well as Kerr, says:

> Kerr obviously believed that if he did this [called Whitlam in] he'd be sacked. For my own part I doubt that . . . I thought at the time that Whitlam had a messianic approach. I thought he was slightly unbalanced but I had a deep respect for his intellect . . . He knew that

THE SOLUTION

smashing the Senate had an almost revolutionary type of appeal . . . But I always thought that his bark was worse than his bite. You see, when Kerr gave him the letter there was a strange reaction. It wasn't this 'smash the Senate' man at all. He walked away and went back to the Lodge . . . I believe, perhaps contrary to what Kerr believed, that Whitlam would have acted more responsibly than Kerr feared. Now that's not a criticism of Kerr.[84]

An acute analysis of the problem comes from Whitlam's speech writer, Graham Freudenberg, who since 11 November 1975 has probably spent more time discussing the event with Whitlam than anybody else. Freudenberg says:

It never occurred to us that Kerr would dismiss us. So obviously, we did not consider our response to that action. As they say, none so blind as those who will not see.

Kerr's fear of dismissal is really a reflection of his own psychology and insecurity. It is not based on anything that Whitlam would have done. It is outrageous that Kerr should have made his own fate the major factor.

If you asked me to speculate about what we would have done if Kerr had said to Gough some time before 11 November that he was concerned about the situation and wanted fresh advice to resolve the deadlock, then we would have considered our options afresh. My view is that in this situation Whitlam would have told Kerr that he believed the Senate could be brought to vote to either accept or reject the budget and that the Senate would not vote for a rejection. That is, Whitlam would have asked for more time. I don't think his response would have been related to Kerr. It would have been related to the Senate.[85]

My judgement—and it can be no more—is that Whitlam would not have approached the Palace to dismiss Kerr, though he would have been tempted to do so. The reason is that offered by Whitlam himself—it would have made him more unpopular. In fact, there would have been uproar in the country. Whitlam would have been seen as sacking the umpire. It would have doomed the government and blackened his name. The Palace would have delayed. Fraser would have been more determined than ever—and Labor's unity would have been threatened. The British political scientist, Dr David Butler, remarked that 'the howls of indignation, the innuendos of dictatorship would have been overwhelming'.[86] Another problem would have been a split within the cabinet.

Prominent Whitlam minister John Wheeldon says: 'I would have resigned from the cabinet if Whitlam had moved against Kerr. I don't believe for one moment that I would have been the only minister doing this.'87 Sacking the Governor-General would have fractured the government. Ministers such as Wheeldon, Hayden, Wriedt, Frank Stewart and Joe Berinson were the likely candidates to protest or to revolt.

Who would Whitlam have made Governor-General?

He had no candidate in mind. But the question is academic. There would not have been time to approach a nominee, offer the job, receive an acceptance and perform the official swearing-in ceremony before the crisis was resolved. Who would have accepted the post in the climate of November 1975? Presumably the task would have fallen upon the senior Governor, Sir Roden Cutler from New South Wales, who would have become Administrator of the Commonwealth pending the appointment of a new Governor-General.

The political, logistical and practical consequences of trying to sack Kerr would have weakened, not strengthened, Labor's position.

John Kerr's conclusion on the evening of 6 November was that both leaders were holding fast to their positions. His final judgement of Whitlam was that 'if he felt the need the Prime Minister would have me recalled before I could dismiss him', and of Fraser that he 'feared I might not have the strength to do what he believed my duty required, but intended to put me to the test'.88

In political terms Whitlam and Fraser had gone so far that the cost of retreat was extremely high; neither was prepared readily to accept that price. Yet there was a greater imperative at work—each leader believed he would triumph. Each had made this assessment based upon his dialogue with Kerr.

The Governor-General now decided to force an election by dismissing Whitlam under section 64 of the Constitution and commissioning Fraser on a caretaker basis. The task of Fraser as caretaker would be to advise the Governor-General to call a general election. Kerr knew that there were 21 bills that could provide the basis for a double dissolution. He drew the obvious conclusion that Fraser, if commissioned on this basis, would advise a double dissolution on these bills—even though they had been opposed by the Coalition in the Senate.

So Kerr decided upon three courses—to dismiss Whitlam, to commission Fraser and to accept advice from Fraser for a general election.

The Governor-General consults the Chief Justice

The Governor-General, not surprisingly, then sought confirmation of his conclusion. On Sunday 9 November Kerr decided to consult the Chief Justice, Sir Garfield Barwick. He said this was a 'natural' decision; yet it was a contentious move.

Whitlam insists that he had told Kerr not to consult Barwick during the crisis, a point Kerr disputed. However, since Kerr was about to dismiss Whitlam, he did not feel bound by any Prime Ministerial instruction. As Kerr explained: 'It is only on those rare but real occasions when he [the Governor-General] can act constitutionally contrary to the Prime Minister's advice, the extreme example of which is dismissal of a Prime Minister and his Government, that he is entitled to such consultation if he feels the need for it and, in my opinion, on a matter of such great importance he can go where he believes he will get the best help.'[89]

Kerr noted that Hasluck, in his William Queale Lecture, had sanctioned a Governor-General's seeking advice from the Chief Justice, particularly if he had doubts about the advice being tendered by a Prime Minister. Kerr said later: 'The Prime Minister has no power and no right to control my decision as to whom I, as Governor-General, would consult in considering the exercise of the reserve powers.'[90]

Whitlam said later that Kerr had been 'quite shattered' by the High Court's judgements in the *Petroleum and Minerals Authority Case* because the Court reviewed decisions taken by the Governor-General Sir Paul Hasluck.[91] 'That is why he wanted to tie in Barwick', Whitlam says.[92] Perhaps.

Presumably Kerr wanted to lock in Barwick and the High Court anyway. His discussion with Barwick in September is the giveaway. Kerr had decided from the start that any use of the vice-regal powers would be backed by Barwick in a constitutional sense. Now it was time to close the circle.

Barwick had firm views about the crisis; they were similar to Kerr's. Barwick said later:

> I concluded that whilst the Prime Minister came under an obligation to resign or advise a dissolution when the Senate had failed to pass the Appropriation Bills, the Governor-General was under no obligation to act until he was satisfied that the Prime Minister could not secure Supply or perhaps until he concluded that the risk of the consequences of an ultimate failure of Supply could no longer be taken.[93]

Barwick also says that during the crisis he assessed the propriety of the Chief Justice's advising the Governor-General—which suggests that he expected, sooner or later, that he would be involved. Kerr had asked him in September whether he would be able to offer advice and he had left the door open.[94]

Barwick now concluded that:

> ... if the matter on which advice was sought was not a justiciable matter, the advice given would in reality *not* be advice given in a

judicial capacity. It would rank no higher than personal advice though undoubtedly, because of the office of Chief Justice, it might appear to carry more weight and even to be the likelier to be correct . . . To give such advice to the representative of the Crown at his request did not seem to me to compromise the independence of the Chief Justice, including his independence of the Executive, or that of the Judiciary nor, to any reasonable and informed person, should it appear to do so.[95]

But Barwick had also decided that if he were asked to give advice on a justiciable question—one that could be answered before the High Court—then 'I would decline to give it'.[96]

Barwick was aware, he says, of how 'party political elements' could misrepresent such involvement. This meant that the safe course 'would be to do nothing—to refuse to advise the Governor-General on a non-justiciable question'. Barwick says that if 'personal comfort' were the sole measure used then the safe option would be taken. But the safe option was not for Barwick. He declares: 'To my mind, such a course would only be attractive to craven spirits, persons too timid and too self-protective to exhibit any spirit. For my own part, I became convinced that I ought to give such advice if it were sought. I believed that both my office and my own reputation would more than survive any unreasonable and partisan assault.'[97]

These words suggest that Barwick was eager to be consulted; they are redolent of a Chief Justice keen to be an influence in this historic contest.

On the Sunday evening Kerr rang Barwick at his Sydney home. He said that he had come to certain conclusions but did not state them. Kerr asked whether Barwick was prepared to advise him constitutionally on what he had in mind. It was arranged that Barwick would call on Kerr at Admiralty House the following morning. This was the first talk between the two men during the crisis.[98]

That night Barwick again turned over in his mind the propriety of advising the Governor-General. He would have realised that Kerr was planning a dismissal. Barwick says he assessed the likely denigration of him stemming from such action, but decided to proceed. He probably found Kerr's invitation irresistible.

The next morning when they met at Admiralty House Kerr briefed Barwick on the parliamentary situation. He told Barwick that his intention was to secure a general election through dismissing Whitlam and commissioning Fraser with the latter recommending a general election. He wanted to know whether Barwick could advise on whether this was a course constitutionally open to the Governor-General. That is, Kerr was seeking advice only on whether he had the constitutional power for his proposed action. In short, Kerr wanted the legal support of the Chief Justice before he acted. This would strengthen Kerr's position given the controversy that the dismissal would inevitably arouse.[99]

Barwick told Kerr that he was able to advise him. Barwick felt that Kerr 'was really asking me whether, in the circumstances he had outlined, he could lawfully withdraw a Prime Minister's commission. That was *not* a question which a court could decide as it did not involve a justiciable matter'. Barwick specified two conditions—that his call at Admiralty House be notified in the daily vice-regal list and that his advice be exclusively in writing to avoid any misunderstandings. Kerr accepted both points.[100]

Barwick was in court that day from 10.15 am. He agreed to return to lunch with Kerr to outline his advice. Barwick prepared a draft of his advice over the next couple of hours and brought the draft to lunch. He told Kerr that he would answer his question in the affirmative. But Barwick was not completely satisfied with his draft. He returned to his chambers and then to the bench for the afternoon session. Kerr had told Barwick that he wanted the advice that day. Barwick signed his letter in the afternoon and it was delivered by car to Admiralty House before Kerr left for Canberra and an appointment with destiny.[101]

The crucial part of the letter said:

> . . . the Senate has constitutional power to refuse to pass a money bill; it has power to refuse supply to the government of the day. Secondly, a Prime Minister who cannot ensure supply to the Crown, including funds for carrying on the ordinary services of government, must either advise a general election (of a kind which the constitutional situation may then allow) or resign. If, being unable to secure supply, he refuses to take either course, Your Excellency has constitutional authority to withdraw his Commission as Prime Minister.

Barwick explained that there was 'no analogy' with the United Kingdom parliament. In Great Britain a government with the confidence of the House of Commons can secure Supply despite a recalcitrant House of Lords; in Australia a government having the confidence of the House of Representatives but not that of the Senate cannot secure Supply. In short, Barwick argued that 'there is an analogy between the situation of a Prime Minister who has lost the confidence of the House of Commons and a Prime Minister who does not have the confidence of the Parliament, ie, of the House of Representatives and of the Senate'. Once the Prime Minister 'ceases to retain his commission' the Governor-General's 'authority and duty would be to invite the Leader of the Opposition, *if he can undertake to secure supply* [author's emphasis], to form a caretaker government . . . pending a general election'.[102]

So Kerr returned to Canberra with the complete backing of the Chief Justice for his plans.

Barwick was operating in a personal capacity. He pointed out later that the advice he gave related to the Governor-General's authority to dismiss and appoint ministers and that this issue 'could not have been answered by the Court in a litigation brought with respect to it'. That is, 'no court has decided who should be the Crown's adviser'. This non-justiciable matter was separate from the justiciable issue—which had already come before the High Court—of whether, in certain circumstances, the conditions had been met under section 57 for a double dissolution.[103]

However, Barwick's intervention was criticised later by many analysts. They argued that Barwick was compromising his judicial independence from the Executive as well as the independent standing of the High Court. The Chief Justice was giving advice in a situation where the Governor-General did not have the consent of the Prime Minister; indeed, Whitlam said that such consent was refused. As Geoffrey Sawer noted, the Chief Justice was a former senior Coalition minister and a relation of Bob Ellicott who had produced a legal opinion for Fraser favouring dismissal, facts that would further compromise Barwick's opinion in the eyes of many people. The High Court did not give advisory opinions but Barwick was prepared to give a personal opinion on the dismissal question. Finally, Sawer claimed the issue could have come before the High Court if Fraser had failed to obtain Supply as caretaker Prime Minister and, in this situation, Whitlam made resort to the High Court.[104]

Kerr rejected any suggestion that his dismissal of Whitlam could have been reviewed by the High Court: 'It is not open to any court to tell the Governor-General that he has made a mistake in dismissing the Prime Minister. If he has made a mistake the votes of the people will tell him . . .'[105] This is a fundamental point and Kerr and Barwick are surely correct—the High Court would not intervene where the Governor-General was exercising a discretion in relation to the Prime Minister's commission. Barwick explained later that bringing a question before the High Court did not imply it was justiciable—the test was whether it was in the Court's jurisdiction to decide.[106] Kerr's concern to lock in the High Court was profound. Barwick was not the only High Court judge to whom Kerr spoke. Kerr was a personal friend of Anthony Mason, a former Solicitor-General who had been appointed to the bench by the McMahon Government in 1972 and was later appointed Chief Justice by the Hawke Government. Gerard Henderson reports that Kerr informed him that he consulted directly with Mason prior to the dismissal.[107] Separately and in addition, Kerr sought to lock in Mason to Barwick's opinion. Barwick tells the story:

> I received a telephone call from Sir John Kerr. He acknowledged receipt of my letter and he then said that he was curious to know what former Solicitors-General would have thought of the matter. He said he knew what one of them, Robert Ellicott, thought because he had publicly stated his views. But he would like to know what the other retired Solicitor-General, Sir Anthony Mason, thought. He asked me would I mind asking him. I said I did not mind doing that and after I had concluded the conversation I went downstairs to Sir Anthony's chambers ... I told him what had occurred and I told him the substance of my letter ... He said he quite agreed with the view I had expressed and I may say he did so without any reluctance. I returned to my chambers and phoned Sir John and informed him of what had passed between Sir Anthony and myself.[108]

According to Bob Ellicott: 'Mason and Kerr were close in the early days. Kerr would have deeply respected Mason's viewpoint.'[109] The story of Mason's involvement was a secret for nearly twenty years—until revealed by Barwick in a 1994 interview on the ABC. Barwick was unimpressed by Kerr's request: 'Tony [Mason] said that my advice was right. And that to me was a great sign of weakness in him [Kerr]. That he wanted to be reassured by someone who was friendly with him; that he wouldn't have regarded me exactly as a friend.'[110]

In his memoirs Kerr referred to his direct consultation with Mason—but did not name him. He said: 'My solitude was tempered by conversation with one person only other than the Chief Justice.' Kerr said that this person—presumably Mason—'sustained me in my own thinking as to the imperatives within which I had to act'.[111]

That Mason, at Kerr's request and through Barwick, approved Barwick's advice offers only one interpretation—that Mason also endorsed Kerr's plans. This must be the position until Mason makes a qualifying public statement on the affair; Mason's full role will not be clear until this occurs.[112]

So Kerr had made significant progress in enlisting the High Court on his behalf—he had the Chief Justice and another, future, Chief Justice. Did he consult further High Court judges, notably Sir Ninian Stephen, a future Governor-General? Stephen rejects this notion: 'The whole thing [the dismissal] came as a complete surprise to me. I have no recollection of being consulted. I think I am quite clear in my own mind that I knew nothing until the news broke publicly.'[113]

Barwick provides different interpretations on whether he influenced Kerr's decision:

> KELLY: When he [Kerr] contacted you do you think his mind was completely made up or do you think you influenced his final decision?
>
> BARWICK: No. I don't think I had any part in that. I think he had made up his mind by that time . . .
>
> KELLY: If it had no influence why did Kerr seek the opinion?
>
> BARWICK: Simply because that was the nature of the man—wanting to gather opinions.
>
> KELLY: But yours was more than an opinion. You suggested to him it was the proper course and he had a duty to take that course?
>
> BARWICK: I wrote that.
>
> KELLY: So you were strengthening his resolve in that letter?
>
> BARWICK: If you like, yes.
>
> KELLY: Did you feel the need to strengthen his resolve?
>
> BARWICK: No. He'd made up his mind. He tried to avoid making up his mind but he had made up his mind . . .
>
> . . . if you think that I actively entered into any conversation with Kerr to encourage him to do what he had to do, I think you'd be wrong.
>
> KELLY: Were your views coloured by your dislike of Whitlam?
>
> BARWICK: No, I don't dislike Whitlam . . . the trouble with [Whitlam] was he'd have taken the rest of us down with him. You don't realise what the situation would have been if Gough had not been displaced. We'd have had chaos, public servants unpaid, bills unpaid, absolutely terrifying.[114]

Reassurance was Kerr's motive—this was certainly Barwick's belief. He says: 'Kerr's trouble was that he had, I think, distinct Labor sympathies and he wanted to delay the matter in the hope that the cup would pass from him. That was my thought—not that he was weak but that he was tempted to temporise.'[115] In an earlier interview with Gerard Henderson, Barwick declared that 'anyone who thought that I stiffened him wouldn't be wrong'.[116]

The fact is that Barwick's letter went beyond advising Kerr that he had the constitutional authority to dismiss Whitlam. Barwick asserted that Kerr had a duty. He was trying to put the steel into Kerr; he wanted to ensure that Kerr didn't weaken. Clyde Cameron who spent dozens of hours with Barwick recording oral history tapes for the National Library says that Barwick told a colleague in early October

1975 that 'Kerr should sack Whitlam but doesn't have the guts to do it'.[117]

In his 1995 memoirs Barwick offers a more personal insight into his views:

> It has been said that the Whitlam ministry was 'toughing it out'. This was in order to put pressure on the Senators so that at least a significant number of them would defect . . . Brinkmanship of this kind might be accepted in the factional infighting in a political or industrial group, but to my mind not in an assembly of honourable representatives of the people . . . it may be that Sir John delayed too long in taking action. I incline to the view that he ought to have acted, at the latest, by 25 October. I think this because by the delay after that date the Prime Minister had a party-political advantage enabling him to indulge in brinkmanship to coerce some, no doubt the weaker, of the Senators.[118]

It was not Barwick's decision. It was Kerr's. Kerr used Barwick to fortify and to assist him to justify a decision already reached. Kerr would have known Barwick's advice without asking. He wanted to lock in the Chief Justice and to recruit Barwick's skill as an advocate to justify his decision. Anne Kerr downplays the influence of Barwick: 'John had made up his mind as to what he had to do and wished only for formal confirmation from the Chief Justice as to his power to do it.'[119]

Bob Ellicott says: 'Barwick gave Kerr comfort. It wasn't the thing that triggered the dismissal.'[120] It is, however, a telling fact that Kerr's statement of explanation for the dismissal followed Barwick's opinion almost to the letter. The intellectual justification for the dismissal was a joint Kerr–Barwick case.

For twenty years the ALP has argued that Kerr had no right to consult Barwick. The fact, however, is that given the magnitude of the decision Kerr had reached—resort to the reserve powers to dismiss the Prime Minister—there can be no decisive argument against his consultation with the supreme judicial figure. In such an extreme circumstance the Crown must possess the right to such consultation. If the Crown possesses the discretions involved in the reserve powers then, clearly, the Governor-General can seek an opinion from the Chief Justice. Of course, there are risks in this process, notably to the standing of the High Court, and a Chief Justice must carefully consider any such request from a Governor-General. Propriety suggests that a Governor-General would inform a prime minister of an intention to consult the Chief Justice.

There is no evidence of a conspiracy involving Barwick and the Opposition via Ellicott—contrary to Whitlam's later claim. Kerr and

Barwick say they did not speak to each other during the crisis until 9 November. Nor did either man speak to Ellicott, a point confirmed by Ellicott. Of course, Fraser spoke to Kerr at length. During the crisis and afterwards Whitlam seemed unable to accept that it was Fraser who outsmarted him. It was Fraser who read Kerr correctly and Whitlam who misread him.

Whitlam, unable to accept psychologically the blame for his 1975 blunder with Kerr, has sought for twenty years to find scapegoats. One of the most celebrated is Anne Kerr. In Whitlam's mind she is the dark force who intervenes between Whitlam's appointment of Kerr and Kerr's dismissal of Whitlam; she is the Lady Macbeth who brings Kerr to the act of constitutional murder—thereby corrupting a decent and compliant man. Whitlam still insists twenty years later that Kerr's second wife 'is as much to blame as Kerr'.[121] Jim McClelland echoes this view: 'I knew Kerr's first wife Peg very well. Peg really controlled him. I don't believe she would have let him sack Gough. If she'd been around Peg would have said, "Don't you think you should mention this to Gough?"'[122]

It is tempting to conclude that Whitlam still underestimates Kerr; despite the sacking he cannot grasp that it was Kerr's own decision—not Barwick's or Ellicott's or his wife's. Anne Kerr says:

> I am not a political animal. I did not ever think in terms of influencing John. Certainly I felt no wish or impulse to do so. My role as his wife was in my view to support him. He was a man who made up his own mind—a powerful mind, well capable of making its own decisions. To claim that I was some kind of Lady Macbeth in the background manipulating John is utterly ludicrous. I am certainly astounded to learn that Whitlam believed I had some such role and actually blames me for his dismissal. I was, however, aware that Margaret Whitlam had attacked me bitterly on the same implausible grounds. When I learned that I felt rather disgusted and let down.[123]

Bob Ellicott says that Anne Kerr 'is a person of strong views' and that while 'she gave support to John, she's not a dictator'.[124] While the decision was Kerr's the question, however, must remain open whether its atmospherics or style were influenced by his wife who was not a political person but had very strong views about people.

Anne Kerr says that her husband told her on Sunday 9 November of his plan to dismiss Whitlam.

By this stage the Senate had deferred the Appropriation bills three times. Kerr discerned correctly that both leaders were 'staking all on winning the vital game'. The pressures on both now intensified.

THE SOLUTION

Fraser remained astute until the end. On Sunday 9 November he was still anxious to depict himself as searching for a reasoned compromise. That afternoon he announced he was willing to meet Whitlam to discuss a solution based upon a House of Representatives election. But Fraser got a surprise: Whitlam accepted. The Prime Minister was now ready to play another card—a half Senate election.

Whitlam had virtually settled on the Senate election option the previous Thursday, 6 November. Now he decided to accept Fraser's offer of a meeting and use the Senate poll as a lever to try to extract a backdown from Fraser. But Whitlam had no hope; he did not grasp the confidence within the upper ranks of the Coalition. Whitlam released a statement saying that he would be willing to meet Fraser, Anthony and Lynch at 9 am on 11 November before the regular party meetings.

Unbeknown to Labor, the Opposition had obtained another legal opinion which further fortified its leadership. The opinion was prepared for the Sydney firm Freehill, Hollingdale and Page by Keith Aickin QC, later to become a High Court judge, Murray Gleeson QC from the Sydney Bar and Professor Pat Lane from the University of Sydney. The opinion considered a situation where the government was denied Supply and was not prepared to advise an election. It said:

> There is precedent to support the view that in such a case it would be within the power of the Governor-General to dismiss his ministers and to seek the advice of other ministers if it is available . . . For a Governor-General to dismiss ministers who command the support of a majority from the House of Representatives has such serious implications that one would normally say that it would only be likely to occur in a case where the Governor-General is satisfied that the majority in the House of Representatives did not also represent a majority in the electorate . . . Nevertheless, the power is there . . . It is possible to envisage a situation where the basis of the dissolution was not the opinion of the Governor-General that the electorate would not support the majority in the lower house, but rather that the parliamentary situation had become such that it ought to be resolved by the electorate.[125]

In his own intervention, Kerr acted on the belief that he could put the issue before the people, rather than making an assumption about the electorate. It is not known whether Kerr read this opinion before the dismissal; but certainly Malcolm Fraser had.

Kerr's timing

Two moods pervaded the Coalition parties—confidence within the leadership and alarm within the ranks. The face that Kerr saw was the leadership. Fraser had convinced him about the Coalition's solidarity.

Doug Anthony says: 'I felt throughout the crisis that we would prevail and I was very determined that Malcolm should continue to hang in.'[126] Bob Ellicott told a Liberal Party gathering in Sydney on the evening of Monday 10 November that he believed the Governor-General would intervene 'in the next day or two', saying 'I've known him for a long time'. Ellicott's prediction proved to be highly accurate.[127]

But apprehension within the ranks of the Coalition parliamentary parties led to widespread speculation that Fraser would have to retreat. These members and Senators were privy to none of the close dialogue between Whitlam, Fraser and Kerr that constitutes the bulk of this book. They were influenced by the opinion polls which revealed that the deferral of the budget was a negative for the Coalition. They saw that Whitlam had rallied party and community support on the platform of democracy and justice, and that the media was critical of their position; they feared the consequences when Supply was exhausted and that the Coalition would suffer the blame. This mood was described in my 1976 account of the crisis:

> In the Opposition lobbies frontbench Liberals were openly dissociating themselves from Fraser's course of action. The overwhelming majority of Liberal members and Senators believed that the Opposition would have to back down and accept a compromise. A number of Fraser's closest supporters on the backbench were already trying to assess the extent to which his leadership would be undermined by a defeat.[128]

Did Kerr believe the Opposition would hold? He says:

> As to Mr Fraser, the Opposition and the Senate, some people claim that there might have been weakening on their side, but the meeting of 1–2 November in my view had provided a firm top-level policy decision. Responsibility for it was widely spread in the councils of the Opposition parties. If there was any possibility of defection I could not know of it and I had to deal with realities as I could best assess them.[129]

This statement reveals the impact that the Coalition summit meeting in Melbourne had upon Kerr as a show of solidarity. So impressed was Kerr that he later ventured: 'For anyone on the Coalition side to go against what this phalanx of Coalition leaders had determined would undoubtedly be political suicide . . . Not once, not twice, but three times they had denied Supply. I had to accept this as their political decision.'[130]

But Kerr's statement leads directly to one of the central disputes concerning the dismissal—his timing.

Jim McClelland says: 'I have the clearest possible recollection of Kerr saying to me in the early days of the crisis that he was not obliged

THE SOLUTION

to do anything about it until the money actually ran out.' McClelland passed this message to Whitlam.[131]

Kerr deliberately chose to dismiss Whitlam *before* Supply started to expire. The constitutional situation on 11 November was no different from that of 16 October—the Senate was deferring the Appropriation bills and the Commonwealth Government, short of a solution, would soon be unable to meet its obligations. It was a political crisis on 16 October and it remained a political crisis on 11 November. The Senate had denied Supply. The government would have no funds from near the end of November. Kerr had to intervene if Supply was exhausted or if Whitlam acted illegally—but this possibility was still a fortnight away.

There were two factors that determined the timing of the dismissal: (1) that if a general election were to be conducted before Christmas that election had to be called by 11 November due to administrative factors; and (2) that the Senate had held fast since 16 October and Kerr had decided that Whitlam could not obtain Supply.

Both assumptions need careful evaluation.

Kerr's Official Secretary, David Smith, had spoken to the Chief Electoral Officer, Frank Ley, and the Governor-General knew that 11 November was the deadline for a pre-Christmas election. In his statement on the dismissal Kerr said the deadlock needed to be resolved 'as promptly as possible'. In fact, he had waited 27 days.

A decision to procure a pre-Christmas election by Whitlam's dismissal meant that a great constitutional event was being staged at this time merely to fit Australia's social and recreational calendar or, to quote Whitlam, to avoid 'disturbing the great Australian summer torpor!'

Supply would be passed the day Whitlam was dismissed or Fraser cracked or a compromise was struck. The only difference between a solution in mid-November and one in late November is that the former would produce an election before Christmas and the latter an election in the New Year. The actual date of the election was quite unrelated to the passage of Supply. Supply would be passed as soon as an election was agreed upon; this would be an election condition. The notion that Whitlam was dismissed on 11 November merely to secure a pre-Christmas poll was branded by Geoffrey Sawer as a 'trivial' reason for the taking of such a momentous decision.[132]

The defect in using 11 November as the deadline was that Whitlam still had Supply for another fortnight. In his determination to secure a pre-Christmas election Kerr was dismissing a government that was still able to meet all its financial obligations.

Kerr's second consideration was contained in his statement on the dismissal: 'The decisions I have made were made after I was satisfied that Mr Whitlam could not obtain Supply.'[133]

Kerr *had* to be satisfied. Barwick had made this clear in his advice. The Barwick letter said: 'my opinion is that, if Your Excellency is *satisfied* in the current situation that the present Government is unable to secure Supply, the course upon which Your Excellency has determined is consistent with your constitutional authority and duty.'[134]

But how could Kerr be satisfied? How could he be sure that a solution would not emerge over the next fortnight?

In justifying his decision not to wait any longer Kerr says:

> It has been claimed that such a consideration should not have prevented me from waiting one week—perhaps two weeks—before acting, in the hope that some solution would thus have had time to manifest itself. On what grounds could I have entertained such a hope? Speculation about the possibility of the Senate breaking was fruitless.[135]

The problem here is Kerr's 'onus of proof'. It was his responsibility to explore all avenues for a political settlement before the resort to a constitutional solution. The question is not 'on what grounds' could Kerr have entertained a hope for a political settlement; it was on what grounds could he rule out a political solution over the next fortnight? The fact, of course, is that a political solution could not be ruled out. There was only one person who ruled it out—John Kerr.

The weakness of Kerr's defence on timing is betrayed by the hyperbole of his language: 'To time my action differently would in my view have been to wait until the country was over the edge of the precipice.'[136]

This is not the case. The 'precipice' was the exhaustion of funds and that was still a fortnight away.

The Senate had held for nearly four weeks but *nobody* knew whether it could hold for another day, a week or a fortnight. At that time 24 hours, let alone two weeks, was a long time. How could Kerr be 'satisfied' that Whitlam could not secure Supply? According to Barwick, Kerr 'had to use his own judgement on the facts as he knew them'. Ellicott agrees: 'The discretion of when to act and how to act in exercising the Reserve Powers is a matter for the Governor-General. It is difficult or presumptuous for anybody else to make that judgement.'[137]

Fraser told Kerr that the Senate would hold; Whitlam told him that the Senate would crack. Kerr accepted Fraser's judgement and rejected Whitlam's.

THE SOLUTION

A balanced assessment is that there was at least as much evidence that the Senate would crack as that it would hold. The one certainty is that the immediate future was unpredictable. Kerr's implication that there were no grounds for a political solution is inconsistent with the volatile mood of the time. Kerr says that because the Senate had denied Supply three times he had to accept this 'as their decision'. Yet many Coalition figures did not accept this as the 'final' decision and expected a backdown.

In Kerr's 1978 memoirs he gives considerable weight to another factor in the timing of the dismissal—the threat of illegality. He says:

> If I did not act, very great suffering on a nation-wide scale would follow. I was not prepared to gamble with the future of the Constitution, the economy, and the financial security of very great numbers of people, indeed directly and indirectly the whole nation. I did not believe that I had to wait until this suffering and these illegalities occurred. I conceived it to be within my discretion to take action in time to avoid them. I was not prepared to delay until after the disaster came to pass in order to get a watertight ground for action based upon visible chaos. The price to the community would be too great.[138]

It is, at first glance, a powerful argument. But it is a justification for dismissing a government because it might commit illegalities. Kerr propounds, in fact, a theory of preventative intervention: a government can be dismissed because it might break the law or threatens to break the law. This, despite formal advice that the proposed alternative arrangements were constitutional. It is not surprising that Kerr did not offer this as a reason for the dismissal in his formal statement of 11 November. It was introduced into the argument later and its status appears to be polemical not constitutional.

There is a final confusion in Kerr's defence of his timing—the claim that it was Whitlam, not Kerr, who determined the timing.

In his interviews with *The Bulletin* in 1985 Kerr elevated this as a new factor in determining his timing:

> The moment for action was chosen by Mr Whitlam himself, when he said on November 11 that he would seek a half Senate election at what he conceded was the last practicable time for any election in 1975 . . . Mr Whitlam's foreshadowed advice was no solution to the crisis. I could not have accepted it. Mr Whitlam made November 11 the day for decision. He chose the date of his dismissal himself.[139]

The implication is that Kerr would not have dismissed Whitlam on 11 November if the Prime Minister had not sought a Senate election. A close confidant of Kerr says: 'If Whitlam had not sought the Senate poll on 11 November there would have been no dismissal that day. That is, Whitlam would have had more time.'[140]

But these comments are inconsistent with Kerr's own earlier account in his memoirs. When on 10 November he was contemplating his plans for the next day Kerr says: 'I thought it likely that Mr Whitlam would come to see me on Tuesday to report the result of the morning's meeting and to advise a half Senate election. If he were not to come of his own accord I should, on the worst view of it, have to send for him.'[141]

So Kerr was going to sack Whitlam on 11 November whether or not he advised a Senate poll.

Would the Senate have cracked?

The question of how much longer the Senate would have held is, by definition, a speculative debate. But this is central to Kerr's intervention since he reached a judgement on this question.

Reg Withers, in an interview with me for the tenth anniversary of the dismissal, conceded that the Senate might have broken the next day—12 November.

> For all I know, my blokes might have collapsed on the 12th. I don't know. You'd just hope day after day you'd get through until the adjournment . . . There were two Senators who told me they were prepared to go . . . I reckon we had another week. If I had got through that week then you'd look at the following week. I would have lost them sometime about November 20 onwards. I know I would have lost them in the run-up to November 30 but it wouldn't have been two then, it would have been ten.[142]

Interviewed for the twentieth anniversary and asked whether the Senate would have cracked, Withers replied:

> I don't know for sure. I was living from day to day. That's how we operated. It was very close and very tight. It's hard to say how much longer we could have held . . . A number of Senators were pretty terrified. The pressure on them was immense. It was also on their wives with calls to their homes. Labor had targeted the weak links.[143]

But Withers is open about the internal pressure on the Senators to hold firm: 'If some people didn't have the guts to go on and wanted to cross the floor and chicken out . . . it would be on their head and they would bear the mark. I'll tell you this, they'd be expelled from the Liberal Party.'[144] Withers' political aide and former journalist, Russell Schneider, says: 'My personal view is that another 24 hours and the bills would have been passed.'[145]

The assessment of the late Sir Philip Lynch, deputy Liberal leader, was that 'we will never know if our Senate numbers would have held until the end of the week'.[146] Fraser's confidant from those days, Tony Staley, asked whether the Senate would have soon broken, replies: 'I just don't know. I can't assert that people would have held.'[147]

Country Party leader, Doug Anthony—one of the 'hard men' of the 1975 crisis—says: 'They certainly wouldn't have held for another week. I think that some of the Senators wouldn't have lasted for much longer. But then again, Supply wouldn't last much longer either. The important thing is that our Senators gave no public indication that they would give it away.'[148]

There is an honesty about the assessments of senior figures like Withers, Staley, Lynch and Anthony. They illuminate the sheer unpredictability of the situation. They also reveal the defects in Kerr's stance. Kerr was sufficiently satisfied of the Senate's solidarity that he used the reserve powers—yet three of the four senior Coalition leaders—Anthony, Lynch and Withers—cannot testify that the Senate would have held out for another week. It is clear that the Coalition, in particular Malcolm Fraser, had persuaded Kerr to a greater confidence in the Senate's solidarity than actually existed. That is a tribute to Fraser's political skill.

Two former Liberal Senators interviewed for this book—Neville Bonner and Don Jessop—state that they were ready to cross the floor. Bonner says:

> I wasn't prepared to continue blocking the budget and I was going to cross the floor. I had gone to Fraser and told him about my worries and that I couldn't support the position any more. What happened, in fact, is that Kerr beat me by a few hours.
>
> I had support from the late Eric Bessell and the late Alan Missen. We'd stayed in touch with each other during the crisis. Whether the three of us would have moved at exactly the same time I can't say. But I was going to cross the floor and I think that they would have joined me.
>
> I spoke to Fraser about my concerns. I explained to him my fears about what was happening. Unless the budget was passed then social security payments, pensions payments and all sorts of payments would not be made. The country was facing chaos. There could be riots in the streets, blood in the streets.
>
> Of course, Kerr didn't know that there were people in the Opposition prepared to cross the floor. There was no way he could have that information. I was certainly going to cross the floor the next day. I was under pressure from my own conscience. You don't vote against your own party without a lot of thought and heartburn and I had gone through that. I'd gone through hell on this issue.[149]

In 1985, too, Bonner told me of his discussion with Fraser. His version then was that he told Fraser his doubts but not that he intended to cross the floor.[150]

Don Jessop says:

> I had felt strongly enough about the issue to speak against it in the party room at the start. Frankly, I had great worries when the Opposition moved to block Supply in 1974. I was determined that if they tried to do it again then I would resist it. On Sunday 9 November I rang Malcolm Fraser. I said to him: 'I just want to tell you, Malcolm, that I have conducted my own poll with twenty or thirty people and I can only find one or so in favour of our position. I want to tell you that I think you should present firm evidence to me next week showing that the government is behaving illegally, and if you are unable to do this you should pass Supply.' Malcolm then said to me: 'I think you'll find that everything will be alright within a few days time.' I left the situation there. But my position was quite clear. I would have crossed the floor and voted for Supply if the events of 11 November had not occurred. I believe that there were a number of Senators with reservations and that others may well have done the same.[151]

Fraser rejects the comments of Bonner and Jessop. He says:

> They did not inform me along those lines. In both cases their remarks are categorically incorrect. Nobody at any stage told me they were going to defect. The point is that several people were worried and we all knew that. But if anybody had told me that they intended to defect then that would habe been a serious matter and I would remember— but nobody told me.[152]

For the tenth anniversary of the dismissal I interviewed Senator Alan Missen—the man most critical of the decision in mid-October. Missen said:

> If it hadn't been resolved then, that day, then the whole thing would have crumbled. Many Senators were panic-stricken, even those who had once been gung-ho. At morning tea on November 11 I spoke with two Liberals who were to become senior ministers in the Fraser cabinet and they were concerned that the public would no longer tolerate it. They wanted to find a way out. This view was common at that time.

Missen told me that his position was to work for a change in the Opposition stance rather than resort to unilateral action.[153]

Missen's widow, Mollie, interviewed for this book, says: 'Alan believed that the tactics of the Opposition . . . were dangerous, opportunistic and cynical . . . In the final week Alan spoke to me about the growing unease among the Opposition's Senators.' She reports that

THE SOLUTION

Missen was optimistic towards the end that Fraser would pass the budget.[154]

Fraser remained confident that Missen would stay loyal. He says now: 'Missen came to see me after the decision was taken. He said, "As you know, I don't like it. But you should know that you don't have to worry about me. There may be others that you do have to worry about. But I will stick with the decision."' Fraser concedes that Don Jessop was a 'weak reed'—but says that Jessop could be brought into line by reference to South Australian opinion, a Fraser code for pressure tactics. Asked whether there were any other Senators about whom he'd been worried, Fraser is tightlipped: 'Look, there were people you'd have to watch, for God's sake, probably three or four. You'd have somebody watching them all the damn time. But it's just team management, that's all.'[155]

Withers says:

> Missen and Jessop were always worries. They were both loose cannons. Missen had campaigned against Menzies in 1951. It's people who have gone against the party in the past that you worry about. Jessop was certainly wobbly. I don't think Condor Laucke would have gone. He was under pressure and he thought we were wrong. But Harold Young, another South Australian, was helping me to keep South Australia in line. Frankly, I didn't know that Neville Bonner was so shaky.[156]

Phil Lynch once reflected: 'It was my job to hold Missen and Bonner and others in line and I did it, but it was not easy. Fortunately, I understood the arguments on both sides. I felt a bit each way myself.'[157] Ian Macphee reports: 'On the very day Kerr acted, many Liberal members and Senators were becoming very uneasy about the deadlock and in another week or so Fraser may have had to find a face-saving backdown.'[158]

The most penetrating perspective comes from Margaret Guilfoyle and Kathy Sullivan, Liberal Senators at the time. Guilfoyle says: 'It was very difficult for Reg Withers. Any speculation about how much longer it could have held is really just speculation. Withers held them long enough for Kerr to be satisfied and that's what mattered.'[159]

Sullivan reports:

> I was deputy whip to Fred Chaney and my job was to monitor opinion the whole time. The place was filled with incredible rumours on a daily basis and towards the end everyone was very tired. Missen and Jessop were always problems. But my view is that people weren't game to act as one or two. They wanted safety in numbers before they went against the tide. Towards the end there was great concern about pensions. Neville Bonner was very agitated about pensions being cut and

he refused to accept assurances from any of us. I think he tracked down Malcolm to try to get an assurance. If Whitlam had allowed things to get to the stage where pensions were affected then everything would have collapsed. As I recollect, Eric Bessell and John Marriott had concerns on constitutional issues. But asking me how long the Senate would have held is a false question. The fact is that the Senate held long enough.[160]

In 1978 Withers first told me that, at the swearing-in ceremony on 12 November for the Fraser Government ministers, Kerr said to some of them: 'I had to do it. It was obvious that you fellas weren't going to crack'—a remark that prompted Guilfoyle to observe in an aside 'if only he knew' or 'we could tell him something else'. I wrote a version of this story in 1985 after re-checking with Withers. Guilfoyle told me at that time: 'If I did make any comment it would have been referring to Withers' difficulties in holding together such a precarious margin.'[154]

Asked about his technique for holding people, Withers says: 'It was peer group pressure. Whenever I heard about a potential waverer I'd send out his closest mate to talk. Also, we had some people who were great strengths—Ivor Greenwood, Harold Young, Margaret Guilfoyle and Kathy Martin [now Sullivan]. The Country Party was never in doubt.'[162] But Withers says that if the crisis had continued beyond 20 November towards 30 November then Opposition Senators 'would have melted away like snow in the desert'.[163]

His successor as Liberal Senate leader, Sir John Carrick, disagrees. Carrick highlights the contrary case—if the Senate had held for nearly four weeks then why could it not continue to hold? Carrick says: 'There was no falling away. I'm aware of the names mentioned as waverers. It would be dishonest if I said everybody had a lack of doubt. But my firm view is that they would have held together . . . the fact that we had persisted for so long suggests how determined we were.'[164]

What is the conclusion to be drawn from these comments from the Coalition side? If the remarks of Bonner and Jessop are accepted then Whitlam was only a day from the greatest victory of his career when Kerr dismissed him.

Some might still conclude that the Senate may have held; others that it would have broken. The real point, of course, is that Whitlam needed more time to prevail; Fraser won because Kerr intervened when he did. This was Whitlam's tactical failure and Fraser's tactical triumph. Whitlam failed to persuade Kerr to give him more time; Fraser persuaded Kerr to close off the issue on 11 November. Kerr chose the timing Fraser wanted. Kerr listened to the Opposition leader, not the Prime Minister.

This means that Whitlam squandered his greatest advantage. The key to securing more time for Whitlam was to build a trusting relationship with Kerr. Yet he hardly even tried. Whitlam did not grasp the need to win Kerr's trust. He was guilty of a double failure—to manage Kerr as a man or advise him with skill as a Prime Minister.

On 16 October Whitlam should have provided Kerr with written legal advice (which he never did) that the Representatives were not obliged to go to an election at the behest of the Senate, and should have gone to Yarralumla for a long and friendly private conversation. He should have educated Kerr about the historic dimensions of the crisis and explained his thinking. Whitlam could have spoken in these terms:

> The Senate's action is without precedent since Federation. This is the greatest threat to the constitutional basis of responsible government. My intention as Prime Minister is to secure a political settlement of this political crisis. I intend to remain in office in the name of the House of Representatives and responsible government. I have no doubt that I will prevail and that the Senate will retreat. I have several weeks before Supply expires in which to achieve this objective and it is my intention to report to you regularly on progress. These tactics, of course, mean that there is no role for the Governor-General to play since I am informing you that I have decided that this deadlock will be settled by political means. Accordingly, I foreshadow now that if the Senate has not cracked as the date for the exhaustion of government funds nears, then I will tender to you alternative advice to resolve the deadlock.

This approach would have taken Kerr into Whitlam's confidence. It would have exposed Kerr to Whitlam's thinking. It would have helped to bring Kerr into Whitlam's plan. It would have established trust because Whitlam would reveal to Kerr a private strategy underlining his public strategy. It would have flattered Kerr. It would have had two lasting consequences—maximising the time that Kerr gave Whitlam to crack the Senate, and holding Kerr to Whitlam instead of sending him to Fraser.

This would have been achieved by giving Kerr some assurance. Once Kerr assumed or suspected that Whitlam, in the end, *would* advise an election from the brink of the Supply precipice—then his mind would be eased. Kerr would see Whitlam's gameplan—and he would not agonise about Whitlam's future moves. Kerr would realise that his own responsibilities as Governor-General under the Constitution would not be compromised by Whitlam—hence he would be more tolerant towards Whitlam's tactics. As a consequence Whitlam would maximise his time to break the Senate and Fraser.

This analysis exposes Whitlam's two great mistakes.

The first was to think he could remain in office after the funds expired. That was a fatal conclusion. The best result Whitlam could have obtained from the Governor-General was a decision to let him remain as Prime Minister and not advise an election until the funds expired. The second mistake was that Whitlam's public position was also his private position with Kerr—that he would not call an election at the behest of the Senate. Whitlam can hardly complain that Kerr believed him. After all, Whitlam's purpose was to convince everyone. His gameplan was that the Senate, once convinced, would fold. But Kerr, once convinced, only grew agitated. The Governor-General feared the Whitlam mission—his threat to stay in office, 'tough it out' without parliamentary approval of Supply, and introduce alternative financial arrangements. This only drove Kerr into Fraser's arms. The deeper Kerr's alarm about Whitlam, the more likely his move against him.

It is clear that Whitlam frightened Kerr. The Governor-General felt at risk. He wasn't privy to Whitlam's tactics—and Kerr, left alone and under pressure, was vulnerable to extreme interpretations further nourished by Whitlam's Napoleonic predilections and Fraser's alarmist predictions.

Whitlam should have made Kerr feel secure. A secure Kerr would have given Whitlam time and flexibility. But Whitlam did the opposite; he contributed to Kerr's own insecurity. An insecure Kerr decided on three courses—to abandon any formal 'advise and warn' procedure; to dismiss Whitlam; and to do so according to a timetable designed to allow a general election before Christmas, although Whitlam still had funds lasting another fortnight.

If the Senate would have cracked in the immediate period after 11 November—and nobody can know the answer to this conundrum—then the timing of Kerr's intervention was the difference between defeat and victory for Whitlam.

On Monday 10 November Whitlam flew to Melbourne to address the Melbourne Press Club lunch. That afternoon he met senior figures from the Victorian ALP—Bob Hawke; State Opposition leader, Clyde Holding; Victorian president, Peter Redlich; and Victorian secretary, Bill Tracey. The Victorians were Senate election hawks. They argued with Whitlam in the hotel bar that the party had never been more united and that there was a pro-Labor surge across the nation. It was time to strike. Whitlam put his massive arms around Hawke and Holding on either side of him and told them as they left the bar: 'I agree with you, comrades'.[165]

THE SOLUTION

Whitlam's plans, in fact, were advanced. The Prime Minister's Department had sent to Government House a draft letter from Whitlam to Kerr requesting the Senate election—ahead of the formal advice. This was normal procedure. Kerr knew Whitlam's intentions.

Late on Monday Government House distributed the vice-regal notice. It reported that Kerr had met Barwick at Admiralty House and then later had entertained the Chief Justice at lunch. It was clear that there had been two meetings. The notice would be published in newspapers on 11 November. The press contacted Whitlam's press secretary, David Solomon, with the news. Solomon mentioned it to Whitlam; here, surely, was another warning sign. Whitlam was a little puzzled. But he dismissed its significance. Kerr had been so reassuring throughout the crisis. Whitlam felt there was no need for concern. Another warning went unheeded.

Meanwhile, late on Monday, drafts were completed at Government House of two documents—Kerr's dismissal letter and a statement of his reasons. They were locked in the Official Secretary's safe overnight.

That night Whitlam attended and addressed the Lord Mayor's Banquet in Melbourne. It is a tribute to the underlying strength of Australian democracy that during such a crisis the Prime Minister extended an invitation to the senior Liberals attending the function to return to Canberra in his own VIP plane. Fraser, Lynch, McMahon and Andrew Peacock travelled back with Whitlam. Peacock told the journalist George Negus, also on board, that 'Malcolm's got us into this terrible mess'. They landed just after midnight—the start of a new day, 11 November 1975.[166]

Whitlam was driven to the Lodge. His plan, within the next twelve hours, was to visit Yarralumla and seek a half Senate poll. Whitlam calculated that, once granted, the Senate poll would intensify the pressure on Fraser. Whitlam did not dream that a letter dismissing him was sitting at Yarralumla.

Fraser and Lynch were driven from the airport by a Commonwealth car driver, Eric Kennedy. They spoke quietly, but Kennedy later relayed what he recalled them saying. A version was published by Whitlam several years later—but it was not clear whether it was attributed to Fraser or to Lynch: 'He doesn't seem to know anything about it. All we have to do now is hope the press doesn't get hold of it, because then it could all blow up in our faces.'[167]

The Liberal and Country Party leaders reject unanimously any suggestion that Fraser had been tipped off about the dismissal. Fraser insists that before 11 November Kerr never gave him any signal about his plans. This is confirmed by all the senior Coalition figures. Withers, who affirms this position, adds: 'Malcolm can keep a secret. If Fraser did know then he wouldn't have told his wife or mother.'[168]

There are claims and counter-claims about prior knowledge of the dismissal. In an October 1995 interview with me John Menadue reported that on Friday 7 November 1975 he had lunch with his former boss Rupert Murdoch. Menadue says of the dismissal: 'I believe he [Murdoch] was very actively involved in it, directly and indirectly through his papers. He told me, in effect, the Government would be dismissed . . . and in a friendly sort of way he said, "Well, John, don't worry, you'll be appointed as ambassador to Tokyo" which turned out to be right on both counts.' Menadue describes Kerr as a 'weak man' and says that Murdoch 'could see a weak man . . . and how he could be manipulated'.

Rupert Murdoch, in turn, rejects such claims. 'I have no memory of that lunch', he says. 'I had nothing to do with Sir John Kerr at that time. Indeed, I don't think that I met Sir John Kerr more than six times in my life. My concern at that time was that Malcolm Fraser, having taken the country to the brink, might lose his courage and back off. Maybe if *The Australian* hadn't been so firm on the constitutional issue then Fraser might have lost courage.'

Any assessment of the issue of prior knowledge should include Menadue's 28 January 1976 note of his discussions that day with Fraser. This records Fraser telling Menadue that in Fraser's initial talk with Kerr, the Governor-General signalled his distrust of Whitlam and his fear that Whitlam might move against him. It is an account that Fraser denies. Fraser insists that Kerr never said to him that he feared his own sacking by Whitlam—a remark that would have virtually given the game away.

It was already clear some days before 10 November that Fraser was confident that Kerr would dismiss Whitlam; the tantalising question is whether he *knew*.

10
Dismissal

We shall all have to live with this.

Sir John Kerr, on dismissing Mr Whitlam,
11 November 1975

TUESDAY 11 NOVEMBER 1975 broke as a crystalline late spring morning in Canberra, a day usually devoted to ceremony. It was the 57th anniversary of the Armistice. The Remembrance Day schedule at the War Memorial, conducted at 11 am, required the Governor-General's attendance. Kerr had a busy day: he had to remember the fallen and conduct an execution of his own.

At 9 am Fraser, Lynch and Anthony arrived at the Prime Minister's Parliament House office for the arranged meeting with Whitlam, Frank Crean and Fred Daly. Whitlam immediately proposed that if the Senate passed the budget he would hold the Senate election sufficiently close to mid-1976 so as never to constitute an interim Senate in which the ALP might have the numbers. If the Opposition rejected this offer, Whitlam made clear, he would call a normal half Senate election.

Whitlam felt that the choice for Fraser was either to retreat and grant Supply now or to face the ignominy of a five week Senate election campaign during which his Senators would almost certainly cave in. Whitlam assumed that he was operating from a position of strength.

Fraser rejected the offer—just as he had previously—though Whitlam formed the mistaken impression that Anthony could be interested. Whitlam says: 'My recollection is that Anthony wasn't "in the know".' Fraser asked Whitlam if this was the only option. Fraser then repeated his own previous concession. 'Why not accept the offer I've made—elections for both houses in May next year?' But Whitlam was not interested.[1]

The Opposition leaders asked Whitlam whether he would be seeking Supply to cover the election period and Whitlam said that he would not be doing so. Fraser felt that Kerr would not give Whitlam a Senate election without Supply.

A confident Fraser now cautioned Whitlam:

> I said, 'You know, Prime Minister, there are people who think that the Governor-General has got an independent duty and obligation to make up his own mind'. Whitlam said, 'It's nonsense'. 'But you can't necessarily assume that he'll just do as you advise', I told him. I don't know if they are the exact words I used, but I certainly did offer a caution to Whitlam, and he just wasn't disposed to listen.[2]

Fraser asked Whitlam not to give either the Prime Minister's proposition or the Opposition's response to the press. Whitlam agreed since he felt the Governor-General should hear first of his request for a Senate election.[3] The Opposition leaders left Whitlam's office at 9.45 am. It was agreed they would call Whitlam to confirm their position.

Both Daly and Crean were concerned about the confidence Fraser had displayed during the meeting. Daly says that Fraser, Lynch and Anthony 'gave me the impression of trying to find out what we knew whilst at the same time knowing all the answers. If they did not know what the future held politically they seemed to have a very good idea that it would turn out all right for them.' As they were leaving, Crean expressed his own fears: 'By gee, they seem very confident. They're pretty cocky.'[4]

The focus of the two Labor ministers was on securing a Senate election from Kerr; they never remotely considered a dismissal. And Whitlam reassured his colleagues.

But Doug Anthony left a worried man—for other reasons. Whitlam's intransigence suggested to him that the Prime Minister would never call a general election and would merely let the services of government grind to a halt. Anthony recalls: 'I didn't know where we were going . . . I hadn't anticipated that the Governor-General would take any action. But Whitlam seemed fanatical at this meeting. He was absolutely adamant that he would not bow to the Senate. I felt we were dealing with a fellow who wouldn't play by the rules.'[5]

Fred Daly, a hardheaded politician, had his own fears. Now he told Whitlam he thought a Senate election would achieve little. He asked Whitlam how he knew that Kerr would grant the Senate election. 'It's the normal procedure because they must be held before 30 June 1976', Whitlam replied.[6]

This was Whitlam's dogmatism at its worst. A request for a Senate election which would see Supply exhausted before polling day was unprecedented in Australia's parliamentary history. If Whitlam couldn't talk frankly to his own electoral minister and most experienced colleague on this issue it is unlikely that the Prime Minister was able to evaluate options or make cool assessments. Whitlam had substituted willpower for analysis, a fatal mistake.

Fraser and Lynch conferred briefly before speaking to senior members of the shadow cabinet. They realised that Whitlam's Senate election threat, if he proceeded with it, would intensify further the pressure on the Coalition and its Senators. They determined to keep holding the line. Fraser felt confident that Kerr would deny Whitlam's request. At 10.05 am Fraser rang Whitlam to confirm that 'there'll be no deal'.[7]

Whitlam immediately rang Kerr.

The Governor-General had been busy. Kerr had risen early that morning to finalise the dismissal documents. He walked urgently into the bedroom where his wife was sitting in bed drinking tea and showed her the copy of his statement explaining the reasons for the dismissal. He said to her: 'I want you to read this. From today, if I have to use it, I am going to be execrated by one half of Australia.'[8]

Anne Kerr says, in retrospect, that her husband was 'seeking to prepare me for the unpopularity to come . . . But . . . execrated? I was incredulous.'[9] Despite Kerr's comments to his wife the evidence overall is that he misjudged the extent of animosity that his action would generate.

Anne Kerr found the document extremely formal and legal. She felt that Kerr needed to explain his action to the people in simple terms. She had a suggestion, and the upshot was a clear sentence in Kerr's statement: 'It is for the people now to decide the issue which the two leaders have failed to settle.'

Vice-regal life had its own schedule which continued simultaneously with Kerr's preparations to invoke the reserve powers. Sir John and Lady Kerr had to dress for the Remembrance Day ceremony being held at the War Memorial at 11 am. Just as Kerr was about to dress he had a phone call from his daughter Gabrielle saying that one of his grandchildren had been taken to hospital with a serious illness. This is why he was unable to take Whitlam's first call.

Whitlam rang Kerr on his direct line. He said that the Opposition had again rejected the compromise he had proposed. He wanted an early meeting with the Governor-General to advise a Senate election. Whitlam also proposed to submit the referendum proposal for simultaneous elections on the same day. Kerr apologised for not having been able to take Whitlam's first call since he had been worried about a grandchild's illness. He explained to Whitlam that he had to prepare for the Remembrance Day ceremony at the War Memorial. Whitlam said that he had parliamentary obligations during the late morning because there was a censure motion against the government. That meant he could not see Kerr until the luncheon adjournment. In the interim there was a caucus meeting at which Whitlam would have to announce his Senate election decision. The story would become public. Whitlam said he would prefer to advise Kerr first but events made this difficult. Would Kerr mind? Kerr agreed with Whitlam's proposed sequence.[10] Whitlam would come to Yarralumla at 1 pm after the Representatives adjourned for lunch and give his advice. Kerr's deception of Whitlam was elaborate. The Governor-General encouraged Whitlam to believe his Senate election would be approved when Kerr's real intention was to sack Whitlam.

In response to a question from Kerr, Whitlam confirmed that Supply was still not available. Whitlam did not address the fact that Supply would expire during the Senate election campaign.[11]

Kerr then made a fateful telephone call to Malcolm Fraser—a call whose contents are a matter of profound dispute between Fraser and Kerr. This goes directly to the question of whether or not Fraser had prior knowledge of the dismissal.

Kerr says that he called Fraser to confirm for himself that there was no change in the Opposition's position as a result of the 9 am meeting between the two sides. But Fraser's version of this discussion is more substantial.

The background, of course, is that Kerr had begun to prepare to dismiss Whitlam and to commission Fraser. Once he knew when Whitlam was coming to Yarralumla Kerr could refine those plans. He took little interest in Whitlam's intended advice for a Senate election. But it was at this point that the difficulties in Kerr's solution began to emerge. The reason for dismissing Whitlam was to commission Fraser to enable Fraser to advise a general election and obtain Supply.

The easiest task, though the most unpleasant, was the dismissal of Whitlam. After that there was a series of difficulties with Kerr's plan—though to this day it is unclear whether Kerr ever appreciated that these hazards had the potential to humiliate him. After Whitlam was dismissed Kerr had to: (1) commission Fraser as Prime Minister as soon as possible; (2) rely upon Fraser to secure Supply for his own government, thereby ending the Supply crisis; (3) receive and act upon advice from Fraser for a general election; and (4) dissolve the Parliament.

This meant that Kerr had to be sure that Fraser would accept a prime ministerial commission on the terms proposed.

Kerr rang Fraser around 10.15 am. It is described by Fraser's official biographer, Philip Ayres, as 'the most momentous call Fraser had ever taken'. Fraser confirmed that the Opposition's position had not changed and that temporary Supply would not be provided for a Senate election. He would grant Supply only for a House election. According to Fraser, Kerr then asked him four questions:

1. If commissioned as caretaker Prime Minister could Fraser guarantee to provide Supply?
2. And if so commissioned would he immediately recommend an election for both houses?
3. Would he be prepared to agree to undertake no new policies and make no appointments of significance before an election?
4. And would he also be prepared to agree, while caretaker Prime Minister, to initiate no inquiries into the activities and policies of the Whitlam Government?

Fraser answered yes to each question.[12]

Fraser believed that Kerr was acting properly and prudently in establishing these matters for himself. Fraser said later:

> He [Kerr] can't go to the end of the road with Whitlam and find that he's got an unacceptable situation as far as I'm concerned . . . But he made it very plain in the conversation that no final decisions had been made, that all he was seeking to do was to clarify his own mind so that he would know as much as possible of the total situation before that decision was made.[13]

Ayres says that after this conversation Fraser 'now felt sure of the outcome—though he did not yet have knowledge of it'. For most people this distinction is not plausible. Fraser now knew that Kerr was planning to dismiss Whitlam and commission him that very day.[14]

But Kerr rejects Fraser's version of the conversation.

Kerr says that in this conversation he did not ask Fraser the four questions that Fraser outlined. In his book he makes clear that the purpose of this telephone call was to confirm that the Opposition position remained the same and that Supply was not available. Kerr asserts that he said 'nothing else' to Fraser about the situation.[15]

After the Ayres book was published Kerr said in an interview with *The Australian* that it was 'quite inconceivable that, at the very height of the crisis and after I had made my decision as to what I would do if the situation remained unchanged, I would on the telephone have asked him [Fraser] the substantive formal questions listed by Dr Ayres as having been asked . . . The notion . . . that I actually warned Mr Fraser of my intentions in advance is without foundation.'[16]

Kerr says that he did put these questions to Fraser—but in his study at 1.15 pm when he was about to commission the Liberal leader as Prime Minister.

Kerr's office later produced a 12 page note handwritten by Kerr, dated 16 November 1975 and titled 'Notes by Governor-General on Discussions with Mr Whitlam and Mr Fraser'. The notes say, in relation to the disputed conversation: 'I rang Mr Fraser to find out whether it was true that they [Whitlam and Fraser] had got nowhere and whether it was the Opposition intention to continue to refuse Supply. His answer to both questions was "Yes".'[17]

It appears, furthermore, that Kerr's Official Secretary, David Smith, was in the room with Kerr when he had this conversation with Fraser. Smith has told colleagues that Kerr's version of the discussion is correct.[18]

Fraser gave his account of the conversation to Philip Ayres in 1985. He also gave the details in an interview recorded with Clyde Cameron for the oral history unit of the National Library. Fraser said that he took notes during this conversation with Kerr but did not keep them. Fraser has insisted that the discussion occurred in the way he described. He has pointed out that of all the conversations in his political life this is one that he would be least likely to forget. Fraser has no ulterior motive in revealing the conversation with Kerr. Indeed, it is an embarrassment for him to the extent that it casts doubt on his own claims from 11 November onwards that he had no prior knowledge of the dismissal.

During my May 1995 interview with Malcolm Fraser we talked about the phone conversation:

KELLY: This account of Kerr putting these four questions to you on the phone that morning. Is that still your recollection?

FRASER: Yes. That is what happened.

KELLY: There is no doubt in your mind about that?

FRASER: No, none at all.

KELLY: Well, Kerr has said that he never asked you the four questions on the phone, that he only asked them in his study when he was commissioning you.

FRASER: He asked them again then.

KELLY: I would like to get this right. You've got a clear recollection in your mind?

FRASER: Yes. On this point, absolute. There is no doubt.

KELLY: What did you feel when Kerr asked you those questions on the phone?

FRASER: I felt then that unless Whitlam changed and recommended something sensible Whitlam was going to get dismissed. But the conversation didn't end up like that. He just asked the questions. It was, 'Well, thank you very much'. There was no 'I will be seeing you later' or anything like that. There were some people in my office at the time. I think Withers, Lynch and Anthony were the most likely ones. They wouldn't have heard. They would have seen me take a few notes on a piece of paper which I haven't kept, I promise you that.[19]

There was a motive for Kerr to put these questions to Fraser—to ensure that his plans would be smoothly implemented. Kerr, as a prudent man, may have felt the need to ensure that, before he got Fraser into the room for a swearing-in, there would be no difficulty with the conditions that Kerr attached to a caretaker commission.

On the other hand, Kerr was only implementing the position Fraser had put in their talks during the crisis, so the Governor-General may have assumed that Fraser would accept them and that there was no need for a prior 'sounding out'.

If Fraser's version is correct it means that Kerr's solution to the crisis was now based not just on Whitlam's ignorance but on Fraser's knowledge. Whitlam would be ambushed; Fraser would be prepared. Whitlam was deliberately never warned by Kerr; but Fraser, according to his own version, was carefully warned by Kerr what to expect.

The conflict over this crucial conversation reveals that the disputes over the facts of the 1975 constitutional crisis are not limited to Kerr and Whitlam but extend also to Kerr and Fraser.

Whitlam then spoke to the regular ALP caucus meeting, reported on his earlier meeting with Fraser and announced that he intended to call a Senate election for 13 December. The caucus was excited and almost euphoric to hear of a circuit-breaker in the crisis. It applauded Whitlam's announcement. It was assumed that the Senate election would further intensify the pressure on Fraser to break the deadlock. It was also assumed that Kerr would grant the election. Although the caucus meeting was relatively brief the news of the Senate election was being broadcast by the electronic media before it ended. In the close confines of the old Parliament House there was no news like election news. It spread quickly, intensifying the mood and range of rumours. With election news Kings Hall was busy with journalists plying their trade.

But Fraser and Lynch believed they were on the verge of a great victory.

Lynch, who was very close to his staff, called his press aide Brian Buckley into the office. According to Buckley, a tired Lynch said: 'I think something might happen today to break the deadlock. Can't tell you the details. Don't know them all myself. But we should get a result today. Could you discreetly pass on to the troops word to that effect without going into any explanations.'[20]

But Fraser, as usual, gave nothing away. None of his staff had a similar story and none believed that Fraser had any prior knowledge.

At 10.30 am the Coalition parties met. This meeting coincided with the ALP caucus meeting and began before the media had confirmed the expected Senate election. Fraser and Lynch had decided not to inform their own meeting of Whitlam's intention to call a Senate election. Indeed, they decided not even to report on their meeting with Whitlam. This was in order to contain any pressure within their own ranks. A party room containing several dozen anxious politicians has a potential for volatility. Fraser insisted upon discipline.

He spoke to the party room as a leader who felt that the resolution of the crisis was at hand.

Fraser opened by saying that his wish was that there be no discussion on the decision taken a month earlier to block Supply. This revealed his extreme concern to prevent any internal criticism of the Opposition's stand. He told the parties that he wanted them to hold tight for a while longer. Fraser said that events might sort themselves out within hours. He expected that before very long he would be able to give them 'a definitive statement about the total position'.[21]

Doug Anthony reinforced Fraser's appeal. According to Ayres' account the minutes of the meeting revealed Anthony saying: 'It's all building to a crisis in the next 24 hours. Just stay firm and resolute.' Another account had Anthony saying: 'We must stay firm and resolute. The next 24 hours are the most vital in the entire history of our parties.'[22]

It was natural for the Opposition leaders to suppress any discussion of Whitlam's Senate election proposal. But the comments of Fraser and Anthony have an urgency that transcends this concern. The two principal features of their remarks are, first, an absolute insistence that there be no discussion—the only time they had required this of the party room during the crisis; and, second, a belief that the month-long crisis must soon be resolved.

Fraser and Anthony would not have made these comments to the party meeting unless they felt that the coming hours would be decisive.

Fraser was acting like a leader who believed that a resolution of the crisis was imminent. His comments were consistent with his account of his phone conversation with Kerr just a few minutes before the party meeting. If Fraser felt he was about to be commissioned as Prime Minister then he would be desperate to prevent any party room discussion. Kerr's intervention was premised on one assumption—that the Opposition was firm on Supply. If Opposition MPs or Senators began to express doubts or call for a retreat at this party meeting then the news would spread through Parliament House within a short time. It would be broadcast immediately on the electronic media; it would be fanned by the government; and it would reach Yarralumla. Kerr could hardly proceed to dismiss Whitlam and commission Fraser if Coalition members were calling for a retreat or threatening to revolt against their leaders. For Fraser, discipline at this party meeting could mean the difference between victory and defeat.

When the meeting broke Coalition backbenchers surged across Kings Hall and a series of fragmented conversations occurred with various journalists. The media was stunned to discover that Coalition backbenchers knew nothing about the Senate election. There was some hilarity at their ignorance. 'There's a Senate election, don't you blokes know?', was the refrain. 'Fraser's been too scared to tell them', journalists joked with each other. The media was in complete ignorance of Fraser's reasons, like the Coalition.[23]

A few minutes later Lynch conducted the usual party room briefing in the Whip's office for the media. My own account of this briefing was as follows:

> Lynch smiled as they [journalists] all came in. He opened the briefing by saying he was afraid it would be an anti-climax. It had been a routine meeting and he went through the business. There was no discussion of the crisis . . . The deputy leader parried a series of questions. Did he know the Prime Minister was seeking a Senate election? Had the Opposition parties been told this? Why not? 'We believe events will work themselves out', Lynch told journalists. 'We believe that the present course is sound for reasons which will become apparent to you later'.[24]

Whitlam, described by Graham Freudenberg as 'confident and ebullient', suggested to Kep Enderby that Whitlam himself might attend the Remembrance Day ceremony at the War Memorial. But Enderby wanted to go.[25] He represented the government at the solemn ceremony of the eleventh hour of the eleventh day of the eleventh month. Enderby stood beside Sir John Kerr who wore full morning dress and decorations. Enderby walked down the stairs with Kerr at the end of the ceremony and then turned quickly, expecting to shake hands. But Kerr climbed into his car. Lady Kerr said, 'Goodbye Mr Attorney'. Kerr drove off, his mind on other matters. Labor would later invest Anne Kerr's comments with a political edge—but she replies, 'What on earth else would I have said?'.[26]

Malcolm Fraser now placed a phone call to the Chief Electoral Officer, Frank Ley. He wanted to know the last date on which a federal election could be held before Christmas. Ley nominated 13 December and said that, in order to meet this deadline, writs would have to be issued within a couple of days at the latest.[27] Ley then rang Whitlam, as a correct public servant, to inform his Prime Minister of this discussion. Why would Fraser be making this call? Whitlam's alarm system still failed to ring.

The House of Representatives sat at 11.45 am and Fraser moved his first motion of censure against the government during the crisis. He began:

> The evasion and contempt of Parliament and of the Constitution have become a critical issue in the attempt of the Prime Minister (Mr Whitlam) to hang on to power. He believes that he alone is the Constitution; that he alone is the Parliament. The Parliament is very clearly the Queen—in our case the Governor-General—the Senate and the House of Representatives. All have a proper part and proper powers under the Constitution.

During his speech Fraser attacked Whitlam, saying:

> He has not said that he would accept the Governor-General's decision taken in accordance with his constitutional prerogative. There are circumstances, as I have said repeatedly, where a Governor-General may have to act as the ultimate protector of the Constitution. He ignores that prerogative.[28]

At 12.34 pm Whitlam, in reply, and unknowingly delivering his last speech as Prime Minister, moved an amendment censuring Fraser and calling upon him to desist from blocking the budget. Whitlam said:

> The whole tactic of the Leader of the Opposition has been to bypass this House, to undermine its established rights and authority . . . which have never been challenged since Federation . . . The new preposterous claim is that the Senate—not even an elected majority but a mere accidental half of the Senate—can dictate to the House of Representatives our own dissolution. That is, the Senate claims the right to send this House to the people without itself facing the people . . . This House has no power to dissolve the Senate. Yet the Senate now purports to have such power over this House.[29]

The debate was an anti-climax. The focus of attention was the looming Senate election. I strolled down to Kings Hall towards the end of the censure debate and fell into discussion with a small group of Labor MPs. They were supremely confident. But I voiced doubts over the Supply issue. I pointed out that this was the real test of whether Kerr would do Whitlam's bidding; it was a substantial step for a Governor-General to give a Prime Minister a Senate election without any guarantee of Supply. But the ALP caucus smelt a victory.

On returning to Yarralumla from the War Memorial, Kerr had his staff make arrangements with both Whitlam's and Fraser's offices for them to come to Government House. Kerr claimed the set times were Whitlam at 12.45 pm and Fraser at 1 pm. The logistics, obviously, were risky. Kerr's plan was to dismiss Whitlam and then commission Fraser *as fast as possible*. But Kerr's version of the appointment times differs from that of Whitlam who assumed a 1 pm appointment after their morning phone call.[30]

The House adjourned at 12.55 pm. Whitlam was running a little late; he was still aiming for a 1 pm appointment at Yarralumla—the time he had mentioned to Kerr that morning. Even worse for Kerr, Fraser was early.[31]

Fraser arrived at Yarralumla before Whitlam.

His senior aide, Tony Eggleton, had been too efficient. The message from Government House when setting Fraser's appointment had been that Kerr wanted to see Fraser only after he saw Whitlam. Fraser's office felt that no time had been fixed. So Eggleton posted a lookout on Whitlam's white Mercedes.

Journalist Peter Bowers later told the story:

> The Whitlam car pulled away, word was passed to Eggleton and Mr Fraser was on his way to Yarralumla within minutes. No sooner had Mr Fraser left than Mr Whitlam's car returned to Parliament House. It had not had time to go to Yarralumla. Mr Whitlam apparently was still in his office. Mr Fraser could not be reached by two-way radio in his car. To the consternation of officials at Yarralumla Mr Fraser arrived before Mr Whitlam.[32]

Fraser's driver, Harry Rundle, was asked by the aide-de-camp (who knew nothing of the purpose of Fraser's visit) to park his car in the area outside the Official Secretary's office—a natural direction given the geography of Yarralumla. In this location it was also largely out of the sight of new arrivals to the Governor-General's residence.[33] Whitlam arrived a few minutes after Fraser. He said later: 'Had I known Mr Fraser's car was there, I could at once have instructed my driver, Robert Millar . . . to turn around and drive me back to Parliament House.

Had I known Mr Fraser was already there, I would not have set foot in Yarralumla.'[34]

Could such a simple logistical matter have been decisive? It is doubtful. Fraser was driving in a Ford LTD from the car pool; such cars were often parked at Yarralumla and it is far from certain that the car, if sighted, would have triggered the notion that Fraser was already inside.[35]

Kerr's aide, Captain Stephens, met Whitlam and escorted him to the Governor-General's study. Making polite discussion, Stephens, who was soon to leave Yarralumla, said as they passed a closed door that a 'successor is being selected in there'—a comment that Whitlam later misinterpreted to refer to his own job rather than Stephens's.

What manner of man walked to his execution that day?

Freudenberg confesses: 'An ambush succeeds partly because the victim is too self-confident. If there was ever a leader, over-confident and convinced of his capacity to prevail, it was Gough. Gough is a man notable for his lack of suspicion, unlike Doc Evatt who was suspicious of everybody.'[36] Whitlam's 'crash through' days were behind him; he was about to crash.

The dismissal

Kerr had thought through his tactics for the face-to-face encounter. They are summarised by a Kerr confidant:

> The Governor-General's intention was to have the issue resolved then and there in his study. He was determined not to let Whitlam get away from Yarralumla without an election. He wouldn't let Whitlam get away on the pretext of consultations with colleagues and then set in train events to dismiss Kerr.[37]

This account is consistent with Kerr's behaviour.

Whitlam entered the study and was asked by Kerr to take a seat, as usual. On the desk, face down, were the documents dismissing Whitlam. The Prime Minister reached into his inside coat pocket for the letter advising a Senate election. He began to say that he had the letter with the advice he had foreshadowed that morning. But Kerr quickly came to the point.

There are differences in the versions provided by the two men of what Kerr now said to Whitlam, but not of substance.

According to Whitlam, Kerr said: 'Before we go any further I have to tell you that I have decided to terminate your commission. I have a letter for you giving my reasons.'[38]

Kerr's version is as follows:

> 'Before you say anything Prime Minister, I want to say something to you. You have told me this morning on the phone that your talks with the leaders on the other side have failed to produce any change and that things therefore remain the same. You intend to govern without parliamentary supply.' He said 'Yes'. I replied that in my view he had to have parliamentary supply to govern and as he had failed to obtain it and was not prepared to go to the people, I had decided to withdraw his commission.[39]

From this stage on their versions contain greater differences.

Kerr insists that at this point Whitlam was still not dismissed and that whether 'I would do this or not was to depend upon his reaction'.[40] Kerr's understanding was that the moment of dismissal was when he told Whitlam he was dismissed and handed him the dismissal letter.

According to Whitlam, Kerr passed him the document. Whitlam asked: 'Have you discussed this with the Palace?'. Kerr replied: 'I don't have to and it's too late for you. I have terminated your commission.' As Whitlam rose to leave, he says, Kerr added: 'The Chief Justice agrees with this course of action.' Whitlam replied: 'So that is why you had him to lunch yesterday. I advised you that you should not consult him on this matter.'[41]

Kerr's version is far more dramatic:

> Things then happened as I had foreseen. Mr Whitlam jumped up, looked urgently around the room, looked at the telephones and said sharply, 'I must get in touch with the Palace at once.' . . . The documents, duly signed, were face down on my desk. I now knew there would be no changed advice, only the certainty of constitutional disruption if any time were allowed to elapse. I therefore made my final decision to withdraw his commission and hand him the signed documents . . . When he said, 'I must get in touch with the Palace at once,' I replied, 'It is too late.' He said 'Why?' and I told him, 'Because you are no longer Prime Minister. These documents tell you so and why.' I handed them to him and he took them. He did not read them. There was a short silence after which he said, 'I see,' and stood up. He made no gesture towards discussion.[42]

Both men agreed almost exactly on their final exchange. Kerr said: 'We shall all have to live with this.' Whitlam replied: 'You certainly will.' Kerr wished Whitlam good luck in the election and extended his hand. Whitlam accepted it. They shook hands. Whitlam left. He never spoke to Kerr again.[43] (In my 1976 account of this meeting which drew upon a background interview with Whitlam I wrote that Whitlam replied,

'I will contact the Queen' when notified by Kerr of his dismissal intention.[44])

Could Whitlam have defied Kerr and just torn up the letter? Kerr replies: 'The lawyer in Mr Whitlam would have told him this was impossible. His only option was to seek to negotiate . . .'[45]

Kerr, unlike Whitlam, has placed great significance on their exchange in his study.

The Governor-General says that during the exchange he gave Whitlam an opportunity to save himself. Kerr says that Whitlam was dismissed only when he was given the dismissal letter. Kerr's assertion is that, after telling Whitlam he had decided to dismiss him but before giving him the letter, Whitlam had an opportunity to change his mind and advise an election as Prime Minister—an opportunity that Whitlam declined. Kerr says that during these moments Whitlam 'still had time in which to act'; that Whitlam could have sought 'to negotiate to go to the people as Prime Minister by agreeing to an election'—in the few seconds before he was handed the letter. But Whitlam's remark about contacting the Palace confirmed for Kerr that Whitlam's reaction was not to advise an election but to seek the Governor-General's dismissal.[46]

Kerr's account of this meeting suggests that even when he made his final decision Whitlam could still have negotiated. According to Kerr: 'He could still say, "Let us talk about this. If you are determined to have an election, I would rather go to the people myself as Prime Minister." Had he done so I would have agreed, provided he committed himself by action then and there.'[47]

But how much of an opportunity was Kerr extending? A few seconds while Whitlam was in a state of shock between being told he was being dismissed and being handed the letter of dismissal? Kerr is obviously correct—it was an opportunity for Whitlam to change his mind. But it was, at best, a minuscule opportunity.

Kerr, however, points to Whitlam's failure to negotiate as more proof of his intransigence. Kerr says: 'He made it obvious what his actions would be; not to seek to discuss with me any change of attitude, not to seek to go to the people in an election as Prime Minister . . . This [to negotiate] he could not bring himself to do and he did not do it.'[48]

Whitlam's so-called option—crammed into a few seconds—came after a four week crisis during which Kerr could have raised this option with him at any time. But Kerr had deliberately decided not to raise the option. He had concealed his thoughts and intentions from Whitlam from a time before Supply was deferred and had ignored throughout the crisis the Governor-General's discretion to advise, warn and counsel Whitlam. On the morning of 11 November Kerr had deliberately encouraged Whitlam to think he would accept advice for a Senate election. Finally, according to Fraser he had given the Opposition leader notice of his intentions—but had kept the plan a secret from Whitlam until he had the Prime Minister in his study to be dismissed, with Fraser waiting in another room to be commissioned. At this point, Kerr claims, Whitlam was given an opportunity to go to an election as Prime Minister, and his failure to seize it only confirmed Whitlam's intransigence and his determination not to negotiate.

Kerr's further claim is that Whitlam's response—wanting to contact the Palace—was 'as I had foreseen'. Kerr argues that this response was 'to move at once for my dismissal by so advising the Queen'. This is designed to validate the assumption on which Kerr operated throughout the crisis: that he could not reveal his thinking to Whitlam because Whitlam would have immediately sought Kerr's dismissal by the Queen.[49]

It may well be that Whitlam's reference to the Palace was as Kerr outlined. Assuming that Kerr's version is correct, it proves little. It would mean that Whitlam, ambushed in a dismissal, instinctively thought aloud of contacting the Palace. Of course, Whitlam could not contact the Palace. He was on Kerr's territory. He had no staff, no phone numbers. He could not ring the Queen in the middle of the night to sack Kerr. The Palace could not save him from Kerr then—and it would not have saved him earlier.

When Kerr offered his hand to Whitlam it was accepted. That was another instinctive response. Whitlam shook hands with his executioner. It meant nothing—Kerr was his mortal enemy from that moment until Kerr's death.

I asked Whitlam about Kerr's claims:

KELLY: You didn't think of trying to do a deal with him?

WHITLAM: No, no, no.

KELLY: But did the idea come into your head or not?

WHITLAM: No, it didn't . . . he'd made up his mind . . . I wouldn't have thought there was much prospect of him—no use arguing with him . . .

KELLY: The point here is that Kerr is actually arguing that in the study he gave you an option . . . some moments to change your mind. Now what's your response to that?

WHITLAM: He never put it to me . . . he said, before you give me that (my letter) I've got a letter for you . . .

KELLY: And what did you think when he said that to you?

WHITLAM: I thought, I'd better get out of here . . .[50]

Referring to Kerr's account of their exchange, Whitlam says: 'He was plainly obsessed by the fear that I would procure his own dismissal by the Queen . . . he saw every action and statement of mine through the distorted focus of his own fears.'[51]

In his 1985 interview with *The Bulletin* Kerr, aware that the weakness in his intervention was the lack of any warning to Whitlam, insists that he did give Whitlam a warning in his study. Kerr says:

> On that fateful day, I did not dismiss Mr Whitlam out of the blue, without warning . . . He had his warning. The ball was in his court. He did not try to get me to change my mind . . . It belittles Mr Whitlam to imagine that he was struck dumb. Not at all.

Sir John reveals that he made a record that day of Whitlam's reaction. He says that the drama of the scene within his study 'is engraved upon my mind'.[52]

A full acceptance of Kerr's account of the exchange in his study means that Whitlam, at the penultimate moment, was given an ultimatum by Kerr. But an ultimatum is not a warning.[53]

Jim McClelland is surely correct when he argues:

> A warning is a notice of what will occur if certain events happen or certain conduct is persisted in . . . If Kerr had said to Whitlam at their meeting on 11 November: 'Go away and discuss what I have just said to you with your colleagues and then get back to me,' that could have been classified as a warning, belated though it would have been.[54]

But this is precisely what Kerr wanted to avoid.

Kerr's comprehensive plan was to dismiss Whitlam—from the consultation with Barwick to the nearby presence of Fraser. If Kerr had been serious about warning Whitlam then he would not have arranged for Fraser to be coming to Yarralumla for an immediate swearing-in. He had prejudged the result of his meeting with Whitlam. Kerr's claim that his initial comment to Whitlam (to the effect that he had decided to withdraw his commission) constituted a genuine warning is unsustainable. Nor could Whitlam's reaction be interpreted as a considered response to a warning.

The final evidence lies in the discrepancy between Kerr's dismissal letter and his remarks to Whitlam. The letter assumed that Whitlam had been given a choice. It said:

You have previously told me that you would never resign or advise an election for the House of Representatives or a double dissolution *and that the only way in which such an election could be obtained would be by my dismissal of you and your ministerial colleagues.* As it appeared likely that you would today persist in this attitude I decided that, *if you did,* I would determine your commission and state my reasons for doing so. *You have persisted in your attitude* and I have accordingly acted as indicated.[55]

Kerr wrote the letter before he saw Whitlam. Its ostensible purpose is clear—in Kerr's words to allow Whitlam to 'change his advice if it were still in him to do so'. According to the letter Whitlam was dismissed because he 'persisted' in his attitude.[56]

But Kerr, according to his own version, did not put the question to Whitlam in his study in the same terms that appear in this letter. The question Kerr had an obligation to ask was: 'Prime Minister, is your position still that you will not resign or advise an election for the House of Representatives or a double dissolution and that the only way such an election can be obtained is by my dismissal of you and your ministerial colleagues?'. Having decided to attribute this attitude to Whitlam, Kerr ought to have put this question. It was necessary to verify the attitude in which Kerr claimed Whitlam had 'persisted' and for which he was dismissing Whitlam.

If Kerr failed to put the question he could not know that his letter of dismissal was accurate. It was the necessary and appropriate question. But it was not asked—according to Kerr's own version.

Kerr's failure to ask that question means that his dismissal letter to Whitlam is unsubstantiated in its essential premise—Whitlam's persistence on the issue warranting dismissal.

According to Kerr's version he asked Whitlam whether it was still his intention to govern without Supply. Whitlam had been governing with a deferral of Supply for four weeks. He would obviously answer 'yes' and he did. Kerr then told Whitlam that he had 'decided to withdraw his commission'. When, according to Kerr, Whitlam said he wanted to contact the Palace, Kerr dismissed him.[57]

So Kerr assumed from Whitlam's behaviour that he was persisting in his attitude and should be dismissed.

Just imagine, for a moment, what would have happened if Kerr had tested Whitlam on the attitude that he attributed to him.

Asking Whitlam with a face-down document on the desk whether he still refused to advise a general election and still insisted that 'the only way in which such an election could be obtained would be by my dismissal of you' would have created a very different chemistry. Whitlam would have realised what was coming. He would have realised that Kerr was thinking of dismissal before Kerr informed him that he had decided to withdraw his commission. It would have meant giving Whitlam much more of a choice, albeit by ultimatum.

There is no certainty whatsoever that Whitlam would have answered this question 'yes' and been dismissed.

The reason is that Whitlam denies that he ever made this statement to Kerr at any stage of the crisis. To repeat such a declaration when in the study at that time would have been *knowingly* to provoke dismissal. Would Whitlam do this? Perhaps—but it must be unlikely. Whitlam had no reason knowingly to provoke his own dismissal. The logic of Kerr's position means that Whitlam not only courted dismissal but preferred dismissal!

It is at this point that the defect in Kerr's stance is best revealed. He refused during the crisis to put to Whitlam what he saw as the real issue—call an election or be sacked. But Kerr, presumably worried about this deception, felt that he had an obligation to put the choice at the time of dismissal. He wrote it in his letter; but, even then, he was unable to put the question to Whitlam face to face in a frank way.

The Governor-General wanted his dismissal of Whitlam to be a watertight case; but he also wanted to be seen as a reasonable man. Kerr aspired both to trap Whitlam and to be a fair man offering a choice. The aims were irreconcilable. The judgement to be made of Kerr based on the events in his study and the letter he gave Whitlam is that his primary purpose was to dismiss Whitlam rather than give him a choice. Kerr's claim that he did give Whitlam a genuine warning is unconvincing on all counts.

With his letter of dismissal Kerr provided a longer 'Statement by the Governor-General' which sought to explain the background to his decision.[58]

Whitlam walked out of Government House and drove to the Lodge—not to his Parliament House office. He accepted the dismissal; he did not tear up the letter, defy the Governor-General, or return to his office to ring Buckingham Palace. Asked at his media conference later that day whether he was tempted to say something else to Kerr, Whitlam replied: 'No. I knew the right course.' This idea of Whitlam's acceptance is fundamental to the subsequent course of events on the day and has been overlooked by his rhetoric on the front steps.

Whitlam said later: 'If my overwhelming preoccupation had been to contact the Palace, I would have gone back to Parliament House and my staff . . . the Lodge has no switchboard, no office and only domestic staff.'[59]

It was a perfect illustration of Australia's bizarre system of government. While Australia's Head of State slept in her Buckingham Palace bed, unbeknownst to her the Crown's representative on location had dismissed the Prime Minister, an action that had not occurred in Britain since 1783.

Kerr asked Captain Stephens to escort Fraser to the study. He informed Fraser that Whitlam had been dismissed. Fraser's face was expressionless; he showed no reaction. The Governor-General offered to commission Fraser as caretaker Prime Minister.[60]

Kerr informed Fraser that if he accepted the commission then, according to constitutional principle, he would also be accepting the political responsibility for Kerr's action. Kerr then put to Fraser the four questions that, according to Fraser, he had put hypothetically during their phone conversation that morning. These concerned the conditions of the caretaker commission—that Fraser had to secure Supply; recommend an immediate double dissolution election; undertake no new policies; and initiate no inquiries into the previous government. Fraser agreed. In his memoirs Kerr insisted that this was the first time he had put such conditions to Fraser and that he had had no need to raise them earlier because 'there was no doubt he would accept: his whole tactic had been to arrive at this result'.[61] David Smith brought in the prepared documents. Fraser signed a letter agreeing to the conditions and was then sworn in as Prime Minister.[62] Kerr shook his hand and wished him good luck. The Governor-General said that in the circumstances they might forgo the traditional glass of champagne.[63] At this point Fraser allowed himself a slight smile. As they walked towards the door he told Kerr that he believed he could obtain Supply during the afternoon. Fraser hoped to see the Governor-General later in the day to advise the double dissolution.

Fraser recalls: 'It was probably overwhelming to be sworn in as Prime Minister under any circumstances. It was slightly more overwhelming to be sworn in under those circumstances. There was work to be done, cleanly and quickly.'[64]

Lady Kerr had been preserving an image of calm for their lunch guests. Kerr strode in at 1.30 pm, apologised for the delay and said that he had been dismissing the government. There was a stunned silence. The butler caught Lady Kerr's eye. 'We went in to lunch', she recorded, observing later that there was 'a certain automatism'.[65]

It should be pointed out, in theory at least, that Fraser did not have to accept all Kerr's conditions although it was clearly in his interests to accept them. For instance, Fraser could have said that he wanted to advise an election for the House of Representatives alone (or the Representatives and half of the Senate) rather than a double dissolution election, for the reason that if Labor won it would be denied the chance to pass its 21 double dissolution bills at a Joint Sitting. Kerr observed that if Fraser had done this then 'I would have accepted that advice'.[66]

Kerr's use of section 57 to secure a double dissolution election was a legal technique and a political nonsense. The bills were Whitlam's, not Fraser's. Fraser had opposed all 21 bills. Fraser was advising a double dissolution on Whitlam's bills that were deadlocked because of his own Opposition tactics. Kerr was forcing an election not because of these bills, but because of a Supply crisis. Once the budget was passed, the Supply crisis was over. But Fraser, under the terms of his commission, had to advise an election. It would be an embarrassment for Kerr if the whole of the Senate did not face the people. But the only way Kerr could despatch the whole of the Senate to the voters was by resort to this section 57 device.

Kerr knew that a double dissolution election—as distinct from an ordinary Representatives election—was a vital political requirement. Given that Supply had been denied by the Senate it was only appropriate that the Senate face the people. But there was another factor. Kerr had a high opinion of Whitlam's electoral capacity. He did not rule out Whitlam's chance of winning the election. In this situation he felt it appropriate to grant a double dissolution on the 21 deadlocked bills. If Whitlam did win and still lacked a Senate majority then he would be able to put all the bills through a Joint Sitting.

On arriving at the Lodge Whitlam called his wife, Margaret, who was hosting a lunch at Kirribilli in Sydney, to break the news. The Whitlams had no comprehension that 11 November would be a day of crisis for them; otherwise husband and wife would have been together. He rang his departmental head John Menadue and office chief John Mant, asking them to invite colleagues to the Lodge. The dismissed Prime Minister then ate his lunch, reflecting upon his tactics. Whitlam joked later: 'I had my steak *after* the execution.'

After the dismissal Whitlam had fled to his home. It was a natural move. But his retreat to the Lodge cost him dearly. It destroyed any remote chance he had of thwarting Fraser.

Fraser secures Supply

There was little time as both houses were reconvening at 2 pm. Whitlam's ministerial and party colleagues began to arrive. Mant and Freudenberg drove out together. They had heard on the radio news that there would be a half Senate election and that the non-Labor

Premiers were threatening not to issue the writs. At the Lodge they saw Whitlam eating his lunch alone in the summer room; Freudenberg flashed him the victory sign. When they walked in Whitlam declared, 'I've been sacked'. Freudenberg and Mant both laughed. 'I'm serious, the letter's over there', Whitlam said, pointing to a bench.

The Secretary of the Prime Minister's Department, John Menadue, arrived and was instructed by Whitlam to 'get hold of Harders'—whereupon Menadue suggested that Whitlam call Enderby, not the Secretary of the Attorney General's Department. Crean, Daly and Enderby, along with the Speaker of the House Gordon Scholes and the ALP National Secretary David Combe, arrived to the same news. To Enderby, Whitlam said: 'He's done a Game on us.' The group's initial response was either laughter or incredulity, then demoralisation. Freudenberg described their condition as 'catatonic'; Fred Daly used 'stunned mullets'.

Daly recalled: 'Whitlam said, "I'll sack Kerr". I can still see David Combe rolling his eyes towards heaven. But it was too late for that even if it were possible. Kerr had king hit us.'[67]

Menadue's secretary rang twice saying that Fraser wanted him. The first time he said 'say you can't find me', but the second message was ominous—the exact words being 'the Prime Minister, Mr Fraser, wants you urgently'—so Menadue withdrew from the presence of the new Opposition leader.[68]

It was just after 1.30 pm. Fraser was arriving back at Parliament House, as Prime Minister. But the Governor-General's plan was still only half executed. Labor still possessed a capacity to deny Fraser. But in the shock of this lunch hour Whitlam made two fatal mistakes.

First, he failed to appreciate fully what had happened—that Fraser was already Prime Minister, that the government had already changed hands and that it was now Fraser who had to obtain Supply. Fraser and Kerr both understood that Fraser could not advise an election—the sole reason for commissioning him—until he had obtained Supply. It was Whitlam's task, above all, to deny Supply to Fraser; their roles had been completely reversed. However, in that lunch hour shock had disarmed the brain. Whitlam, his ministers and his advisers were not thinking clearly. They failed to recover quickly enough from dismissal trauma.

Their dilemma betrayed Whitlam's absolute confidence during the crisis. Labor had not prepared contingency plans or given even cursory thought to the issues it might have to address if the government were dismissed. They were, in essence, elementary. Kerr's only motive in dismissing Whitlam was to secure advice from a Prime Minister who, after securing Supply, would advise a general election.

Whitlam's tactics should have been twofold—to deny Fraser Supply and then move a motion of no-confidence in him in the House.

There should be no misunderstanding of the vulnerability of Kerr's solution. It could be ruined easily. In fact, it was a simple though dangerous undertaking to destroy Fraser's prime ministership. It is unrealistic, however, to think that such a tactic could have been devised solely in the 45 minutes before Parliament reconvened. A prudent government would have drafted a contingency plan during the crisis as political insurance in case Whitlam's confidence in Kerr was misplaced.

Whitlam now framed a resolution to move when the Parliament reconvened:

> That this House declares that it has confidence in the Whitlam Government and that this House informs Her Majesty the Queen that, if His Excellency the Governor-General purports to commission the honourable member for Wannon as Prime Minister, the House does not have confidence in him or in any government he forms.[69]

The draft motion suggests that Whitlam did not realise that Fraser was already Prime Minister. It signals his plan—to try to regain office by using his majority in the House and to appeal to the Palace. Crean was despatched back to Parliament House to stonewall during the ongoing censure debate which resumed at 2 pm, while the others finalised their tactics.

Whitlam's second mistake was his failure to invite the Senate leadership to the Lodge. Whitlam was a victim of his own parliamentary philosophy; he was a champion of the House of Representatives and his purpose had been to defend the rights of the House against the Senate. After his dismissal Whitlam still placed his tactical reliance upon the House. But the Senate, as before, remained vital. Whitlam did not think to invite his Senate leadership to the Lodge and, as a consequence, the ALP had no chance to prepare its Senate tactics. Fred Daly said: 'I did not give the Senate a thought and evidently no one else did, least of all Whitlam.'[70] Freudenberg conceded later that 'nobody around that table at the Lodge thought of the Senate'.[71]

If Whitlam had returned from Yarralumla to Parliament House, not the Lodge, it seems certain that far more ALP parliamentarians from both chambers would have been told that Whitlam was dismissed and would have realised that Fraser was Prime Minister. By returning to the Lodge Whitlam isolated Parliament House from this critical information. ALP Senate leader Ken Wriedt had no idea that Whitlam was dismissed, or indeed that he was no longer the government leader in the Senate.

The first Opposition member to guess that history had been made during the lunch break was Peter Nixon. He sighted Fraser returning through Kings Hall with a Bible in his hand. Nixon knew it was tradition that a newly sworn Prime Minister kept the Bible used in the ceremony.[72] Fraser rang his wife Tamie. Then he called his Coalition partner. Doug Anthony recalls: 'I was absolutely stunned. Malcolm told me, "We are now the government, Whitlam's been dismissed". Frankly, I couldn't believe it.'[73]

The new Prime Minister called his senior colleagues into his office. Fraser, unlike Whitlam, knew Supply was the key; he had to satisfy the terms of his commission.

Now he had a stroke of luck.

Reg Withers explains:

> I was having a sandwich in my room with Magnus Cormack. I think they'd been trying to get me but had kept missing me. About a quarter to two I was walking across Kings Hall and I bumped into Doug McClelland, the manager of government business in the Senate. He told me, 'I'm going to put a motion as soon as we start that the Appropriation bills be passed forthwith'. I said, 'Righto, Doug', and kept walking into the Reps corridor and then into Malcolm's office. Well, it was bedlam in there. 'Where the hell have you been? We've been looking for you', Fraser said. After explaining that he was now Prime Minister Malcolm's concern was to get Supply. They were pretty anxious about this. 'How do we get Supply? How long will it take?', Fraser asked me. 'Just leave it to me, Malcolm', I said. 'How will you do it?', they asked. 'Don't you blokes worry', I said, and left.[74]

Withers knew that Doug McClelland was ignorant of the change of government and that he planned to resubmit the Appropriation bills within minutes. McClelland, unknowingly, was busy trying to secure Supply for the *Fraser* Government! Withers began to feel that this could be his lucky day.

Just before 2 pm word began to spread through Parliament House that Whitlam had been sacked. A few minutes later the senior ALP Senators—Ken Wriedt, Don Willesee and Doug McClelland—walked into the Senate for the afternoon session unaware that Whitlam had been dismissed or that Fraser was Prime Minister. They were terribly unlucky. By this time journalists were milling around the press boxes on the Representatives side amid word of the dismissal. Just before the Senate sat, the veteran journalist Alan Reid, on hearing of the dismissal, had gone to Kings Hall where he saw Doug McClelland. Reid called out and as they began to move together for a chat McClelland got diverted and missed the moment at which Reid would have told him about the dismissal. There must have been several such near misses, given the nature of the old Parliament House. It was improbable in its close quarters, where news travelled at such pace, that somewhere, somehow, through someone, the ALP Senate leadership had not been told. But the improbable had happened.

Meanwhile Whitlam and his advisers were just about to leave the Lodge, having drafted a motion to move in the House within a few minutes. The Senate had not crossed their minds.[75]

Wriedt and Withers now faced each other across the main bench of the Senate. Here was an irony that mocked Labor's competence. Wriedt and Withers, the Senate protagonists, were both trying to secure Supply![76]

The shock of discovery of the dismissal has coloured the memories of what happened in the Senate that day. Wriedt and Withers help to capture the mood in their respective accounts. According to Wriedt:

> I said to Withers across the table, 'Come on Reg, let's get this thing over and done with and the bills passed.' To my great surprise he replied, 'Oh yes, I think we can do that.' So he agreed to pass the bills. I didn't like his manner or the way he was talking. I turned and spoke briefly to Don Willesee and Doug McClelland: 'There's something strange here. He's saying he'll pass the bills but I can't understand why they've changed their minds.' We were all in the dark. I was signalled from the side of the chamber and went across to see John Button. He said to me, 'There's a story going around that the government's been sacked'. I replied, 'Don't be bloody ridiculous. Send someone to check it out.' I asked my staff to check. But within moments the Supply bills were called on and within what seemed to be a few seconds they were voted. I wasn't completely sure the government had been sacked. I think that if we had stopped Supply that day the Army would have been called out. Kerr and Fraser knew they had public support and they had committed themselves to a course of action.[77]

According to Withers:

> I said to Wriedt, 'Put the question, we'll vote for it this time'. He looked stunned. Just couldn't believe it. Then I said, 'Whitlam's been sacked. Fraser's Prime Minister. We're going to pass the bills.' Wriedt said to me, 'You're a funny bastard, Reg. You'll say anything.' Then the bills came on. Doug had given us the motion. You can be lucky in life. All Gough could do at the end was to go to the House of Representatives and make a grand speech. But he had no strategy and it was all nonsense.[78]

Alan Reid provided his own account much closer to the event:

> The first McClelland, manager of the ALP's Senate business, knew of the dismissal was when a sheet of paper was handed to him. It read:

'The Governor-General has dismissed the government.' McClelland thought it was a joke. McClelland and Willesee crossed the chamber to talk to Withers. McClelland said, 'What's the strength of this?'. Withers said, 'It's right'. Willesee said, believing he was being facetious, 'And I suppose he has appointed Fraser Prime Minister'. Withers said, 'That's right'. Both McClelland and Willesee laughed. 'Now pull the other leg', said McClelland. But it was not a leg-pull and it was too late to pull back the Appropriation bills.[79]

It was less than 75 minutes since Whitlam had been dismissed. The theme common to all accounts is Labor's incredulity at the dismissal, followed by confusion.

By 2.10 pm journalists sitting in the House of Representatives gallery were reading Kerr's statement explaining the reasons for his action. That statement had been delivered to the press boxes on the Representatives side slightly after 2.05 pm. The news was about to be flashed on radio. But Labor's Senate leaders were struggling to discover the facts.

The Appropriation bills were reintroduced into the Senate. Once this happened Labor had lost control of the bills since they would be dealt with according to the numbers. It seems clear from accounts published in 1976, based on interviews with the principals, that Wriedt had been told at about 2.15 pm that Labor was dismissed. He was distressed and placed in a quite impossible position. According to one report Withers asked, 'Are you going to move these bills or will we?'. At 2.20 pm exactly Wriedt moved that the bills be passed. The President of the Senate put the motion. It was resolved in the affirmative. This was the last act of the Senate before its dissolution. The Senate adjourned at 2.24 pm. Stunned ALP Senators streamed from the chamber. Wriedt had helped to secure Supply for the Fraser Government. Such a swift passage of Supply was a triumph for Fraser and for Kerr's stratagem. Labor's hope of thwarting Fraser and forcing Kerr to recommission Whitlam was undermined by the rapidity of these events.[80]

In the Representatives, which also reconvened at 2 pm, Labor had been wasting time on the censure motion. Its tactics were aimless and passive. The censure motion debate drifted on; then there were three divisions—the gag, the amendment and the question. By the time the vote was taken members on both sides were aware of the change of government. The pent-up emotions were given free licence when Malcolm Fraser rose from his Opposition leader's chair at 2.34 pm—ten minutes after his government had secured Supply. Fraser said: 'Mr Speaker, this afternoon the Governor-General commissioned me to form a government until elections can be held . . .', whereupon he was drowned out by jeering and cries from the government benches.

Eventually Fraser continued: 'The purpose of the commission is to permit a deadlock between the Houses of Parliament to be resolved and to return Australia to stable government. It will be my sole purpose to ensure that Australia has the general election to which it is constitutionally entitled and which has so far been denied it.' At the conclusion of his five minute speech Fraser said 'it is inappropriate that further business be done by this House' and he moved that the House adjourn.[81]

Fraser lost the division 64–55; the announcement of these numbers provoked another round of jeering from the ALP benches. Fred Daly, acting with despatch and using Labor's numbers, then suspended standing orders to allow Whitlam to move a motion. At 3.00 pm Whitlam rose and moved: 'That this House expresses its want of confidence in the Prime Minister and requests Mr Speaker forthwith to advise His Excellency the Governor-General to call the honourable member for Werriwa [Whitlam] to form a government.'[82]

In his brief speech Whitlam argued that there was no longer a deadlock on the budget between the houses since Supply had been passed. Accordingly the government could now govern. Therefore the Speaker should advise the Governor-General to recommission Whitlam as the leader of the party that had the confidence of the House of Representatives. The words of Whitlam's motion had been rewritten from the draft prepared at the Lodge. The vote was carried 64–54. The Speaker said that he would convey the message of the House to the Governor-General.

Even while debate continued in the House, the dismissed Labor executive was evacuating its offices. Ministerial staff were filling boxes with papers of all variety—secret, confidential, mundane. It was a picture of confusion, chaos and, in some cases, panic. There was a fear that Labor's ministerial quarters might be occupied at any moment by Fraser's own staffers. Labor was on the run. Its sense of disempowerment was pervasive.

The two Appropriation bills were returned from the Senate without amendment. Then Labor made another tactical mistake. It adjourned the House at 3.15 pm until 5.30 pm. Joe Riordan recommended to Whitlam and Daly that the House not adjourn until Kerr saw the Speaker, but: 'Gough would not agree. He believed that the dissolution of Parliament was at that stage a formality and he would not damage the institution of Parliament.'[83]

The focus now moved to the Speaker, Gordon Scholes. Even before the vote was taken to recommission Whitlam, Scholes asked his office to seek an appointment with the Governor-General. On returning to his office Scholes was told that the Official Secretary had reported that Kerr was busy and might not have time for the appointment. This was an obvious signal that Kerr would stick by his course of action and ignore the vote of the Representatives. An angry Scholes then conveyed to Yarralumla the fact that unless he got the appointment he would recall the House, inform members of the situation and seek further guidance. It was the only threat the former government made to save itself. Scholes got his appointment for 4.45 pm, more than an hour later. At this point Labor made another mistake.[84]

The normal procedure was for the Speaker to send a request to the Governor-General that he sign the Appropriation bills—the final step in passing them into law. But this was not a normal situation. Kerr needed the bills for signature in order to secure Supply and Scholes had a message from the House calling on Kerr to reinstate Whitlam. Scholes might have been tempted to present this situation as a quid pro quo—Supply for reinstatement. But he did not. Nor did the Representatives seek to pass a motion instructing the Speaker and the Clerk of the House not to transmit the bills to Yarralumla. The proper procedure was followed to the letter by the Speaker.[85]

Scholes recalls: 'It was my view at this stage that Whitlam had accepted the reality of a dissolution and an election. The game was up. I had some hurried talks with Gough that afternoon. But he never suggested to me that the Supply bills not be sent to the Governor-General.'[86]

If Whitlam or Scholes had delayed the transmission of the bills to Kerr then that, in turn, would have delayed Fraser's securing of Supply—a move that would have created difficulties for all sides.

The bills were transmitted to Government House from the Speaker's office, arriving at 3.50 pm—even though the Speaker was being forced to wait to see the Governor-General to convey the House's message.[87] Whitlam said later that 'with the wisdom of hindsight' it would have been 'wiser if Mr Scholes had taken the Appropriation Bills together with the resolution of the House to his appointment with the Governor-General, instead of sending the bills ahead with the usual written message. This would have been a legitimate and, even against Sir John Kerr, an effective tactic.'[88]

Such a tactic would have accentuated the conflict between the Governor-General and the House of Representatives and it would have deepened further the drama and bitterness of the day. It would have created problems for Kerr. This act alone, however, would not have been sufficient to persuade Kerr to dismiss Fraser and recommission Whitlam, the main reason being that Prime Minister Fraser had secured the Appropriation bills through the Senate.

By sending the bills ahead Scholes allowed Kerr to give the Royal Assent, thereby securing their passage into law. The 1975 Supply crisis had been terminated.

After the House's sitting was suspended at 3.15 pm Fraser prepared to advise Kerr on the double dissolution. He subsequently returned to Yarralumla, as envisaged, to tender the advice. By the time Fraser left Parliament House a large and emotional crowd had gathered, including scores of demonstrators. With a slight smile breaking his stern features Fraser walked past the angry protesters, the Fascist salutes, and climbed into his car. People ran alongside pounding the roof as the car slowly moved off. 'They clearly had a lot of venom when they saw me', Fraser remarked later.[89]

Fraser went to Yarralumla with the Secretary of the Attorney General's department, Clarrie Harders. After Kerr had given Royal Assent to the Appropriation bills he then signed the Proclamation dissolving the two Houses of Parliament. That document listed the twenty-one bills on which Fraser was advising Kerr to grant a double dissolution under section 57 of the Constitution. These were the Whitlam Government's bills which the Coalition had opposed so resolutely during the previous eighteen months. Fraser gave Kerr oral advice that the bills met the requirements of section 57 which, in turn, was supported by Harders. Fraser made it clear that written confirmation of this advice would be provided later.[90]

According to his memoirs Kerr then addressed the parliamentary situation—the resolution passed in the House *for* Whitlam and against Fraser—and asked whether there was any legal or constitutional difficulty in his proceeding with the decisions that he had made before lunch. Kerr wrote: 'Mr Harders said he had spoken to Mr Byers and both of them were of the view that, as I had exercised the reserve power in the morning, I could complete its exercise and could accept the advice of the Prime Minister in favour of a double dissolution.' Kerr continued:

> If I had had no power to do what I had done in dismissing the previous government it would have been the duty of Mr Byers and Mr Harders to advise the Prime Minister and me that what I had done before lunch was invalid and in those circumstances, as Supply had been granted and Mr Whitlam had the confidence of the House, my duty would have been to undo my invalid act, withdraw Mr Fraser's commission and send for Mr Whitlam. This they did not do.'[91]

Asked about Kerr's remarks, Harders replies: 'I didn't doubt that the Governor-General had such a discretion. The problem was the way it was done. In my opinion that was quite wrong. You would not expect a Governor-General to act like that without warning. I don't think any Prime Minister was deserving of that sort of treatment.'[92]

Kerr signed the Proclamation dissolving both Houses. David Smith, present during this conversation, left for Parliament House to read the Proclamation.[93]

Speaker Scholes arrived at the gates of Government House at 4.25 pm. He was kept waiting until Smith drove out to Parliament House to read the Proclamation and dissolve the two houses. Scholes was then kept waiting until his 4.45 pm appointment—the very time that Smith reached the front steps of the Parliament.[94] The Governor-General was treating the Speaker with orchestrated contempt.

Scholes says: 'It was arrogant and improper for the Governor-General to sign the proclamation and send his Secretary to dissolve the Parliament while the Speaker waited at his front gate to convey a message from the House. Can you imagine the uproar if Bill Hayden did this to a Liberal Government?'[95]

Scholes gave Kerr a letter with the resolutions of both houses. Kerr says he told Scholes that he had already dissolved both houses and that there was nothing more to say.[96] A short time later Scholes made a detailed written record of this discussion. It is clear from this record that the Speaker was in a determined and persistent mood. Gough Whitlam writes:

> Mr Scholes said [to Kerr] that he considered it improper for the representative of the Crown to dissolve Parliament without first receiving and hearing from the Speaker . . . He considered that the Governor-General had acted in bad faith. Sir John responded that his mind was made up and as Mr Fraser had, as promised prior to his being commissioned, delivered Supply, he saw no reason to delay the double dissolution which Mr Fraser had requested.
>
> Mr Scholes said that he considered that the Governor-General had acted to dissolve the House without having first taken all action necessary to resolve the deadlock. He considered the Governor-General's first action should have been to write to the President of the Senate, indicating his concern at the refusal of the Senate to consider the Appropriation Bills and thus its refusal to carry out its constitutional obligation. He considered that a request from the Governor-General to the Senate to consider the Appropriation Bills and thus indicate its view on the Supply question would have been a proper first step by the Governor-General. Sir John indicated that he had no power to make such a request . . . He [Scholes] then raised the resolution of the House about my reinstatement and said that that portion should be

complied with irrespective of the dissolution of the Parliament . . . Sir John indicated that for him to comply with the resolution of the House after Mr Fraser had had Supply passed would be viewed as part of a pre-arranged plan between himself and me. Mr Scholes records that the only other significant remark made during the interview was Sir John's comment that his action in sacking me would result in my re-election as Prime Minister.[97]

When interviewed for this book Scholes noted that Kerr told him he had no authority to ask the Senate to cast a decisive vote on the budget bills—yet he was prepared to dismiss the government!

Whitlam insists that Kerr was obliged to act on the motion of the Representatives and recommission him. According to Whitlam: 'Whatever you think about the sacking during the luncheon adjournment, Kerr and Fraser didn't anticipate what would happen in the Parliament after lunch. They stuck to their script . . . but Kerr acted completely unconstitutionally . . . The person you've appointed as Prime Minister has been disowned by the Parliament! You can't retain that Prime Minister.'[98]

But Whitlam's argument is unconvincing.

It was not possible, once Fraser had obtained Supply, for Kerr to recommission Whitlam. This is because Kerr's application of the reserve powers—and Fraser's commission as Prime Minister—were made on the basis that Fraser would obtain Supply and recommend a general election. Fraser had met the terms of his commission; Kerr could hardly respond to this situation by sacking Fraser. The Senate passed Supply *on the assumption* that Fraser as Prime Minister would advise a general election. Kerr could not dishonour the reasons for his commissioning of Fraser in the first place. The House vote had demonstrated what Kerr knew from the start—that Whitlam had its confidence. Kerr knew he was commissioning Fraser as a minority Prime Minister. He did so in order to allow Fraser to obtain Supply and then advise an election. The only way Whitlam could have been recommissioned was by making it impossible for Fraser to meet the conditions of his commission—that is, by delaying him Supply for a sufficient time so that Fraser's position became untenable.

By 4.30 pm the news of Whitlam's dismissal had spread throughout Canberra. The crowd, emotional and angry, growing all the time, mingled with politicians, staffers and journalists and spilled across the road in front of the building, on to the steps and into Kings Hall. About this time a podium and microphone were set up at the top of the front steps. At 4.40 pm David Smith, dressed in formal black jacket, arrived at the entrance to Parliament House to read the Proclamation. His words were drowned out by demonstrators who then broke into the chant 'We want Gough', reinforced by the waving of makeshift banners.

Behind Smith to his right was the tall figure of the former Prime Minister, tense and redfaced, a looming presence amid the masses which included many police who were trying to keep a path open down the steps. Smith finished, and pushed his way out of the crowd.

The Parliament was dissolved. Fraser was a caretaker Prime Minister and Whitlam, dismissed from office, was the Opposition leader. It was just three and three quarter hours since Whitlam had walked into Kerr's study as Prime Minister. The implementation of Kerr's transfer of power and his instigation of a general election had proceeded fairly smoothly. Labor had not recovered from the blow of dismissal. Now Whitlam took the microphone. His cue was Smith's last phrase, 'God save the Queen'—Australia's head of state in whose name, ultimately, Kerr had acted.

Whitlam delivered a short and famous speech:

> Well may we say 'God save the Queen', because nothing will save the Governor-General! The Proclamation which you have just heard read by the Governor-General's Official Secretary was countersigned Malcolm Fraser, who will undoubtedly go down in Australian history from Remembrance Day 1975 as Kerr's cur. They won't silence the outskirts of Parliament House, even if the inside has been silenced for a few weeks. The Governor-General's proclamation was signed after he had already made an appointment to meet the Speaker at a quarter to five. The House of Representatives had requested the Speaker to give the Governor-General its decision that Mr Fraser did not have the confidence of the House and that the Governor-General should call upon me to form the government . . . Maintain your rage and enthusiasm for the campaign for the election now to be held and until polling day.

Whitlam said later that his words were 'a remarkable exercise in restraint and moderation'—given the events. Like the political professional that he was, Whitlam was now gearing his efforts to the campaign.[99]

A political veteran, Doug Anthony, was apprehensive about the crowd's mood: 'It was quite frightening. I was on the front steps and the crowds were running across the road. I think there was a risk that it could have got out of control. People were cursing us. I was being cursed. If something had snapped it could have changed the course of Australian history. It was one of the few times when I felt a sense of danger.'[100]

But Whitlam noted of the crowd: 'I daresay I could have stirred them up a lot more than I did . . . just the night for a pleasant walk to Yarralumla'.[101]

Could Labor have destroyed Sir John Kerr's stratagem in the few hours after he dismissed Whitlam at 1 pm?

It is most probable that Whitlam could have ruined it. Kerr's plan succeeded for three reasons: (1) it was a complete surprise; (2) Whitlam had no contingency plan to handle a dismissal; and (3) luck ran with Kerr and Fraser and against Whitlam.

As a concept Kerr's plan was unsound. It was flawed in theory and could have been countered in practice. The essential element was for Whitlam to have prepared a contingency plan to counter a dismissal. But Whitlam never entertained the need for such a plan because he did not regard dismissal as a possibility.

The flaw in Kerr's intervention as a practical exercise is that a minority government lacking the confidence of the House cannot obtain Supply. Fraser had told Kerr throughout the crisis that he would be able to obtain Supply, but such advice—if Whitlam had thought about Fraser's position—could be countered.

Whitlam's first action when the House sat at 2 pm should have been to move a motion rescinding the House's previous motions carrying the Appropriation bills. The Representatives would have denied Supply to the minority Fraser Government. Whitlam's actual response on 11 November was proper, parliamentary and rhetorical. But it was ineffective and conceptually inadequate. Kerr and Fraser were not following the normal rules. A government without the confidence of the Representatives cannot secure Supply. Whitlam was better placed to deny Supply to a Fraser Government than Fraser had been to deny Supply to the Whitlam Government. The dismissal merely reversed the situation. Fraser had the numbers for Supply in the Senate but he could not command Supply through the Representatives. Fraser had a temporary advantage because the House had already secured the Appropriation bills on behalf of the now dismissed Whitlam Government. So Whitlam's first task should have been to cancel this temporary advantage by rescinding in the Representatives the passage of the Appropriation bills. This could have been done immediately without debate, with Fred Daly moving the gag. It would have been accomplished by 2.15 pm at the outside.[102]

It was appropriate from a parliamentary and moral perspective that Whitlam implement such a tactic. The Appropriation bills that had passed the House were those of the Whitlam Government based upon the Hayden budget. Since the Whitlam Government no longer existed it was correct to insist that a new government should carry its own Supply bills. By rescinding its previous votes on the Supply bills the Representatives would be conveying this message to the new Prime

Minister. In addition, Whitlam could have successfully moved that the Representatives send a message to the Senate informing that chamber that previous votes had been rescinded and requesting the return of the former government's Appropriation bills.

This scenario was outlined by the former Clerk of the Senate, J R Odgers, who said:

> In reality, no Opposition leader or other Member not commanding a majority in both Houses can guarantee Supply because, even if Supply has passed the House of Representatives and a caretaker Government is confident of its passage through the Senate, a dismissed Prime Minister, still having the numbers in the House of Representatives, could cause the recission of all votes in the House on Supply and bring about stalemate.[103]

Whitlam could have also carried a motion to the effect that if the Senate defied the message from the House and passed the Appropriation bills the Speaker of the House of Representatives be instructed not to forward such bills to the Governor-General for Royal Assent. Whitlam could have then carried a no-confidence motion in the Fraser Government and sought his own reinstatement as Prime Minister on the grounds that Supply had been denied to Fraser who therefore could not meet the terms of his commission. Finally, the Representatives could have voted to remain in continuous sittings until the Governor-General acted on the denial of Supply to Fraser. All these motions could have been put and carried in the House before 3 pm. The Fraser Government might have resorted to a court order to compel the Speaker to comply, but the High Court surely would not have intervened in such a situation.

In the meantime Labor's tactic in the Senate should have been to use every possible procedural motion, plus the advantage of controlling the chair, to rearrange business, seek an adjournment of the Senate or delay the introduction of the Supply bills. The longer Labor could have delayed the passage of these bills the more likely Fraser and Kerr would have retreated in the face of the series of motions carried through the Representatives. The President of the Senate was Labor's Justin O'Byrne and this would have given the ALP a considerable advantage in thwarting the Coalition for some time. Ultimately, if Fraser and Withers insisted, they would have had the numbers in the Senate to carry Supply. But the Representatives would have merely stood upon its own motions and its rights as the House that made and unmade governments according to the practice of responsible government. At this point Whitlam could have sought an appointment with Kerr to advise him that the House was denying Supply to Fraser and would sit until he was recommissioned.

This integrated approach should have terminated Fraser as Prime Minister and destroyed Kerr's strategy. The most effective method, of course, would have been for Whitlam to accept the advice of his officials and include a provision in the Appropriation bills that, after passing the Senate, they had to pass the Representatives again. This would have made the dismissal meaningless since Fraser could not have advised Kerr that he could secure Supply.

It is a violation of responsible government for a minority leader lacking the confidence of the popular house to be commissioned on the condition that he *guarantees* Supply. It is also a contradiction in terms. This is the strongest criticism of Kerr's solution. Fraser was not in a position to guarantee Supply; he secured Supply only because Whitlam declined to respond ruthlessly by resort to every parliamentary weapon, just as Fraser and Kerr had ruthlessly used the powers available to them against Whitlam. In effect, Whitlam did not deploy against Fraser the 'denial of Supply' device that Fraser deployed against him. Labor's failure to have a contingency plan meant that the cause of responsible government was diminished when it should have been more vigorously defended.

If Whitlam had ruthlessly implemented a contingency plan to thwart his dismissal, then Australia's system of government would have come close to the point of breakdown. Kerr was lucky in that his solution was not seriously resisted. If Whitlam had resisted as outlined, then Kerr's nerve would have probably cracked before Whitlam's or Fraser's—given the nature of the three men.

There were several options in this situation. First, that Kerr would still have held out, even for a considerable period of time, until somehow the Supply bills were sent to Yarralumla for the Royal Assent. He would then have dissolved the Parliament on Fraser's advice. Second, that facing a stalemate, Kerr would have modified his position and accepted advice from Fraser for a general election without Supply. This would have been extremely dangerous for both Fraser and Kerr. Fraser would have faced a general election as Prime Minister with Supply expiring in mid-campaign, and most people blaming him. Kerr would have been responsible for the precise situation he professed his intervention was designed to avoid—an expiry of Supply. Third, Kerr, given Fraser's failure to secure Supply, would have recommissioned Whitlam, and presumably would have then resigned as Governor-General. If he had failed to resign, then Whitlam would have approached the Palace to seek his removal. Given the situation,

Whitlam might have accepted the intended double dissolution and gone to a general election as Prime Minister. Alternatively, depending upon the extent of Fraser's humiliation, the Opposition might have promptly passed the budget in the Senate without an election, thereby ending the crisis with Whitlam as Prime Minister and Kerr dismissed as Governor-General. (There is another possibility—that in a stalemate the Palace would have been asked to intervene, although it is most unlikely that the Queen would have done anything.)

Constitutional government requires the consent of the principals in order to operate successfully. That is one reason why legal rules alone cannot suffice. The conclusion about the events of 11 November is that Kerr and Fraser pushed the system to the limit and that Whitlam, on the other hand, did not deploy all his power as majority leader in the House. This conclusion is based upon an analysis of power, not an impression of rhetoric.

Later that afternoon Whitlam held a press conference which was restrained despite the emotions of the day:

> Q: Are you saying that at no stage of the talks you had with the Governor-General did he give you the impression that he thought a general election was the proper course?
>
> A: On the contrary. He gave me the other impression . . .
>
> Q: Are you going to contact London?
>
> A: The Governor-General prevented me getting in touch with the Queen by just withdrawing the commission immediately. I was unable to communicate with the Queen, as I would have been entitled to if I had any warning of the course that he, the Governor-General, was to take . . .
>
> Q: Are you suggesting that the Governor-General may have misled you?
>
> A: No, I'm not saying that . . .
>
> Q: Mr Whitlam, are you satisfied that the Governor-General had the right under the Constitution to withdraw your commission?
>
> A: Oh no. On the contrary, I am certain the Crown did not have the right to do what the Governor-General did on this occasion . . . Let's be frank about it—the Queen would never have done it . . . There's no Act which says it can't happen, but it hasn't happened for 200 years in the Westminster system.

A short time later Fraser also met a sullen press gallery:

> Q: Did you have any advice beforehand?
>
> A: No, none at all . . .

Q: How do you think history will judge this action of yours in precipitating this election?

A: It will be vindicated by the judgement of history because Australia will get a responsible government again . . .

Q: You said on *This Day Tonight* that the Governor-General could speak for himself 'and he will'. Why did you make such a firm and definitive statement?

A: Only because I have a proper understanding that the Parliament of Australia is comprised of the Queen, in her case represented by the Governor-General, the Senate and the House of Representatives.

A few hours earlier, just after 1 pm Canberra time, David Smith had rung the Queen's staff and broken the news of the dismissal. The Queen, presumably, was told when she awoke. But the Queen's private secretary, Sir Martin Charteris, was told directly by Whitlam.

That afternoon—early morning in London—Whitlam rang Sir Martin who confirmed that the Queen had known nothing before Kerr acted. Charteris recalls: 'It was late at night, probably after midnight, when I took a call from Gough Whitlam. I had returned from the Lord Mayor's Banquet. I remember clearly that he introduced himself as the member for Werriwa. He informed me that Sir John had terminated his commission. That was the sole purpose of his call.' Asked if Whitlam had made any requests of or complaints to the Palace, Sir Martin says: 'He didn't ask me to do anything.' Sir Martin confirms that there was 'plenty of drama' at the Palace after the news became known.[104]

Kerr ended the Whitlam era in Australian history. The election on 13 December 1975 confirmed Whitlam's demise. The people voted overwhelmingly against Whitlam, as Malcolm Fraser believed they would. The dismissal made Whitlam a hero to the 'true believers' but, for many others, Kerr's dismissal of Whitlam merely confirmed the ALP's lack of legitimacy. There is no reason to believe that the dismissal had anything but a damaging electoral impact for Whitlam. He fought the election as a dismissed Prime Minister against a caretaker Prime Minister. Fraser emerged from the election not just victorious but dominant. His Liberal–National Coalition won 91 seats compared to Labor's 36 and Fraser had 35 Senators in a 64-strong Senate.

11
1975

Looking at everything that has happened I must say that I would do it all again.

Sir John Kerr on his dismissal of Gough Whitlam

WHILE WHITLAM AND FRASER fought an election campaign that oscillated between the bitter and the dreary, the Kerrs cancelled nearly all official functions, repaired to the swimming pool and made plans to evacuate Yarralumla if Whitlam won. Sir John Kerr decided that if Labor were re-elected then he would resign as Governor-General before Whitlam's inevitable move to sack him. Anne Kerr went to Sydney before election day and purchased an apartment. It was prudent planning; the Kerrs were taking no chances lest the opinion polls pointing to a Fraser victory were misleading.[1]

This was an admission of the obvious—that Kerr's action had destroyed his ability as Governor-General to serve as a symbol of unity beyond partisan politics. Sir John saw the election result as a vindication of his action: 'It was heartening to me to see that, with these matters squarely before the people, their vote could not fail to be recognised as an expression of approval of my action.'[2]

So the Crown's representative judged his success by the triumph of one party against another—a repudiation of the Crown's place beyond party politics.

The Labor Party was opposed to Kerr's remaining as Governor-General and imposed a boycott of vice-regal functions that began with the opening of the new Parliament in February 1976. In addition, there was a vigorous nationwide protest movement against Sir John which curtailed his appearances and role as Governor-General. Kerr kept inviting Whitlam to Government House without success until he refused an invitation in honour of the Queen, described by Anne Kerr as 'a discourtesy which, we felt, released us from further efforts'.[3]

After the election, Kerr says, he spoke to Malcolm Fraser whose 'firm advice was against resignation'.[4]

It is a fair judgement of Kerr to say that he was debilitated by the passions aroused against him and anxious—during the rest of his tenure and of his life—to vindicate his dismissal of Whitlam. Sir John was placed in a difficult position. Any decision to resign as Governor-General in the interests of maintaining the impartiality of the office would be interpreted in some quarters as an admission of Kerr's culpability. On the other hand, the decision to remain, heavily inspired by the motive of defying his critics, ensured that Sir John and his office became the focus of a bitter political dispute that could be resolved only by his eventual retirement. Kerr justified his decision by insisting that 'it had to be proved that a Governor-General who had properly exercised the reserve powers could not be driven from office'.[5]

It was unrealistic to think that Kerr might resign after the election. After all, the entire rationale for his behaviour during the crisis—keeping his counsel secret from Whitlam—was designed to protect his own position from a prime ministerial sacking. Having prevailed in this contest with Whitlam, Kerr was not going to surrender his office afterwards.

The depth of feeling about Sir John within the ALP is revealed in the reflections of former Whitlam minister, Joe Riordan—not a principal figure in the 1975 crisis, but a decent man and a realistic politician:

> There are very few people that I have met in my lifetime for whom I have had a higher regard. When he was appointed Governor-General I wrote and congratulated him. I have never been so shocked as I was on the afternoon of 11 November when Gough told me what had occurred. I did not believe him and he showed me the letter . . .
> There has never been an occasion in my life when I have experienced such a feeling of betrayal and deception . . . I regarded John Kerr as a friend and he was a guest at my wedding. I had complete and unqualified trust in his integrity. I never spoke to him again because I could not do so. I adhere to the view that Kerr's action was planned in advance and that he set out to deceive, which was essential to his treachery.[6]

Kerr was indulged by Fraser with overseas trips and imperial honours—but not with personal support. Doug Anthony says: 'I felt that Malcolm was never kind enough to him. I think the events affected him terribly and that his life was pretty miserable. I can't forgive Gough for crucifying him.'[7] Other Liberals say that afterwards Fraser took Kerr's intervention for granted! Reg Withers, who became vice-president of the Executive Council under Fraser, reports that 'Kerr spent all his time afterwards justifying what he did'.[8]

Anne Kerr called the situation confronted by the Kerrs after the December 1975 election as a 'new irrational scene swarming with instant enemies'.[9] Despite Kerr's claims that he anticipated the hostility that the dismissal would provoke, his behaviour was that of a man succumbing to pressure. The spectacular example occurred at Australia's famous sporting event, the Melbourne Cup, in 1977, when an intoxicated Governor-General was captured on television presenting the cup. Whitlam would quip that a million viewers 'may have thought that the horse would have made a better proconsul'.[10]

John Menadue, who remained Secretary of the Prime Minister's Department during the initial period of Fraser's rule and who continued to visit Yarralumla to brief Kerr on government business, paints a graphic portrait: 'My impression of John Kerr afterwards was that he was a beaten man. He was obsessed about security. There was a sense of physical fear, that people might jump the walls. When I would go to Yarralumla to brief him I found that Lady Kerr would often join us. She was a source of much needed support.'[11]

One minister, John Wheeldon, who had been friendly with Kerr, says: 'Afterwards I think Kerr was in a sad and dismayed condition. I personally felt very sorry for him. I think he was as full as a boot a lot of the time.'[12]

In late 1977 Kerr granted an early Representatives and half Senate election to Fraser—a proper exercise of his power based upon ministerial advice. Kerr says he would have 'almost certainly' resigned beforehand 'had there been any prospect of a Labor victory'.[13] It was further proof that the Crown's representative was hostage to party-political forces—a situation incompatible with Australia's system of constitutional monarchy.

Asked about his relationship with Kerr, Fraser ruminates:

> We didn't talk much about the dismissal. I probably should have tried to talk to him more about it. That might have made it a bit easier for him. He felt that he'd done the right thing and that he was paying a terrible price for it, as we know . . . I suppose the Labor Party, in part, made him a symbol of division. But you can't entirely ignore the way he was handling the situation.[14]

Fraser sounds ungrateful; but the impression is misleading. He was a professional politician and had made his judgement. By 1977 Fraser wanted Kerr to take his departure.

It was an irony. Fraser, the beneficiary of Kerr's intervention, was embarrassed, finally, by Kerr's tenure.

Kerr insists that resignation was his own decision anyway. In the first part of 1977, Kerr says, he discussed resignation with both the Queen and Fraser—at his own initiative.[15]

Kerr wanted another position. He had negotiated with Whitlam a ten year term as Governor-General that would have taken him through to mid-1984, so it 'did not occur to me for a moment' that a premature retirement as Governor-General would mean retirement from public life.[16] In Paris in mid-1977 the Kerrs inspected at length the new Australian embassy building, designed by Harry Seidler. On 14 July 1977 it was announced that Sir John would be retiring as Governor-General—and he left office in December. Fraser explained later that the reason was to allow the 'scars on the Australian body politic' to heal 'more quickly'. The political correspondent of the *Age*, Michelle Grattan, wrote: 'Sir John Kerr leaves the office of Governor-General mourned by no one in politics.' In February 1978, three months after Kerr granted Fraser his early election, a re-elected Prime Minister announced that Sir John would become ambassador to a revived UNESCO post based in Paris. The condemnation was universal and virulent—by individuals and by newspapers, many of whom had supported the dismissal. The ALP leader, Bill Hayden, said the appointment was 'a further demonstration of the degree by which the high office of Governor-General has been abused by the former incumbent for personal gain'.[17] Whitlam said the principle was simple—that former Governors-General should not accept appointments from governments with which 'they have stood in a constitutional relation'.

On 1 March 1978 Kerr wrote to Fraser withdrawing from this post and the next day Fraser announced Sir John's decision to Parliament. Both men blamed the unremitting campaign against Sir John which Kerr branded as 'trial by innuendo and falsehood'. The aborted appointment was a humiliation for both Fraser and Kerr.[18]

The Kerrs left Australia for six and a half years—apart from holidays back home. Sir John said that after leaving Yarralumla they always intended 'to live in Europe for a longish period' and that 'it was not an enforced exile'.[19]

Sir John's successors were both distinguished lawyers, Sir Zelman Cowen and Sir Ninian Stephen, and they engaged in what became known as 'the healing process'—the restoration of faith in the office.

In his defence Kerr's resort was the scapegoat plea. He declared:

> It was my fate to be regarded by the Labor Party—and not only by them—as a scapegoat. Other people's sins were heaped upon my head. It was as though, through vilifying one individual, all others could be cleansed of their responsibility for that great national crisis. I was the scapegoat—the sacrificial animal. It was as if I was to blame for 1975—not the Senate denying Supply; not Mr Whitlam refusing to go to the people; but the Governor-General for ending the crisis, averting terrible chaos, and letting the people decide . . . Because he could not blame a whole people, Mr Whitlam chose to blame one man.[20]

Many have found this argument persuasive.

It raises, ultimately, two questions about 1975. How should responsibility for the crisis be allocated and how valid was Kerr's solution of dismissal?

The issue of responsibility—Fraser and Whitlam

Legal opinions about powers do vary but there exists a majority view among jurists that the three powers exercised were valid. That is, the Senate had the power to defer the budget on behalf of Fraser's Opposition; Whitlam was entitled to remain in office and 'tough it out' *for some time* while he had Supply, rather than resign or advise a general election; and the reserve powers upon which Sir John Kerr relied do exist and include the dismissal power.

Not everyone will agree with these three propositions. None of them enjoys universal support; but each of them enjoys majority support. However, the argument is academic. Each of these powers was exercised in 1975 and therefore it is a fact that they do exist. The Senate did block the budget; Whitlam did remain in office for 27 days waging a political campaign against the Senate; and the Governor-General did dismiss the Prime Minister. For better or worse these events occurred and it will be difficult to argue that the powers involved do not exist. The 1975 crisis, despite the claims of the protagonists, is not about the occurrence of unconstitutional behaviour.

The Constitution is an imperfect document which contains conflicts and inconsistencies. No political system can endure relying upon just a legal skeleton; it is the working rules and conventions that keep the system operational and shape constitutional interpretation. The events of 1975 are best understood in terms of a contradiction, embedded in the Constitution, being exposed by a power and personality clash involving three wilful men—Fraser, Whitlam and Kerr. Former Whitlam minister John Wheeldon says: 'We were really dealing with three crackpots here. We were just lucky that between them they didn't sink the country.'[21]

The contradiction within Australia's Constitution originated with the efforts of the founding fathers to reconcile the Westminster model of responsible government with the United States notion of federalism. The attempt to marry the Westminster and Washington models produced a unique system for the Commonwealth of Australia.

Responsible government is the notion that the party that obtains the confidence of the lower house elected directly by the people is entitled to govern, and that governments are made and unmade in the lower house to which they are responsible. But the tradeoff agreed by the founding fathers in order to secure a new Commonwealth was a Senate to uphold the interests of the States—a Senate with powers almost co-equal with those of the Representatives.

The founding fathers were aware of the contradiction and struggled to find a solution. Their conclusion was that the two institutions were 'theoretically incompatible' but 'both were practically necessary, and moreover . . . they could be made to work together'.[22]

The salient points arising from the Federation debates are:

- the Constitution embodies responsible government and this belief was fundamental to the Senate's being denied the power to initiate or to amend money bills
- the financial powers of the Senate were granted on the assumption by most delegates that such powers were necessary to safeguard the smaller States
- it was envisaged that the Senate would reject discrete tax or money bills on specific policy or State-interest grounds—such bills not being the Supply bills which would halt the daily process of government—and that a dispute between the houses might mean a general election
- a mechanism was provided for such deadlocks through section 57, which allowed a double dissolution if the Senate failed to pass the same bill after a three month interval
- it was not envisaged by most delegates that the Senate would reject or block Appropriation bills and no particular mechanism was provided for such a deadlock—which was described by a New South Wales conservative, McMillan, as a step that 'would mean revolution' and was dismissed by Sir Samuel Griffith with 'I do not think the matter is worth discussing'.[23]

One analyst says: 'The founders had provided no adequate mechanical means for breaking supply deadlocks because they never envisaged politicians would engineer such dangerous things for short run gains'.[24]

Such a deadlock never arose until 1975 and Sir John Kerr's answer was to 'invent' a solution.[25]

The precedent-making potential of the 1975 crisis cannot be overlooked. Suppose Malcolm Fraser had announced on 15 October 1975 that, despite the state of the economy and the resignation of Rex Connor, he would not block Whitlam's budget because the architects of the Constitution did not envisage resort to this power and such action would undermine the Representatives. Had Fraser done this he would probably have gone far to confirm such a convention, which over time would have influenced constitutional interpretation.

But Fraser responded as a party politician and he reflected a party-political culture. He used the powers available in an effort to destroy the Whitlam Government and return the Liberal–Country Party Coalition to office. In the process he confirmed the Senate's constitutional power in relation to financial bills and rejected any convention that the Senate did not use this power for party interests.

It is Malcolm Fraser who must carry the major responsibility for initiating the 1975 crisis. A different but significant responsibility resides with Whitlam. This is because a more competent ALP government would not have provided such a tempting target; it was Whitlam's electoral weakness that attracted Fraser. However, there was no obligation upon Fraser in terms of the national interest or a personal interest to force an election in late 1975 by blocking the Appropriation bills. Fraser had a choice. If he had let the Parliament run its term then Whitlam would have been defeated, Fraser would have enjoyed a victory at the usual time and there would have been no crisis for the Constitution or animosity towards the Coalition because of its tactics.

Fraser's own claim is that another year or 18 months of Whitlam should not have been tolerated. He concedes that Australia would have 'survived' but asks: 'Should Australia have been asked to endure another year of *that* government?' However, Fraser's invocation of the national interest to justify his action is not persuasive. The economic policy changes instituted by the Fraser Government were only marginally different from those being piloted by the Whitlam–Hayden–McClelland team. The evidence is unconvincing that a further year of Whitlam's government would have left Australia in a seriously worse condition than having Fraser in government during this same period. Malcolm Fraser was inspired by power and, like most leaders in such situations, convinced himself of the national interest imperative.

Fraser used the Senate not to review or halt policy—but to send the Representatives to an election. This was a derogation of responsible government, an undermining of the House of Representatives and a damaging imposition on the democratic institutions. It was a power that, once invoked, could lead to a constitutional 'no man's land' since there was no constitutional mechanism to handle this deadlock.[26] It was also a power that the founding fathers had believed would only be exercised, if ever, on behalf of the States—not by the Opposition leader in the House of Representatives. Fraser manipulated the Senate from his position in the lower house. The vote carried in the Senate was possible only because of the death of a Labor Senator and the corruption of the Senate's numbers—a fact that severely undermined Fraser's moral position. Not only was Fraser the first Opposition leader in 75 years to force an election by blocking Supply but, when Whitlam resisted, Fraser became the first Opposition leader to tell the Governor-General to dismiss the Prime Minister because of the Senate's actions.

Twenty years later Fraser defends his decision:

People like to dramatise and claim that our social and constitutional fabric has disintegrated. I just don't believe that. I can name two instances as being more serious for the body politic than the Supply issue. One was Evatt and the split in the Labor Party in the 1950s and the hatreds which poured out as a result of that with the social divisions it created. An earlier one was Billy Hughes' treatment of Archbishop Mannix and his turning the referendums in World War I into anti-Catholic and anti-Irish votes. It was at that time that the Federation could have been destroyed. I don't think that 1975 deserves prominence in this context.[27]

Fraser's argument carries much weight. The issue, however, is not whether 1975 caused more social and political divisions than did other great crises. It is, rather, whether the 1975 crisis that Fraser initiated was necessary. The compelling interpretation is that Fraser, by forcing the crisis, put a premium on short-term gain at the cost of responsible government, community division and the alienation from his prime ministership of a significant minority within the electorate upset at the way in which he got the job. Moreover, as Menzies implied to Barwick when he criticised Fraser for blocking the budget, it was unnecessary as judged against the Coalition's political interest.[28] Fraser would win the next election anyway. So his own political interest would have been equally served by waiting for an election, not forcing a crisis.

The second stage of the crisis was Whitlam's decision to remain in office and attempt, through political pressure, to force Fraser and his Senate to retreat. Whitlam's initial motive was elemental—survival itself. Whitlam knew that Labor would lose an immediate election and that is the reason why he refused to accede to the Senate.

But Whitlam had another motive which originated within the constitutional system. For nearly three years his government's legislative reform program had been thwarted by the Senate; the non-Labor Premiers had refused to fill ALP Senate vacancies with ALP appointees; they were threatening to advise their Governors not to issue writs for a late 1975 Senate election; and, finally, Fraser was using the Senate's biannual approval of Supply to force the Whitlam Government to the people despite its majority within the Representatives. The consequences were potentially fatal to Whitlam's government and, beyond that, detrimental to the cause of responsible government and the influence of the Representatives—the people's house.

Whitlam's stand was designed not just to save his own government; not just to thwart the triumph of the 'federalism' interpretation of the Constitution implicit in any success by Fraser. Beyond this, Whitlam intended to use the crisis triggered by Fraser to defeat the Senate in such a comprehensive manner that no future Senate would contemplate such action, and to ensure that the contradiction within the Constitution since the inauguration of the Commonwealth was finally resolved with the victory of the Representatives over the Senate and of responsible government over federalism. Whitlam would become the last of the founding fathers. He would resolve the contradiction that they had been unable to resolve.

Whitlam sought to achieve this by a political victory. Fraser had begun this battle but Whitlam intended to finish it. Whitlam's aspirations were outlined in his speeches in the Representatives during the crisis.

There was no constitutional provision that required a Prime Minister, faced with the Senate's deferral of Supply, to call an election. Sir John Kerr believed that Whitlam was entitled to remain in office and seek a political solution to the crisis. The Governor-General did not suggest and never suggested that Whitlam's action was unconstitutional at the time he launched his 'tough it out' campaign on 15 October. Whitlam was under pressure from the Opposition to call a general election when the Appropriation bills were blocked. But there was neither a constitutional obligation nor a political convention that obliged him to call an election at this point.

Whitlam argued, with considerable effect, the reverse proposition—that there was a constitutional obligation upon him to defeat the Senate's manoeuvre. This obligation arose to the extent that the concept of responsible government, as reflected in the Constitution, was being put at risk by the Coalition's tactic.

Two senior ministers, Wriedt and Wheeldon, recommended a general election. They did so not because they believed the Opposition was correct. Their argument was that one wrong should not be matched by another; that Australia's democratic institutions were being put under strain and that Labor should not compound the structural stresses being imposed by Fraser. That is an honourable argument. But a combination of self-interest and political belief drove Whitlam to remain in office. He responded in kind to Fraser. Whitlam decided that the House of Representatives in October 1975 was neither the place nor the time for Labor to surrender to the Coalition campaign and buckle before Fraser's election ultimatum.

That put the issue squarely before Sir John Kerr.

The issue of responsibility—Sir John Kerr

The idea has gained currency that Kerr was a victim of two headstrong leaders, Fraser and Whitlam, neither of whom would retreat or compromise and that, finally, he had no alternative but dismissal.

It is an interpretation that cannot be sustained.

The Crown and the Crown's representative will be called upon, periodically, to address a crisis. That is the nature of monarchy and the role of the Sovereign; it is the role of the Governor-General in Australia's system of constitutional monarchy.

Most successful leaders can be headstrong and, in Australia's competitive party system, they will wield constitutional powers that can be used to their advantage. The 1975 crisis was both a challenge and an opportunity for Kerr as Governor-General—a man who had aspired to leave his mark upon the nation. It is easy to open a flower show; the 1975 crisis demanded judgement—the quality that makes a successful Sovereign and for which Governors-General are chosen.

The argument against Sir John Kerr is that he chose an extreme solution—dismissal of the Prime Minister without warning and with damaging consequences for his own office and the parliamentary system—when a better solution was available. It is an argument about his competence.

Sir John Kerr's argument that no political solution was available is not convincing. It originates within Kerr's view that his office carried little influence but an ultimate sanction. As a consequence he failed to influence and applied the sanction. Sir John explored options for a compromise during the crisis; but he did not commit his office to this task.

There are four dimensions in which Kerr's judgement undermined a political solution—the timing of his intervention was unnecessarily premature; instead of approaching the reserve powers as a solution of 'last resort' he was attracted to their use before more orthodox processes; he failed in the Crown's obligation to warn the Prime Minister of a possible vice-regal intervention and thus to encourage Whitlam to reassess; and the principle upon which he acted—that if the Prime Minister did not resign or advise a general election then he had to be dismissed—was substantiated neither by the Constitution nor by political practice. The startling point about the dismissal is how unusual were the premises on which Kerr acted.[29]

Sir John chose to become a constitutional innovator. The lawyers have obscured this reality by defending his application of the reserve powers. The mere claim that the reserve powers exist is a truism; it is also irrelevant to the questions of what are these powers and in what circumstances can they be used; the claim cannot serve as justification for a dismissal on 11 November. It is widely, though not universally, accepted, by both believers and disbelievers in the reserve powers that they should be used only as a last resort or in an 'emergency', when all ordinary processes cannot solve the problem.[30]

The starting point in assessing the dismissal is the principle on which Kerr acted. It is explained in his statement: 'A Prime Minister who cannot obtain Supply, including money for carrying on the ordinary services of government, must either advise a general election or resign.' So Kerr insisted that if the Senate blocked Supply the Prime Minister's options were an election or resignation—or dismissal.

Professor Geoffrey Sawer put this statement into context:

> The problem is difficult because the Governor-General's action was completely without precedent. It is clear from the documents that he acted for one reason only—because Mr Whitlam was unable to get Supply from the Senate. On no previous occasion in Britain, Australia or any British-derived parliamentary system has the Monarch or a Governor dismissed a ministry having a majority in the Commons, Representatives or similar House, because that ministry has been denied Supply by the Lords, Senate or similar House.[31]

Sir John, in fact, took the argument a step further—he asserted a 'duty' to dismiss the Prime Minister in this situation. Again, there is neither a constitutional provision nor a political convention to support this assertion. So Kerr's dismissal of Whitlam on these grounds was a constitutional innovation of considerable audacity.

Sir John's defence of his principle relies upon the argument set out in Sir Garfield Barwick's letter. Sir Garfield said that in Australia a Prime Minister required the confidence of both the House of Representatives and the Senate to govern. His memoirs further elaborate the political theory on which the Chief Justice and the Governor-General relied. Barwick says that from the day Whitlam's government was denied Supply,

> ... it had lost the confidence of the Parliament, though it still had the confidence of the House of Representatives. It then came under a Parliamentary obligation to resign or advise a dissolution. From that date it had no *legitimate* claim to govern.[32]

Sir John, in his dismissal statement, said: 'The position in Australia is quite different from the position in the United Kingdom. Here the confidence of both Houses on Supply is necessary to ensure its provision.' This is the Kerr–Barwick justification for the dismissal; it is Kerr's central argument.

(Kerr did not dismiss Whitlam for any illegality and there was no illegality. He did not dismiss Whitlam for any threat of illegality—although Sir John later defended his action by saying that he 'was not prepared to delay until after disaster came to pass'. Sir John knew that a theory of preventative intervention—dismissing a government because it might break the law in future—was not a valid basis for dismissal. He did not offer such a justification in his statement explaining his action and this notion was only used sometime later as a polemical device.)

What happened is that Kerr and Barwick invented a new political convention to justify the dismissal. Their convention is that in Australia a Prime Minister needs the confidence of both the Representatives and the Senate to govern. This theory was not heard before 1975; it has not been heard since. The notion that a Prime Minister faced with denial of Supply by a Senate is obliged to resign because he has lost the confidence of the Parliament has no precedent.[33]

At the Federal Conventions the founding fathers—in the teeth of small-State resistance—implanted responsible government in the Constitution by ensuring that only the Representatives can originate or amend money bills. The logic is clear: a government cannot be based in the Senate because the Senate cannot initiate a money bill. The founders assumed that ministers 'would be primarily located in, and be entirely responsible to, the House of Representatives'.[34] The situation was documented by Quick and Garran:

> The cabinet depends for its existence on its possession of the confidence of that House directly elected by the people, which has the principal control over the finances of the country. It is not so dependent upon the favour and support of the second Chamber, but at the same time a cabinet in antagonism with the second Chamber will be likely to suffer serious difficulty, if not obstruction, in the conduct of public business.[35]

So a government is responsible to the Representatives. It is the Representatives that determines who governs. If a government loses the confidence of the Representatives then it falls. But a government is *not* responsible to both Representatives and Senate. Once a government is formed then it must manage its relations with the Senate where it could face difficulty or obstruction.

Lest there be any doubt that a government is responsible to the Representatives only, Quick and Garran surveyed the arguments put forward during the Federation debates by staunch federalists who asserted, in fact, that 'the State House could, as effectively as the primary Chamber, enforce its want of confidence by refusing to provide the necessary supplies'. These champions of the States made two proposals to prevent the entrenchment of responsible government in the Constitution. They were, first, that the Senate should approve the appointment of federal ministers and, second, that federal ministers should be elected for a fixed term at a joint sitting of both houses. Quick and Garran conclude:

> It is not our province to comment on the opinions and contentions of these eminent federalists. Their views have not been accepted; and, for better or for worse, the system of Responsible Government as known to the British Constitution has been practically embedded in the Federal Constitution, in such a manner that it cannot be disturbed without an amendment of the instrument.[36]

How is responsible government safeguarded? There is no law that says that government must be conducted on behalf of the will of the people as expressed through the lower house. There is no reference in the Australian Constitution to either the Prime Minister or the cabinet. The answer to this conundrum is that the sanction, ultimately, is Supply. A government without the confidence of the Representatives cannot govern because it cannot obtain Supply. As Dicey argued, Supply is a sanction ensuring that a government can endure only with the confidence of the lower house.[37]

The technique used by Kerr and Barwick was to argue in the reverse direction—to construct a constitutional theory from a legal power. They said that because the Senate had the power to defer Supply a government was therefore responsible to both the Senate and the Representatives. Kerr could only dismiss Whitlam because Whitlam lacked the confidence of the Parliament. There was no other ground existing on 11 November 1975. But Whitlam clearly had the confidence of the Representatives. He could only lack the confidence of the Parliament if a government was responsible not to the Representatives but to both houses. Accordingly, this Kerr–Barwick theory was constructed not only to justify the dismissal but to require the dismissal.

So Kerr treated the denial of Supply as equivalent to a vote of no-confidence in the government. He says: 'There is a sense in which a Government must retain the "confidence" of the Senate to be able to continue in government. It must have the confidence of the Senate expressed by the passing of Supply by the Senate'.[38]

It is one thing to insist that a government denied Supply by the Senate cannot remain in office without funds to provide for the ordinary services of government. It is quite another to insist that a government denied Supply has therefore lost the confidence of the Parliament and, unless it resigns or advises an election, must be dismissed. Geoffrey Sawer explains:

> Denial of Supply by a Lower House is one of the many ways by which loss of confidence in the Government may be expressed, and has always been considered in that context. Denial of Supply by an Upper House, like any other expression of no confidence in a Government with a Lower House majority, has ever since the Reform Act of 1832 been regarded as irrelevant to the principles governing responsible government . . . the 'responsibility' of an Australian Commonwealth Government is solely to the House of Representatives.[39]

A government cannot be responsible to both the Senate and the Representatives—since these chambers may have majorities supporting different parties. The Kerr–Barwick theory confuses law and constitutional convention. In the process it can generate political absurdities. For example, under this constitutional theory the Senate, whose members may have been elected three and six years earlier, by blocking Supply can vote no-confidence in an elected government, force the Representatives to the people without having to face any election itself and, if it dislikes the government formed after the subsequent election, vote no-confidence six months later thereby repeating the process. (Kerr was able to despatch the Senate to the people in 1975 only because the grounds existed for a double dissolution under section 57.)

These absurdities are accentuated because, given the party system, the Senate may be manipulated on behalf of the interests of the minority party in the Representatives.

The Kerr–Barwick working rule is unlikely to be acceptable to the political parties, to the people or to future Governors-General. Sir John's solution had the effect of undermining the position of an elected government, the notion of responsible government and the standing of the House of Representatives.

By his action Kerr adopted a staunch federalist view of the Constitution against responsible government. He gave little sign of having absorbed Quick and Garran. Indeed, his statement on the dismissal was mildly contemptuous of responsible government and referred to 'how far the conventions of responsible government have been grafted on to the federal compact . . .'

Sir Maurice Byers says: 'I think Kerr was put in a very difficult position. I think that he believed that what he was doing was right. I don't doubt that. But I don't think his decision really accords with notions of responsible government and that's what this whole thing is about.'[40]

According to historical precedent, constitutional provision and political theory, the Governor-General should not have treated the deferral of Supply by the Senate as a want of 'confidence' in Whitlam and therefore as grounds for a dismissal. He should have treated the situation as a test of the Senate's financial power to obstruct a government which, if persisted in to the point where funds might expire, would require a general election.

The confusion over law and convention is at the core of Kerr's second mistaken judgement—over timing. It is because Sir John regarded the deferral of Supply by the Senate as tantamount to a vote of no-confidence, and therefore an issue of 'responsibility', that he was prepared not just to dismiss the government but to dismiss it before the money ran out. If there was no issue of confidence then there was no ground for dismissal until the issue of illegality arose—that is, when the money began to expire. This would not happen until a fortnight past 11 November.

Sir John's defence of his timing is noticeably weak. It seems clear from his calculations and the sequence that his timing was designed to procure a general election before Christmas.[41] He acted on the last or close to the last possible date, just as Whitlam was acting on the same date in seeking his pre-Christmas Senate election. But this was a purely administrative reason. It was not a substantial reason for the timing of such a spectacular use of the reserve powers.

The feature of the Kerr–Barwick rule in relation to timing is its arbitrary nature. In his memoirs Barwick declares that he thinks Kerr should have intervened 'at the latest by 25 October' to deny Whitlam the opportunity 'to indulge in brinkmanship to coerce some, no doubt the weaker, of the Senators to break ranks'.[42]

Why 25 October? Why 11 November? There was no difference in the situation between these dates. The Senate had deferred Supply and the government was governing on the premise that there would be a political solution before any illegality occurred. Sir John says:

> I believe I had a discretion on timing. I had to protect the country from the incredible chaos resulting from there being no money available to pay the Commonwealth's obligations . . . I had to prevent the chaos, not try to pick up the pieces later. But I believed I should wait to see how the political mess developed, how firm was the Senate's will and whether a compromise short of absolute deadlock could be found. I waited almost four weeks—from October 16 to November 11. It was clear to me on November 6 that no compromise could be found . . . I had to accept what they did in the Senate and what their leader, Mr Fraser, told me they would continue to do.[43]

The trouble with this statement is that nobody apart from Sir John had decided that there would be no political compromise. There was no reason why he 'had to accept' the advice provided him by the leader of the Opposition. These are extraordinary claims by any measure: a Governor-General who is supposed to act on the advice of his Prime Minister asserts that he had no option but to act on the advice of the Opposition leader on an issue that involved dismissal.

It is apparent that Kerr was influenced by Fraser's command over his parliamentary wing, notably his Senators. It is also apparent that Kerr was apprehensive about Whitlam's alternative financial measures and feared their consequences.

Barwick's letter said that Kerr had to be 'satisfied' that Whitlam could not secure Supply—so Kerr asserted such a condition when explaining the dismissal. The truth is that it was impossible to be 'satisfied' about this matter on 11 November. A stranger visiting Parliament House at this time who chatted to a few politicians would have rapidly concluded that the situation was unstable and unpredictable. The statements made by many Coalition figures over the past twenty years confirm this. In interviews for this book two Liberal Senators say they had decided to cross the floor; the remarks from senior Coalition figures confirm that the situation was volatile and unpredictable. It would seem, however, that the closer the deadline for the expiry of funds the more intense was the pressure on the Opposition to retreat or negotiate.

Sir John's decision on timing must be set in context. He was contemplating the ultimate application of the reserve powers against a government with a clear majority in the Representatives, on behalf of a Senate whose ongoing resolve was unpredictable, in a manoeuvre that would split the country, damage the Crown and provoke claims that the Governor-General had been partisan.

Given this situation, it was prudent for Kerr to wait as long as possible and be as sure as possible.[44] Sir John had waited for 27 days; he decided that was enough. But the chance of a political settlement over the next ten days must have been at least 50 per cent. Given the issues, it is difficult but to conclude that Kerr intervened prematurely.

The third element in the critique is the Kerr–Barwick claim that the Governor-General had a 'duty' to dismiss Whitlam. This elevates the reserve powers from a 'last resort' solution to a more favoured priority. It implies that when a deadlock over Supply cannot be easily resolved then the expected solution is an intervention by the Governor-General to put the issue before the people.

Kerr approached the office as a jurist; he failed to grasp that the Crown is not a jurist. Indeed, he argued that the Governor-General must come 'to a correct result, be it for one side or the other'.[45] Gerard Henderson, who discussed the matter with Kerr, asserted that Kerr saw the office of Governor-General as 'not all that dissimilar to his role as a Chief Justice'—an extraordinary perception.[46] Kerr used the reserve powers to solve the crisis; he failed to understand that the reserve powers are best exercised by not being exercised—that they guarantee the influence of the Crown and it is that influence that enables the Crown to secure a political solution. Kerr's approach reflected his legal background and his long study of the reserve powers—as a student through Evatt and as Governor-General through Forsey. His discussion with Barwick in September 1975 before the crisis began is a further pointer—Kerr would have known that Barwick would support the application of the reserve powers. Maurice Byers reflects: 'Kerr was Governor-General. Nearly everyone who possesses an office tends to look upon it as his own private property and to ascribe to it powers that don't fit to the situation. That's a human failing.'[47]

One consequence is that Kerr seemed to have given insufficient weight to the dilemma arising from the exercise of the reserve powers. To the extent that the Crown is seen as partisan by the community, its integrity and ultimately its existence is in question. Given that the last clear case in the United Kingdom of the dismissal of a government with a Lower House majority was in 1783, and that the ground on which Kerr was acting—denial of Supply by an Upper House—had never been the occasion of a dismissal before, greater care should have been exercised in ensuring that the reserve powers were used only as a last resort.

There was an alternative to the reserve powers. It was the orthodoxy expected from the Crown or the Crown's representative: advising, warning and mediating to secure a political solution. This highlights the fourth criticism of Kerr's behaviour which, twenty years later, remains the most emotional point in the dismissal—Kerr's failure to warn, and as a consequence, the belief of Whitlam and his ministers that they were deliberately misled as part of a strategy of dismissal.

Bill Hayden, drawing upon his own experience as Governor-General, criticises Kerr for his failure to follow conventional procedure: 'I think that Kerr should have had the courage and conviction about his own role in the crisis to express himself frankly to Whitlam.'[48]

The Secretary of the Attorney General's Department at the time of the crisis, Sir Clarence Harders, says: 'Kerr should have advised Whitlam that in his opinion Whitlam was not doing the right thing... You would not expect a Governor-General to act like that [dismiss the Government] without warning.'[49] The former Liberal Premier of Victoria, Sir Rupert Hamer, says that the Governor-General 'had a duty and a right to warn his Prime Minister in the situation'. Hamer reports that the then Victorian Governor and former Supreme Court judge, Sir Henry Winneke, in private discussion with Hamer, was a strong critic of Kerr's act of dismissal on exactly the same grounds.[50] The former Solicitor-General, Sir Maurice Byers, puts the core proposition: 'The Governor-General was under an obligation to allow Whitlam to go to the election as Prime Minister.'[51]

The former New South Wales Governor, Sir Roden Cutler, who would have handled the crisis from Yarralumla if Kerr had proceeded with his planned overseas trip, says:

> I thought it was wrong for the Governor-General to dismiss Whitlam when he had a majority in Parliament. I thought that the Parliament had created the problem and the Parliament should solve it... My view was that he did not have to act at that time. I felt that he would not be in a position to act as a conciliator if he insisted on being the arbitrator... I feel that the dismissal created great division in the country. My impression is that Kerr acted from a sense of *folie de grandeur*. I think that Kerr liked being in the job and that he didn't want to leave it. In one sense I think he welcomed the opportunity to be the political dictator of Australia... He looked upon this generally as an occasion on which as Governor-General he would be the number one citizen and I think he saw that as a role he rather welcomed. I got the impression that Kerr's approach was to act as Whitlam was expecting.[52]

Kerr's failure to warn has sunk deep into the culture of the Labor Party. It leads to an even more serious charge—that he deceived his ministers. It is this conviction that is the reason why Whitlam and McClelland and other ministers reacted so strongly; it is the reason why Labor boycotted Kerr in such a comprehensive fashion while he remained in office. Their charge against Kerr is that he was dishonourable because he was deceiving.

Whitlam says: 'Nothing will explain or justify Kerr's deception. He was not just being secretive, he was deceptive. He deceived not just me. He deceived John Menadue. He deceived Jim McClelland. He deceived Joe Riordan.' The three named by Whitlam confirm his claim that they were deceived personally and separately. Whitlam also argues:

> Sir John Kerr's deception was two-fold. At all stages, he failed to 'counsel and warn'; he never disclosed to his constitutional advisers his concerns or the course he had in mind. It follows by necessary inference that he deliberately misled us: at the very time he had determined to dismiss us, he consciously and deliberately left us to believe that he understood and supported what we were doing. His was a double deceit—by omission and by commission.[53]

McClelland says: 'I wouldn't have held it against Kerr if he had just been honest. If he had said to Gough, "Prime Minister, I'm in a dilemma and I might soon have no option but to dismiss you". But he didn't. Instead he planned an ambush. He did his best to deceive us and mislead us about his intentions on the reserve powers.'[54]

In repudiating such accusations Kerr says: 'Mr Whitlam knew of the danger that I might dismiss him . . . At no time did I say anything that could be taken as ruling out that possibility.'[55] Only a fool of a Governor-General would reject this possibility and Sir John was anything but a fool.

So Kerr did not rule out the option of dismissal. But the common theme that runs through the accounts given by different ministers of their dialogue with the Governor-General is his impression of sympathy and support. This is conveyed in detail in the accounts provided by Whitlam and McClelland. One of the best examples of Kerr's technique is provided by John Wheeldon:

> It was at an early stage of the trouble. I was at Government House chatting to Kerr . . . He said to me, 'How are we going?' It struck me at once—how are *we* going? When I got back to Parliament House I bumped into Jim McClelland and said to him, 'Well, your friend Kerr is on side alright. We don't have to worry about him. He just said to me, 'How are *we* going?'. McClelland replied, 'That's good. I'm just on my way to see Gough, so I'll tell him'.[56]

This story from a minister who had opposed Whitlam's 'tough it out' policy and had been friendly towards Kerr captures the Governor-General's style. There are too many separate examples to dispute the evidence. Kerr portrayed himself as sympathetic towards Whitlam and Whitlam concluded that Kerr was sympathetic. But Kerr did not rule out a dismissal as such. Whitlam was unwise enough not to probe the Governor-General to discover his real attitude.

Sir John was determined to conceal that attitude. He defended himself against the charge of deception, but admitted to concealment. He acknowledged that he practised it against Whitlam throughout the crisis. When all the accounts given by the participants are read and re-read this looms as the extraordinary and pervasive factor. It is not about the law or the Constitution—it is about the trust between two men. Kerr distrusted Whitlam; so he declined to enter a frank dialogue.

The benchmark was set on 14 October, just before the budget was blocked, when Kerr, after two discussions with Whitlam, concluded that:

> ... an implacable element began to appear in the Prime Minister's approach ... From that time forward my opinion was that he was beyond the reach of any argument of mine, or even discussion.[57]

Kerr's failure *during the crisis* to counsel or warn Whitlam was an abdication of the responsibility of the Crown's representative. It violates the classic texts on the spirit and technique that the Crown should bring to a crisis. (Kerr makes the unsubstantiated claim in his own defence that Walter Bagehot's dictum about 'warning' does not apply to the exercise of the reserve powers.)[58] The contrast between Kerr's performance and Hasluck's doctrine of vice-regal behaviour is stark: 'With the Prime Minister the Governor-General can be expected to talk with frankness and friendliness, to question, discuss, suggest and counsel.'[59]

The justification advanced by the Governor-General for his behaviour was his conviction that Whitlam was prepared to sack him. Kerr felt that if Whitlam sensed that he was anything other than a 'rubber stamp', the Prime Minister would immediately approach the Palace. This is the bedrock issue. But if Kerr was seen as a 'rubber stamp' it was his own fault, which he should have corrected by being firm with Whitlam.

In a magazine article ten years after the dismissal, Kerr advanced a series of reasons which he claimed 'confirmed' his assessment of Whitlam's intention.[60] They were: (1) the Prime Minister's 16 October 'joke' in Tun Abdul Razak's presence about who sacked whom first; (2) Whitlam's statement late on 11 November that his dismissal meant that he could not get in touch with the Queen on the matter; (3) a passage contained in my 1976 book to the effect that 'a number of people' close to Whitlam were convinced he would sack Kerr; (4) that after being dismissed Whitlam called the Palace in the middle of the night and spoke to the Queen's private secretary; (5) that Fred Daly reported Whitlam as saying 'I'll sack Kerr' when they met at the Lodge after Whitlam's dismissal; and (6) Whitlam's reaction in the Yarralumla study at the moment of dismissal when he jumped up and allegedly said, 'I must get in touch with the Palace at once'.

As a lawyer Kerr would know that such evidence did not prove his case. It was both circumstantial and speculative. Twenty years later opinions still differ among those close to Whitlam at the time on whether he would have sacked Kerr. Whitlam denies that he would have done so. But Kerr was obsessed by the threat. Kerr insisted he was certain that Whitlam would sack him—yet there cannot be certainty on this issue. Kerr had his fears and suspicions of Whitlam. But that is all they can be; Kerr could not have *knowledge*.

The point, however, is that this risk or danger or probability was neither a sufficient nor a proper ground for misleading the Prime Minister and refusing to treat him in the way expected of the Crown's representative.

What should Kerr have done?

He should have unflinchingly and courageously met his responsibility to the Crown and to the Constitution. He should have spoken frankly with his Prime Minister from the start. He should have warned whenever and wherever appropriate. He should have realised that, whatever his fears, there was no justification for any other behaviour. He should have demonstrated to Whitlam at the outset that he was a Governor-General who would not be intimidated. He should have sought, throughout the crisis, assessments from Whitlam on his evolving plans for a solution. A situation in which Prime Minister and Governor-General were informed of each other's thinking would have maximised the basis for a political compromise and minimised the grounds for misunderstanding and any resort to the reserve powers.

An implicit element in this would have been an acceptance that if the Prime Minister acted with headstrong stupidity then Kerr might be dismissed as Governor-General. The Palace would have probably played for time but it had to accept the advice. Bill Hayden, reviewing the situation from Yarralumla, says that if Whitlam had tried to sack Kerr, Buckingham Palace 'would have taken an inordinately long time to get back, by which time the issue would have been sorted out one way or another.'[61] This is possible but by no means certain. Of course, it was far easier and faster for Kerr to dismiss Whitlam by handing him a letter than it was for Whitlam to write to the Palace to secure Kerr's dismissal.

If his own dismissal was the price that Kerr might have to pay for honouring his responsibilities then he should have accepted that price. It was still a 'less worse' option for Australia's system of government than the one he finally took. In a moment of candour, Kerr later told a confidant, 'he thought he had "out-marshalled" Whitlam'—only to withdraw this word quickly.[62] However, one of Kerr's closest friends, James McAuley, concludes that Kerr would have derived a sense of personal satisfaction from the dismissal. Offering an insight into Kerr's character, McAuley says:

> I concluded that John Kerr would act in the way he soon after did. He would enjoy the opportunity for a grand dramatic moment; he would appreciate the opportunity, such as few Governors-General are given, to enter the history books. But he would not make his decision for these reasons . . . [63]

Anne Kerr paints a different portrait of her husband during the crisis—that of a worried and lonely man, heavy with his responsibility, re-reading Evatt and Forsey, following his habits of a lifetime and sometimes rising at 2 am and reading and contemplating for two hours in the Yarralumla solitude on the decision closing upon him.[64]

Kerr's obsession is captured by a Whitlam critic, John Wheeldon, who says in an exasperated tone:

> After the dismissal I said to Kerr, 'Why didn't you talk to your ministers? You could have told us that unless the ministry obtained Supply, then you might have to dismiss us.' But Kerr just said to me, 'If I'd done that, Whitlam would have sacked me'. I said to Kerr, 'I'm very disappointed that you were more concerned about your own dismissal than dismissal of your 27 ministers.[65]

Kerr decided that it was his responsibility to prevent *at all costs* Whitlam recommending his own dismissal, and he sought to achieve this by dismissing Whitlam. In the finality, Kerr should have given Whitlam the opportunity to go to a general election as Prime Minister. That was Whitlam's right as Prime Minister; it was Kerr's obligation to the Constitution's commitment to responsible government.

There is, however, another step in this analysis. Kerr's refusal to deal frankly with him misled Whitlam into believing throughout the crisis that Kerr was supporting his approach. Fraser was equally convinced that Kerr would act to validate his own position and from 6 November onwards Fraser was predicting a dismissal based upon his discussions with Kerr.

So each leader, Whitlam and Fraser, was convinced that he would prevail and, accordingly, each rejected any further compromise. Both leaders assumed a victory and their calculations were based explicitly on their view of Kerr. This is the principal reason why the crisis was so prolonged. Both Whitlam and Fraser concluded that Kerr was on their side. Neither man was interested in political suicide; both would have changed tack if it became apparent that their assumptions were false. That is the nature of politics.

There can be no doubt that Kerr encouraged both sides. There are too many former ALP ministers on record to permit any other conclusion in relation to the government. Fraser's own accounts of his talks with Kerr and the judgements he formed permit no other conclusion in relation to the Opposition.

Kerr encouraged both sides. It might initially seem curious behaviour but, on the evidence, it is an irresistible conclusion.

It is salutary to recall the view of Sir Maurice Byers:

> John was a man who liked pleasing people. Smoothing them over and getting a favourable response. The articulation of an unpleasant truth, I think, he found difficult. He would have found it particularly difficult putting it to a man with such a dominant and extravagant temperament as Gough.[66]

Kerr's priority was to protect the Palace and his own position—not to solve the deadlock through mediation. If Fraser *had* cracked then Whitlam would always have been grateful to Kerr in the false belief that Kerr had been supportive. Kerr, in fact, was too accommodating to both leaders during the crisis. He should have been tougher with both in the cause of settlement.

The obligation upon Kerr was to achieve a settlement before the parliamentary appropriation started to expire. At this point there would be one of three unacceptable consequences: breaches of government contracts and social upheaval; illegal remedies being applied; or unacceptable financial innovation to bypass the Parliament.

Kerr's sense of the office and the law told him that a solution was imperative before any such breakdown was reached. There were three types of political solution—a loss of nerve by the Coalition; a compromise involving the timing of Senate or Representatives elections; or an admission of political defeat by Whitlam and his calling of a general election. If Kerr had waited another fortnight until the eve of the expiry of funds then the possibility of either a Coalition retreat or a compromise would have intensified. If Kerr had also warned Whitlam that he could not continue to 'tough it out' when the money began to expire, and that vice-regal intervention would be required at that point, then Whitlam would have been compelled to change tactics at this stage. Presumably he would have either moved against Kerr or called a general election.

The view that Kerr should have waited and warned—thereby putting more pressure on both leaders for a compromise—is not a judgement made in retrospect; it was the conventional response. The crisis was political in its origins and nature and it required a political solution. It was Kerr's task to force Fraser and Whitlam to confront the consequences of their actions. For Fraser that meant confronting the fact that denial of the budget would threaten the nation with profound hardship for which he would be held accountable; for Whitlam it meant confronting the fact that as Prime Minister he could not remain in office once the funds began to expire. Kerr was too weak in his dealings with both men and failed to put either leader under face-to-face pressure. When he found that the leaders failed to compromise between themselves he was trapped by his own interpretation of the crisis and view of his powers into a dramatic and exaggerated intervention.

Sir Paul Hasluck, in his appreciation of the crisis, wrote:

> As I saw the events, the faults in our system of government appeared, not in the crisis that had its immediate outcome in the dismissal of the Prime Minister, but, firstly, in the apparent inadequacy of communication and consultation (and perhaps lack of confidence in each other) in the relationship between Governor-General and Prime Minister . . . I suggest that if there had been more talking and a higher measure of confidence between the Governor-General and Prime Minister it is probable that no crisis would have arisen. The role of the Crown (and hence the Governor-General) to be consulted, to encourage and to warn can only be fulfilled if they talk to each other in terms which reflect that they have respect for each other . . . The essence of a political judgment on the events of 1975 is whether it was either necessary or wise to use the reserve powers. The fault in the smooth working of the Australian Constitution did not come with the use of a power of dismissal but with an apparent breakdown in consultation between the Governor-General and Prime Minister . . . The consultation, advice and warning precede any use of reserve powers . . . 'Reserve Powers', if one may give a double meaning to their description, are powers to be held in reserve and not used in the frontline except in extreme and unpredictable situations.[67]

Whitlam's approach towards Kerr was insensitive in personal terms and humiliating in constitutional terms. It was guaranteed to provoke resentment, suspicion and the temptation towards retaliation. It was comprehensively incompetent.

The conclusion must be that Whitlam made little or no effort to persuade Kerr to accept the Prime Minister's view of the crisis, namely that it was a threat to responsible government which Whitlam felt an obligation to defend. Instead Whitlam delivered public and private homilies that Kerr could act only on the advice of his ministers.

Whitlam took Kerr for granted. He failed either to respect Kerr or to show the necessary respect for the Governor-General's office.

Jim McClelland speculates: 'If Gough had not treated Kerr with such blatant contempt—my viceroy, my creature—it is possible though not certain that Kerr might have discussed all the possibilities with us. You can imagine how Kerr with his overblown sense of self-importance must have bit his lip when Gough made it clear that he saw Kerr as a cypher.'[68] Kerr's friend, Ken Gee says: 'Whitlam mismanaged John because he mismanaged most people.'[69]

A prudent Prime Minister would have sought to engage Kerr. This process should have begun before Supply was blocked. Once the Senate voted then Whitlam should have provided a detailed prime ministerial briefing to Kerr to explain his approach to the crisis. This should have established the personal chemistry between the two men for the decisive period ahead. It should have ensured that their dialogue would be honest and open. A wise Whitlam would have flattered Kerr and, above all, confided in him. Whitlam should have made Byers available to Kerr, offered immediate written legal advice to the Governor-General and then further opinions on responsible government and, if necessary, on the reserve powers. Whitlam's blunder was to underestimate Kerr. He thought all this was unnecessary.

Whitlam was mesmerised by his belief that Kerr was a weak man whose courage had never matched his ambition. This personal judgement was reinforced by Whitlam's arrogance towards the office—he could not conceive that a Governor-General had an influential role in this situation let alone a power to dismiss. A more astute appreciation on Whitlam's part would have been that Kerr, as an eminent jurist and a proud man, would require his time and his careful management. Yet Whitlam offered neither.

Even worse, Whitlam adopted towards Kerr a technique of casual intimidation. The best instance is the dismissal quip made in front of Tun Abdul Razak. If it was thoughtless then it reveals Whitlam's naive insensitivity in dealing with people; if it was casual intimidation then it reveals Whitlam's misjudgement of both Kerr and his own situation. Whitlam should have told Kerr that as Prime Minister he would ensure that Kerr would not be embarrassed as a man or as Governor-General by any action taken by his government. He should have sought to build the trust between them; but where Whitlam needed Kerr to trust him there was only mistrust.

However, Whitlam's strategy was undermined in its constitutional foundations. It seems clear that the Prime Minister believed that his 'tough it out' strategy could be applied not just in the period before the expiry of Supply, but in the period *after* the funds ran out. This was an unwarranted assumption which no responsible Governor-General would be likely to accept. A recognition that his 'tough it out' strategy had this limitation should have informed Whitlam's dialogue with the Governor-General.

A paradox of Whitlam's epic defiance of the Senate is that he translated the same vehemence into his dealings with Kerr. Yet Kerr was not the Opposition leader. There was no point in behaving towards Kerr in an implacable manner. It was not Kerr whose retreat Whitlam needed, it was Fraser's. Whitlam's manner only alarmed Kerr. It discouraged him from talking frankly with Whitlam; because it was so difficult, Kerr stopped trying. If Whitlam was going to be this bloody-minded then he could live with the consequences! Where Whitlam should have encouraged Kerr to confide in him, he drove Kerr away. Eventually he drove Kerr to Fraser. Ultimately, Kerr had to try to resolve the crisis in conjunction with either Whitlam or Fraser. He chose Fraser because he felt that the prospect of working with Fraser to secure a settlement was a better proposition than working with Whitlam.

It was a startling demonstration of misjudgement destroying the advantage of incumbency.

Whitlam's dismissal gave him an heroic status among the true believers and the Kerr critics. But if Whitlam is a hero then he is a tragic hero in the Shakespearian sense: a man of great capability undermined by a fatal flaw.

Whitlam's flaws, however, cannot absolve Kerr as executioner. Kerr's difficulty was considerable but far from intractable. His response to his dilemma is the key; it is the essential insight into his character. By this response Kerr compounded his own difficulties. It is his inactions and actions that prolonged the crisis. Finally, Kerr assumed the role of Crown's executioner against a majority leader of the Representatives. That guaranteed a divided community, an alienated Labor Party and a campaign against him until his own resignation. It was a solution that was neither inevitable nor satisfactory.

The Governor-General and the Crown

Kerr's justification for the manner of his intervention lay in his determination to protect the Queen. What happened on 11 November is that, in his desire to safeguard the Queen, Sir John prejudiced the office of Governor-General. It is an exquisite irony.

During the crisis Kerr reported regularly to the Queen by letter—a detailed correspondence that will one day provide fascinating material for historians.

The constitutional position is that the Queen is Australia's head of state. But the powers of the Crown are not exercised by the Crown itself but by the Governor-General as the Crown's representative. This view was implanted in the Constitution. In this sense Australia's system of government could be called a Governor-Generalate.[70] The power of the Crown resides in the office of Governor-General rather than with the Queen.

After the dismissal Speaker Scholes wrote to the Queen asking her to intervene to restore Whitlam as Prime Minister, a foolish request. On 17 November the Queen's private secretary replied:

> As we understand the situation here, the Australian Constitution firmly places the prerogative powers of the Crown in the hands of the Governor-General as the representative of the Queen in Australia. The only person competent to commission an Australian Prime Minister is the Governor-General, and the Queen has no part in the decisions which the Governor-General must take in accordance with the Constitution.[71]

The events of 1975 highlight the nature of Australia's constitutional monarchy and its evolution. In 1901 there was no Queen of Australia in law or in fact. Australia was not an independent country; Federation did not deliver genuine independence to Australia. In a legislative, judicial and foreign policy sense Australia remained subservient to Britain. The Australian colonies federated under the Queen 'of the United Kingdom of Great Britain and Ireland'. The Queen appointed the Governor-General on the advice of British ministers and his task, among others, was to safeguard Britain's interests in Australia. However, Australia's 'Head of State' system had been evolving since Federation. The disappearance of the British Empire meant that the British Monarch became Sovereign of a number of separate countries. Australia's Federal Parliament passed laws in the 1950s and 1970s that enshrined the notion of the 'Queen of Australia'. Laws made in 1986 removed the vestiges of British authority over the States. The most visible change in Australia's 'Head of State' system has been the acceptance that the office of Governor-General should be filled by an Australian and that its essential task is to represent the nation to itself.[72]

Sir John Kerr acted on the basis that it was the Governor-General's task to discharge the obligations of the Crown during the 1975 crisis. While keeping the Queen informed of developments he did not inform her of his decision. Sir John said: 'I did not ask her approval. The decisions I took were without the Queen's advance knowledge.'[73]

Precisely.

Informing the Queen beforehand meant that the Monarch herself would be blamed for the dismissal or blamed for not preventing the dismissal.

Using the same logic, Sir John ensured that Whitlam was not in a position to approach the Palace seeking his removal as Governor-General. The Queen, confronted by a recommendation from her Prime Minister, would be plunged into the controversy. Kerr's belief was that the Queen had to act on Whitlam's advice, that it would be given with such force that any period of delay would be difficult, and that 'the country and its institutions would have been placed under almost impossible stress'.[74]

Accordingly, Kerr concluded that in exercising the reserve power of dismissal he must ensure that Whitlam did not have an opportunity to consider his position and respond with a recommendation to the Palace that the Governor-General be removed.

The source of the problem, according to Kerr's analysis, is the Governor-General's lack of tenure. In truth, it is a legacy of a monarchical system without a monarchy. If Australia had a true monarchy then the problem would not have existed, since Whitlam could not have sacked a Queen. Moreover, if Australia had been a republic the problem would not have existed, since a President would have security of tenure against removal by a Prime Minister. The problem was the system of Governor-Generalate. The Governor-General had the powers of the Queen but not the security. According to the Kerr–Barwick rule such a system dictated a dismissal by ambush. However, a better solution is to change the system. There will be many Australians who conclude that the Kerr–Barwick system is unsatisfactory if its logic delivers this result. A King or a President could have handled the problem. But Kerr's conception of the office of Governor-General proved unsatisfactory.

If the Governor-General had been a Sovereign bent upon employing the reserve powers the decision would have been clear—the Sovereign would have simply advised the Prime Minister to call an election; that is, there would have been a forced dissolution. If the Prime Minister refused then the Sovereign would obtain a new Prime Minister to give such advice. The Sovereign, in effect, would have put the issue before the people. The Prime Minister would have gone to the election as Prime Minister unless he had a compulsion to become the Leader of the Opposition. Such simplicity was denied by Sir John's assumptions within Australia's Governor-Generalate. Sir John protected the Queen, but he exposed the limitations in Australia's system of constitutional monarchy.

The legacy

The blocking of the budget and dismissal of Whitlam was a very successful tactic for the Fraser-led Coalition. Fraser won the 1975 election by a large majority, a confirmation of his electoral judgement, and then repeated the result at the 1977 election. One of the senior party critics of Fraser's action, the former Victorian Premier, Sir Rupert Hamer says: 'I think the Liberal Party felt vindicated by the result. The election was a landslide. It would have justified, in the view of most people, all the actions taken.'[75]

Malcolm Fraser also saw these results as his vindication. Asked twenty years later whether his method of becoming Prime Minister compromised his performance Fraser says: 'People like to dramatise this, but I don't really think so.'[76]

Ian Macphee, a Fraser supporter but opponent of the deferral of the budget, puts a different view. Macphee says:

> I supported Fraser to the end and after the loss in 1983 to Hawke, urged him to remain in Parliament . . . Fraser's sense of direction for our society and nation and his absolute commitment to expunge racism and protect the environment was correct . . . He did not love to be hated, however, and I always believed that his policy daring was quelled by the anger directed at him pursuant to the dismissal. Fraser was the dominant person in his Government but his inability to gain a rapport with the general public reduced the quality of government decision-making. Much of the media hostility to Fraser stemmed from the dismissal and even his better policies were rarely presented by the media with the credit they deserved . . . the dismissal soured us for seven years![77]

Many Liberals will reject Macphee's analysis. But there is weight in his assessment. Macphee and John Howard rarely agree. But Howard, a minister throughout the Fraser years who succeeded Lynch as Fraser's deputy leader, puts a similar argument. Howard says that the blocking of Supply in 1975 was damaging for the Liberals and that if Fraser had waited until the normal time for an election then his government would not have been 'so tentative'. According to Howard the problem is that Fraser 'really pushed the thing to the limit getting there'. He recalls an example in the first few weeks of government when Fraser told him to 'go soft' on the Coalition's promise to abolish the Prices Justification Tribunal because 'we need to give Bob Hawke a win'.[78]

The legacy of the dismissal on the Fraser Government should not be exaggerated. It would be wrong, for instance, to see the dismissal as the principal or a major factor in the policy mindset of Fraser's Government since there were many other factors shaping it.

One consequence for the Coalition, particularly the Liberals, has been a legacy of guilt, which probably became deeper after Fraser's departure. Bob Ellicott, an intellectual moving force in the events of 1975, identifies the difficulty: 'There's a feeling about, generated since, that there was some element of shame in being involved, as if it was a counter-revolutionary right-wing coup . . . As both a constitutional lawyer and a liberal I've never had any problem with what we did. I would have rather it didn't happen, but I think there was a justifiable view that the government had to go.'[79] Reg Withers fingers the 'guilt' legacy with his contemptuous remark that 'not one Liberal Senator has caused the Labor government the slightest trouble since 1983'.[80]

Fraser carries the personal and political responsibility for the legacy of 1975. The decision to block the budget was quintessentially a leader's decision. Once he was defied by Whitlam, Fraser then urged the Governor-General to resort to the reserve powers and to dismiss Whitlam. According to Kerr when he commissioned Fraser as caretaker Prime Minister he informed Fraser that he did so on the basis that Fraser would 'accept the political responsibility for my decision to dismiss'. When Kerr swore-in the Fraser ministry on 12 November he reported:

> I said to them: 'Gentlemen, the Prime Minister before being commissioned yesterday assumed responsibility for my dismissal of the previous government . . . He has told me you are all prepared, with him, to assume that responsibility. To emphasise the importance of the matter I will ask each of you to confirm it before I administer the oath of office.' All confirmed it.[81]

Fraser was fortunate that he had a Governor-General who was prepared to intervene decisively on 11 November because a further delay could have prejudiced the Opposition's position. On the other hand, Fraser suffered from having a Governor-General whose intervention on his behalf was so divisive.

The crisis left a legacy of paranoia and bitterness on both sides of the great divide. Fraser had a great majority but he forfeited the tolerance of a powerful minority that included the ALP, the unions, much of the media and the opinion-making elite and many ordinary Australians. In each of the three following campaigns that he waged—1977, 1980 and 1983—Fraser was forced to defend his deferral of the budget and, under questioning, said he would repeat it if necessary.

Twenty years later opinion has mellowed. Jim McClelland says: 'I think we were wrong about Fraser. I regarded him as a loathsome figure, a megalomaniac. I suspect he may be a bit ashamed about what he did and that it showed when he was Prime Minister.'[82] This is an unsubstantiated theory.

In a deeper sense Fraser's deferral of the budget represented the last gasp of the Menzian 'born-to-rule' Liberal Party. Fraser embodied two streams of thought that have since disappeared—that the Coalition was Australia's true governing party, and that it was possible for competent governments to overcome the problems of the age.

The dismissal and its 1975 election rejection left the ALP discredited and divided. These events terminated the Whitlam era. Born in optimism and idealism, it finished in despair and anger. A pessimistic interpretation of the Whitlam age was offered two years later by one of its principal voices, Whitlam's speechwriter, Graham Freudenberg:

> What happened on 11 November was simply the crowning point of all that had gone before: the denial of legitimacy of a Labor Government. The dismissal of that Government by the Governor-General, the Queen's representative, the Crown in Australia, was merely the ultimate expression of that denial of legitimacy. The denial began first with the assertion in April 1973 that the election of 1972 was just an aberration, 'an act of lunacy by the larger states', as Senator Withers had put it. Then began the process of Senate obstruction, even on matters like health insurance and the Schools Commission . . . This led to the Double Dissolution of 1974. Yet, even by its own re-election and the strengthening of its position in the Senate, the Labor Government was still unable to establish its legitimacy. It remained a government under siege, under question, under doubt as to its legitimacy. By November 1975, a climate had been created in which the Crown, the fount of authority, could at one stroke declare that the Labor Government was indeed illegitimate.[83]

On another occasion Freudenberg asserted: 'It is my basic proposition that the anti-Labor establishment—the controllers of the main sources of power and influence in the ruling institutions, the law, the media, business and higher education, had never accepted the legitimacy of Labor governments, especially federal Labor governments.'[84]

Freudenberg's view had a powerful currency in its time. But it has not been verified over the past twenty years. That is tribute to the recuperative ability of the Labor Party because Labor declined to self-destruct after the dismissal. It defied this setback, rebuilt in adversity and revealed its maturity as a political institution. Under the leadership of Bill Hayden and then Bob Hawke, Labor returned to power eight years later in 1983.

The origins of the Hawke–Keating party were fashioned in the furnace of the Fraser–Kerr–Barwick rules. Three messages were drawn—that Labor was primarily responsible for its own failure; that

Fraser's ruthlessness must be matched; and that ALP policy and presentation must win the confidence of voters, not frighten them. Above all, the Hawke–Keating ALP believed that legitimacy was earned, not bestowed by right.

After the dismissal the ALP had two constitutional objectives—to correct the preference that the Fraser–Kerr–Barwick outcome gave to federalism over responsible government, and to reform the powers of Governor-General. Over the last twenty years virtually no real progress has been made on either front.

Responsible government was to be enshrined by removal of the Senate's power over Supply. The ALP became pledged to this goal. But it required a referendum and Labor declined to put the question because it lacked confidence that it would be carried. Such a referendum, so close to the events of 1975, would have been seen as a vote on both the Senate's action and Kerr's dismissal decision; the contest would be polarised along party lines; and the prospects for success which typically require a bipartisan approach would be dismal.

The truth is that the unresolved issue from Federation—federalism versus responsible government—remains unresolved. Sir Samuel Griffith said during the Convention debates that 'we should not make difficulties in advance' hoping that the conflict between these ideas could be managed. That might have been possible—but the 1975 crisis brought the latent contradiction into the sunlight and the Kerr–Barwick solution favoured one interpretation of Australian democracy against another.[85]

The Kerr–Barwick solution is a conservative interpretation; it is a view that favours the Senate; it is a view that militates against popular democracy and diminishes the Constitution's faith in responsible government; it creates an unacceptable situation in which the Senate can force the Representatives to the people without facing the people itself; it is a view opposed by one side of politics; finally, it is an interpretation that many Australians do not accept. The contradiction has again been consigned to 'cold storage' but it remains a tension within Australia's Constitution and the community over the nature of Australian democracy. The question about what sort of democracy Australians want, which lies at the core of the use of the Senate's power, has been neither confronted nor properly debated by the nation post-1975. It is certain that events and politicians will interact at some time in the future to force another showdown between these concepts.

Sir Maurice Byers ruminates on 1975:

> The situation can always re-occur. It is possible if you have people very strongly committed or people who are unscrupulous as to the means

to achieve power. But it all depends upon the personality of the Governor-General. I think, frankly, it is unwise to appoint a lawyer. The type of person needed is a former politician who realises the lack of rules and appreciates that his function is to preserve the peace.[86]

There is a greater recognition since 1975 of the demands of the office. Its supreme requirement concerns the judgement of a Governor-General—where Sir John Kerr was found wanting.

Sir Paul Hasluck ventured that the problem was not the Senate's power nor the reserve powers but the personal breakdown between Kerr and Whitlam. This is correct—though it is unwise to pretend the question of powers is irrelevant. It highlights the second focus of post-1975 reform, the office of Head of State, in particular, what sort of Head of State Australians want.

Sir John's dismissal of the Whitlam Government revealed three features of Australia's 'Head of State' system that, taken together, are the nourishment for change. First, that the power of the Crown in Australia was exercisable by the Governor-General. Second, that the Governor-General used a power—dismissal of a government with the confidence of the Lower House—that would neither be assumed nor exercised by the Crown in Britain thereby forcing the conclusion that the Governor-General, whose powers originate with the notion of the Crown, possesses greater powers than the Crown itself. Third, that the Governor-General, unlike the Queen, has no tenure and can therefore become entangled in political 'rivalry' with the Prime Minister.

These features are 'shocks' that undermine our system of constitutional monarchy and provide intellectual momentum for a change. But Labor found the reform of the Governor-General's power too difficult and too divisive and, ultimately, it focused upon the need to break the link between the Governor-General and the Crown.

Gough Whitlam captured the ethos of the 1990s debate when he referred to the Queen's trip to Russia in 1994:

> By their presence in Russia, the Queen, an incomparably experienced, competent and gracious Head of State in and for Britain, and her consort, a descendant of Nicholas I, the gendarme of Europe, symbolised the reconciliation of the most western and eastern states, and two of the oldest states, in Europe. In the Kremlin they saw the great coach which Elizabeth I sent to Ivan the Terrible. In St Petersburg they visited the cathedral where Russia's last Emperor and Empress, both of whom were George V's cousins, are to be laid to rest this year. The Queen and Prince Philip were invited and welcomed by Russia's first elected head of state. One thing is certain among all these symbols of change and continuity: nobody noted that the Queen was also Queen of Australia.[87]

Paul Keating became the first Australian Prime Minister pledged to the republic as an article of policy. In his 1993 election policy speech Keating sought a mandate to pursue the republican cause with the intention of putting a referendum to achieve a republic by the centenary of Federation in 2001. By this action Keating has established a unique place for himself as the Prime Minister who launched the transition from constitutional monarchy to a republic.

In 1995 Malcolm Fraser, still emotionally attached to the monarchy, declared nonetheless that in his view a republic was 'inevitable and right'.[88] The Coalition leader, John Howard, adopted a flexible position—which recognised the move of the Coalition away from firm support for the monarchy—and advocated a People's Convention as a means of adjusting to the momentum for change.

Keating was driven by the conviction that Australia had reached a stage of national maturity where it aspired to become a truly independent nation thereby removing the final link with a colonial past. Significantly, he was not motivated by the spectre of 1975 and was careful not to narrow the appeal of the republic by tying its rationale to the dismissal. That would have been a serious political blunder that would have belittled the republican cause. The republic did not need the 1975 crisis to gather its momentum.

It is a fact, however, that the dismissal did encourage the republic by persuading many people that Australia's Head of State system was unsatisfactory. Immense powers were deployed in the Crown's name in a partisan fashion contrary to the tradition of monarchy with the Queen not involved whatsoever.

In an historic meeting with the Queen at Balmoral Castle, Keating helped to shape the public response of the Crown and Prince of Wales to the issue, namely, that the decision rested solely with Australia. The Prince of Wales said he felt the debate was a sign of Australia's maturity and responded to the prospect of a republic by saying: 'I'm not going to run around in small circles, tear my hair out, boo-hoo and throw a fit on the floor, as if somehow like a spoilt child your toy's been taken away.'[89]

The Palace is not a participant in the process. Neither the Queen nor her successor will defend her constitutional and family position as Australia's Head of State. After the dismissal the Palace conveyed to Sir John Kerr its appreciation that he had kept the Crown out of the crisis.[90] The Prince of Wales wrote a personal letter to Sir John in 1976 expressing his appreciation to the Governor-General and conveying his moral support. Prince Charles urged Sir John 'not to lose heart' in the face of such hostility.[91] But these expressions of support or sympathy—it is hard to draw the line—should not be misunderstood. They represented a conscientious effort to uphold an existing system; not a commitment to its future.

In June 1995 Keating outlined his blueprint for a republic—an Australian President to take over the Governor-General's constitutional duties—elected by a two-thirds majority of a joint sitting of the House of Representatives and the Senate. Keating said that the reserve powers that would be retained in the new office would not be codified for two reasons. It would be too difficult to reach agreement on them and such codified powers could become justiciable. He also pledged that in the transition the Senate's powers would be untouched thereby upholding the federal nature of the Constitution.

Bill Hayden told me: 'It is a monumental breakthrough. I agree that the reserve powers can't be codified, but in the process their existence is being acknowledged. That's against Whitlam's previous position that there are no such powers.'[92]

It was a watershed for Labor—and for Whitlam who embraced the blueprint. Indeed, the implications were heavy with irony. In his statement outlining the republic Keating accepted the reserve powers and the Senate's financial powers—the principal instruments which led to the destruction of the Whitlam government. A cynic would say that the republic had reconciled Labor to the powers that had undermined Whitlam and that had proved too difficult to change. Labor, in fact, had shifted the focus of its reform from the Senate and reserve powers to the logic implicit in the office of Governor-General—that is autonomy invited its conversion into a presidency.

With twenty years of hindsight there were three questions the dismissal raised for the Labor Party. First, the Senate and federalism versus the Representatives and popular democracy. Second, the powers within the office of Governor-General and their use against a government. Third, the constitutional link between Australia and Britain—and this is the issue upon which Labor has finally settled. The ALP's solution of a republic achieves not just independence but severs this link that was fundamental in Whitlam's dismissal. However, Labor has declared that it will acquiesce in the Senate's financial power and that it accepts the existence of the reserve powers. In short, Labor has been unable to resolve the question of powers at the heart of the dismissal because the community remains fundamentally divided about them.

The republic will achieve Australian independence. But its ability to resolve outstanding constitutional issues must not be exaggerated. Of course, by guaranteeing a President tenure against the whim of a Prime Minister, a President would be more secure than a Governor-

General. This removes the fear of insecurity that influenced Kerr so much in Whitlam's dismissal.

The republic renders redundant the argument of Kerr that the manner of the dismissal was necessary to protect the Crown. Ultimately, there is no place for this sort of argument in Australia. As time advances, it will be seen as one of the bizarre aspects of the dismissal typifying an obsolete approach to the Constitution.

Sir John Kerr said in early 1975 that 'The Governor-Generalship in Australia is an Australian institution and nothing else'.[93] But this is not right—yet. It recalls the recent defence of Australian constitutional monarchy by Justice Michael Kirby, namely that Australia is really a 'crowned republic', so there is no need to change![94] This is really an argument for taking the final step—making the office of Governor-General into an Australian Presidency and making Australia's 'crowned republic' a true republic.

However, no such innovation can guarantee against human nature. The 1975 crisis is a reminder that Governors-General, like Presidents, bring their characters to their offices. Ultimately, it is these personal qualities that dominate—the frailties, ego and prowess. Fraser, Whitlam and Kerr each deployed massive institutional power on calculations of personal psychology. These were ambitious men, with flaws to match their vigour. Their triangular rivalry is unmatched for its intensity and brinkmanship.

Whitlam's mistake was to isolate himself in a political and legal sense. He did this by saying the Senate had acted unconstitutionally by seeking alternative finance to parliamentary approval, and by denying the reserve powers. Whitlam's insistence on these three propositions, given the history of his government, united the business and financial establishment against him in a recognition that the people would also vote against Labor. Kerr, on the other hand, was meticulous in ensuring that the legal establishment was on his side and that his dismissal of Whitlam was based on a firm constitutional foundation.

The personal divisions were never healed. After Kerr was diagnosed with a terminal illness, Ken Gee tried to arrange a meeting between Kerr and Whitlam. A reconciliation in the evening of their lives. Before agreeing, Kerr asked 'What is the point?'. But his health deteriorated, so Gee did not proceed.[95]

In 1975 Whitlam became a political martyr to the ALP faithful—yet it was his own folly that provoked Kerr and his arrogance that blinded his judgement. He secured a paradoxical triumph: the shadow of the dismissal has obscured the sins of his government. Fraser won the tactical battle of 1975 but his prime ministership was blighted by the technique he used to achieve power. Beset by an aloof manner, Fraser had denied himself any hope of uniting the nation, the secret ambition of each Prime Minister. Kerr depicted himself as a reluctant victim when he was a willing executioner. He achieved in the dismissal the historical fame of which he had dreamt but in the process betrayed a fatal strand of self obsession. His moment of destiny revealed a judgement that left a nation divided and the Australian constitutional monarchy contemplating the next stage of its evolution.

Appendix A

A statement by Opposition front-bencher Mr R J Ellicott, QC

THE GOVERNOR-GENERAL'S basic role is the execution and maintenance of the Constitution and of the laws of the Commonwealth. He performs this role with the advice of Ministers whom he chooses and who hold office during his pleasure.

The Prime Minister is treating the Governor-General as a mere automaton with no public will of his own, sitting at Yarralumla waiting to do his bidding.

Nothing could be further from the truth. It is contrary to principle, precedent and commonsense. The Governor-General has at least two clear constitutional prerogatives which he can exercise—the right to dismiss his Ministers and appoint others, and the right to refuse a dissolution of the Parliament or of either House.

These prerogatives, of their very nature, will only be exercised on the rarest occasions. They have been exercised in the past and the proper working of the Constitution demands that they continue. One only has to think of extreme cases to realise the sense behind them, e.g. the case of an obviously corrupt Government.

The maintenance of the Constitution and of the laws of the Commonwealth require that the Government have authority from Parliament to spend money in order to perform those functions. A Government without supply cannot govern.

APPENDIX A

The refusal by Parliament of supply, whether through the House or the Senate, is a clear signal to the Governor-General that his chosen Ministers may not be able to carry on. In the proper performance of his role, he would inevitably want to have from the Prime Minister an explanation of how he proposed to overcome the situation. If the Prime Minister proposed and insisted on means which were unlawful or which did not solve the problems of the disagreement between the Houses and left the Government without funds to carry on, it would be within the Governor-General's power and his duty to dismiss his Ministers and appoint others.

In the current situation now facing us, the Governor-General, in the performance of his role, would need to know immediately what steps the Government proposes to take in order to avert the problem of it being without supply in the near future, so endangering the maintenance of the Constitution and of the laws of the Commonwealth. He is not powerless and the proper exercise of his powers demands that he be informed immediately on this matter. The Prime Minister should inform him on his own initiative. If he does not, the Governor-General would be justified in sending for him and seeking the information.

The Governor-General is entitled to know:

(1) when it is that the Government will or is likely to run out of funds under the current Supply Acts; and
(2) how the Government proposes to carry on after those funds run out; and
(3) how the Government proposes that the disagreement between the two Houses should be resolved.

These questions cannot properly be left to be considered at a later date because of the consequences which lack of authorised appropriations will have on the Government's capacity to govern, the public service of the Commonwealth and public order.

If he is informed by the Prime Minister that the Government proposes that a half Senate election be held and that by this means (as a result of the election of Territory Senators) the Government hopes to have a majority in the Senate, the Governor-General will need to be satisfied:

(i) that having regard to the proposed date of the election, the Government will have sufficient supply to carry on until the result of that election has been ascertained.
(ii) that the election is likely to resolve the difference between the two Houses by giving the Government a majority in the Senate.

In being satisfied of the first matter a number of factors would be relevant and he would be entitled to be informed about them, eg.:

(i) the date when the Government would or would be likely to run out of supply. Because of the seriousness of the Government not having supply the Governor-General should not be expected to rely nor should he rely on mere estimates. He is entitled to and should be satisfied what supply the Government still has and when it will in the ordinary course run out; and
(ii) the date when the result of the poll is likely to be known having regard to possible events such as a large number of candidates or postal voting. Because of the seriousness of the Government being without supply before that date the assessment should err on the conservative side.

In being satisfied of the second (the likelihood of the Government obtaining a majority in the Senate as a result of the election) he will need to have information which justifies that conclusion. He would also be entitled to consider how those who will be in the Senate immediately after the election are likely to vote if the Appropriation Bills were re-submitted. If it was thought that some of the States were not prepared to hold the elections he would be entitled to consider, for instance, the likely votes of those casual Senators who would remain, e.g. Senator Field. The fact that Senator Field's seat is under challenge would only add uncertainty as to whether the Government can hope to get a majority as his replacement would be a matter for the Queensland Government.

In view of the Government's complaint that the Senate has consistently blocked its legislation the Governor-General would be entitled to consider whether the dispute would really be solved by a half term election or whether the only practicable course was for the Government to seek a double dissolution so that the matter could be resolved by the people.

If the Governor-General was not satisfied that the Government would have supply until the election result in the Territories was known he would only have one option open to him in the interests of good government. He is entitled to and should ask the Prime Minister if the government is prepared to advise him to dissolve the House of Representatives and the Senate or the House of Representatives alone as a means of ensuring that the disagreement between the two Houses is resolved.

If the Prime Minister refuses to do either it is then open to the Governor-General to dismiss his present Ministers and seek others who are prepared to give him the only proper advice open. This he should proceed to do. The proper advice in the circumstances is to dissolve both Houses of the Parliament or the House of Representatives alone with or without a half Senate election.

Appendix B

Opinion dated 4 November 1975 and signed by Maurice Byers

Opinion

MR R. J. ELLICOTT, Q.C., M.P. at the Attorney-General's request made available to him a copy of a press statement relating to the Governor-General's powers. We have been asked by the Prime Minister to provide an opinion upon the legal propositions which that statement contains or assumes. The statement expresses Mr Ellicott's view that His Excellency is legally obliged to take certain steps because of, and as a result of, the current dispute between the House and the Senate. A short recapitulation of that dispute is necessary so that our view of what the situation is which confronts His Excellency may be understood.

2. We set out hereunder a statement in chronological order of the formal steps taken in relation to the introduction and disposition of the Bills by the Representatives and the Senate including the relevant resolutions passed by each of the Houses.

1975

19 August Appropriation Bill (No. 1) 1975–76 and Appropriation Bill (No. 2) 1975–76 were introduced into the House of Representatives, accompanied in each case by a message from the Governor-General, in accordance with the requirements of section 56 of the Constitution, recommending an appropriation of the Consolidated Revenue Fund for services set forth in the Bills.

8 October The House of Representatives passed Appropriation Bills (No. 1) and (No. 2) 1975–76.

16 October The Senate, after reading Appropriation Bill (No. 1) a first time, amended a motion by the Leader of the Government in the Senate 'that the bill be now read a second time' by leaving out all words after 'that' and inserting:

> 'this Bill be not further proceeded with until the Government agrees to submit itself to the judgment of the people, the Senate being of the opinion that the Prime Minister and his Government no longer have the trust and confidence of the Australian people because of—
> (a) the continuing incompetence, evasion, deceit and duplicity of the Prime Minister and his Ministers as exemplified in the overseas scandal which was an attempt by the Government to subvert the Constitution, to by-pass Parliament and to evade its responsibilities to the States and the Loan Council;
> (b) the Prime Minister's failure to maintain proper control over the activities of his Ministers and Government to the detriment of the Australian nation and people; and
> (c) the continuing mismanagement of the Australian economy by the Prime Minister and this Government with policies which have caused a lack of confidence in this nation's potential and created inflation and unemployment not experienced for 40 years'.

Appropriation Bill (No. 2) was similarly dealt with.

On 16 October the House of Representatives adopted a resolution in the following terms:

> '*Considering* that this House is the House of the Australian Parliament from which the Government of Australia is chosen;
> *Considering* moreover that on 2 December 1972 the Australian Labor Party was elected by judgment of the people to be the Government of Australia; that on 18 May 1974 the Australian Labor Party was re-elected by judgment of the people to be the Government of Australia; and that the Australian Labor Party continues to have a governing majority in this House;
> *Recognising* that the Constitution and the conventions of the Constitution vest in this House the control of the supply of money to the elected Governments;
> *Noting* that this House on 27 August 1975 passed the Loan Bill 1975 and on 8 October 1975 passed the Appropriation Bill (No. 1) 1975–76 and the Appropriation Bill (No. 2) 1975–76 which, amongst other things, appropriate moneys for the ordinary annual services of the Government;

Noting also that on 15 October 1975, in total disregard of the practices and conventions observed in the Australian Parliament since Federation, the Leader of the Opposition announced the intention of the Opposition to delay those Bills, with the object of forcing an election of this House; that on 15 October 1975 the Leader of the Opposition in the Senate announced that the Opposition parties in the Senate would delay the Bills; and that on 15 October 1975 the Senate, against the wishes of the Government, decided not to proceed further with consideration of the Loan Bill 1975;

Considering that the actions of the Senate and of the Leader of the Opposition will, if pursued, have the most serious consequences for Parliamentary democracy in Australia, will seriously damage the Government's efforts to counter the effect of world-wide inflation and unemployment, and will thereby cause great hardship for the Australian people:

1. This House *declares* that it has full confidence in the Australian Labor Party Government.
2. This House *affirms* that the Constitution and the conventions of the Constitution vest in this House the control of the supply of money to the elected Government and that the threatened action of the Senate constitutes a gross violation of the roles of the respective Houses of the Parliament in relation to the appropriation of moneys.
3. This House *asserts* the basic principle that a Government that continues to have a majority in the House of Representatives has a right to expect that it will be able to govern.
4. This House *condemns* the threatened action of the Leader of the Opposition and of the non-government parties in the Senate as being reprehensible and as constituting a grave threat to the principles of responsible government and of Parliamentary democracy in Australia.
5. This House *calls upon* the Senate to pass without delay the Loan Bill 1975, the Appropriation Bill (No. 1) 1975–76 and the Appropriation Bill (No. 2) 1975–76.

21 October The House of Representatives resolved as follows:

'(1) That the House of Representatives having considered Message No. 276 of the Senate asserts that the action of the Senate in delaying the passage of the Appropriation Bill (No. 1) 1975–76 and the Appropriation Bill (No. 2) 1975–76 for the reasons given in the Senate resolution is not contemplated within the terms of the Constitution and is contrary to established constitutional convention, and therefore requests the Senate to re-consider and pass the Bills without delay.

APPENDIX B

(2) That a message be sent to the Senate acquainting it of this resolution.'

22 October The Senate, having received by message the resolution adopted by the House of Representatives on 21 October, resolved as follows:

'Leave out all the words after "That", insert—"the Senate having considered Message No. 380 of the House of Representatives asserts'
(a) That the action of the Senate in delaying passage of the Appropriation Bill (No. 1) 1975–76 and the Appropriation Bill (No. 2) 1975–76 for the reasons given in the Senate resolution communicated to the House of Representatives in Message No. 276 is a lawful and proper exercise within the terms of the Constitution of the powers of the Senate.
(b) That the powers of the Senate were expressly conferred on the Senate as part of the Federal Compact which created the Commonwealth of Australia.
(c) That the legislative power of the Commonwealth is vested in the Parliament of the Commonwealth which consists of the Queen, the Senate and House of Representatives.
(d) That the Senate has the right and duty to exercise its legislative power and to concur or not concur, as the Senate sees fit, bearing in mind the seriousness and responsibility of its actions, in all proposed laws passed by the House of Representatives.
(e) That there is no convention and never has been any convention that the Senate shall not exercise its constitutional powers.
(f) That the Senate affirms that it has the constitutional right to act as it did and now that there is a disagreement between the Houses of Parliament and a position may arise where the normal operation of Government cannot continue, a remedy is presently available to the Government under section 57 of the Constitution to resolve the deadlock.
(2) That the Senate reaffirms to the House of Representatives its resolution set out in Senate Message No. 276 in respect of each of the two Appropriation Bills, namely—"this Bill be not further proceeded with until the Government agrees to submit itself to the judgment of the people, the Senate being of the opinion that the Prime Minister and his Government no longer have the trust and confidence of the Australian people because of —
(a) the continuing incompetence, evasion, deceit and duplicity of the Prime Minister and Ministers as exemplified in the overseas loan scandal which was an attempt by the Government to subvert the Constitution, to by-pass Parliament and to evade its responsibilities to the States and the Loan Council;
(b) the Prime Minister's failure to maintain control over the activities of

his Ministers and Government to the detriment of the Australian nation and people; and

(c) the continuing mismanagement of the Australian economy by the Prime Minister and this Government with policies which have caused a lack of confidence in this nation's potential and created inflation and unemployment not experienced for 40 years."

(3) That the foregoing resolutions be transmitted to the House of Representatives by message.'

Bills identical with the original Appropriation Bills and entitled Appropriation Bill (No. 1) 1975–76 [No. 2] and Appropriation Bill (No. 2) 1975–76 [No. 2] were introduced in and passed by the House of Representatives and forwarded to the Senate. These Bills were accompanied by messages from the Governor-General recommending the appropriation of the Consolidated Revenue Fund accordingly as required by section 56 of the Constitution. The Senate read the [No. 2] Bills for the first time.

23 October The motion of the Leader of the Government in the Senate that the [No. 2] Bills be now read a second time was amended to the effect that the Bills were not to be further proceeded with until the Government agreed to submit itself to the judgment of the people. The motion as amended and passed then went on to refer to the same matters as were contained in the Senate's motion of 16 October.

28 October The House of Representatives resolved as follows:

'(1) That the House of Representatives, having considered Message No. 279 of the Senate—

(a) again asserts that the action of the Senate in delaying the passage of the two Appropriation Bills is contrary to established constitutional convention;

(b) denounces the blatant attempt by the Senate to violate section 28 of the Constitution for political purposes by itself endeavouring to force an early election for the House of Representatives;

(c) resolves that it will uphold the established right of the Government with a majority in the House of Representatives to be the Government of the nation; and

(d) again calls on the Senate to reconsider and pass the Bills without further delay in order to avoid the possibility of widespread distress occurring within the Australian community.

(2) That a message be sent to the Senate acquainting it of this Resolution.'

3. We conclude this recital with the list of Appropriation and Supply Bills which had been passed by the Senate where the Government of the day did not have a Senate majority.

APPENDIX B

Appropriation and Supply Bills

1913
  Appropriation 1913–14
  Appropriation (Works and Buildings) 1913–14
  Supplementary Appropriation 1911–12
  Supplementary Appropriation (Works and Buildings) 1911–12
  Supplementary Appropriation 1912–13
  Supplementary Appropriation (Works and Buildings) 1912–13
  Supply (No. 1) 1913–14
  Supply (No. 2) 1913–14
  Supply (No. 3) 1913–14
  Supply (No. 4) 1913–14
  Supply (No. 5) 1913–14

1930
  Appropriation 1930–31
  Appropriation (Works and Buildings) 1930
  Supply (No. 1) 1930–31

1931
  Appropriation 1931–32
  Appropriation (Unemployment Relief Works)
  Appropriation (Works and Buildings) 1931
  Supplementary Appropriation 1927–30
  Supplementary Appropriation (Works and Buildings) 1927–30
  Supply (No. 1) 1931–32

1956
  Appropriation (No. 2) 1955–56
  Appropriation 1956–57
  Appropriation (Works and Services) (No. 2) 1955–56
  Appropriation (Works and Services) 1955–57
  Supplementary Appropriation 1954–55
  Supplementary Appropriation 1955–56
  Supplementary Appropriation (Works and Services) 1954–55
  Supplementary Appropriation (Works and Services) 1955–56
  Supply (No. 1) 1956–57
  Supply (Works and Services) (No. 1) 1956–57

1957
  Appropriation (No. 2) 1956–57
  Appropriation 1957–58
  Appropriation (Works and Services) (No. 2) 1956–57
  Appropriation (Works and Services) 1957–58
  Supply 1957–58

Supply (No. 2) 1957–58
Supply (Works and Services) 1957–58
Supply (Works and Services) (No. 2) 1957–58

1958
Appropriation (No. 2) 1957–58
Appropriation 1958–59
Appropriation (Works and Services) (No. 2) 1957–58
Appropriation (Works and Services) 1958–59
Supply 1958–59
Supply (Works and Services) 1958–59

1962
Appropriation (No. 2) 1961–62
Appropriation 1962–63
Appropriation (Works and Services) (No. 2) 1961–62
Appropriation (Works and Services) 1962–63
Supply 1962–63
Supply (Works and Services) 1962–63

1963
Appropriation (No. 2) 1962–63
Appropriation 1963–64
Appropriation (Works and Services) (No. 2) 1962–63
Appropriation (Works and Services) 1963–64
Supply 1963–64
Supply (Works and Services) 1963–64

1964
Appropriation (No. 2) 1963–64
Appropriation 1964–65
Appropriation (Works and Services) (No. 2) 1964–65
Appropriation (Works and Services) 1964–65
Supply 1964–65
Supply (Special Expenditure) 1964–65

1965
Appropriation (No. 3) 1964–65
Appropriation (No. 1) 1965–66
Appropriation (No. 2) 1965–66
Appropriation (Special Expenditure) (No. 2) 1965–66
Supply (No. 2) 1965–66

1966
Appropriation (No. 3) 1965–66
Appropriation (No. 4) 1965–66

Appropriation (No. 1) 1966–67
Appropriation (No. 2) 1966–67
Supply (No. 1) 1966–67
Supply (No. 2) 1966–67

1967
Appropriation (No. 3) 1966–67
Appropriation (No. 4) 1966–67
Appropriation (No. 1) 1967–68
Appropriation (No. 2) 1967–68
Supply (No. 1) 1967–68
Supply (No. 2) 1967–68

1968
Appropriation (No. 3) 1967–68
Appropriation (No. 4) 1967–68
Appropriation (No. 1) 1968–69
Appropriation (No. 2) 1968–69
Supply (No. 1) 1968–69
Supply (No. 2) 1968–69

1969
Appropriation (No. 3) 1968–69
Appropriation (No. 4) 1968–69
Appropriation (No. 1) 1969–70
Appropriation (No. 2) 1969–70
Supply (No. 1) 1969–70
Supply (No. 2) 1969–70

1970
Appropriation (No. 3) 1969–70
Appropriation (No. 4) 1969–70
Appropriation (No. 1) 1970–71
Appropriation (No. 2) 1970–71
Supply (No. 1) 1970–71
Supply (No. 2) 1970–71

1971
Appropriation (No. 3) 1970–71
Appropriation (No. 4) 1970–71
Appropriation (No. 1) 1971–72
Appropriation (No. 2) 1971–72
Appropriation (No. 3) 1971–72
Supply (No. 1) 1971–72
Supply (No. 2) 1971–72

Supply (No. 3) 1971–72

1972
Appropriation (No. 4) 1971–72
Appropriation (No. 5) 1971–72
Appropriation (No. 1) 1972–73
Appropriation (No. 2) 1972–73
Supply (No. 1) 1972–73
Supply (No. 2) 1972–72 [*sic*]

1973
Appropriation (No. 3) 1972–73
Appropriation (No. 4) 1972–73
Appropriation (No. 5) 1972–73
Appropriation (No. 6) 1972–73
Appropriation (No. 1) 1973–74
Appropriation (No. 2) 1973–74
Supply (No. 1) 1973–74
Supply (No. 2) 1973–74
Supply (No. 3) 1973–74

1974
Appropriation (No. 3) 1973–74
Appropriation (No. 4) 1973–74
Appropriation (No. 5) 1973–74
Appropriation (No. 1) 1974–75
Appropriation (No. 2) 1974–75
Appropriation (Urban Public Transport) 1974
Supply (No. 1) 1974–75
Supply (No. 2) 1974–75

1975
Appropriation (No. 3) 1974–75
Appropriation (No. 4) 1974–75
Appropriation (No. 5) 1974–75
Appropriation (No. 6) 1974–75
Appropriation (No. 1) 1975–76
Appropriation (No. 2) 1975–76
Appropriation (Development Bank) 1975
Supply (No. 1) 1975–76
Supply (No. 2) 1975–76

4. The resolutions we have set out define the conflict between the Houses. The Senate asserts that it may consistently with the Constitution and the practices or conventions governing the relations between the

APPENDIX B

Houses defer Supply to compel an election of the Representatives. This the Representatives deny. That House says the Senate's action violates its position relating to the Senate under the Constitution and the practices and conventions necessary for its working. The reasons referred to in the Senate's resolution are themselves matters of political dispute as to the truth of which opinion is divided. There has been no authoritative determination upon any one of them. Indeed there cannot be, for they are stated not as matters of law upon which a Court could pass but as matters only determinable politically. To accept one or more of them as established is therefore to enter the area of political dispute.

5. The question thus is whether the deferring of Supply by the Senate solely to procure the resignation or, failing that, the dismissal of the Ministry as a step in a forced dissolution of the Representatives compels His Excellency to dissolve that House. The existence, nature or extent of the Governor-General's reserve powers of dismissal or dissolution in other circumstances does not arise. On those questions we express no opinion. By forced dissolution we mean one occurring 'when the Crown insists on dissolution and, if necessary, dismisses Ministers in order to procure others who will tender the desired advice': (Forsey: *The Royal Power of Dissolution of Parliament in the British Commonwealth*, 1943, p. 71).

6. We have set out in paragraph 4 what may be regarded as the essence of the dispute between the Houses. But a closer analysis of the opposing contentions is called for. It will be remembered the Representatives' first resolution of 21 October says 'that the action of the Senate in delaying the passage of Appropriation Bill (No. 1) 1975–76 and Appropriation Bill (No. 2) 1975–76 for the reasons given in the Senate resolution is not contemplated within the terms of the Constitution and is contrary to established constitutional convention'. The Senate's reply of 22 October denies this and in doing so refers in paragraph (c) to the undoubted fact that the legislative power of the Commonwealth is vested in the Queen, the Senate and the House of Representatives. That, of course, is the language of section 1 of the Constitution and reference to it but emphasises the validity of the Representatives' complaint set out at the beginning of this paragraph. For the Senate's resolutions of 16 and 22 October made clear its refusal to participate with the Representatives in relation both to these Bills and their successors in the exercise of legislative power with which the Constitution entrusts both Houses except upon satisfaction of a condition which it has no express constitutional authority to impose. Nor is there any implied authority. What justification under the Constitution

would there be for the Representatives to refuse to perform its part in law-making unless the Senate agreed to a periodical election of half its members?

7. This is not to say that the Senate's actions are in any way invalid or inoperative. It is but an assertion of the view that the Constitution envisages the Houses of Parliament as engaged in legislative action alone, and that save perhaps to the extent that a refusal to embark upon consideration of the measure may amount to a failure to pass it for the purposes of section 57, does not contemplate either House as refusing to undertake that task whether conditionally or unconditionally. But when one says that a refusal to entertain consideration of a measure may amount to a failure to pass it for the purposes of section 57, the necessary consequence follows, we think, that that dispute between the Houses has a constitutional solution which envisages the interposition of a period of three months between the first and second failures to pass the measure. To this we later return.

8. It clearly cannot be said that the Representatives in asserting the existence of the convention are acting unreasonably or without the most solid foundation. This particular power of the Senate has never before been exercised—a fact suggesting the convention exists. There is no doubt that the principle of responsible government permeates the Constitution (*Amalgamated Society of Engineers v. Adelaide Steamship Co. Ltd* (1920), 28 C.L.R. 129 at pp. 146–7). Indeed a number of the principles of responsible government, for example that Supply is voted only on message from the Crown, and that appropriation and taxation law may only originate in the popular House, are expressly provided for by the Constitution. Neither the existence of the Prime Minister nor the necessity for his membership of the Representatives is the subject of express provision, but that such requirements exist and have been observed for the same period as has the disputed convention or practice is incontrovertible.

9. The Senate's resolution indicates an intention to defer passage of the Appropriation Bills until either the Ministry resigns or the Governor-General acting against its advice dismisses it and, upon advice of Ministers in a minority in the Representatives, dissolves it. The Ministry has not resigned and will not do so. That leaves only a forced dissolution. Dr Jennings (*Cabinet Government*, 3rd edn 1969) observes (at page 403) that 'No Government has been dismissed by the Sovereign since 1783', and points out that there was no dismissal in 1834 of Lord Melbourne's Government (pp. 403–5). Dr Forsey (*The Royal Power of Dissolution of Parliament*, 1943) says that 'In the overseas Empire

APPENDIX B 333

there appears to have been only one instance of this: New Brunswick in 1853' (page 71). The passage continues—

> The dissolutions in Newfoundland in 1861, New Brunswick in 1866, Quebec in 1878 and 1891, British Columbia in 1900, Queensland in 1907 and New South Wales in 1932, like the British dissolution of 1807, were not true forced dissolutions. Ministers were not dismissed because they refused to advise dissolution; they were dismissed for quite other reasons, and dissolutions granted to their successors because they could not hope to carry on government with the existing Lower House.

10. We have referred to forced dissolutions only to indicate that their very rarity and the long years since their exercise cast the gravest doubt upon the present existence of that prerogative.

11. But we would emphasise that we understand the question for His Excellency to be not which of the disputants is correct in its views, but rather that the two Houses are in real dispute about momentous matters. For it can hardly be doubted that the Crown will not as a general rule take sides in such disputes for 'while it should be the governor's earnest desire to contribute, as far as he can properly contribute, to the removal of existing differences between the two Houses, it is clearly undesirable that he should intervene in such a manner as would withdraw these differences from their proper sphere, and so give to them a character which does not naturally belong to them of a conflict between the majority of one or another of the two Houses, and the representative of the Crown:' (Todd: *Parliamentary Government in the British Colonies*, 2nd edn 1893 p. 722). To this we later return.

12. Before turning to a consideration of Mr Ellicott's press statement, we think it relevant to observe that by section 28 of the Constitution every House of Representatives shall continue for three years from the first meeting of the House and no longer but may be sooner dissolved by the Governor-General. Whether the power of dissolution referred to in section 28 is independent of that conferred by section 5 is not, we think, material to resolve. What is significant is that, while the power to refuse a dissolution is one 'for which the representative of the Crown is alone responsible, although it is sometimes stated that the incoming Ministry assumes the responsibility of the refusal by undertaking to carry on the Queen's Government for the time being', it is equally clear that 'A grant of a dissolution is an executive act, to which the Crown assents, and for which the Ministry tendering the advice and doing the act are responsible to Parliament and the country' (*Quick and Garran*, section 118, p. 464). A passage to the same effect

appears in section 63 of the *Annotated Constitution of the Australian Commonwealth* by the same authors at page 407. The point of this, of course, is that the Crown in dissolving the House of Representatives acts upon ministerial advice—that is to say, upon the advice of Ministers chosen from the political party with the majority in the Representatives. The only exception presently material is the doubtful case of the forced dissolution. In such cases the Crown in dissolving has acted upon advice of a minority Ministry.

13. The central point taken by Mr Ellicott is that a Government without Supply cannot govern, for the maintenance of the Constitution and of the laws of the Commonwealth require that the Government have authority from Parliament to spend money to perform those functions. The Governor-General is sought to be immediately engaged upon a refusal of Supply by the assertion that His Excellency's basic role is the execution and maintenance of the Constitution and Commonwealth laws, one which he exercises upon the advice of a Ministry chosen from the majority party in the Representatives, but holding office during His Excellency's pleasure.

14. Before proceeding further some comments should be made. Section 61 of the Constitution enacts that—

> 61. The executive power of the Commonwealth is vested in the Queen and is exerciseable by the Governor-General as the Queen's representative, and extends to the execution and maintenance of this Constitution, and of the laws of the Commonwealth.

Section 62 provides for a Federal Executive Council to advise the Governor-General 'in the government of the Commonwealth' who shall hold office during his pleasure and section 64 for the appointment of officers to administer such departments of State as the Governor-General in council may establish. These officers must be members of the Federal Executive Council and hold office during the Governor-General's pleasure. They are the Queen's Ministers of State for the Commonwealth and must sit in the Parliament. In this way the Cabinet system was incorporated into the Constitution. What these sections make clear is that the Executive power of the Commonwealth exerciseable by the Governor-General may only be so exercised on advice of a Ministry which, because responsible government permeates the Constitution, will be drawn from the majority party in the Representatives.

15. The point of this is that section 61 affords no ground for the conclusion that upon the Senate deferring or rejecting Supply solely to procure the resignation or dismissal of the Ministry possessing a majority in the Representatives, His Excellency is constitutionally

obliged immediately to seek an explanation of the Prime Minister of how he proposes to overcome that situation.

16. Nor do we agree with the suggestion that were the Prime Minister unable to suggest means which would solve the disagreement between the Houses and left the Government without funds to carry on, it would be His Excellency's duty to dismiss his Ministers.

17. We do not suggest that, should a case exist for his intervention, His Excellency in considering the course he will take must disregard the fact that the Senate's deferring or refusal of Supply will impede the business of government. We do suggest that His Excellency is not confined to a consideration of that fact. He may consider others. After all the constitutional provisions but recognise that the Ministry holds office during His Excellency's pleasure (section 64) and that he may dissolve the Representatives before the expiry of its term (sections 5 and 28); they do not, considered alone, afford any guide as to the circumstances when the extreme and abnormal reserve powers of dismissal of a Ministry and consequent dissolution of the Representatives should or may be exercised or even that they still exist. This is the field of convention and discretion.

18. But it is, we think, not correct to treat the exercise of those powers as demanded when refusal of Supply is threatened or when it occurs. To do so is to deny, for example, a Vice-regal authority to offer suggestions where the circumstances have reached a stage sufficiently grave to warrant His Excellency's adoption of that course, bearing in mind that the cardinal rule is that the Crown should not 'withdraw these differences from their proper sphere': (*Todd, supra*).

19. We have quoted in paragraph 11 above the view expressed by Governor Bowen in relation to his duty where a conflict between the two Houses arose in the State of Victoria in 1877. We shall later refer to Mr Asquith's memorandum to His Majesty the King containing more recent and more forceful observations to like effect. Dr Jennings remarked of this memorandum (*Cabinet Government*, 3rd edn 1969) that it 'so far as it goes, is incontrovertible' (page 409).

20. It is perhaps relevant to bear in mind that the Legislative Council in that dispute, possessing an express constitutional power to reject financial measures, in fact rejected the Appropriation Bill and that the response of the Government of Victoria was the dismissal of civil servants, an act in which the Governor acquiesced. The important consideration for present purposes is that the Governor was advised by the Colonial Secretary, Sir Michael Hicks Beach, that he must follow his Ministers' advice though in case of necessity he should take legal opinion: Jennings: *Cabinet Government*, 3rd edn 1969 p. 407. This, of

course, supports the view we have expressed that the mere threat of or indeed the actual rejection of Supply neither calls for the Ministry to resign nor compels the Crown's representative thereupon to intervene.

21. It is, we think obvious enough that since the Imperial Conference of 1926 the Governor-General is the representative of the Crown and holds in all essential respects the same position in relation to the administration of public affairs in the Dominion as is held by His Majesty the King in Great Britain, and that he is not the representative or agent of His Majesty's Government in Great Britain or of any Department of that Government. Thus, as Sir Kenneth Bailey suggested in his introduction to the first edition of Dr Evatt's work *The King and His Dominion Governors*, it is necessary in the Dominions now to discover the principles which have underlain the action of the King himself in recent constitutional crises and that the most important sections of Dr Evatt's book are those which analyse the action of the Crown in Great Britain during the critical years 1909–14: Evatt: *The King and His Dominion Governors*, 2nd edn 1967 pp. xxxvi–xxxvii. We would not suggest, of course, that the constitutional authority of the House of Lords is as great as that of the Senate for, amongst other factors, the power to reject money measures has been removed. But when that power still existed and was exercised the constitutional crisis thus caused continued for a number of years. It could hardly be disputed that a factor of the first importance is the relationship between the Governor-General and the two Houses and that that relationship is the stronger when a judicious abstention from intervention is exercised, as the present crisis perhaps indicates.

22. It is with such considerations in mind that Mr Asquith, in his memorandum on the King's position in relation to the Home Rule Bill, wrote:

> Nothing can be more important, in the best interests of the Crown and of the country, than that a practice, so long established and so well justified by experience, should remain unimpaired. It frees the occupant of the throne from all personal responsibility for the acts of the Executive and the legislature. It gives force and meaning to the old maxim that 'the King can do no wrong'. So long as it prevails, however objectionable particular Acts may be to a large section of his subjects, they cannot hold him in any way accountable. If, on the other hand, the King were to intervene on one side, or in one case—which he could only do by dismissing ministers in *de facto* possession of a Parliamentary majority—he would be expected to do the same on another occasion, and perhaps for the other side. Every Act of Parliament of the first order of importance, and only passed after acute controversy,

would be regarded as bearing the personal *imprimatur* of the Sovereign. He would, whether he wished it or not, be dragged into the arena of party politics; and at a dissolution following such a dismissal of ministers as had been referred to, it is no exaggeration to say that the Crown would become the football of contending factions.

This is a constitutional catastrophe which it is the duty of every wise statesman to do the utmost in his power to avert. Jennings: *Cabinet Government* 3rd edn 1969 p. 408.

23. To the above positive considerations, in themselves perhaps compelling enough, another remains to be added, one valid whether or not our analysis of the nature of the dispute be right or not. There is or is threatening a legislative deadlock. Section 57 of the Constitution enshrines the constitutional solution 'of the spectre of legislative deadlock' which possession by the Senate of the power to reject legislation including money bills necessarily gave rise to. The language we use has been borrowed from the judgment of the Honourable Mr Justice Stephen delivered in the case of *The State of Victoria and Her Majesty's Attorney-General for the State of Victoria v. The Commonwealth and another* (not yet reported). As His Honour said in *Cormack v. Cope* (a passage quoted with approval by the Honourable Mr Justice Mason in his judgment in the first mentioned case):

> It (section 57) serves an obviously useful purpose: avoidance of deadlock is what the section is concerned with and the interval of three months, in providing a time for attempted reconciliation of differences must begin after the deadlock occurs.

24. That the section applies to money bills is obvious not only from its language ('any proposed law') and the opinion of the most persuasive writers upon the Constitution ('It covers every proposed law which may have been passed by the National Chamber', *Quick and Garran* p. 685) but also, explicitly (the Honourable Mr Justice Gibbs and the Honourable Mr Justice Stephen and, perhaps, the Honourable Mr Justice Mason) and implicitly in the judgments of the other Justices who considered that case first referred to.

25. It seems likely that the refusal of the Senate to entertain consideration of the Appropriation Bills may have amounted to a failure to pass them within the meaning of the section. But, if that is or may be so, the full operation of the section requires that a period of three months elapse between that failure to pass by the Senate before the first limb of the section has fully operated. The section 'relies, after the first occurrence of deadlock, upon providing opportunity for second, and perhaps wiser, thoughts and for negotiation and

compromise between the chambers', to use again the language of the Honourable Mr Justice Stephen in the case first cited.

26. If such be the section's purpose and intended operation, how is it possible consistently with the Constitution that a reserve power of uncertain existence and unknowable constituents must be exercised in a way necessarily denying effect to the one constitutional provision expressly directed to the solution of deadlock between the Houses? We do not find it possible ourselves to accept that view and to the extent that Mr Ellicott does so he is, we think clearly wrong.

27. That neither or either House intends to compromise is not to the point, should it be the fact. The section exists to permit that opportunity and to allow a joint sitting to be held whose decision finally resolves the difference.

28. We have, so far, confined our remarks to what the press release expressly says. We turn now to consider what it assumes. Those assumptions include at least the following:

(1) that the Senate's legal power to reject Supply may in point of law be exercised whenever and for whatever reason commends itself to the Senate and whatever the consequences;
(2) the express provisions of the constitution, construed taking into account the principle of responsible government which pervades it (to use the language of the High Court in the *Engineers' Case (1920) 28 C.L.R. 129* at pp. 146-7) contain nothing which implies any restraint upon the untrammelled use of the Senate's legal power to reject Supply for any reason; and lastly
(3) that no practice or convention relating to the exercise of that power solely to determine the life of the Representatives exists, or, if existing, is relevant for Vice-regal consideration.

29. We have referred to an untrammelled use of the power to reject Supply. By that expression we mean one legally and in point of constitutional practice of the nature we have described in (1) above and naturally intend to include an exercise solely to determine the Representatives' term. Such is the present exercise, as the Senate's resolution makes clear. It is not, we think, unfair or inaccurate on our part to suggest that the press statement demands the making of such an assumption amongst others. For if the Senate's power to reject is subject to any restraint, that restraint is not in words imposed upon the power which section 53 contains and thus must be found in a practice or convention which would then become a factor offsetting the weight that would otherwise attach to a denial of funds and the hardships necessarily thereby involved without a forced dissolution. None such is suggested. The power which Mr Ellicott assumes in the

Senate must, therefore, be one legally and conventionally untrammelled.

30. How does this assumption accord with other provisions of the Constitution? We have already mentioned on 57 and do not here repeat what we have said of it. We would wish again to refer to sections 5 and 28. The relevant part of section 5 is in the following terms:

> 5. The Governor-General may appoint such times for holding the sessions of the Parliament as he thinks fit, and may also from time to time, by Proclamation or otherwise, prorogue the Parliament, and may in like manner dissolve the House of Representatives.

Section 28 provides as follows:

> 28. Every House of Representatives shall continue for three years from the first meeting of the House, and no longer, but may be sooner dissolved by the Governor-General.

31. We have also referred to the voting of Supply only on a message from the Crown and to the Representatives' exclusive authority to initiate laws imposing taxation and appropriating revenue or moneys. This last is the subject of express Constitutional provision for section 53 provides (and we quote the relevant parts):

> 53. Proposed laws appropriating revenue or moneys, or imposing taxation, shall not originate in the Senate. But a proposed law shall not be taken to appropriate revenue or moneys, or to impose taxation, by reason only of its containing provisions for the imposition or appropriation of fines or other pecuniary penalties, or for the demand or payment or appropriation of fees for licences; or fees for services under the proposed law.

32. The second paragraph denies to the Senate power to amend proposed laws imposing taxation or proposed laws appropriating revenue or money for the ordinary annual services of the Government. The Senate's power to reject appropriation (which for the purpose of this Opinion we assume to exist) arises from that part of section 53 enacting that except as the section provides the Senate shall have equal power with the Representatives in respect of all proposed laws.

33. The object of section 56 of the Constitution (providing that proposed laws appropriating revenue or moneys may not be passed unless the purpose of the appropriation has been recommended by message of the Governor-General to the House in which the proposal originated) is to retain to the Ministry drawn from the party with a majority in the Representatives (and therefore advising the Governor-General in the exercise of the Executive power which section 61 of the Constitution confers) control over the means to give effect to the

maintenance of the Constitution: 'and the execution of the laws of the Commonwealth.'

34. What emerges from the provisions? In our opinion it is clear enough that the financial provisions (sections 53 and 56) both in terms and in their implications commit to those advising the Governor-General as the Queen's representative and exercising the Executive power of the Commonwealth, authority to decide the amounts necessary for the ordinary annual services and to obtain from the Representatives (for they are envisaged by the Constitution as there possessing a majority) legislation for those amounts. The Senate is denied authority to amend any proposed law giving effect to that decision. It is denied also authority to make that decision itself. It may ask the Representatives to consider its suggestions as to the omission or amendment of any items (section 53, third paragraph). Again, those advisers alone by virtue of their majority in the Representatives may initiate laws imposing the taxation necessary to obtain those amounts. Further, the Constitution envisages in section 28 that the Representatives will normally enjoy a term of three years. Any decision for a shorter term will be taken by the Governor-General on the advice of those from the Representatives' majority.

35. To treat the Senate's power to reject Supply as untrammelled by convention or practice means that sections 28 and 53 are deprived of their intended harmonious co-operation and that continuity in the exercise of the Executive power is disrupted and thus the power itself is weakened.

36. It is germane to recall that several Australian federalists of eminence considered that the Cabinet system of Executive Government which the Constitution enshrines was incompatible with a true Federation. Their contentions are thus described by Quick and Garran at page 706 of their work on the Constitution:

> In support of this contention it is argued that, in a Federation, it is a fundamental rule that no new law shall be passed and no old law shall be altered without the consent of (1) a majority of the people speaking by their representatives in one House, and (2) a majority of the States speaking by their representatives in the other House; that the same principle of the State approval as well as popular approval should apply to Executive action, as well as to legislative action; that the State should not be forced to support Executive policy and Executive acts merely because ministers enjoyed the confidence of the popular Chamber; *that the State house would be justified in withdrawing its support from a ministry of whose policy and executive acts it disapproved; that the State house could, as effectively as the primary Chamber, enforce its want of confidence by refusing to provide the necessary supplies.* The Senate of the

French Republic, it is pointed out, has established a precedent showing how an Upper House can enforce its opinions and cause a change of ministry. On these grounds it is contended that the introduction of the Cabinet system of Responsible Government into a Federation, in which the relations of two branches of the legislature, having equal and co-ordinate authority, are quite different from those existing in a single autonomous State, is repugnant to the spirit and intention of a scheme of Federal Government. In the end it is predicted that either Responsible Government will kill the Federation and change it into a unified State, or the Federation will kill Responsible Government and substitute a new form of Executive more compatible with the Federal theory. In particular, strong objection is taken to the insertion in the constitution of a cast-iron condition that Federal Ministers must be members of Parliament. Membership of Parliament, it is argued, is not of the essence of Responsible Government, but only an incident or an accidental feature, which has been introduced by modern practice and by statutory innovation.

The italics are ours. But as those learned authors said:

Their views have not been accepted, and for better or worse, the system of Responsible Government as known to the British Constitution has been practically embedded in the Federal Constitution in such a manner that it cannot be disturbed without an amendment of the instrument.

Quick and Garran pp. 706–7

In the first passage which we have quoted 'the State House' is, of course, the Senate.

37. The point of quoting the first passage is that those eminent Federalists included Sir Samuel Griffith and Mr Justice Inglish Clark and that the defeat of their objections involved in the minds of those responsible for the Constitution rejection of the notion that the Senate would 'enforce its want of confidence by refusing to provide the necessary supplies'.

38. It seems to us, if we may respectfully say so, that assumptions underlie Mr Ellicott's press statement which present dangers to the orderly working of Government. Those dangers are significant ones. That the possibility of their existence is a disquieting one cannot, we venture to think, be seriously doubted. For they may be indefinitely repeated and may involve deleterious consequences to the working of the constitutional provisions. That that working requires restraint on the part of both Houses is hardly open to doubt. A view which looking only to the existence of the legal power disregards or ignores constitutional practices hitherto apparently governing the exercise of those

powers, requires, we venture to think, the gravest consideration before its adoption could even be contemplated.

39. We have found ourselves for the reasons we have stated firmly of opinion that Mr Ellicott's expressed views are wrong.

Kep. Enderby
Attorney-General of Australia

M. H. Byers
Crown Solicitor

4 November 1975

Appendix C

Letter from the Chief Justice of the High Court to the Governor-General

Dear Sir John,

    In response to Your Excellency's invitation I attended this day at Admiralty House. In our conversations I indicated that I considered myself, as Chief Justice of Australia, free, on Your Excellency's request, to offer you legal advice as to Your Excellency's constitutional rights and duties in relation to an existing situation which, of its nature, was unlikely to come before the Court. We both clearly understood that I was not in any way concerned with matters of a purely political kind, or with any political consequences of the advice I might give.

    In response to Your Excellency's request for my legal advice as to whether a course on which you had determined was consistent with your constitutional authority and duty, I respectfully offer the following.

    The Constitution of Australia is a federal Constitution which embodies the principle of Ministerial responsibility. The Parliament consists of two houses, the House of Representatives and the Senate, each popularly elected, and each with the same legislative power, with the one exception that the Senate may not originate nor amend a money bill.

    Two relevant constitutional consequences flow from this structure of the Parliament. First, the Senate has constitutional power to refuse to pass a money bill; it has power to refuse supply to the Government of the day. Secondly, a Prime Minister who cannot ensure supply to the Crown, including funds for carrying on the ordinary services of Government, must either advise a general election (of a kind which the constitutional situation may then allow) or resign. If, being unable to secure supply, he refuses to take either course, Your Excellency has constitutional authority to withdraw his Commission as Prime Minister.

There is no analogy in respect of a Prime Minister's duty between the situation of the Parliament under the federal Constitution of Australia and the relationship between the House of Commons, a popularly elected body, and the House of Lords, a non-elected body, in the unitary form of Government functioning in the United Kingdom. Under that system, a Government having the confidence of the House of Commons can secure supply, despite a recalcitrant House of Lords. But it is otherwise under our federal Constitution. A Government having the confidence of the House of Representatives but not that of the Senate, both elected Houses, cannot secure supply to the Crown.

But there is an analogy between the situation of a Prime Minister who has lost the confidence of the House of Commons and a Prime Minister who does not have the confidence of the Parliament, i.e. of the House of Representatives and of the Senate. The duty and responsibility of the Prime Minister to the Crown in each case is the same: if unable to secure supply to the Crown, to resign or to advise an election.

In the event that, conformably to this advice, the Prime Minister ceases to retain his Commission, Your Excellency's constitutional authority and duty would be to invite the Leader of the Opposition, if he can undertake to secure supply, to form a caretaker government (i.e. one which makes no appointments or initiates any policies) pending a general election, whether of the House of Representatives, or of both Houses of the Parliament, as that Government may advise.

Accordingly, my opinion is that, if Your Excellency is satisfied in the current situation that the present Government is unable to secure supply, the course upon which Your Excellency has determined is consistent with your constitutional authority and duty.

Yours respectfully,
(sgnd Garfield Barwick)

His Excellency the Honourable Sir John Kerr, K.C.M.G.,
Governor-General of Australia,
Admiralty House,
SYDNEY

10 November 1975

Appendix D
Sir John Kerr's letter of dismissal

Dear Mr Whitlam,

In accordance with section 64 of the Constitution I hereby determine your appointment as my Chief Adviser and Head of the Government. It follows that I also hereby determine the appointments of all the Ministers in your Government.

You have previously told me that you would never resign or advise an election of the House of Representatives or a double dissolution and that the only way in which such an election could be obtained would be by my dismissal of you and your ministerial colleagues. As it appeared likely that you would today persist in this attitude I decided that, if you did, I would determine your commission and state my reasons for doing so. You have persisted in your attitude and I have accordingly acted as indicated. I attach a statement of my reasons which I intend to publish immediately.

It is with a great deal of regret that I have taken this step both in respect of yourself and your colleagues.

I propose to send for the Leader of the Opposition and to commission him to form a new caretaker government until an election can be held.

Yours sincerely,
(sgnd John R. Kerr)

The Honourable E. G. Whitlam, QC, M.P.
11 November 1975

Appendix E

Governor-General's statement of reasons

I HAVE GIVEN careful consideration to the constitutional crisis and have made some decisions which I wish to explain.

Summary

It has been necessary for me to find a democratic and constitutional solution to the current crisis which will permit the people of Australia to decide as soon as possible what should be the outcome of the deadlock which developed over supply between the two Houses of Parliament and between the Government and Opposition parties. The only solution consistent with the Constitution and with my oath of office and my responsibilities, authority and duty as Governor-General is to terminate the commission as Prime Minister of Mr Whitlam and to arrange for a caretaker government able to secure supply and willing to let the issue go to the people.

I shall summarise the elements of the problem and the reasons for my decision which places the matter before the people of Australia for prompt determination.

Because of the federal nature of our Constitution and because of its provisions the Senate undoubtedly has constitutional power to refuse or defer supply to the Government. Because of the principles of responsible government a Prime Minister who cannot obtain supply, including money for carrying on the ordinary services of government, must either advise a general election or resign. If he refuses to do this I have the authority and indeed the duty under the Constitution to withdraw his commission as Prime Minister. The position in Australia is quite different from the position in the United Kingdom. Here the confidence of both Houses on supply is necessary to ensure its provision. In the United Kingdom the confidence of the House of Commons alone is necessary. But both here and in the United Kingdom the duty of the Prime Minister is the same in a most important respect—if he cannot get supply he must resign or advise an election.

If a Prime Minister refuses to resign or to advise an election, and this is the case with Mr Whitlam, my constitutional authority and duty require me to do what I have now done—to withdraw his commission—and to invite the Leader of the Opposition to form a caretaker government—that is one that makes no appointments or dismissals and initiates no policies until a general election is held. It is most desirable that he should guarantee supply. Mr Fraser will be asked to give the necessary undertakings and advise whether he is prepared to recommend a double dissolution. He will also be asked to guarantee supply.

The decisions I have made were made after I was satisfied that Mr Whitlam could not obtain supply. No other decision open to me would enable the Australian people to decide for themselves what should be done.

Once I had made up my mind, for my own part, what I must do if Mr Whitlam persisted in his stated intentions I consulted the Chief Justice of Australia, Sir Garfield Barwick. I have his permission to say that I consulted him in this way.

The result is that there will be an early general election for both Houses and the people can do what, in a democracy such as ours, is their responsibility and duty and theirs alone. It is for the people now to decide the issue which the two leaders have failed to settle.

Detailed statement of decisions

On 16 October the Senate deferred consideration of Appropriation Bills (Nos. 1 & 2) 1975–1976. In the time which elapsed since then events made it clear that the Senate was determined to refuse to grant supply to the Government. In that time the Senate on no less than two occasions resolved to proceed no further with fresh Appropriation Bills, in identical terms, which had been passed by the House of Representatives. The determination of the Senate to maintain its refusal to grant supply was confirmed by the public statements made by the Leader of the Opposition, the Opposition having control of the Senate.

By virtue of what has in fact happened there therefore came into existence a deadlock between the House of Representatives and the Senate on the central issue of supply without which all the ordinary services of the government cannot be maintained. I had the benefit of discussions with the Prime Minister and, with his approval, with the Leader of the Opposition and with the Treasurer and the Attorney-General. As a result of those discussions and having regard to the public statements of the Prime Minister and the Leader of the Opposition I have come regretfully to the conclusion that there is no likelihood of a compromise between the House of Representatives and the Senate nor for that matter between the Government and the Opposition.

The deadlock which arose was one which, in the interests of the nation, had to be resolved as promptly as possible by means which are appropriate in our democratic system. In all the circumstances which have occurred the appropriate means is a dissolution of the Parliament and an election for both Houses. No other course offers a sufficient assurance of resolving the deadlock and resolving it promptly.

Parliamentary control of appropriation and accordingly of expenditure is a fundamental feature of our system of responsible government. In consequence it has been generally accepted that a government which has been denied supply by the Parliament cannot govern. So much at least is clear in cases where a ministry is refused supply by a popularly elected Lower House. In other systems where an Upper House is denied the right to reject a money bill denial of supply can occur only at the instance of the Lower House. When, however, an Upper House possesses the power to reject a money bill including an appropriation bill, and exercises the power by denying supply, the principle that a government which has been denied supply by the Parliament should resign or go to an election must still apply—it is a necessary consequence of Parliamentary control of appropriation and expenditure and of the expectation that the ordinary and necessary services of government will continue to be provided.

The Constitution combines the two elements of responsible government and federalism. The Senate is, like the House, a popularly elected chamber. It was designed to provide representation by States, not by electorates, and was given by Sec. 53, equal powers with the House with respect to proposed laws, except in the respects mentioned in the section. It was denied power to originate or amend appropriation bills but was left with power to reject them or defer consideration of them. The Senate accordingly has the power and has exercised the power to refuse to grant supply to the Government. The Government stands in the position that it has been denied supply by the Parliament with all the consequences which flow from that fact.

There have been public discussions about whether there is a convention deriving from the principles of responsible government that the Senate must never under any circumstances exercise the power to reject an appropriation bill. The Constitution must prevail over any convention because, in determining the question how far the conventions of responsible government have been grafted on to the federal compact the Constitution itself must in the end control the situation.

Sec. 57 of the Constitution provides a means, perhaps the usual means, of resolving a disagreement between the Houses with respect to a proposed law. But the machinery which it provides necessarily entails a considerable time lag which is quite inappropriate to a speedy resolution of the fundamental problems posed by the refusal of supply. Its presence in the Constitution does not cut down the reserve powers of the Governor-General.

I should be surprised if the Law Officers expressed the view that there is no reserve power in the Governor-General to dismiss a Ministry which has been refused supply by the Parliament and to commission a Ministry, as a caretaker ministry which will secure supply and recommend a dissolution, including where appropriate a double dissolution. This is a matter on which my own mind is quite clear and I am acting in accordance with my own clear view of the principles laid down by the Constitution and of the nature, powers and responsibility of my office.

There is one other point. There has been discussion of the possibility that a half-Senate election might be held under circumstances in which the Government has not obtained supply. If such advice were given to me I should feel constrained to reject it because a half-Senate election held whilst supply continues to be denied does not guarantee a prompt or sufficiently clear prospect of the deadlock being resolved in accordance with proper principles. When I refer to rejection of such advice I mean that, as I would find it necessary in the circumstances I have envisaged to determine Mr Whitlam's commission and, as things have turned out have done so, he would not be Prime Minister and not able to give or persist with such advice.

The announced proposals about financing public servants, suppliers, contractors and others do not amount to a satisfactory alternative to supply.

Government House,
Canberra, 2600
11 November 1975

Appendix F
Malcolm Fraser's caretaker commission

Your Excellency,

You have intimated to me that it is Your Excellency's pleasure that I should act as your Chief Adviser and Head of the Government.

In accepting your commission I confirm that I have given you an assurance that I shall immediately seek to secure the passage of the Appropriation Bills which are at present before the Senate, thus ensuring supply for the carrying on of the Public Service in all its branches. I further confirm that, upon the granting of supply, I shall immediately recommend to Your Excellency the dissolution of both Houses of the Parliament.

My government will act as a caretaker government and will make no appointments or dismissals or initiate new policies before a general election is held.

Yours sincerely,
(sgnd J. M. Fraser)

His Excellency the Honourable Sir John Kerr,
A.C., K.C.M.G., K.St.J., Q.C.

11 November 1975

Appendix G
Proclamation

PROCLAMATION
Australia
JOHN R. KERR
Governor-General

By His Excellency, the
Governor-General of
Australia

WHEREAS by section 57 of the Constitution it is provided that if the House of Representatives passes any proposed law, and the Senate rejects or fails to pass it, or passes it with amendments to which the House of Representatives will not agree, and if after an interval of three months the House of Representatives, in the same or the next session, again passes the proposed law with or without any amendments which have been made, suggested, or agreed to by the Senate and the Senate rejects or fails to pass it, or passes it with amendments to which the House of Representatives will not agree, the Governor-General may dissolve the Senate and the House of Representatives simultaneously:

ANDWHEREAS the conditions upon which the Governor-General is empowered by that section of the Constitution to dissolve the Senate and the House of Representatives simultaneously have been fulfilled in respect of the several proposed laws intitled—

Health Insurance Levy Act 1974

Health Insurance Levy Assessment Act 1974
Income Tax (International Agreements) Act 1974
Minerals (Submerged Lands) Act 1974
Minerals (Submerged Lands) (Royalty) Act 1974
National Health Act 1974
Conciliation and Arbitration Act 1974
Conciliation and Arbitration Act (No. 2) 1974
National Investment Fund Act 1974
Electoral Laws Amendment Act 1974
Electoral Act 1975
Privy Council Appeals Abolition Act 1975
Superior Court of Australia Act 1974
Electoral Re-distribution (New South Wales) Act 1975
Electoral Re-distribution (Queensland) Act 1975
Electoral Re-distribution (South Australia) Act 1975
Electoral Re-distribution (Tasmania) Act 1975
Electoral Re-distribution (Victoria) Act 1975
Broadcasting and Television Act (No. 2) 1974
Television Stations Licence Fees Act 1974
Broadcasting Stations Licence Fees Act 1974

NOWTHEREFORE, I Sir John Robert Kerr, the Governor-General of Australia, do by this my Proclamation dissolve the Senate and the House of Representatives.

(L.S.)   Given under my Hand and the Great Seal of Australia on 11 November 1975.

By His Excellency's Command,
MALCOLM FRASER
Prime Minister

God Save The Queen!

Appendix H

Letter from the Queen's private secretary to the Speaker

I am commanded by The Queen to acknowledge your letter of 12th November about the recent political events in Australia. You ask that The Queen should act to restore Mr Whitlam to office as Prime Minister.

As we understand the situation here, the Australian Constitution firmly places the prerogative powers of the Crown in the hands of the Governor-General as the representative of the Queen of Australia. The only person competent to commission an Australian Prime Minister is the Governor-General, and The Queen has no part in the decisions which the Governor-General must take in accordance with the Constitution. Her Majesty, as Queen of Australia, is watching events in Canberra with close interest and attention, but it would not be proper for her to intervene in person in matters which are so clearly placed within the jurisdiction of the Governor-General by the Constitution Act.

I understand that you have been good enough to send a copy of your letter to the Governor-General so I am writing to His Excellency to say that the text of your letter has been received here in London and has been laid before The Queen.

I am sending a copy of this letter to the Governor-General.

17 November 1975

Notes

Chapter 1   Whitlam

1. Gough Whitlam, *The Truth of the Matter*, Penguin, Ringwood, Victoria, 1979, pp. 5–6.
2. Fred Daly, *From Curtin to Kerr*, Sun Books, Melbourne, 1977, pp. 195–97.
3. Graham Freudenberg, *A Certain Grandeur*, Macmillan, Melbourne, 1977, p. 66.
4. ibid. p. 88.
5. Paul Kelly, *The Unmaking of Gough*, Allen & Unwin, revised edition, Sydney, 1994, p. 428.
6. Gough Whitlam, *The Whitlam Government*, Penguin, Ringwood, Victoria, 1985, p. 1.
7. Freudenberg, *A Certain Grandeur*, pp. 35–37. In the event Whitlam later secured the full representation of the parliamentary leaders at Federal Conference and Federal Executive.
8. *Australian Financial Review*, 30 May 1972.
9. Freudenberg, *A Certain Grandeur*, p. 75.
10. This point draws upon James Walter, *The Leader*, University of Queensland Press, St Lucia, 1980, p. 172.
11. Kelly, *The Unmaking of Gough*, p. 424.
12. ibid. p. 424.
13. Laurie Oakes, *Crash Through or Crash*, Drummond, Richmond, Victoria, 1976, p. 25.
14. *Australian Financial Review*, 30 May 1972.
15. Refer Walter, *The Leader*, p. 192, for this argument.
16. John Mant, personal interview, May 1995.
17. Refer Brian Galligan, *Politics of the High Court*, University of Queensland Press, St Lucia, 1987, chapter four.
18. Freudenberg, *A Certain Grandeur*, p. 74.
19. ibid. p. 72.

20 Geoffrey Sawer, *Federation Under Strain*, Melbourne University Press, Melbourne, 1977, p. 4.
21 Freudenberg, *A Certain Grandeur*, p. 79.
22 This is implicit in the Governor-General's speech at the opening of the Parliament. See chapter three.
23 Whitlam, *The Whitlam Government*, pp. 17–19; Freudenberg, *A Certain Grandeur*, pp. 239–45; refer C J Lloyd and G S Reid, *Out of the Wilderness*, Cassell Australia, Melbourne, 1974, chapter two.
24 Whitlam, *The Whitlam Government*, pp. 19–22.
25 Whitlam, *The Truth of the Matter*, pp. 5–6.
26 John Quick and Robert Garran, *The Annotated Constitution of the Australian Commonwealth*, 1901, reprinted by Legal Books, Sydney, 1995, pp. 706–07.
27 In one respect the framers of the Australian Constitution were in advance of the United States, where direct election of Senators in place of election by State legislatures was not introduced until 1913.
28 Quick and Garran, *The Annotated Constitution of the Australian Commonwealth*, p. 414.
29 George Winterton, *Parliament, the Executive and the Governor-General*, Melbourne University Press, Melbourne, 1983, p. 6.
30 Quick and Garran, *The Annotated Constitution of the Australian Commonwealth*, p. 706.
31 Federal Convention Debates, Sydney Session, 1897, p. 584.
32 See Max Walsh, *Poor Little Rich Country*, Penguin, Melbourne, 1979, p. 63.
33 Alan Reid, *The Whitlam Venture*, Hill of Content, Melbourne, 1976, p. 1.
34 See chapter four for an account of the Executive Council minute authorising the $4000 million overseas loan.
35 Paul Keating, personal conversation, May 1976.

Chapter 2 Fraser

1 Refer Philip Ayres, *Malcolm Fraser, A Biography*, William Heinemann Australia, Melbourne, 1987, pp. 6–9.
2 ibid. pp. 24–30.
3 Refer Paul Kelly, *The Unmaking of Gough*, Allen & Unwin, revised edition, Sydney, 1994, pp. 155–59.
4 Ayres, *Malcolm Fraser*, p. 6 and 63.
5 ibid. p. 111.
6 ibid. p. 159.
7 ibid. pp. 160–62.
8 Kelly, *The Unmaking of Gough*, p. 159.
9 ibid. p. 156.
10 Ayres, *Malcolm Fraser*, p. 92–5.

11 ibid. pp. 169–70. The upshot of this incident was that a cabinet meeting *was* held and that it agreed to the order which was never, in fact, invoked.
12 ibid. p. 182.
13 Kelly, *The Unmaking of Gough*, p. 175.
14 J R Odgers, *Australian Senate Practice*, Commonwealth of Australia, fifth edition, Australian Government Publishing Service, Canberra, 1976, p. 476.
15 *The Australian*, 24 May 1973.
16 Hansard, Senate, 18 June 1970, p. 2647.
17 Hansard, House of Representatives, 25 August 1970, p. 463.
18 This assessment is made after considering the account by Jack Kane, *Exploding the Myths*, Angus & Robertson, Sydney, 1989, p. 192. See also Geoffrey Sawer, *Federation Under Strain*, Melbourne University Press, Melbourne, 1977, pp. 124–26.
19 Refer Sawer, *Federation Under Strain*, p. 126.
20 *The Advertiser*, 11 April 1974.
21 ibid.
22 *National Times*, 28 May–2 June 1973.
23 *The Advertiser*, 11 April 1974.
24 *The Australian*, 24 May 1973.
25 R G Withers, Sherrington Memorial Lecture, 21 July 1973.
26 R G Withers, speech to Liberal Party dinner, Perth, 29 October 1973.
27 ibid.
28 ibid.
29 *The Advertiser*, 11 April 1974.
30 Jim McClelland, *Stirring the Possum*, Penguin, Melbourne, 1988, p. 143.
31 Refer L F Crisp, *Ben Chifley*, Longman, Adelaide, pp. 403–05.
32 Kelly, *The Hawke Ascendancy*, p. 57.
33 ibid.
34 Patrick Weller, *Malcolm Fraser PM*, Penguin, Melbourne, 1989, p. 16.

Chapter 3   1974

1 Reg Withers, personal interview, June 1995.
2 R G Withers, speech to Liberal Party dinner, Perth, 29 October 1973.
3 Reg Withers, personal interview, June 1995.
4 Senate, Hansard, 27 February 1973, p. 6.
5 ibid. 8 March 1973, p. 291.
6 J R Odgers, *Australian Senate Practice*, fifth edition, Australian Government Publishing Service, Canberra, 1976, p. 170–71.
7 Refer Laurie Oakes and David Solomon, *Grab for Power: Election '74*, Cheshire, Melbourne, 1974, p. 81–91.
8 ibid.
9 ibid. p. 133.
10 R G Withers, press release, 15 May 1973.
11 Reg Withers, personal interview, June 1995.

12 Senate, Hansard, 5 April 1973, p. 915.
13 Senate, Hansard, 10 April 1974, p. 910.
14 House of Representatives, Hansard, 29 March 1973, p. 901.
15 Senate, Hansard, 21 November 1973, p. 1965.
16 Oakes and Solomon, *Grab for Power*, p. 183.
17 Reg Withers, personal interview, June 1995.
18 Russell Schneider, *War Without Blood*, Angus & Robertson, Sydney, 1980, pp. 16–17.
19 'The Liberals', ABC Television Productions, 1994.
20 C J Lloyd and G S Reid, *Out of the Wilderness*, Cassell Australia, Melbourne, 1974, p. 381.
21 Gough Whitlam, *The Whitlam Government*, Penguin Australia, Melbourne, 1985, p. 315.
22 ibid. p. 318.
23 Oakes and Solomon, *Grab for Power*, pp. 135–36.
24 Peter Blazey and Andrew Campbell, *The Political Dice Men*, Outback Press, Fitzroy, 1974, p. 58.
25 Oakes and Solomon, *Grab for Power*, pp. 7–14.
26 ibid. pp. 9–10.
27 ibid. p. 5.
28 House of Representatives, Hansard, 2 April 1974, p. 805.
29 Oakes and Solomon, *Grab for Power*, pp. 28–29.
30 ibid. p. 31.
31 James Killen, *Inside Australian Politics*, Methuen Haynes, Sydney, 1985, p. 224.
32 Oakes and Solomon, *Grab for Power*, p. 32.
33 Paul Kelly, *The Unmaking of Gough*, Allen & Unwin, revised edition, Sydney, 1994, p. 72.
34 House of Representatives, Hansard, 4 April 1974, p. 1057.
35 Oakes and Solomon, *Grab for Power*, pp. 42–44.
36 ibid. p. 46.
37 Frank McManus, *The Tumult and the Shouting*, Rigby, 1977, p 117.
38 Senate, Hansard, 10 April 1974, p. 902.
39 ibid. p. 894.
40 ibid. p. 890.
41 ibid. p. 891.
42 The bills were: Commonwealth Electoral Bill (No 2) 1973, Senate (Representation of Territories) Bill 1973, Representation Bill 1973, Health Insurance Commission Bill 1973, Health Insurance Bill 1973 and Petroleum and Minerals Authority Bill 1973.
43 Senate, Hansard, 10 April 1974, p. 885.
44 ibid. p. 934.
45 Graham Freudenberg, *A Certain Grandeur*, Macmillan, Melbourne, 1977, p. 302.
46 Oakes and Solomon, *Grab for Power*, p. 495.
47 *The Australian*, 30 May 1974.

48 *Australian Financial Review*, 18 May 1974.
49 *The Australian*, 24 May 1974.
50 J R Odgers, *Australian Senate Practice*, p. xix.
51 (1974) 131 Commonwealth Law Reports 432.
52 Minutes of Proceedings of Joint Sitting, Hansard, 6–7 August 1974, p. 4.
53 ibid. p. 6.
54 Kelly, *The Unmaking of Gough*, p. 149.

Chapter 4 Kerr

1 Gough Whitlam, personal interview, May 1995.
2 For an elaboration of this point see chapters five, six and eleven.
3 Gough Whitlam, *The Truth of the Matter*, Penguin, Ringwood, Victoria, 1979, pp. 17–19; Paul Kelly, *The Unmaking of Gough*, Allen & Unwin, revised edition, Sydney, 1994, pp. 20–22.
4 *Bulletin*, 24 September 1985.
5 Whitlam, *The Truth of the Matter*, p. 17; personal interview, May 1995.
6 The only minister with whom Whitlam discussed the matter was his deputy, Lance Barnard. Gough Whitlam, personal interview, May 1995.
7 Gough Whitlam, personal interview, May 1995. See also Whitlam, *The Truth of the Matter*, pp. 19–20.
8 *Quadrant*, January 1976.
9 Letter from Patti Warn to Gough Whitlam, 11 December 1978.
10 See further Sir John Kerr, *Matters for Judgment*, Macmillan, Melbourne, 1978.
11 *Quadrant*, January 1976.
12 Whitlam *The Truth of the Matter*, p. 28.
13 Lady (Anne) Kerr, personal interview, June 1995.
14 Kerr, *Matters for Judgment*, p. 121.
15 ibid. p. 141.
16 Joe Riordan, personal interview, June 1995.
17 Kerr, *Matters for Judgment*, p. 146.
18 *Quadrant*, January 1976.
19 James McClelland, *Stirring the Possum*, Penguin, Melbourne, 1988, p. 108.
20 Kerr, *Matters for Judgment*, pp. 149–57.
21 Clem Lloyd and Andrew Clark, *Kerr's King Hit*, Cassell Australia, Sydney, 1976, p. 19.
22 Lady (Anne) Kerr, personal interview, June 1995.
23 *Quadrant*, January 1976.
24 Lloyd and Clark, *Kerr's King Hit*, p. 3.
25 Lady (Anne) Kerr, personal interview, June 1995.
26 *Bulletin*, 24 September 1985; James McClelland, *Stirring the Possum*, p. 91.
27 Kerr, *Matters for Judgment*, pp. 186–90.
28 McClelland, *Stirring the Possum*, p. 135.
29 ibid. pp. 172–73.

30 Sir Roden Cutler, personal interview, August 1995.
31 There is an insignificant difference between Kerr and Whitlam over the actual date. But they agree that it was at a state dinner in Sydney about this time.
32 Kerr, *Matters for Judgment*, p. 14.
33 Whitlam, *The Truth of the Matter*, p. 22.
34 Kerr, *Matter for Judgment*, pp. 14–16; Whitlam, *The Truth of the Matter*, pp. 22–24.
35 Kerr, *Matters for Judgment*, p. 16.
36 Graham Freudenberg, *A Certain Grandeur*, Macmillan, Melbourne, 1977, p. 368.
37 Ken Gee, personal interview, June 1995.
38 McClelland, *Stirring the Possum*, p. 173.
39 Kerr, *Matters for Judgment*, p. 17.
40 Whitlam, *The Truth of the Matter*, p. 30.
41 Elizabeth Reid, personal interview, August 1995.
42 Sir John Kerr, address to the Cardinal's dinner, Sydney, 21 August 1975.
43 Whitlam, *The Truth of the Matter*, pp. 25–26.
44 Gough Whitlam, personal interview, June 1995.
45 Kerr, *Matters for Judgment*, pp. 52–53.
46 H V Evatt, *The King and His Dominion Governors*, Oxford University Press, London, 1936; 2nd ed., Frank Cass and Company Limited, 1967; reprinted by Legal Books, Sydney, 1990, pp. 81–83.
47 Refer George Winterton, *Parliament, the Executive and the Governor-General*, Melbourne University Press, Melbourne, 1983, pp. 149–57 for these references and a discussion of the issue.
48 See Kerr, *Matters for Judgment*, pp. 52–82.
49 ibid. p. 16.
50 *Bulletin*, 24 September 1985.
51 Kelly, *The Unmaking of Gough*, pp. 21.
52 *Bulletin*, 24 September 1985.
53 Whitlam, *The Truth of the Matter*, p. 29.
54 Kerr, *Matters for Judgment*, p. 18.
55 Bob Hawke, *The Hawke Memoirs*, William Heinemann Australia, Melbourne, 1994, p. 69.
56 Sir Paul Hasluck, William Queale Memorial Lecture, 24 October 1972.
57 Walter Bagehot, *The English Constitution*, 1867; reprinted by Fontana Press, London, 1993, p. 113.
58 Sir Ivor Jennings, *Cabinet Government*, Cambridge University Press, Cambridge, 1951, p. 361.
59 Harold Nicolson, *King George V*, Constable and Co, London, 1952.
60 This assessment draws directly upon Professor A D Low, Foundation Lecture, University of Adelaide, 12 July 1983.
61 E A Forsey, *The Royal Power of Dissolution of Parliament in the British Commonwealth*, first published 1943, reprinted by Oxford University Press (Canadian Branch), 1968; reprinted by Legal Books, Sydney, 1990.

62 Geoffrey Sawer, *Federation Under Strain*, Melbourne University Press, Melbourne, 1977, p. 155.

Chapter 5   The loan

1 Alan Reid, *The Whitlam Venture*, Hill of Content, Melbourne, 1976; Graham Freudenberg, *A Certain Grandeur*, Macmillan, Melbourne 1977.
2 Malcolm Fraser, personal interview, May 1995.
3 Alan Reid, *The Whitlam Venture*, pp. 9–12.
4 ibid. p. 22.
5 ibid. p. 23.
6 John Kerr, *Matters for Judgment*, Macmillan, Melbourne, 1978, p. 231.
7 ibid. p. 224.
8 Geoffrey Sawer, *Federation Under Strain*, Melbourne University Press, Melbourne, 1977, pp. 102–03.
9 Kerr, *Matters for Judgment*, p. 231.
10 This assessment is based on interviews with senior staff who have worked at Yarralumla.
11 Kerr, *Matters for Judgment*, pp. 230–32.
12 Sir Clarence Harders, personal interview, June 1995.
13 House of Representatives, Hansard, 9 July 1975, p. 3611.
14 Sawer, *Federation Under Strain*, p. 76.
15 House of Representatives, Hansard, 9 July 1975, p. 3598; my emphasis.
16 Sir Clarence Harders, personal interview, June 1995.
17 Sir Maurice Byers, personal interview, June 1995.
18 Freudenberg, *A Certain Grandeur*, pp. 350–51.
19 ibid. p. 351.
20 Refer Sawer, *Federation Under Strain*, chapter five.
21 House of Representatives, Hansard, 9 July 1975, pp. 3644–45.
22 Bob Ellicott, personal interview, June 1995.
23 Kerr, *Matters for Judgment*, p. 233.
24 Sir Maurice Byers, personal interview, June 1995.
25 Kerr, *Matters for Judgment*, p. 234.
26 Gough Whitlam, *The Truth of the Matter*, Penguin, Ringwood, Victoria, 1979, p. 49.
27 Kerr, *Matters for Judgment*, pp. 234–36.
28 ibid. p. 237.
29 ibid. p. 237.
30 ibid. pp. 239–40.
31 Whitlam, *The Truth of the Matter*, p. 52.
32 Sir Paul Hasluck, William Queale Memorial Lecture, 24 October 1972.
33 Sir Clarence Harders, personal interview, June 1995.
34 Address to the Indian Law Institute, India, 28 February 1975.
35 Based on a personal interview, April 1995.
36 James McAuley, *Quadrant*, January 1976.
37 Whitlam, *The Truth of the Matter*, p. 51.

38 Patti Warn, letter to Gough Whitlam, 11 December 1978.
39 ibid.
40 Whitlam, *The Truth of the Matter*, pp. 52–58.
41 Kerr, *Matters for Judgment*, p. 240.

Chapter 6 The deadlock

1 Gough Whitlam, *The Truth of the Matter*, Penguin, Ringwood, Victoria, 1979, p. 61.
2 Speech at Goulburn College of Advanced Education, 12 September 1975.
3 Reg Withers, personal interview, June 1995.
4 Paul Kelly, *The Unmaking of Gough*, Allen & Unwin, revised edition, Sydney, 1994, p. 289.
5 Alan Reid, *The Whitlam Venture*, Hill of Content, Melbourne, 1976, p. 348.
6 This draws on the argument put by Geoffrey Sawer, *Federation Under Strain*, Melbourne University Press, Melbourne, 1977, pp. 130–37.
7 John Wheeldon, personal interview, July 1995.
8 Kelly, *The Unmaking of Gough*, p. 307.
9 ibid. pp. 304–08.
10 Sir Rupert Hamer, personal interview, 20 April 1995.
11 Reg Withers, personal interview, June 1995.
12 Anton Hermann, *Alan Missen, Liberal Pilgrim*, The Popular Press, Canberra, 1993, p. 105.
13 Don Jessop, personal interview, June 1995.
14 Hermann, *Alan Missen*, p. 106.
15 Bill Hayden, personal interview, June 1995.
16 Reg Withers, personal interview, June 1995.
17 Reid, *The Whitlam Venture*, p. 359.
18 Hermann, *Alan Missen*, p. 106.
19 ibid. p. 107.
20 Alan Missen, personal interview, April 1976.
21 Senate, Hansard, 15 October 1975, pp. 1154–60.
22 ibid. pp. 1180 and 1177.
23 Sawer, *Federation Under Strain*, pp. 125–29.
24 ibid.
25 Sir Garfield Barwick, *Barwick: A Radical Tory*, The Federation Press, Sydney, 1995, p. 214.
26 Kelly, *The Unmaking of Gough*, p. 326.
27 John Wheeldon, personal interview, July 1995.
28 Ken Wriedt, personal interview, July 1995.
29 Kelly, *The Unmaking of Gough*, p. 326.
30 Sir Maurice Byers, personal interview, June 1995.
31 Sir Clarence Harders, personal interview, June 1995.
32 This assessment is based on the author's discussions at various times with Sir Geoffrey Yeend.
33 Jim McClelland, personal interview, August 1995.

34 Jim McClelland, personal interview, August 1995.
35 *Quadrant*, September 1989.
36 Anne Kerr, *Lanterns Over Pinchgut*, Macmillan, Melbourne, 1988, pp. 271–72.
37 Whitlam, *The Truth of the Matter*, p. 58.
38 ibid. p. 92.
39 John Menadue, personal interview, April 1995.
40 Sawer, *Federation Under Strain*, p. 54.
41 Many commentators found this reasoning inconsistent. See Sawer, *Federation Under Strain*, chapter four; Leslie Zines, 'The double dissolutions and joint sitting', in Gareth Evans (ed.), *Labor and the Constitution*, Heinemann, Melbourne, 1977.
42 Gough Whitlam, personal interview, May 1995.
43 Sir John Kerr, Australian Law Schools Association speech, 25 August 1975.
44 Sir John Kerr, *Matters for Judgment*, Macmillan, Melbourne, 1978, p. 245.
45 12 September 1975; see mention of it at the beginning of this chapter.
46 Clyde Cameron, personal interview, August 1995.
47 Barwick, *Barwick: A Radical Tory*, pp. 289–90.
48 Jim McClelland, personal interview, February 1976.
49 Joe Riordan, personal interview, June 1995.
50 Sir Maurice Byers, personal interview, June 1995.
51 Barwick, *Barwick: A Radical Tory*, p. 232.
52 Lady (Anne) Kerr, personal interview, May 1995.
53 Patti Warn, letter to Gough Whitlam, 11 December 1978.
54 Elizabeth Reid, personal interview, August 1995; the artist Clifton Pugh spent some time with Kerr in 1975 painting his portrait.
55 Eugene A. Forsey, *The Royal Power of Dissolution of Parliament in the British Commonwealth*, 1943; reprinted by Oxford University Press, 1968, and Legal Books, Sydney, 1990, p. 7 and p. 259. Sir John Kerr confirms in his memoirs (p. 209) that he read Forsey during 1975.
56 Whitlam himself says that he never used the phrase 'smash the Senate' in talks with Kerr. Refer Whitlam, *The Truth of the Matter*, p. 73.
57 Kerr, *Matters for Judgment*, p. 254.
58 ibid.
59 ibid.
60 Sir John Kerr said he made a note of these two conversations and was 'certain of the accuracy'. Refer the *Bulletin*, 10 September 1985.
61 Kerr, *Matters for Judgment*, p. 254.
62 Walter Bagehot, *The English Constitution*, 1867; reprinted by Fontana, London, 1993, p. 113.
63 Kerr, *Matters for Judgment*, p. 254.
64 Whitlam, *The Truth of the Matter*, p. 95.
65 ibid.
66 Ken Wriedt, personal interview, July 1995.

Chapter 7 The battle

1 Sir John Kerr, *Matters for Judgment*, Macmillan, Melbourne, 1978, p. 258.
2 Gough Whitlam, *The Truth of the Matter*, Penguin, Ringwood, Victoria, 1979, pp. 93–94.
3 *Bulletin*, 10 September 1985.
4 Lady (Anne) Kerr, personal interview, June 1995.
5 *Bulletin*, 17 September 1985.
6 Alan Reid, *The Whitlam Venture*, Hill of Content, Melbourne, 1976, pp. 369–70.
7 This quote is based on a personal interview held in April 1995.
8 Whitlam, *The Truth of the Matter*, p. 111.
9 ibid. p. 70.
10 Gough Whitlam, speech at Rotary District Conference for Tasmania, 1 April 1995.
11 Gough Whitlam, personal interview, May 1995.
12 *Bulletin*, 10 September 1985.
13 Kerr, *Matters for Judgment*, p. 246–47.
14 Whitlam, *The Truth of the Matter*, pp. 92–93.
15 Kerr, *Matters for Judgment*, pp. 252–53.
16 Whitlam, *The Truth of the Matter*, p. 94.
17 House of Representatives, Hansard, 15 October 1975, p. 2109.
18 ibid.
19 Kerr, *Matters for Judgment*, p. 82.
20 H V Evatt, *The King and His Dominion Governors*, Oxford University Press, 1936; 2nd ed. Frank Cass and Company Limited, 1967, reprinted by Legal Books, Sydney, 1990, pp. 165–66; Kerr, *Matters for Judgment*, p. 71.
21 Kerr, *Matters for Judgment*, p. 75; my emphasis.
22 ibid. p. 259.
23 Sir Roden Cutler, personal interview, August 1995.
24 Malcolm Fraser, personal interview, May 1995.
25 Lady (Anne) Kerr, personal interview, June 1995.
26 John Menadue, personal interview, April 1995.
27 Graham Freudenberg, *A Certain Grandeur*, Macmillan, Melbourne, 1977, p. 375.
28 John Mant, personal interview, May 1995.
29 Gough Whitlam, personal interview, May 1995.
30 *Bulletin*, 10 September 1985.
31 John Menadue, personal interview, April 1995.
32 Paul Kelly, *The Unmaking of Gough*, Allen & Unwin, Sydney, revised edition, 1994, p. 346; Also Kep Enderby, personal interview, August, 1995.
33 *Bulletin*, 24 September 1985.
34 See Kelly, *The Unmaking of Gough*, p. 328.
35 John Menadue, personal interview, April 1995.
36 Clyde Cameron, personal interview, August 1995.
37 Sir Maurice Byers, personal interview, June 1995.

38 Lady (Anne) Kerr, personal interview, June 1995.
39 John Menadue, personal interview, April 1995.
40 John Mant, personal interview, May 1995.
41 Clyde Cameron, personal interview, August 1995.
42 Gough Whitlam, personal interview, May 1995.
43 *Bulletin*, 24 September 1985.
44 House of Representatives, Hansard, 16 October 1975, pp. 2199–202.
45 House of Representatives, Hansard, 16 October 1975, pp. 2202–204.
46 House of Representatives, Hansard, 16 October 1975, pp. 2209, 2214.
47 Malcolm Fraser, personal interview, May 1995.
48 Refer David Butler, *Current Affairs Bulletin*, University of Sydney, vol. 52, no. 10, March 1976.
49 Refer Kelly, *The Unmaking of Gough*, pp. 329–30.
50 Bob Ellicott, personal interview, June 1995.
51 Refer Appendix A for the text.
52 My emphasis.
53 Bob Ellicott, personal interview, June 1995.
54 Kerr, *Matters for Judgment*, p. 271.
55 ibid.
56 Kelly, *The Unmaking of Gough*, p. 7.
57 Bob Ellicott, personal interview, June 1995.
58 Sir Paul Hasluck, William Queale Memorial Lecture, 24 October 1972.
59 Jim McClelland, *Stirring the Possum*, Penguin, Melbourne, 1989, p. 170.
60 Bob Ellicott, personal interview, June 1995.
61 ibid.
62 Kerr, *Matters for Judgment*, p. 271; Whitlam, *The Truth of the Matter*, p. 83.
63 John Mant, personal interview, May 1995.
64 Sir Maurice Byers, personal interview, June 1995.
65 ibid.
66 ibid.
67 Graham Freudenberg, *A Certain Grandeur*, Macmillan, Melbourne, 1977, p. 377.
68 Sir Maurice Byers, personal interview, June 1995.
69 Freudenberg, *A Certain Grandeur*, p. 378.
70 Sir Clarence Harders, personal interview, June 1995.
71 John Menadue, personal interview, April 1995.
72 *Bulletin*, 3 September 1985; John Menadue, personal interview, April 1995; refer Freudenberg, *A Certain Grandeur*, p. 378.
73 Freudenberg, *A Certain Grandeur*, p. 381.
74 John Menadue, personal interview, August 1995.
75 Kelly, *The Unmaking of Gough*, p. 333.
76 See Whitlam, *The Truth of the Matter*, pp. 90–91.
77 ibid.; see also Kelly, *The Unmaking of Gough*, p. 29.
78 *Bulletin*, 10 September 1985.
79 Sir Maurice Byers, personal interview, June 1995.
80 Kerr, *Matters for Judgment*, p. 271.

81 House of Representatives, Hansard, 16 October 1975, p. 2206.
82 Senate, Hansard, 16 October 1975, p. 1239.
83 Kelly, *The Unmaking of Gough*, pp. 330–31.
84 Kerr, *Matters for Judgment*, p. 263; my emphasis.
85 Whitlam, *The Truth of the Matter*, p. 90.
86 Kerr, *Matters for Judgment*, pp. 263–64; Kerr's emphasis.
87 See chapter five for an account of this earlier discussion.
88 Philip Ayers, *Malcolm Fraser: A Biography*, William Heinemann Australia, Richmond, Victoria, 1987, p. 278.
89 ibid. p. 279.
90 ibid. pp. 279–80; the footnotes in the Ayers book indicate that this information comes from the Fraser Papers.
91 Don Jessop, personal interview, July 1995.
92 Ayers, *Malcolm Fraser*, p. 280.
93 Malcolm Fraser, personal interview, May 1995.
94 ibid.
95 See Kerr, *Matters for Judgment*, pp. 272–73.
96 Ayers, *Malcolm Fraser*, pp. 281–82.
97 ibid. p. 282.
98 Malcolm Fraser, personal interview, June 1995.
99 Kerr, *Matters for Judgment*, p. 265.
100 ibid. p. 266.
101 ibid. p. 265.
102 Sir Ivor Jennings, *Cabinet Government*, Cambridge University Press, 1951 edition, Cambridge, pp. 360–61.
103 *Bulletin*, 10 September 1985.
104 Sir Maurice Byers, personal interview, June 1995.
105 Kerr, *Matters for Judgment*, p. 266; Kelly, *The Unmaking of Gough*, pp. 333–34; G Evans (ed.), *Labor and the Constitution*, Heinemann, Melbourne, 1977, p. 325.
106 Kerr, p. 266.
107 Malcolm Fraser, personal interview, May 1995.
108 House of Representatives, Hansard, 21 October 1975, p. 2305.
109 Refer Whitlam, *The Truth of the Matter*, p. 91.
110 House of Representatives, Hansard, 21 October 1975, p. 2309.
111 ibid. p. 2323.
112 Ayers, *Malcolm Fraser*, p. 282.
113 Malcolm Fraser, personal interview, May 1995.
114 Kerr, *Matters for Judgment*, pp. 267–68; my emphasis.
115 Ayers, *Malcolm Fraser*, p. 283.
116 ibid.
117 David Smith, personal discussion, 21 October 1975.
118 'The Liberals', ABC Television documentary, 1994.
119 ibid.
120 See Kerr, *Matters for Judgment*, p. 269.
121 ibid.

Chapter 8 Failed compromises

1 House of Representatives, Hansard, 23 October 1975, p. 2448.
2 Gough Whitlam, *The Truth of the Matter*, Penguin, Ringwood, Victoria, 1979, pp. 84–85.
3 ibid. p. 85.
4 Joe Riordan, personal interview, June 1995. Riordan's contact with Marriott arose from their respective posts as chairman and deputy chairman of the Joint Committee on Pecuniary Interests of Members of Parliament.
5 Paul Kelly, *The Unmaking of Gough*, Allen & Unwin, revised edition, Sydney, 1994, p. 305.
6 Gough Whitlam, personal interview, May 1995.
7 Gough Whitlam, *The Truth of the Matter*, p. 84.
8 Joe Riordan, personal interview, June 1995.
9 Kelly, *The Unmaking of Gough*, p. 340.
10 Kerr, *Matters for Judgment*, Macmillan, Melbourne, 1978, p. 263.
11 Whitlam, *The Truth of the Matter*, p. 90.
12 *The Australian*, 1 November 1975.
13 Kelly, *The Unmaking of Gough*, pp. 344–45.
14 Michael Sexton, *Illusions of Power*, George Allen & Unwin, Sydney, 1979, p. 223.
15 ibid. pp. 223–24.
16 ibid. p. 229.
17 Malcolm Fraser, personal interview, May 1995.
18 Geoffrey Sawer, *Federation Under Strain*, Melbourne University Press, Melbourne, 1977, p. 216.
19 Kerr, *Matters for Judgment*, p. 289.
20 House of Representatives, Hansard, 4 November 1975, p. 2720.
21 ibid. p. 2724.
22 ibid. p. 2723.
23 Malcolm Fraser, personal interview, May 1995.
24 House of Representatives, Hansard, 5 November 1975, p. 2784.
25 Kelly, *The Unmaking of Gough*, p. 344.
26 Ken Wriedt, personal interview, July 1995.
27 Bill Hayden, personal interview, June 1995.
28 Joe Riordan, personal interview, June 1995.
29 David Butler, *Current Affairs Bulletin*, University of Sydney, vol. 52, no. 10, March 1976.
30 Graham Freudenberg, *A Certain Grandeur*, Macmillan, Melbourne, 1977, p. 380.
31 Kerr's original invitation to Whitlam was extended to McClelland at Whitlam's request when it became known that McClelland was coming to Yarralumla for the Executive Council meeting.
32 Whitlam, *The Truth of the Matter*, p. 95.
33 Kerr, *Matters for Judgment*, p. 288.

34 Kelly, *The Unmaking of Gough*, p. 9; Senate, Hansard, 18 February 1976, p. 56.
35 Whitlam, *The Truth of the Matter*, p. 95.
36 Senate, Hansard, 18 February 1976, p. 56.
37 *Bulletin*, 24 September 1985.
38 ibid.
39 Kelly, *The Unmaking of Gough*, p. 341. Based on personal interviews with Gough Whitlam and Jim McClelland in February 1976.
40 Jim McClelland, *Stirring the Possum*, Penguin, Melbourne, 1989, p. 171.
41 Jim McClelland, personal interview, August 1995.
42 *Bulletin*, 10 September 1985.
43 Lady (Anne) Kerr, personal interview, June 1995.
44 *Bulletin*, 24 September 1985.
45 ibid.
46 Alan Reid in his book *The Whitlam Venture* (Hill of Content, Melbourne, 1976, p. 383) suggests that the call occurred 'about or shortly after' 30 October 1975.
47 Senate, Hansard, 18 February 1976, p. 56.
48 McClelland, *Stirring the Possum*, pp. 175–76.
49 *Bulletin*, 24 September 1985.
50 ibid.
51 *Bulletin*, 10 September 1985. Kerr also says that his version of his talks with McClelland during the crisis were based on his own notes taken at the time.
52 Kerr, *Matters for Judgment*, p. 288.
53 Philip Ayres, *Malcolm Fraser: A Biography*, William Heinemann Australia, Richmond, 1987, p. 285.
54 *Bulletin*, 10 September 1985.
55 *Bulletin*, 24 September 1985.
56 Gough Whitlam, personal interview, November 1975.
57 Bill Hayden, personal interview, June 1995.
58 'The Liberals', ABC Television documentary, 1994.
59 Reg Withers, personal interview, June 1995.
60 Sir Rupert Hamer, personal interview, April 1995.
61 Gough Whitlam, personal interview, May 1995.
62 Ayres, *Malcolm Fraser*, p. 286.
63 Malcolm Fraser, personal interview, May 1995.
64 Reg Withers, personal interview, June 1995.
65 Kerr, *Matters for Judgment*, p. 291.
66 Ayres, *Malcolm Fraser*, p. 288.
67 Malcolm Fraser, press statement, 3 November 1975.
68 Kerr, *Matters for Judgment*, p. 292.
69 Whitlam, *The Truth of the Matter*, p. 87.
70 Kelly, *The Unmaking of Gough*, p. 336.
71 Reg Withers, personal interview, June 1995.
72 Bob Ellicott, personal interview, June 1995.

73 Kerr, *Matters for Judgment*, p. 292.
74 Gough Whitlam, personal interview, June 1995.
75 Lady (Anne) Kerr, personal interview, June 1995.
76 Gough Whitlam, personal interview, May 1995.
77 Lady (Anne) Kerr, personal interview, June 1995.
78 See chapter nine.
79 *Bulletin*, 10 September 1985.
80 Bob Ellicott, personal interview, June 1995.
81 Kerr, *Matters for Judgment*, p. 270.
82 *Bulletin*, 10 September 1985.
83 McClelland, *Stirring the Possum*, p. 176.

Chapter 9   The solution

1 Malcolm Fraser, personal interview, May 1995.
2 Philip Ayres, *Malcolm Fraser, A Biography*, William Heinemann Australia, Richmond, Victoria, 1987, p. 287.
3 Reg Withers, personal interview, June 1995.
4 Ayres, *Malcolm Fraser*, pp. 288–89.
5 ibid. p. 289.
6 Gough Whitlam, *The Truth of the Matter*, Ringwood, Victoria, 1979, p. 133.
7 Sir Rupert Hamer, personal interview, April 1995.
8 Sir Roden Cutler, personal interview, August 1995.
9 I have confirmed with senior officials that Kerr and Winneke discussed the crisis and its possible resolution.
10 Sir Rupert Hamer, personal interview, April 1995.
11 Sir Roden Cutler, personal interview, August 1995.
12 House of Representatives, Hansard, 4 November 1975, p. 2726.
13 ibid. 5 November 1975, p. 2785.
14 ibid. 5 November 1975, p. 2832.
15 ibid. 5 November 1975, p. 2834.
16 ibid. 5 November 1975, pp. 2833–34.
17 ibid. 5 November 1975, pp. 2835–37.
18 Sir John Kerr, *Matters for Judgment*, p. 297.
19 Malcolm Fraser, personal interview, May 1995.
20 ibid.
21 Ayres, *Malcolm Fraser*, p. 290.
22 ibid. p. 290.
23 Kerr, *Matters for Judgment*, p. 297.
24 Malcolm Fraser, personal interview, May 1995.
25 ibid.
26 *Bulletin*, 1 October 1995.
27 Tony Staley, personal interview, June 1995.
28 Malcolm Fraser, personal interview, May 1995.

29 Paul Kelly, *The Unmaking of Gough*, Allen & Unwin, revised edition, Sydney, 1994, pp. 30–31 and 442.
30 Malcolm Fraser, personal interview, May 1995 and August 1995.
31 Ayres, *Malcolm Fraser*, p. 290.
32 Kerr, *Matters for Judgment*, p. 297.
33 Malcolm Fraser, personal interview, May 1995 and August 1995.
34 Personal interview, April 1995.
35 Malcolm Fraser, personal interview, August 1995.
36 Kelly, *The Unmaking of Gough*, p. 349.
37 Kerr, *Matters for Judgment*, p. 297.
38 ibid.
39 Bill Hayden, personal interview, June 1995.
40 Whitlam, *The Truth of the Matter*, p. 101.
41 Bill Hayden, personal interview, June 1995.
42 Whitlam, *The Truth of the Matter*, p. 102.
43 Bill Hayden, personal interview, June 1995.
44 Gough Whitlam, personal interview, May 1995.
45 Kerr, *Matters for Judgment*, pp. 307–08.
46 ibid. p. 300.
47 ibid. p. 293.
48 Kelly, *The Unmaking of Gough*, pp. 345–46.
49 Kerr, *Matters for Judgment*, p. 302.
50 ibid. pp. 302–03.
51 Kep Enderby, personal interview, August 1995.
52 Kelly, *The Unmaking of Gough*, p. 346.
53 Sir Maurice Byers, personal interview, June 1995.
54 Kerr, *Matters for Judgment*, p. 303.
55 See Appendix B for full text.
56 Kerr, *Matters for Judgment*, pp. 303–07.
57 ibid. p. 307.
58 Paul Kelly, *The Unmaking of Gough*, p. 5.
59 Kerr, *Matters For Judgment*, p. 317.
60 ibid. pp. 312–28.
61 ibid. p. 315.
62 House of Representatives, Hansard, 30 October 1975, p. 2701.
63 Kerr, *Matters for Judgment*, p. 323.
64 See chapter eleven.
65 Kerr, *Matters for Judgment*, p. 330.
66 ibid. p. 330.
67 ibid. p. 310.
68 ibid. p. 331.
69 Sir Martin Charteris, personal interview, June 1995.
70 Comment based on a personal interview, May 1995.
71 Bill Hayden, personal interview, June 1995.
72 See chapter seven for a discussion about Sir Colin Hannah.
73 H V Evatt, *The King and His Dominion Governors*, Oxford University Press,

1936; second edition, Frank Cass and Company Limited, London, 1967; reprinted by Legal Books, Sydney, 1990, pp. 164–65.
74 Whitlam, *The Truth of the Matter*, pp. 110–11.
75 Malcolm Fraser, personal interview, May 1995.
76 ibid.
77 Gough Whitlam, personal interview, May 1995.
78 ibid.
79 John Mant, personal interview, April/June 1995.
80 Bill Hayden, personal interview, June 1995.
81 *The Bulletin*, 24 September 1985.
82 Jim McClelland, personal interview, August 1995.
83 Sir Roden Cutler, personal interview, August 1995.
84 Bob Ellicott, personal interview, July 1995.
85 Graham Freudenberg, personal interview, September 1995.
86 *Current Affairs Bulletin*, University of Sydney, vol. 52, no. 10.
87 John Wheeldon, personal interview, June 1995.
88 Kerr, *Matters for Judgment*, p. 333.
89 ibid. p. 339.
90 *Bulletin*, 10 September 1985.
91 See chapter six.
92 Gough Whitlam, personal interview, May 1995.
93 Garfield Barwick, *Sir John Did His Duty*, Serendip Publications, Wahroonga, NSW, 1983, p. 76.
94 See chapter six.
95 Barwick, *Sir John Did His Duty*, pp. 76–77; emphasis Barwick's.
96 ibid. p. 78.
97 ibid. p. 77.
98 Kerr, *Matters for Judgment*, pp. 341–42; Barwick, *Sir John Did His Duty*, p. 75.
99 Kerr, *Matters for Judgment*, p. 342; Barwick, *Sir John Did His Duty*, p. 79.
100 Barwick, *Sir John Did His Duty*, pp. 79–80; emphasis Barwick's.
101 ibid. pp. 79–80.
102 See Appendix C for full text of Barwick's letter.
103 Barwick, *Sir John Did His Duty*, pp. 82–84.
104 Geoffrey Sawer, *Federation Under Strain*, Melbourne University Press, Melbourne, 1977, pp. 157–58.
105 *The Bulletin*, 10 September 1985.
106 *Quadrant*, January–February 1985.
107 Gerard Henderson, *Menzies' Child*, Allen & Unwin, Sydney, 1994, p. 244.
108 Sir Garfield Barwick, *A Radical Tory*, Federation Press, Sydney, 1995, p. 298.
109 Bob Ellicott, personal interview, June 1995.
110 Henderson, *Menzies' Child*, p. 244.
111 Kerr, *Matters for Judgment*, p. 341.
112 Sir Anthony Mason declined to be interviewed for this book.
113 Sir Ninian Stephen, personal interview, September 1995.

114 Sir Garfield Barwick, personal interview, June 1995.
115 ibid.
116 Henderson, *Menzies' Child*, p. 244.
117 Clyde Cameron, personal interview, August 1995.
118 Barwick, *A Radical Tory*, pp. 293–97.
119 Lady (Anne) Kerr, personal interview, May 1995.
120 Bob Ellicott, personal interview, June 1995.
121 Gough Whitlam, personal interview, May 1995.
122 Jim McClelland, personal interview, August 1995.
123 Lady (Anne) Kerr, personal interview, May 1995.
124 Bob Ellicott, personal interview, July 1995.
125 Michael Sexton, *Illusions of Power*, Allen & Unwin, Sydney, 1979, p. 220.
126 Doug Anthony, personal interview, July 1995.
127 Kelly, *The Unmaking of Gough*, p. 30 and p. 349; confirmed by Bob Ellicott, personal interview, June 1995.
128 Kelly, p. 350.
129 Kerr, *Matters for Judgment*, p. 334.
130 *The Bulletin*, 10 September 1985.
131 Kelly, *The Unmaking of Gough*, p. 17; *The Bulletin*, 24 September 1985.
132 Sawer, *Federation Under Strain*, p. 161.
133 See Appendix E.
134 See Appendix C; my emphasis.
135 Kerr, *Matters for Judgment*, p. 336.
136 ibid. p. 336.
137 Bob Ellicott, personal interview, July 1995.
138 Kerr, *Matters for Judgment*, p. 335.
139 *The Bulletin*, 10 September 1985.
140 Personal interview, April 1995.
141 Kerr, *Matters for Judgment*, p. 346.
142 *The Australian*, 6 November 1985.
143 Reg Withers, personal interview, June 1995.
144 *The Liberals*, ABC Television Productions, 1994.
145 ibid.
146 Brian Buckley, *Lynched*, Salzburg Publishing, Melbourne, 1991, p. 88.
147 Tony Staley, personal interview, June 1995.
148 Doug Anthony, personal interview, July 1995.
149 Neville Bonner, personal interview, 8 July 1995.
150 *The Australian*, 6 November 1985.
151 Don Jessop, personal interview, June 1995.
152 Malcolm Fraser, personal interview, August 1995.
153 *The Australian*, 6 November 1985.
154 Mollie Missen, personal interview, June 1995.
155 Malcolm Fraser, personal interview, May 1995.
156 Reg Withers, personal interview, June 1995.
157 Buckley, *Lynched*, p. 88.
158 Ian Macphee, personal interview, August 1995.

159 *The Australian*, 6 November 1985.
160 Kathy Sullivan, personal interview, June 1995.
161 *The Australian*, 6 November 1985.
162 Reg Withers, personal interview, June 1995.
163 *The Australian*, 6 November 1985.
164 ibid.
165 Laurie Oakes, *Crash Through or Crash*, Drummond, Melbourne, 1976, p. 199.
166 Whitlam, *The Truth of the Matter*, p. 104.
167 ibid.
168 Reg Withers, personal interview, July 1995.

Chapter 10 Dismissal

1 Refer Philip Ayres, *Malcolm Fraser: A Biography*, William Heinemann Australia, Richmond, Victoria, 1987, pp. 291–92; Paul Kelly, *The Unmaking of Gough*, Allen & Unwin, revised edition, Sydney, 1994, pp. 352–53; Gough Whitlam, *The Truth of the Matter*, Penguin, Ringwood, Victoria, 1979, p. 104; also Gough Whitlam, personal interview, May 1995.
2 Ayres, *Malcolm Fraser*, p. 292; Kelly, *The Unmaking of Gough*, p. 353.
3 Whitlam, *The Truth of the Matter*, p. 105.
4 Fred Daly, *From Curtin to Kerr*, Sun Books, Melbourne, 1977, p. 230.
5 Doug Anthony, personal interview, July 1995.
6 Daly, *From Curtin to Kerr*, p. 230.
7 Whitlam, *The Truth of the Matter*, p. 105; Ayres, *Malcolm Fraser*, p. 292.
8 Anne Kerr, *Lanterns Over Pinchgut*, Macmillan, Melbourne, 1988, p. 283.
9 ibid.
10 Whitlam, *The Truth of the Matter*, p. 105.
11 Sir John Kerr, *Matters for Judgment*, Macmillan, Melbourne, 1978, p. 355.
12 Ayres, *Malcolm Fraser*, pp. 292–93.
13 ibid. p. 293.
14 ibid.
15 Kerr, *Matters for Judgment*, p. 355.
16 *The Australian*, circa 5 November 1987.
17 Gerard Henderson, *Menzies' Child*, Allen & Unwin, Sydney, 1994, pp. 239–240. Henderson reports that he was able to read these notes in Kerr's office.
18 A relevant question here is whether Kerr and Fraser had more than one phone conversation that morning.
19 Malcolm Fraser, personal interview, May 1995.
20 Brian Buckley, *Lynched*, Salzburg Publishing, Melbourne, 1991, p. 87.
21 Ayres, *Malcolm Fraser*, pp. 293–94; Kelly, *The Unmaking of Gough*, p. 354.
22 ibid.
23 Kelly, *The Unmaking of Gough*, p. 354.
24 ibid. pp. 354–55.

25 Graham Freudenberg, *A Certain Grandeur*, Macmillan, Melbourne, 1977, p. 391.
26 Anne Kerr, *Lanterns Over Pinchgut*, p. 285.
27 Whitlam, *The Truth of the Matter*, p. 106.
28 House of Representatives, Hansard, 11 November 1975, pp. 2913–16.
29 ibid. pp. 2917–21.
30 Kerr, *Matters for Judgment*, p. 356.
31 Freudenberg, *A Certain Grandeur*, p. 393.
32 ibid. p. 109.
33 Sir David Smith, 'The 1975 Dismissal', address to The Samuel Griffith Society, 1 April 1995.
34 Whitlam, *The Truth of the Matter*, p. 108.
35 Whitlam, *The Truth of the Matter*, p. 108; Ayres, *Malcolm Fraser*, p. 295.
36 Graham Freudenberg, personal interview, September 1995.
37 Personal interview, April 1995.
38 Whitlam, *The Truth of the Matter*, p. 110.
39 Kerr, *Matters for Judgment*, p. 358.
40 ibid. p. 346.
41 Whitlam, *The Truth of the Matter*, p. 110.
42 Kerr, *Matters for Judgment*, pp. 358–59.
43 Whitlam, *The Truth of the Matter*, p. 110; Kerr, *Matters for Judgment*, p. 359.
44 Kelly, *The Unmaking of Gough*, p. 10.
45 Kerr; *Matters for Judgment*, p. 359.
46 ibid. pp. 358–59.
47 ibid.
48 ibid.
49 ibid.
50 Gough Whitlam, personal interview, May 1995.
51 Whitlam, *The Truth of the Matter*, pp. 110–11.
52 *Bulletin*, 10 September 1985.
53 This line and this argument come directly from Jim McClelland, *Stirring the Possum*, Penguin, Melbourne, 1989, p. 179.
54 ibid.
55 My emphasis; see Appendix D for full text of the letter.
56 Kerr, *Matters for Judgment*, p. 347.
57 ibid. p. 358.
58 See Appendix E for text.
59 Whitlam, *The Truth of the Matter*, p. 112.
60 Kerr, *Matters for Judgment*, p. 364.
61 ibid.
62 See Appendix F for text.
63 Kerr, *Matters for Judgment*, pp. 364–66; Ayres, *Malcolm Fraser*, pp. 295–96.
64 Malcolm Fraser, personal interview, May 1995.
65 Anne Kerr, *Lanterns Over Pinchgut*, p. 285; personal interview, June 1995.
66 Kerr, *Matters for Judgment*, p. 366.
67 Daly, *From Curtin to Kerr*, p. 231.

68 Freudenberg, *A Certain Grandeur*, p. 395.
69 Whitlam, *The Truth of the Matter*, p. 112.
70 Daly, *From Curtin to Kerr*, p. 232.
71 Freudenberg, *A Certain Grandeur*, p. 396.
72 Ayres, *Malcolm Fraser*, p. 296.
73 Doug Anthony, personal interview, July 1995.
74 Reg Withers, personal interview, June 1995; see also Clem Lloyd and Andrew Clark, *Kerr's King Hit*, Cassell, Sydney, 1976, p. 228.
75 Alan Reid, *The Whitlam Venture*, Hill of Content, Melbourne, 1976, pp. 416–17.
76 Kelly, *The Unmaking of Gough*, p. 358; Reid, *The Whitlam Venture*, pp. 417–18.
77 Ken Wriedt, personal interview, July 1995.
78 Reg Withers, personal interview, June 1995.
79 Alan Reid, *The Whitlam Venture*, pp. 418–19.
80 Refer Paul Kelly, *The Unmaking of Gough*, p. 358, and Lloyd and Clark, *Kerr's King Hit*, p. 229.
81 House of Representatives, Hansard, 11 November 1975, pp. 2928–29.
82 ibid. pp. 2930–31.
83 Joe Riordan, personal interview, June 1995.
84 Whitlam, *The Truth of the Matter*, p. 114.
85 Refer H O Browning, *1975 Crisis*, Hale & Iremonger, Sydney, 1985, p. 206.
86 Gordon Scholes, personal interview, August 1995.
87 Whitlam, *The Truth of the Matter*, p. 114.
88 ibid. p. 117.
89 Philip Ayres, *Malcolm Fraser*, p. 297.
90 Kerr, *Matters for Judgment*, pp. 369–70.
91 ibid. p. 371.
92 Sir Clarence Harders, personal interview, June 1995.
93 See Appendix G for the text of the Proclamation.
94 Whitlam, *The Truth of the Matter*, p. 114.
95 Gordon Scholes, personal interview, August 1995.
96 Kerr, *Matters for Judgment*, p. 374.
97 Whitlam, *The Truth of the Matter*, pp. 115–16; this account is confirmed by Gordon Scholes, personal interview, August 1995.
98 Gough Whitlam, personal interview, May 1995.
99 Whitlam, *The Truth of the Matter*, p. 119.
100 Doug Anthony, personal interview, July 1995.
101 Whitlam, *The Truth of the Matter*, p. 119.
102 This argument draws on J R Odgers, *Australian Senate Practice*, sixth edition, Commonwealth of Australia, 1991, pp. xxvii–xxviii.
103 ibid. p. xxvii.
104 Sir Martin Charteris, personal interview, June 1995.

Chapter 11   1975

1. Lady (Anne) Kerr, personal interview, June 1995.
2. Sir John Kerr, *Matters for Judgment*, Macmillan, Melbourne, 1978, p. 377.
3. Anne Kerr, *Lanterns Over Pinchgut*, Macmillan, Melbourne, 1988, p. 288.
4. ibid. p. 380.
5. Kerr, *Matters for Judgment*, p. 421.
6. Joe Riordan, personal interview, June 1995.
7. Doug Anthony, personal interview, July 1995.
8. Reg Withers, personal interview, June 1995.
9. Anne Kerr, *Lanterns Over Pinchgut*, p. 289.
10. Gough Whitlam, *The Truth of the Matter*, Penguin, Melbourne, 1979, p. 169.
11. John Menadue, personal interview, April 1995.
12. John Wheeldon, personal interview, July 1995.
13. Kerr, *Matters for Judgment*, p. 398.
14. Malcolm Fraser, personal interview, May 1995.
15. Kerr, *Matters for Judgment*, pp. 398–99.
16. ibid. p. 399.
17. House of Representatives, Hansard, 28 February 1978, p. 207.
18. ibid. 2 March 1978, p. 422.
19. *Bulletin*, 10 September 1985.
20. ibid.
21. John Wheeldon, personal interview, July 1995.
22. Brian Galligan, 'The founders' design and intentions regarding responsible government', in Patrick Weller and Dean Jaensch (eds) *Responsible Government in Australia*, Drummond Publishing, Melbourne, 1980, p. 9.
23. This analysis draws upon Colin Howard and Cheryl Saunders, 'The blocking of the Budget and dismissal of the Government', in Gareth Evans (ed.) *Labor and the Constitution*, Heinemann, Melbourne, 1977, pp. 256–60; refer *Australasian Federal Convention*, first session, Sydney, 2 March to 9 April 1891, p. 428 for Griffith, and *Australasian Federal Convention*, third session, Melbourne, 20 January to 17 March 1898, volume two, p. 2165 for McMillan (see Volumes I and V respectively of *Official Record of the Debates of the Australasian Federal Convention*, Legal Books, Sydney, 1986).
24. Galligan, 'The founders' design and intentions regarding responsible government', p. 9.
25. ibid.
26. If grounds for a double dissolution existed when the Senate blocked Supply then a means was available to send the Senate to an election as well.
27. Malcolm Fraser, personal interview, May 1995.
28. See chapter six.
29. In these arguments I have drawn upon Professor Geoffrey Sawer, *Federation Under Strain*, Melbourne University Press, Melbourne, 1977, chapter eight.
30. ibid. p. 153.

31 ibid. p. 145.
32 Sir Garfield Barwick, *A Radical Tory*, The Federation Press, Sydney, 1995, p. 288. My emphasis.
33 Howard and Saunders, 'The blocking of the Budget and dismissal of the Government', p. 282.
34 Galligan, 'The founders' design and intentions regarding responsible government', p. 8.
35 John Quick and Robert Garran, *The Annotated Constitution of the Australian Commonwealth*, Legal Books, Sydney, 1995, p. 706.
36 ibid. pp. 706–07.
37 A V Dicey, *Law of the Constitution*, Macmillan, tenth edition, London, 1965, chapter fifteen.
38 Kerr, *Matters for Judgment*, p. 315.
39 Sawer, *Federation Under Strain*, p. 146.
40 Sir Maurice Byers, personal interview, August 1995.
41 See chapter nine.
42 Sir Garfield Barwick, *A Radical Tory*, Federation Press, Sydney, 1995, p. 297.
43 *Bulletin*, 10 September 1985.
44 See Sawer, *Federation Under Strain*, p. 161.
45 *Bulletin*, 10 September 1985.
46 Gerard Henderson, *Menzies' Child*, Allen & Unwin, Sydney, 1994, p. 237.
47 Sir Maurice Byers, personal interview, July 1995.
48 Bill Hayden, personal interview, June 1995.
49 Sir Clarence Harders, personal interview, June 1995.
50 Sir Rupert Hamer, personal interview, April 1995.
51 Sir Maurice Byers, personal interview, June 1995.
52 Sir Roden Cutler, personal interview, August 1995.
53 Gough Whitlam, personal interview, April 1995; and see chapters eight to ten; also Whitlam, *The Truth of the Matter*, p. 89.
54 Jim McClelland, personal interview, August 1995.
55 *Bulletin*, 10 September 1985.
56 John Wheeldon, personal interview, July 1995.
57 Kerr, *Matters for Judgment*, p. 254.
58 *Bulletin*, 10 September 1985.
59 William Queale Memorial Lecture, 24 October 1972.
60 *Bulletin*, 10 September 1985.
61 Bill Hayden, personal interview, June 1995.
62 Gerard Henderson, *Menzies' Child*, p. 247.
63 *Quadrant*, January 1976.
64 Lady (Anne) Kerr, personal interview, June 1995.
65 John Wheeldon, personal interview, August 1995.
66 Sir Maurice Byers, personal interview, June 1995.
67 Sir Paul Hasluck, 'Tangled in the harness', *Quadrant*, November 1983.
68 Jim McClelland, personal interview, August 1995.
69 Ken Gee, personal interview, July 1995.

70 This term was used initially by Donald Horne, but the meaning I give to it is not the same as Horne's.
71 Whitlam, *The Truth of the Matter*, p. 176; see Appendix H.
72 This idea of the office draws upon an interpretation put forward by the former Governor-General, Sir Ninian Stephen.
73 Kerr, *Matters for Judgment*, p. 330.
74 ibid. p. 331.
75 Sir Rupert Hamer, personal interview, April 1995.
76 Malcolm Fraser, personal interview, May 1995.
77 Ian Macphee, personal interview, August 1995.
78 Gerard Henderson, *Menzies' Child*, p. 260.
79 Bob Ellicott, personal interview, July 1995.
80 Reg Withers, personal interview, June 1995.
81 Sir John Kerr, *Matters for Judgment*, p. 364 and p. 376.
82 Jim McClelland, personal interview, August 1995.
83 Graham Freudenberg, *A Certain Grandeur*, Macmillan, Melbourne, 1977, pp. 402–403.
84 Graham Freudenberg in 'Whitlam, Wran and the Labor tradition', *Labor History Essays*, volume two, Pluto Press, Sydney, 1988, p. 8.
85 Colin Howard and Cheryl Saunders, 'The blocking of the Budget and dismissal of the Whitlam Government', p. 258.
86 Sir Maurice Byers, personal interview, July 1995.
87 Gough Whitlam, speech at Rotary District Conference for Tasmania, 1 April 1995.
88 *The Australian*, 30 August 1995.
89 Interview with Paul Kelly, *The Australian*, 7 February 1994.
90 This information draws upon two confidential discussions in 1995.
91 I have spoken to two people who have read the letter.
92 Bill Hayden, personal interview, June 1995.
93 Address to the Indian Law Institute, 28 February 1975.
94 'The Australian constitutional monarchy and its likely survival', *New Zealand Law Journal*, vol. 1, 1993, pp. 201–206, June 1993.
95 Ken Gee, personal interview, July 1995.

Index

ACTU, 49, 81, 178
Admiralty House, 89, 92, 101–2, 119, 224–5
Advertiser, 171
Age, 200, 284
Age–Herald poll, 172
Aickin QC, Keith, 231
ALP, 1; *see also* Whitlam Government
   1972 election, 2
   Constitution, and the, 9, 11, 13, 15, 21
      section 96, 11
   dismissal, lesson from, 311–12
   federal conferences, 7
      abolition of Senate, 12
      unification position, 12
   Federal Executive, 5
   federalism, and, 12
   Federation, and, 9
   High Court, and the, 11
   mandate, 1
   responsible government, and, 17
   Senate, and the, 33
      abolition of, 12
      bills opposed, 33
      Gair affair, 52
      numbers, 1972, 44
   socialist objective, 10, 11
   State Aid, 5
   Whitlam, E G and, 4–6
   Withers, Reg and, 35, 37
   years in government, 30
alternative financial arrangements, 190, 207, 216, 296
   draft Law Officers' opinion, 211
   Kerr/Fraser discussions, 187
Anderson, Kenneth, 34, 111, 197
ANOP, 172, 178
Anthony, Doug, 24, 31, 39, 45, 48, 55–6, 63, 106, 231–2, 237, 245–6, 251–2, 275
   concedes cracking, 237
   foreknowledge?, 245–6, 252, 267
   Kerr, Sir John on, 282
   Supply and, 49
   Whitlam, E G and, 246
ASIO, 19, 45–6
   Murphy 'raid', 19, 45
Askin, Sir Robert, 49, 73
Asquith, H H, 78, 155, 159, 161, 163
Attorney General's Department, 87, 88, 91, 92, 118, 173, 174, 208, 210, 272
Australian Capital Territory Senators, 109
Australian, The, 33, 58, 61, 151, 249
Australian Financial Review, 200
Australian School of Pacific Administration, 70

Ayres, Philip, 182, 187, 249–50, 252

Bagehot, Walter, 82–3, 99, 127–8, 147, 168, 300
Bailey, Sir Kenneth, 78
bank nationalisation, 11
Bank of New South Wales, 174
Bankers' Association, 210
banks, 172–8, 210
Barbour, Peter, 46
Barnard, Lance, 9, 14, 43, 67, 73, 80, 106
Barwick, Sir Garfield, 72, 117, 122–4, 145, 151–3, 206, 215, 223–30, 234, 260, 288, 291–2, 294–7, 308, 311–12
   1951 opinion on GG discretion, 140
   Cameron, Clyde and, 228
   Chief Justice as 123–4
   Kerr, Sir John and, 122–3, 222–3, 227, 243
      advice, 223–6, 228, 229
      Kerr asks to consult, 151–2
   Menzies, R G and, 117
   Murphy, Lionel views of, 123
   new political theory, 116, 292–5, 312
   Parliament, 225
   Supply and, 117, 123–4
   view of crisis, 223
   Whitlam, E G and, 123, 152, 228
Bass by-election, 9, 106
Baume, Peter, 197
Beazley, Kim (Snr), 8, 13, 51, 169
Bell, Tom, 210
Berinson, Joe, 222
Bessell, Eric, 111, 158, 171, 237, 240
   Senate, and the, 240
Bjelke-Petersen, Johannes, 54, 107, 111, 184, 198
   Gair affair, 54
   Senate and the, 107–9
Black Friday, 89
Blamey, General Sir Thomas, 70
Bonner, Neville, 111, 237, 239–40
   crossing the floor, 237
   Fraser, Malcolm and, 237–40
   Senate, and the, 239–40
born to rule, 23, 29, 42, 311
Bowen, Lionel, 8
   education policy, 51
Bowers, Peter, 255
British Constitution, 16, 168, 225, 293
   1909–1911 crisis, 16
British High Commissioner, 199
Buckley, Brian, 252
Budd, Dale, 40
Bulletin, 235, 260

INDEX

Bunting, Sir John, 151
Bunton, Cleaver, 107, 109–10, 115, 198
Burns, Tom, 108
Burton, Dr John, 70–1
Butler, Dr David, 178, 221
Button, John, 115
  dismissal, and, 268
Byers, Sir Maurice, 92, 95, 124, 139, 149–50, 152–3, 159, 211–15, 272, 295, 297, 305, 312
  Ellicott, Bob and, 149
  Governor-General, on, 313
  Kerr and Barwick, on, 123
  Kerr, Sir John and, 96, 152, 303
  legal opinion
    alternative financial arrangements, 173
    dismissal and reserve powers, 149
    response to Ellicott, 211–12
    Senate's powers, 149
    Supply, advice to PM, 118
    temporary purposes, 95
    on Whitlam sacking Kerr, 220
  reserve powers, and, 149
  Supply and, 118
  temporary purposes, 92
  views on dismissal, 295, 298, 312
  Whitlam, E G and, 149

Cairns, Jim, 6, 8–9, 19, 63, 87, 89, 102
  loans affair, 94
  Whitlam, E G and, 6
Calwell, Arthur, 6, 11
Cameron, Clyde, 8, 19, 122, 138, 140, 228, 250
  Barwick, Sir Garfield and, 228
  Kerr, Sir John and, 122
    GG powers, 140
    swearing in as Science minister, 140
Cameron, Rod, 172
caretaker government, 226
caretaker Prime Minister, 263
  terms of commission, 263
Carleton, Richard, 138
Carrick, Sir John
  Senate, and the, 240
Carrington, Lord, 156
Casey, Lord (Richard), 25, 80, 99
Cass, Moss, 8
Certificate of Indebtedness, 173
Chaney, Fred, 239
Charles, HRH Prince of Wales, 314–15
  Kerr, Sir John and, 314
Charteris, Sir Martin, 217, 280
  Whitlam, E G, and, 280
Chief Electoral Officer, *see* Ley, Frank
Chief Justice, 74, 80, 122–3, 215, 222–3, 243, 257
  Governor-General and, 74, 123, 151–2, 224–6, 228–9
  Sir Samuel Griffith, 151
Chifley, Ben, 10, 11, 13, 21, 32, 35, 80, 138
Churchill, Winston, 7
class politics, 9
Coalition, 3, 21, 23, 30, 31, 36, 42, 47–8, 58, 60, 65, 142, 145, 153, 197, 199, 222, 231, 253, 287, 296; *see also* Liberal Party, Country Party, blocking of Supply; *see* Chapter 6 *passim*
  cessation of, 24, 49
  communique, 184
  electoral laws and, 48
  ramshackle, reactionary, 5
  Senate and the, 20–2, 33, 43
  solidarity, 232
  Whitlam Government and, 31
  Withers, Reg and, 36
colonies, 12, 16, 307
Colston, Dr Malcolm, 108
Combe, David, 172, 178, 265
Commercial Banking Company, 175
Conlon, Alf, 69, 70
Connor, Rex (R F X), 8, 19, 86–7, 89–90, 93, 97, 112, 125, 287
  loans affair, 87, 91–3, 112
  misleads Parliament, 112
  misleads PM, 112
  personality, 87
  resignation, 112
  Whitlam, E G and, 9, 87, 93, 112
Constitution, 1, 285; *see also* Quick and Garran. For UK Constitution *see* British Constitution
  ALP and, 9, 11, 13, 15, 21, 189
  casual vacancies, 107
  Commonwealth powers, 4
  conventions, 117
  crown and, 125
  deadlock, 115, 129, 133, 146, 159, 287, 288
    Supply, 116
  democracy and, 10
  executive power, 88, 99
  federalism, 15, 105, 189, 286
  Federation debates, 286
  founding fathers, 15, 16, 58, 116
  Fraser, Malcolm and, 42, 115–16
  Governor-General salary, 74
  High Court and, 10
  joint sitting, 63
  nature of, 9
  Parliament and, 116
  Prime Minister and, 116–17
  Quick and Garran, 162, 293
  referenda
    postwar reconstruction, 4
    prices and incomes, 48–9
  reserve powers, 213, 216
  responsible government, 15–16, 105, 286, 293, 295
  section 1, 1
  section 2, 1
  section 5, 213
  section 15, 53, 107
  section 28, 213
  section 53, 105, 143, 201, 215
    Menzies' view, 158
  section 57, 52, 59, 62, 213, 226, 264, 272; *see also* double dissolution
    justiciability, 121
    legal opinion, 59

PMA case, 121
section 61, 88, 213, 216
section 62, 88, 213
section 63, 88
section 64, 213, 222
section 92, 10
section 96, 11
Senate and the, 16–18, 34, 58, 105
  powers of, 116
States and, 10
two party system and, 17
Whig view of, 78, 211
Whitlam, E G and, 9, 22, 189, 202
constitutional monarchy, 77, 83, 127, 168, 290, 307, 314, 316
Cooley, Alan, 102
Cormack v Cope, 62
Cormack, Sir Magnus, 46, 60, 267
Cotton, Robert, 34
Country Party, 1, 12, 23–5, 30, 36, 39, 45, 47–9, 51, 55, 58, 113, 166, 181, 237, 240, 243, 287
  DLP and, 49
  education policy, 51
  Fraser, Malcolm and, 31
  Gair, Vince and, 54
  Supply and, 49
Court, Sir Charles, 111
Cowen, Sir Zelman, 79, 82, 284
Crean, Frank, 8, 19, 67, 80, 245–6, 265–6
Crichton-Browne, Sir Robert, 174
crossing the floor, 237–40
Crown, 77, 82, 88, 125, 149, 160–1, 180, 225, 313; *see also* Queen, Monarch, Sovereign, Constitution
  advise and warn, 126, 192
  influence, 194
  powers of, 279
  reserve powers, 204
    dismissal, 194
  rights of, 229
  role of, 83, 98–9, 128, 151, 194, 290, 297, 301
Curtin, John, 4, 35
Cutler, Sir Roden, 73, 77, 81, 122, 134, 198–9, 222
  discussions with governors, 199
  issue of writs, 198
  Kerr, Sir John and, 73, 134–5, 298
    discussion on crisis, 199
    dismissal by PM possibility, 135
    Kerr's proposed overseas trip, 134
  personality, 135
  relations with his premier, 198
  role of Governor, 198
  view of crisis, 135, 298
  Whitlam, E G and, 73
    view of, 220
    view on Whitlam sacking Kerr, 220

Daly, Fred, 2, 48, 129, 169, 245–6, 265, 266, 270, 276, 300
  Whitlam, E G and, 246
De Lisle, Viscount, 80

Deakin, Alfred, 17, 27, 78
Deane, Sir William, 82, 174
democracy, 1, 10, 13–14, 57, 118, 189, 243, 312, 315
democratic socialism, 11
Dicey, A V, 293
Directorate of Research and Civil Affairs, 69
Dismissal, the, 256–9, 261–3, 265; *see* Chapter 10 *passim*
  Hasluck's view of, 304
Disraeli, Benjamin, 84
DLP, 20, 36, 44–6, 49, 52–5, 57–8, 60, 71
  Kerr, Sir John and, 70, 81
'do a Game', 191, 194, 219, 265
double dissolution, 2, 22, 37, 47, 51, 56–7, 59, 62, 79, 106, 117, 121, 133, 156, 163, 186, 222, 226, 261, 263–4, 272–3, 279, 286, 294; *see also* Constitution, section 57
  1914, 2, 59, 151
    bill, 59
  1951, 2, 37, 59, 138, 140
  1974, 2, 47, 52, 56, 59–60, 63, 107, 121
    bills, 56–7, 59, 62
    bills rejected, 47
  1975, 2
  bills
    end 1974, 63
    June 1975, 64
    October 1975, 115, 186
    11 November 1975, 264, 272
  joint sitting, 52, 56
    1974, 62
  justiciability, 121
  Odgers, J R, 62
  stockpiling, 63
Drake-Brockman, Tom, 36
Duke of Wellington, 14
Dunrossil, Lord, 80
Dupruytren's contracture, 52
duumvirate, 14–15, 43

education policy, 50–1
Egbert, King of Wessex, 99
Eggleston, Sir Richard, 201
Eggleton, Tony, 157, 255
elections
  13 December 1975, 280
  1914, 151
  1949, 37
  1951, 70
  1961, 11
  1967, 36
  1972, 2, 7, 13, 23, 31, 58, 141
    ALP vote, 44
    State results, 37
  1974, 22, 43, 47, 48, 52–3, 56, 58, 141
    results, 60
  Balcatta by-election, 49
  Bass by-election, 9, 106
  deadlock and, 115
  double dissolution, 2
  Greensborough by-election, 49
  half Senate election, 106, 115, 117, 143, 231
    Governors and, 111

INDEX

Territory Senators, 109–10
New South Wales, 49
Parramatta by-election, 48–9
possible 1973, 50
Victoria, 48
Western Australia, 49
Electoral Office, 205
Ellicott, Bob, 89, 95, 145–9, 151–2, 161, 164–5, 193, 206, 211, 213–15, 226–7, 229–30, 232, 234, 310
   Barwick, Sir Garfield and, 145
   Byers, Sir Maurice and, 149
   foreknowledge?, 232
   Kerr, Sir John and, 94, 145, 147–8, 151
   assessment of, 148
   legal opinion, 16 October 1975, 145
   loans affair and, 94, 163
   McClelland, Jim and, 148
   speech to parliament 21 October, 163
   Whitlam, E G and, 190, 193
      view of, 220
      view on Whitlam sacking Kerr, 220
   Whitlam Government and, 163
Enderby, Kep, 78, 97, 124, 137, 148–9, 152, 207, 208, 211–12, 253, 265
   Kerr, Sir John and 6 November, 207, 211
   legal opinion, alternative financial arrangements, 173
   Remembrance Day, 253
Evatt, H V, 14, 69–70, 72, 74, 77–9, 84, 125, 138, 143, 163, 256, 288, 297, 302
   Kerr, Sir John and, 69–70
   monarchy, view of, 78
   reserve powers and, 84
EXCO, *see* Executive Council
Executive Council, 86, 88
   13 December 1974 meeting, 86, 88–91
      Kerr's view, 90
      Sawer's view, 90
   14 December 1974 minute, 19, 89–92, 95
   21 March 1974 meeting, 53
   21 October 1974 meeting, 160
   30 October 1975 meeting, 178
   7 January 1975 meeting, 92, 97
   7 October 1975 meeting, 129
   Governor-General and, 88
   Hasluck, Sir Paul and, 88, 98
   procedures, 88
   role of, 98
Executive Council Minute
   14 December 1974, 86, 88
      justiciability, 96, 101
   7 January 1975, 92, 97

federalism, 1, 12, 15, 17, 105, 189, 214, 286, 289, 295, 315
Federation, 9
   ALP and, 9
Field, Albert Patrick, 107–9, 115, 198
Financial Agreement, 91, 92, 97
folie de grandeur, 298
Forsey, Eugene, 84, 124, 213, 297, 302
founding fathers, 15–17, 45, 58, 116, 214, 286, 288–9, 292

Griffith, Sir Samuel, 151
   Senate and the, 16–17
Fraser, Allan, 13
Fraser Government
   double dissolution bills, 272
   swearing-in, 240
Fraser, Malcolm, 1–2, 6–7, 16, 20, 22–7, 29, 32, 35, 38, 40–3, 55, 62–5, 67, 89, 104–6, 109–14, 116–18, 126, 128, 130, 132–3, 134, 136, 141–5, 148, 150–1, 153–4, 156–72, 175–9, 181–90, 194–207, 209–11, 214–15, 219–22, 224, 226, 230–3, 237–43, 245–56, 259–60, 263–85, 287–90, 296, 302–4, 306, 309–12, 316
   alleged wavering, 184
   alternative financial arrangements and, 176
   as a politician, 40, 42, 203, 204
   background, 25, 38
   banks and, 175
   blocking of Supply, 114, 116, 121
   Bonner, Neville and, 237–8, 240
   born to rule, 23, 29, 42, 311
   Casey, Lord (Richard) and, 41
   challenge to Snedden, 25, 28, 64
   Constitution and, 42, 115–17
   consultation and, 39–40
   Country Party and, 31
   Deakin lecture, 27
   dismissal defence, 288
   double dissolution, 272
   education, 25
   education policy, 51
   Ellicott opinion and, 148
   entry into Parliament, 23
   'extraordinary' circumstances, 23, 41, 64, 112, 117
   foreknowledge, 205–6, 243–4, 246, 248, 249, 252, 279
   former leaders and, 188
   Fraser compromise, 184–99, 201, 245
   Gorton, John and, 27–8, 110
   governing mentality, 38
   Governors-General and, 25, 28, 39, 41
   half Senate election and, 144
   Hall, Steele and, 110
   Hasluck, Sir Paul and, 28, 41
   institutional power and, 39–40, 42
   Jessop, Don and, 157
      crossing the floor, 238
   Kerr compromise, 179, 202–3, 207
   Kerr, Sir John and, 41–2, 151, 156, 161, 165, 206, 222, 230–1, 240, 260, 282–4, 296, 306
      11 November, 250, 263; appointment, 255; telephone call, 248–51
   belief in, 168
   confidence in, 205
   consultations, 159–61; 21 October, 163–4; 3 November, 186; 30 October, 182; 6 November, 196, 202, 204–7; alternative financial arrangements, 187; Fraser raises dismissal, 207
   Fraser pressures Kerr, 161, 203, 204

    Kerr raises theoretical possibility of
      sacking Whitlam, 166
    opinion of, 113
    past acquaintance, 163–4
    personal relations, 187
    Senate, the, 234
  leadership, 25–7, 29, 39–41, 197, 252
  Liberal Party and, 25
  Liberal Party leader, 24, 38, 64
  'life wasn't meant to be easy', 27
  loans affair, 87, 89, 94, 113
  McClelland, Jim and, 310
  Menzies, R G and, 30, 157
    consultations, 196
    Kerr anecdote, 121
  ministerial career, 26
  Missen, Alan and, 239
  personality, 25, 27, 39
    Withers' view, 244
  philosophy, 25–7
  pressure to compromise, 169
  Prime Minister, 263–5, 269–70, 275, 309, 310
    caretaker commission, 263, 274
    Supply, 267, 274
  promotes dismissal option, 151
  propriety, 38
  public demonstrations against, 154, 272
  'reprehensible' events, 41, 112, 117
  republic, 314
  resignation as Minister of Defence, 28
  Senate and the, 38, 41, 65, 109, 116, 234, 239
    does not concede cracking, 237
    tactics, 237
  speech to Parliament
    21 October, 162
    5 November, 202
    11 November, 254
  strategy, 165, 171
  Supply and, 29, 40, 41, 64, 117, 150, 164, 176, 268, 272, 278
    alternative financial arrangements, 173
    blocking of, 112; see Chapter 6 passim, especially 109–16
    floats moving to a reject position, 158
    guarantee of, 164
    options, 156
    tactics, 158
  tactics, 156, 166, 169, 184, 186, 197, 239, 240, 247, 252–3
  three-year term, 23
  Vietnam and, 27
  view of crisis, 135
  Whitlam compromise, 245
  Whitlam, E G and, 6, 25, 39, 40–2, 142, 189, 231, 245
    alternative financial arrangements, 176
    cautions, 246
    on sacking of Kerr, 219
    speech to Parliament 21 October, 162
  Whitlam Government on, 143, 287
  Withers, Reg and, 38
  working style, 26

Fraser, Neville, 25
Fraser, Simon, 25
Fraser, Tamie, 267
Freehill, Hollingdale and Page, 231
Freudenberg, Graham, 4, 12, 86, 93, 137, 149, 151, 178, 214, 221, 253, 264–6, 311
  Whitlam, E G, and
    view of, 7, 256
    view on Whitlam sacking Kerr, 221

Gair Affair, 52, 55, 58
Gair, Vince, 36, 52, 54, 55, 57–8, 60
  Ambassador to Ireland, 53
  Country Party and, 54
  DLP and, 52
  resignation from Senate, 54
  Whitlam, E G and, 52
Game, Sir Philip, 77, 133, 191, 219
  dismissal of Premier, 77, 134
  Whitlam view of, 191
Garran, Robert, see Quick and Garran
Gee, Ken, 74, 76, 119, 305, 316
  Kerr, Sir John on, 74
  McClelland, Jim on, 120
Gibbs, Sir Harry, 215
Gleeson QC, Murray, 231
Gloucester, HRH the Duke of, 80
'God save the Queen', 275
Gorton, John, 11, 28–9, 33–4, 80, 110, 188
  Fraser, Malcolm and, 27, 28
  Hasluck, Sir Paul and, 28
  Independent Senate candidate, 110
Governor
  Cutler, Sir Roden, 198
    relations with his government, 198
  dismissal of Premier, 77, 133–4, 191, 194, 219
    illegality, 134
    warning in writing, 134
  dismissal of, procedures, 132
  Game–Lang crisis, 77, 133–4, 191, 194, 219
  Governors meet with Kerr, 198
  issue of writs, 111, 142, 145, 178, 185, 289
    Cutler's view, 198
    discussions with Kerr, 198
  removal of dormant commission, 132
  role of, 198
  Winneke, Sir Henry, 199
Governor of New South Wales, see Cutler, Sir Roden, and Rowland, Sir James
Governor-General, 1, 6, 12, 14, 21, 29
  Address in Reply, 44–5
  Address to Parliament, 44
  advise and warn, 126–7, 129
  assent to bills, 133
  Casey, Lord (Richard), 25, 41, 80, 99
  ceremonial leadership, 81
  Chief Justice and, 13, 74, 123, 151–2, 224–6, 228–9
  comparison with Monarch, 99
  Constitution and, 6
  Cowen, Sir Zelman, 79, 82
  Crown and the, 82
  De Lisle, Viscount, 80

INDEX

Deane, Sir William, 82
dismissal of Prime Minister, 2
dismissal of, procedures, 132
double dissolution, 56, 59
  1951, 59
  1974, 59, 62
Dunrossil, Lord, 80
Executive Council and, 88, 94, 98
executive power, 88
Fraser, Malcolm and, 41, 166
Gloucester, Duke of, 80
government appointments and, 284
Gowrie, Lord, 80
half Senate election, 53
Hasluck, Sir Paul, 14, 28, 41, 44, 53, 65, 67, 74, 76, 80, 99
  double dissolution, 59
  refusal of Prime Ministerial request, 28
Hayden, Bill, 76, 82
influence, 99–100, 128, 194
Isaacs, Sir Isaac, 80
justiciable issues, 96, 226
Kerr, Sir John, 41–2, 65, 67
  Joint Sitting, 62
  term, 74
lawyers as, 313
loans affair, 94
McKell, Sir William, 80, 138
Munro Ferguson, Sir Ronald, 151
politicians, 80
power to dismiss
  Ellicott opinion, 146
powers of, 128–9, 231, 313
  dismissal, 163
  reserve powers, 77
  Supply, 178
Prime Minister and, 82, 84, 100, 103, 105–6, 126–9, 139, 143, 146–7, 192, 223, 226, 229, 304
  Barwick opinion, 140
  Harders' advice, 150
  mechanism of GG removal, 217
  Whitlam's view, 138
Queen and the, 1, 88, 99
refusal of Prime Ministerial request, 28
requirements for, 73
reserve powers, 42, 77–9, 122, 124–5, 163
  advise and warn, 86, 96
  dismissal, 2
  Evatt view, 78
  Hasluck's view, 122
  Whitlam's view, 78
role models, 80–1
role of, 41–2, 77, 83, 96, 98–101, 151, 160, 193, 194
  Byers' view, 149
  dismissal of ministers, 161
  Ellicott opinion, 146–7
  Executive Council, 88
  Fraser, Malcolm view of, 41
  Hasluck, Sir Paul, 74
  Whitlam's view, 69, 137
  Winneke's view, 199
salary, 74

Slim, Field Marshal Sir William, 25, 80
  soldiers as, 80
  sources of advice, 122
  Speaker and the, 273
Stephen, Sir Ninian, 82, 227
Supply and, 144, 200
tenure, 219, 308
Whitlam E G and, 42, 79, 81
  list of names, 67
Gowrie, Lord, 80
Grattan, Michelle, 284
Greenwood, Ivor, 34, 49, 58, 61, 240
Griffith, Sir Samuel, 151, 286, 312
Guilfoyle, Margaret, 239, 240
  Senate, and the, 240

Hall, Steele, 12, 60, 107, 110, 115, 154, 251
  Supply and, 110
Hamer, Rupert (Dick), 49, 111, 184–5, 198, 298, 309
  Governor's view of crisis, 199, 298
  issue of writs, 198
  Supply and, 55, 111
  Winneke, Sir Henry and, 199
Hannah, Sir Colin, 132–3, 136, 218
Harders, Sir Clarence, 91, 99, 118, 149–50, 153, 265, 272
  advice to PM, 118, 150
  dismissal and, 273
  EXCO meeting, 91
  Supply, blocking of, 118
  temporary purposes, 92
  view of crisis, 298
Harradine, Brian, 6
Hasluck, Sir Paul, 14, 44, 53, 59, 65, 67, 76, 80, 98–100, 121–2, 152, 193
  1974 double dissolution, 121
  Chief Justice and, 152
  dismissal, view of crisis, 313
  double dissolution, 59
  Executive Council and, 88
  Fraser, Malcolm and, 28, 41
  Governor-General, role of, 74, 98–100, 129, 147, 223, 300
  High Court review, 121–2
  list of names for Governor-General, 67
  refusal of Prime Ministerial request, 28
  reserve powers, 122, 304
  view of crisis, 304
  Whitlam, E G and, 59, 67
  William Queale Lecture, 74
Hawke, Bob, 24, 40, 82, 89, 178, 227, 242, 309, 311–12
  Kerr, Sir John and, 81
Hayden, Bill, 9, 48, 82, 104, 112, 129, 153–4, 169, 175–6, 183, 186, 190, 207–10, 212, 218, 220, 222, 284, 287, 311, 315
  alternative financial arrangements, 175–6, 207
  budget, 89, 106, 188, 276
  Governor-General, 76, 82, 218, 273, 298, 301
  Kerr, Sir John and, 175

NOVEMBER 1975

6 November, 207; consultations, 207, 209;
    details of, 208–9
view on Whitlam sacking Kerr, 220
warns Whitlam, 209
Head of State, 39, 263, 275, 307, 313, 314; *see also* Governor-General
Queen, 76
Heenan, James, 208
Henderson, Gerard, 227–8, 297
High Court, 10–11, 13, 21, 39, 54, 63–4, 82, 121–2, 151, 216, 223–4, 226–7, 229, 231, 277
    advisory opinions, 151, 226
    ALP and, 11
    Barwick, Sir Garfield and, 123–4
    Commonwealth and, 124
    Cormack v Cope, 62
    double dissolution and, 121–2
    Governor-General and, 123
    Kerr, Sir John, influence on, 121–2
    Murphy appointment, 107, 123–4
    Murphy, Lionel, 89, 162
    Petroleum and Minerals Authority Case, 121, 215, 223
    review of Governor-General's decision, 121–2
    section 57, 62
    section 92, 10
    Sir John Kerr and, 227
    Supply and, 123
    Territory Senators decision, 109
Holding, Clyde, 242
Holt, Harold, 24, 27, 188
    Supply and, 116
House of Commons, 16, 225
House of Lords, 16, 225
House of Representatives, 1, 10, 15, 21–2, 104–6, 118, 146, 189, 201–2, 254, 287
    16 October speeches, 141
    adjournment, 270
    deadlock, 47
    responsible government, 88
    Senate and the, 2, 32, 36, 42, 47, 59, 61–3, 79, 116
        deadlock, 45, 115; 1974, 47–8
        Menzies, R G on, 37
    Whitlam, E G and, 60
Howard, John, 309, 314
Howard, Professor Colin, 159
Hughes, Billy, 288

interim Senate, 179
Iraqi affair, 9
Ireland, 52
Isaacs, Sir Isaac, 80

Jarman, Alan, 197
Jennings, Sir Ivor, 83, 159, 213
Jessop, Don, 111, 113, 157, 158, 171, 237–40
    crossing the floor, 237
    Fraser, Malcolm and, 157
        crossing the floor, 238
    Supply and, 157
Johnson, President Lyndon, 18
Joint sitting, 22

Karmel, Peter, 50
Keating, Paul, 21, 24, 35, 40, 82, 112, 169, 311–12, 314–15
    Queen, and the, 314
    republic, 314
    swearing in as minister, 160
Kelly, Paul, 61, 120, 136, 147, 183, 191, 205–6, 228, 250
Kennedy, Eric, 243
Kennelly, Pat, 24
Kerr, Lady (Anne), 66, 70–1, 76, 120, 124, 126, 131–2, 137, 139, 180, 191, 229–30, 247, 254, 263, 281–3, 302
    Kerr, Sir John and, 230, 247, 302
    view of John Kerr, 71, 139
Kerr, Peggy, 67–8, 74–5, 191, 230
    death of, 75, 84
Kerr, Sir John, 1, 2, 5, 9, 19, 20, 41, 42, 62, 65–9, 71–92, 94–5, 97, 98, 100–3, 105–6, 113, 117–56, 158–61, 163–9, 172, 178, 179–85, 187–95, 198–292, 294–306, 308, 310–17
    ACT Supreme Court, 72
    address to Senate proposal, 150
    advise and warn prerogative, 129, 193, 218, 242
    advises and warns, 257–63
    ALP and, 69–71, 73, 75
    alternative financial arrangements, 175, 187, 207, 209–10
    appointment as Governor-General, 67
    background, 69–72, 75
    Barwick, Sir Garfield and, 72, 122–4, 222–3, 227–8, 243
        advice, 223–6, 228–9
        request to consult, 151–2
    boycott of, 281
    Byers, Sir Maurice and, 96, 123, 149
    Cameron, Clyde and, 122
    Chief Justice and, 257
    Chief Justice of NSW, 67, 73
    Commonwealth Industrial Court, 68, 72
    compromise, 178–84, 202–3, 207
    Constitution and, 6
    constitutional innovator, 291
    consultative technique, 209
    consults with Governors, 198–9
    Cutler, Sir Roden and, 73, 135, 220, 298
        discussions on crisis, 199
    death of first wife, 75, 84, 100
    deception, 299–300
    decision to dismiss, 214–19, 222, 228, 230, 236
        draft letters, 243
        justification, 240
        timing, 232, 235, 240, 242
    Democratic Labor Party and, 70–1, 81
    dismissal, 245–51, 256–9, 261–3, 265; *see* Chapter 10 *passim*
        timing, 295, 297
    Ellicott opinion and, 147–8, 152
    Enderby, Kep and
        Byers' opinion, 211
        consultations 6 November, 207, 211

INDEX

Evatt, H V and, 69–70, 74, 77
Executive Council meeting
  13 December 1974, 89–90, 100
  7 January 1975, 97
Executive Council Minute
  14 December 1974, 86, 88, 90, 92, 94–5, 99; doubts, 95
failure to warn, 257, 298
fear of sacking, 67, 83, 84, 129–36, 148, 167, 194–5, 205, 207, 217–22, 257, 259, 260, 300–2
folie de grandeur, 298
Fraser compromise, 186–8
Fraser, Malcolm and, 41–2, 161, 165, 167, 206, 230, 231, 240, 260, 282–4, 296, 306
  11 November, 250, 263; appointment, 255; telephone call, 248–51
  consultations, 159, 160–1
    21 October, 163–4; summary, 164
    30 October, 182
    3 November, 186
    6 November, 196, 202, 204–7; summary, 204
  alternative financial arrangements, 187
  Kerr's Menzies anecdote, 121
  Kerr complains of intimidation, 151
  past acquaintance, 163–4
  pressures Kerr, 203–4
  raises dismissal, 207
  raises possibility of sacking Whitlam, 166
  Senate, 234
friendship with Whitlam ministers, 137
Game dismissal of Lang and, 134
Governor-General, 74
  advise and warn, 126
  announcement of appointment, 79, 81
  influence, 74, 99, 156
  jurist's view of, 83–4, 95–6, 98, 121–2, 149, 152, 194, 210, 212, 222, 223–4, 297, 303
  reserve powers, 77–8, 86
  role of, 74–5, 83, 96, 98–9, 122
  rubber stamp, 85–6, 95, 103, 300
  swearing-in, 75
  term, 74, 79
  view of, 76, 82–3, 102
  view of office, 101, 298
Grattan, Michelle on, 284
half Senate election, 200, 243
Hayden, Bill and, 175
  consultations, details of, 208–9
  failure to warn, 210
High Court and, 121, 122–3, 227
industrial barrister, 70
influence and, 76, 83
Joe Riordan's views of, 70, 123
joint sitting, 121–2
Kerr, Anne and, 120, 230, 247, 283, 302
Kerr, Peggy and, 74–5, 230
Lady Kerr's view, 139
Liberal Party and, 71–2, 75
Lieutenant Governor of NSW, 67, 73

loans affair, 89, 95, 99, 119; *see* Chapter 5 *passim*, 100
Lowe and, 70
Mason, Sir Anthony and, 226, 227
McAuley, James and, 71
McClelland, Jim and, 67, 70, 119, 140, 180, 181, 183, 232, 299
  deception, 181–3
Menzies, R G and, 72, 134
Moore v Doyle, 68
new political theory, 116, 291–5, 312
O'Shea, Clarrie and, 72
personality, 71, 75–6, 101, 119, 139
  Barwick's view, 227–9
  Ellicott's view, 148
  Byers' view, 149, 297, 303
  Cutler's view, 298
  Elizabeth Reid's view, 119, 124
  Fraser's assessment, 206
  Freudenberg's view, 221
  Joe Riordan's view, 70, 123, 282
  John Burton's view, 71
  Ken Gee's view, 74
  Lady Kerr's view, 71, 139, 302
  McAuley's view, 302
  McClelland's view, 180, 194, 230, 305
  Menadue's view, 283
  reassuring technique, 121, 187, 209, 299, 303
  Roden Cutler's view, 73
  Wheeldon's view, 283, 299
  Whitlam's view, 137, 220, 305
PMA Case, 223
politics and, 70–2, 74, 75
Prime Minister, pretensions to, 68, 101
Prince Charles and, 314
Queen and, 102, 216, 218, 307–8
  briefings, 216, 306
  Kerr seeks advice on PM/GG sacking, 217
Reid, Elizabeth and, 75, 102, 119, 124
Remembrance Day, 253
removal of Governor's dormant commission, 132
requests talks with Fraser, 160
reserve powers, 84, 124–5, 138–9, 272
Riordan, Joe and, 70, 172
Robson, Anne and, 70, 120
Royal Assent, 271–2
Santamaria, B A and, 70
scapegoat, 285
Senate, and the, 172, 210, 215, 237, 239, 274
  does not concede cracking, 237
  money bills and, 120
'Silver', 71, 148, 183
Smith, David and, 91, 217, 250
Speaker and the, 271, 273
Supply and, 122, 155, 178, 215, 234, 255, 271–2
  blocking improper, 121, 172
tactics, 256
tenure, 284
UNESCO and, 284
view of self, 119, 124

Wheeldon, John and, 299
Whitlam, E G and, 9, 66, 67, 68–9, 75, 79, 82, 83–6, 90–1, 95, 100, 106, 119–20, 123–4, 128, 138–9, 148, 180, 190, 217, 230, 240
  11 November: appointment, 255; telephone call, 247
  advise and warn prerogative, 126–7, 192–3
  advises and warns, 125, 258–63
  alleged conversations concerning PM dismissal, 133, 180
  alleged raising of dismissal option by Whitlam, 155–6
  alleged Supply conversation, 126
  alternative financial arrangements, 173, 175, 177; consultations on, 173
  consultations: 3 November, 188, 191; 6 November, 207; 14 October (alleged), 126, 129; 18 October (alleged), 155; Executive Council meeting 30 October, 178; Port Moresby (alleged), 164; prior 14 October (alleged), 125–6, 129, 300
  deception, 180–1, 183, 192–4, 279, 282, 298–300
  decision to dismiss, 214–19, 222, 230, 236; draft letters, 243; Supply, 234; timing, 233, 235
  dismissal, 245–51, 256–9, 261–3, 265
  dismissal raised, 191–2
  distrust of, 95–8, 101, 103, 125, 127–8, 131, 136, 155–6, 161, 163, 167, 192–4, 207, 219
  'do a Game', 191, 194, 219
  Ellicott opinion, 147
  failure to warn, 96–7, 100–1, 103, 128, 180–1, 193–4, 199, 218, 220, 251, 257–63, 279, 298, 300
  Fraser compromise, 187–92
  half Senate election, 200, 235; advance warning, 243
  initial relationship, 79
  Kerr's remarriage, 120
  Kerr seeks legal advice from Whitlam, 148
  Lady Kerr's view, 139
  loans affair, 97
  lunch 30 October, 179
  McKell reference, 140
  money bills and, 120
  offer of Governor-Generalship, 73
  personal relations, 140, 180, 183, 190–2, 241–2, 304–6
  personality, 156
  possible reconciliation, 316
  Queen dismissal of GG reference, 131–2, 305
  relations, 153
  Senate, the, 234
  timing, 147
  views on Whitlam sacking Kerr, 219–22
Winneke, Sir Henry and, 199
Khemlani, Tirath, 19, 87–8, 93, 106, 112–13, 190
Killen, Jim, 55, 143
  Supply and, 55, 113
King, 82, 160, 308
  rights of, 127
  role of, 83, 99, 160
Kings Hall, 12, 251, 253, 255, 267, 274
Kirby, Justice Michael, 316
Kirribilli House, 68, 101–2, 151

Laird, Mel, 26
Lane, Professor Pat, 231
Lang, Jack, 77, 133, 191, 219
  dismissal by Governor, 134
Laucke, Condor, 111, 158, 171, 239
legal opinions, 285
  Aicken/Gleeson/Lane, 231
  ALP lack of, 152
  alternative financial arrangements, 177, 210
    Attorney General's Department, 208
    Deane QC, William, 174
    draft Law Officers', 211
    Sawer, 175
  Barwick, Sir Garfield
    1951, 140
    dismissal, 225–8
  blocking of Supply
    resignation of government (Byers), 118
    resignation of government (Harders), 118
  Byers, Sir Maurice
    dismissal and reserve powers, 149
    response to Ellicott opinion, 211–12
    Senate's powers, 149
  Byers/Enderby
    alternative financial arrangements, 173
  double dissolution, 59
  Eggleston, Sir Richard, 201
  Ellicott opinion, 145
  Harders, Sir Clarence
    Governor-General's role, 150
    return of bills to H of R, 150
  Kerr, Sir John and, 83
  loans affair, 95
  section 57, 59
  temporary purposes, 92–3, 95
Lewis, Tom, 107, 111, 184, 198
  relations with Governor Cutler, 198
Ley, Frank, 207, 233, 254
  Whitlam, E G and, 254
Liberal Movement, 60, 115
Liberal Party, 1, 12, 23, 25, 28–9, 31, 34–5, 38–40, 55, 58, 142, 156–7, 188, 196, 232, 236, 309
  blocking of Supply, 111
    opponents of, 110–14, 171
  born to rule, 29, 311
  DLP and, 54, 57
  education policy, 50
  Federal Council support for blocking of Supply, 111
  Fraser, Malcolm and, 27
    leader, 38
    philosophy, 25
  Kerr, Sir John and, 72, 75
  Senate and the, 47, 110
  Senate leader election, 34
Supply

INDEX

alternative financial arrangements and, 174
  blocking of, 111
  Supply, blocking of 1974, 55
  Withers, Reg and, 35
Loan Council, 91, 93, 97, 114
loans affair, 19–20, 32, 39, 63, 87, 92–5, 101, 103–4, 112–13, 119, 143, 163; *see* Chapter 5 *passim*
  Connor, Rex and, 112
  temporary purposes, 89, 91–3
Lodge, 88–9, 91, 120–1, 243, 262, 264, 270
Lord Mayor's Banquet, 243
Lowe, 70
Lynch, Philip, 34, 39, 45, 112, 114, 231, 237, 243, 245, 247, 251–3, 309
  foreknowledge?, 246, 252–3
  Senate and the, 239
    concedes cracking, 237

McAuley, James, 68–9, 71, 101, 302
McClelland, Doug, 267–9
  dismissal and, 268–9
McClelland, Freda, 181
McClelland, Jim, 72, 75–6, 80, 104, 119, 123, 137, 140, 148, 172, 179, 180–4, 186, 220, 260, 267, 269, 287, 299, 310
  Ellicott, Bob and, 148
  Kerr, Sir John and, 67, 70–1, 73–4, 119–20, 140, 178, 180–1, 183, 194, 230, 232
    deception, 181–3, 298–9
    lunch, 30 October, 179
  reserve powers, on, 79
  Whitlam, E G and, 183, 233, 299, 305
    on Whitlam sacking Kerr, 220
  Withers, Reg, on, 37
McEwen, John (Jack), 13
McKell, Sir William, 80, 138–9, 140
  double dissolution, 138
  views on dismissal, 159
  Menzies and, 138
McKenna, Nick, 35
McMahon, Sir William, 5, 13, 24, 72, 188, 197, 243
  Mason appointment, 226
McManus, Frank, 54, 57–8
McMillan, William, 286
Macphee, Ian, 111, 196, 197, 239, 309
mandate, 1, 14, 15, 16, 17, 21, 45, 48, 49, 56, 60, 61, 88; *see* Whitlam, E G and Australian Labor Party
Mant, John, 8, 137, 139, 148, 264, 265
Marriott, John, 171
Martin, Kathy, *see* Sullivan, Kathy
Mason, Sir Anthony, 215, 226–7
  Barwick, Sir Garfield and, 227
  Kerr, Sir John and, 226–7
Melbourne Cup, 190, 195, 198, 283
Menadue, John, 89, 118, 121, 137, 138–9, 150, 264, 265, 299
  Kerr, Sir John and, 121, 283
  on Whitlam sacking Kerr, 220
  possibility of Palace briefing, 151
Menzies Government, 27

Menzies, R G, 7, 11, 13, 23–5, 30, 37, 40, 80, 134, 138, 139, 157, 162, 196–7, 239, 288
  1949 election, 37
  Barwick, Garfield and, 117
  double dissolution, 37, 59, 138
    1951, 140
  Fraser, Malcolm and, 117, 157
    consultations, 196
    doubt about tactics, 196
    Kerr's anecdote, 121
  Governor-General, and, 59, 138
  Kerr, Sir John and, 72
    letter to Game, dismissal of Premier, 133
  responsible government, 134
  Senate and, 37, 38, 116, 157
    powers of, 37
  statement of support for Fraser, 158
  Supply and, 116–17
  Whitlam, E G, comparison with, 7, 15, 37–8, 68, 138
Milliner, Bert, 108, 142
Minerals and Energy, Department of, 88
Missen, Alan, 111–14, 237–9
  Fraser, Malcolm and, 239
  Senate and the, 238
  Supply and, 113–14, 238
Missen, Mollie, 238
Monarch, 67, 78, 82
  advise and warn, 127
  comparison with Governor-General, 99
  rights of, 127
  role of, 99, 194
Monarchy, 78, 218
Moore v Doyle, 68
Morosi, Junie, 102
Munro Ferguson, Sir Ronald, 151
Murdoch, Rupert, 244
Murphy, Lionel, 19, 32–4, 44–5, 58–9, 60, 89, 92, 95, 97, 123, 162
  ASIO 'raid', 45, 46
  High Court appointment, 107
  loans affair, 92
  personality, 46
  Senate, and the, 32–4, 46
  Withers, Reg and, 46
Myer, Ken, 67, 81

National Country Party, *see* Country Party
National Party, *see* Country Party
Negus, George, 243
Negus, Sid, 44
Nicolson, Harold, 83
Nixon, Peter, 31, 51, 113, 267
no confidence, 116, 277
Northern Territory Senators, 109–10

O'Byrne, Justin, 52, 277
O'Connell, Professor D P, 147
O'Shea, Clarrie, 72, 76
Oakes, Laurie, 49, 51, 53
Odgers, J R, 33, 54, 62, 277
Official Secretary, 255, 271, 273, 275; *see* Smith, David
OPEC oil shock, 18, 87

Palace, the, 151, 207, 216, 218–21, 257–9, 261, 266, 278, 279–80, 300–1, 303, 314
  Independence Day, 133
Parliament, 1, 12, 62, 162, 187, 189, 254
  Barwick view of, 225
  confidence of, 293
  Constitution and, 116
  deadlock, 115–16
  double dissolution and, 121
  unworkable, 61
Patterson, Rex, 8, 169
Peacock, Andrew, 243
Petrol and Minerals Authority Case, 121
Petroleum and Minerals Authority Case, 215, 223
Playford, Sir Thomas, 111, 157
post-war reconstruction, 4
Premiers
  blocking of Supply and, 111
President, 308, 315
Prime Minister
  Chief Justice and, 226
  Crown and, 88
  Governor-General and, 82, 84, 100, 103, 105, 106, 126–9, 139, 143, 146–7, 192, 223, 226, 229, 304
    Barwick opinion, 140
    Harders' advice, 150
    mechanism of GG removal, 217
    Whitlam's view, 138
  majority in lower house, 105
  mandate, 88
  powers of, 88
  Queen and the, 218
  responsible government and, 116
  role of, 125
  Sovereign and, 84
  Supply and, 225
Prime Minister and Cabinet, Department of, 88–9, 118, 121, 137, 173, 210, 243, 265, 283
Prince of Wales, 314, 315; *see* Charles, HRH Prince of Wales
Privy Council, 64
Proclamation, 273–4
  1974 Joint Sitting, 62
proportional representation, 32
Pugh, Clifton, 124, 138

Queen, the, 1, 69, 74, 76, 84, 99, 131, 138, 156, 217, 219, 259–60, 275, 279, 282, 284, 313
  Cutler, Sir Roden and, 198
  executive power, 88
  Governor, removal of, 132
  Governor-General and, 1, 216
  Prime Minister and, 135, 218, 308
  Queen of Australia, 313
  removal of Governor-General, 135
  Whitlam, E G and, 193, 279
Queen Victoria, 83–4
Quick and Garran, 16, 17, 162, 214, 292–3, 295
  Senate, on the, 16
Quick, John, *see* Quick and Garran

Razak, His Excellency Tun Abdul, 131, 132, 134, 300, 305
Redlich, Peter, 242
referenda
  1944, 4
  1973, 48–9
  postwar reconstruction, 4
  prices and incomes, 48–9
Reid, Alan, 19, 86, 108, 132, 267, 268
Reid, Elizabeth, 76, 102, 119, 124
  Kerr, Sir John and, 75, 102, 119, 124
    Reid warning to Whitlam, 124
  view of, 119
Remembrance Day, 245, 247, 253
republic, 314, 315, 316
Reserve Bank, 210
reserve powers, 77, 79, 84, 124–5, 139, 163, 193, 194, 204, 211, 213, 216, 223, 229, 272, 285, 297, 308, 315
  advise and warn, 86, 96
  Byers' advice, 149
  Evatt, H V, 78
  Hasluck's view, 304
  Lord Esher, 78
  Whitlam's view, 137
responsible government, 15–17, 20, 22, 65, 88, 105, 116, 118, 124, 141, 152, 189, 212, 214, 241, 277, 278, 280, 286, 288–9, 292–5, 304–5, 312
Riordan, Joe, 70, 75, 120, 123, 137, 171–2, 270, 282, 299
  alternative financial arrangements, 177
  Kerr, Sir John and, 70, 282
  Kerr, Sir John on, 123
Robson, Anne (later Lady Kerr), 70, 120
Robson, Hugh, 120
Rowland, Sir James, 82
Royal Assent, 150, 271–2, 277–8
Royal Prerogative, 77, 84
Rundle, Harry, 255

Santamaria, B A, 70
  Kerr, Sir John and, 70
Sawer, Professor Geoffrey, 90, 121, 226, 233, 291, 294
  alternative financial arrangements, 175
  EXCO meeting, 90
Schneider, Russell, 236
Scholes, Gordon, 129, 265, 271, 272–4, 307
  Kerr, Sir John and, 273–4
Scullin, J H, 80
Senate, the, 1, 10, 56, 107, 198, 202, 254, 269
  abolition of, 12
  ALP and, 12, 33, 43, 47
    bills opposed in Senate, 33
    numbers, 44
  Anthony, Doug and, 237
  ASIO 'raid' and, 19, 46
  Bar of, 89
  Bessell, Eric and, 240
  Bjelke-Petersen, Joh and, 107–9
  blocking of Supply, 113, 133
  Bonner, Neville and, 237–40
  Byers' opinion, 212

INDEX

Carrick, Sir John, 240
casual vacancies, 53, 107, 109
  challenge to Field, 109
Chaney, Fred and the, 239
Coalition, 61
  negative majority, 60
committee system, 32
composition of
  1972, 20, 43
  1972–73, 56
  1974, 60
  May 1974, 107
  1975, 107
  July 1975, 107
  October 1975, 109, 115
crossing the floor, 237–40
double dissolution
  1974, 56, 59
election of Territory Senators, 109
forcing an election, 57, 59–60
founding fathers and, 16
Fraser compromise, 197
Fraser, Malcolm and, 39, 197, 238
Guilfoyle, Margaret and, 239–40
half Senate election, 106, 200, 231, 253
  1974, 53
  advice to Government House, 243
  Supply and, 144, 145
Hall, Steele and, 110
hold or crack, 232, 234–7, 296
  cracking possible, 232, 236–40
  crossing the floor, 237–9, 240
  Fraser tactics, 253
  holding long enough, 240
Holt, Harold and, 116
House of Representatives and, 2, 32, 36, 42, 47, 59, 61–3, 79, 116
  deadlock, 45, 115; 1974, 47–8
  Menzies, R G on, 37
independents, 44
interim Senate, 110
Jessop, Don and, 238–9
Kerr's compromise, 179
Kerr, Sir John and, 240, 274
Lynch, Philip and, 237, 239
mandate, 61
Menzies, R G and, 37, 116, 157
Missen, Alan and, 238–9
Murphy, Lionel and, 32
Murphy 'raid' and, 45
negative majority, 107
obstruction, 51
  1973, 44
positive majority, 107, 109
powers of, 17, 18, 34, 37, 45, 58, 105, 116, 143, 149, 201, 287, 292
  Menzies, R G on, 37
Quick and Garran, 16
role of, 17
smell of death, 46
Staley, Tony and, 237
Sullivan, Kathy and, 239
Supply and, 2, 11, 22, 34, 36, 42, 105, 189, 215, 294

1974 double dissolution, 60
blocking of: 1974, 55–6, 59;
  determination, 59; Liberal opponents, 110–14; tactics, 115
conventions, 117
deferral, 49
Fraser, Malcolm and, 239
tainted, 118
Territory Senators, 109–10
voting system, 10, 32
Whitlam, E G and, 43–4, 57, 125, 128, 143, 162, 201, 221
Whitlam Government and, 20–1
Withers, Reg and, 35–8, 43, 236, 239–40
  cracking possible, 240
  tactics, 240
Short, Laurie, 70
Sinclair, Ian, 31, 166
  Kerr raises possibility of sacking Whitlam, 166
Slim, Field Marshal Sir William, 25, 80
Smith, David, 89–91, 147, 165, 217–18, 233, 250, 263, 273, 275, 280
  Kerr, Sir John and, 91, 217, 250
  reads Proclamation, 274
Snedden, Bill, 24, 27, 29, 34, 38, 43, 45, 48–51, 53–7, 62–3, 65, 72, 104, 158, 179, 188
  1973 referenda and, 49
  1974 election, 43, 57, 61–2
  Fraser challenge, 25, 28, 64
  Kerr, Sir John and, 74, 81
  Senate, and the, 61
  Supply and, 55
socialist objective, 10–11
Solomon, David, 46, 49, 51, 243
Southey, R J, 24
Sovereign, 78, 82, 98, 307, 308
  rights of, 127, 168
  role of, 83, 290
Speaker, the, 270–1, 273
  letter to Queen, 307
Staley, Tony, 205
  concedes cracking, 237
Stannard, Bruce, 183
State Aid, 5
  ALP and, 5
Stephen, Sir Ninian, 82, 215, 227, 284
Stephens, Captain, 256, 263
Stewart, Frank, 90, 222
Stone, John, 87
  memo on loan, 87
Sullivan, Kathy, 239; *see also* Martin, Kathy
Supply, 2, 11, 17–18, 21, 22, 104, 110, 225, 246, 255, 273, 289, 291–4
  1974 double dissolution, 60
  alleged discussions between Kerr and Whitlam, 125–9
  ALP and, 33
  alternative financial arrangements, 172–6, 187, 190, 207, 216
  banks, 176
  draft Law Officers' opinion, 211
  Kerr/Fraser discussions, 187

legal opinions, 176; Byers/Enderby, 173; Deane QC, William, 174
States and the, 174
blocking of, 112–13, 145; see Chapter 6 passim, especially 109–16
1974, 55–7, 59, 61–2
Cutler, Sir Roden's view of, 135
effect of, 169
Kerr views as improper, 121
Liberal opponents, 110–14, 171
premiers and, 111
vote, 115
casual Senate vacancies and, 107
conventions, 117
deferral of, 49, 127, 128
DLP and, 57
effects of blocking, 153–4
exhaustion of, 178
Fraser, Malcolm and, 40–1, 267, 278
as Prime Minister, 265
deferral rather than reject, 164
half Senate election and, 144, 200
Hall, Steele and, 110
Holt, Harold and, 116
House of Representatives debate on, 161
Jessop, Don and, 157
Kerr, Sir John and, 155
Menzies, R G and, 116
no confidence and, 116
not expired, 233–4
political solution, 234
Queen dismissal of GG reference, 131–2
refusal of, 104
return of bills to Reps, 150
Royal Assent, 150
Senate and the, 2, 42, 143
voter sentiment, 153
Whitlam, E G and, 125
Withers, Reg, 36

Tange, Sir Arthur, 26
Tawney, R H, 51
This Day Tonight, 138, 162, 176, 280
Tonkin, David, 157
Townley, Michael, 44, 60, 107
Tracey, Bill, 242
Treasury, 87, 173, 210
Tudor House, 25
Turnbull, Senator (Dr) 'Spot', 44–6
two-party system, 4, 17

UK Constitution
1909–11 crisis, 77

Wales, HRH Prince of, 314–15
Walsh, Eric, 54
Ward, Eddie, 13
Warn, Patti, 102
Wentworth, Bill, 53
Westminster system, 16, 65, 279
Wheeldon, John, 8, 109, 117, 222, 283, 289
Kerr, Sir John and, 283, 299, 302
Supply and, 117
view of crisis, 285

views on Whitlam sacking Kerr, 221
Wheeler, Sir Frederick, 56, 87, 89
Whitlam Government, 2, 3, 6, 18–19, 21, 24, 31–2, 35, 39, 42, 52, 63, 65, 112, 114, 143, 169
1972 majority, 13
ASIO 'raid', 46
Cairns budget, 63
Constitution and the, 10
double dissolution bills, 272
duumvirate, 14, 15
education policy, 50
election of, 2
Ellicott, Bob on, 163
Fraser, Malcolm on, 40, 116
Gair affair, 54
Hayden budget, 89, 106, 112, 188, 276
inflation, 58
initial policies, 14–15
legislative program, 10
loans affair, 112
Loans Council, 93
Menzies' view, 158
policies, 11, 30
program, 44
Senate and the, 18, 20–1, 32, 47, 60
States and the, 44
Whitlam, E G, 1–7, 9, 13, 16, 17, 19, 21, 24, 26, 27, 29, 31, 33–7, 40, 42–5, 48–51, 53–7, 59, 61–2, 64, 66–70, 73–86, 89, 90, 92, 95, 97, 98, 100–13, 115, 117–26, 128, 129, 131–73, 175, 176–224, 226, 228, 229–35, 240–1, 242–82, 284–5, 287–93, 295–311, 313, 315–16
1970 vote against budget, 142
ALP and, 3, 6–7, 11–12
ALP deputy leader, 5
alternative financial arrangements, 172–8, 190
as a politician, 5, 8, 51
as Prime Minister, 100
ASIO 'raid', 46
Barwick, Sir Garfield and, 123, 152, 226, 228
blocking of Supply, 115
Cairns, Jim and, 6
Calwell, Arthur and, 6
caucus and, 6, 49
Charteris, Sir Martin and, 280
Commonwealth powers, view of, 4
compromise, 245
Connor, Rex and, 9, 87, 93, 112
Constitution and the, 9–11, 15, 105, 117, 188, 189
view of, 78
crash through or crash, 4–6, 40, 105, 190, 201, 256
Cutler, Sir Roden and, 73, 220
Daly, Fred and, 246
democracy and, 13–14, 57, 189
democratic socialism, 11
DLP and, 60
'do a Game', 265
double dissolution, 51–2, 186

INDEX

1974, 56–7
duumvirate, 14, 43
election as ALP leader, 4
elections
  1972, 2, 13
  1974, 22, 43, 56, 60
electoral reform, 47
Ellicott, Bob and, 193
Ellicott, Bob on, 190
entry into Parliament, 4
EXCO Minute 14 December 1974, 95
Executive Council meeting 13 December 1974, 89, 91
feather duster, 54
federalism and, 12
first ALP Prime Minister re-elected, 60
flaws, 5, 8–9
Fraser compromise, 188–90, 199, 203, 245
Fraser, Malcolm and, 6, 25, 39–42, 116, 128, 176, 188–9, 199, 230–1, 245
  cautions, 246
  Fraser compromise, 186
Gair affair, 54
Gair, Vince and, 52, 54, 58
Game, Sir Philip on, 191
Goulbourn declaration, 104, 122
government, 10
Governor-General and, 67
  list of names, 67
  reserve powers, 77
  role of, 42, 66, 69, 76–7, 161; advice from Harders, 150
  view of, 79–82
half Senate election, 117, 161, 177–8, 185, 200, 207, 231, 235–6, 246, 248, 251
  advice to Government House, 243
Harradine, Brian and, 6
Hasluck, Sir Paul and, 59, 67
1974 double dissolution, 121
Hayden warns Whitlam, 209
House of Representatives and, 21, 39, 60, 64, 118, 201
innovation, 14
Iraqi affair, 9
Kerr compromise, 207
Kerr, Lady (Anne) and, 120, 191, 230
Kerr, Sir John and, 6, 9, 20, 66–9, 74–5, 77, 79, 82–6, 89–91, 95, 98, 100, 119–20, 123–5, 127–8, 139, 148, 167, 189, 222, 230, 240, 260–3, 283
  11 November appointment, 255; telephone call, 247
  advise and warn prerogative, 126–7, 192, 193
  advises and warns, 257–9
  alleged conversations concerning dismissal, 133, 180
  alleged Kerr/Whitlam Supply conversation, 126
  alleged raising of dismissal option by Whitlam, 155–6
  alternative financial arrangements, 173, 175, 177
  assessment of, 137

belief in, 149, 151, 160–1, 168, 190
comparison with Game, 191
consultations, 164; 3 November, 188, 191; 6 November, 207; alleged, 14 October, 126, 129; alleged, 18 October, 155; alleged, Port Moresby, 164; alleged, prior 14 October, 125–6, 129, 300; Executive Council meetings, 129, 160, 178
death of first wife, 84
deception, 180–1, 183, 192–3, 194, 279, 300
decision to dismiss, 236; draft letters, 243; Supply, 234; timing, 233, 235, 240
dismissal, 245–51, 256–9, 261–3, 265
dismissal raised, 191–2
distrust of, 207, 219
'do a Game', 265
Ellicott opinion, 147
EXCO meeting, 103
EXCO minute, 101
failure to persuade, 241
failure to warn, 96–7, 100–1, 103, 128, 180–1, 193–4, 199, 218, 220, 251, 257–63, 298
Fraser compromise, 187–9, 190–2
friendship with ministers, 137
half Senate election advance warning, 243
ignorance of, 129, 136, 138, 161, 192–4, 214, 251
initial relationship, 79
Kerr asks to consult Barwick, 151–2
Kerr compromise, 179, 182
Kerr seeks legal advice, 148
Kerr's assessment of, 208
Kerr's remarriage, 120
Lady Kerr's view, 139
loans affair, 95–7
lunch, 30 October, 179
McClelland on, 180
money bills and, 120
offer of Governor-Generalship, 73
personal relations, 140, 153, 180, 183, 187, 190–2, 241–2, 304–6
PMA Case, 223
possible reconciliation, 316
Queen dismissal of GG reference, 131–2, 305
Senate, 234
term as GG, 74
threat to sack, 265
timing, 147
view of, 68
views on Whitlam sacking Kerr, 218, 220, 221–2
Whitlam defends Kerr, 161, 178
Whitlam denies advise and warn discussions, 129
Whitlam denies he would have dismissed, 132
Whitlam denies he would have sacked Kerr, 136
Leader of the Opposition, 266, 270
leadership, 2, 5–6, 8, 20–2

Ley, Frank and, 254
loans affair, 9, 20, 87, 89, 93, 95; see Chapter 5 passim
mandate, 1, 14–17, 21, 45, 48, 56, 60–1
　Withers' comments, 49
McClelland, Jim and, 183, 220, 233, 299
Member for Werriwa, 270, 280
Menzies, R G, 134
　comparison with, 7, 15, 37–8, 68, 138
middle class and, 3
nationalism and, 31
near expulsion from ALP, 5, 6
Opposition leader, 275
overseas trip 14 December, 88
Parliament and, 12–13, 61, 189
personality, 3–5, 7, 9, 15, 21, 51, 156, 180
　Barwick's view, 228
　Cutler's view, 220
　Ellicott's view, 193, 220
　Freudenberg's view, 256
　Ken Gee's view, 305
　McClelland's view, 220, 305
philosophy in the crisis, 202
policies, 11
possible 1973 election, 50
program, 7, 18, 21, 44
Queen, and the, 258, 279
raises dismissal in Parliament, 161
Reid warning about Kerr, 124
relations with colleagues, 8–9
Remembrance Day, 253
reserve powers and, 79, 137, 149, 315
responsible government and, 16, 17, 20, 22, 65, 116, 124, 152, 189
Senate election, 200
Senate, and the, 12, 18, 20, 32, 34, 38–9, 42–4, 47, 51, 57, 60–1, 65, 108–9, 114, 117, 125, 128, 143, 168, 171, 188–9, 193, 202, 221, 234, 266, 269
　blocking of Supply, 115
　casual vacancies, 108
　half Senate election, 143, 145, 177–8, 185, 186, 231, 236, 246, 248, 251; advice to Government House, 243
　interim Senate, 110
　Supply, 33
socialist objective and, 11
Sovereign and, 84
speech to Parliament
　11 November, 254
　21 October, 161–2
　5 November, 201–2
State Aid, 5
States and, 39, 44, 178
Supply, and, 33, 42, 49, 57, 114, 117–18, 125, 154, 164, 168, 188–9, 216
　1970 speech, 142
　tactics, 143
tactics and timing, 143–5, 177–8, 188–90, 201, 241–2, 266, 268–70, 276–8
toasts Kerr, 214

tough it out strategy, 106, 117–18, 143–5, 175, 190, 202, 210, 215, 242, 289, 299, 303, 305
Whitlam compromise, 245
'Who's party is it?', 6
Whitlam, Margaret, 67, 68, 120, 131, 230, 264
Whitlamism, 3, 19, 25, 55
Willesee, Don, 267–9
William Queale Lecture, 74, 98, 223
Wilson, Harold, 125–6, 129, 208
Winneke, Sir Henry, 198–9, 298
　Kerr, Sir John and, 198–9
　discussions on crisis, 199
　view of crisis, 199, 298
Withers, Reg, 33, 36–9, 43–5, 47, 58, 60–1, 106, 111, 114–15, 171, 184, 186, 197, 236–7, 239–40, 243, 251, 267, 268–9, 277, 283, 310–11
　ALP and, 35, 37, 45
　background, 34, 35
　blocking of Supply, 115
　Coalition and, 36
　Curtin, John and, 35
　Fraser compromise, 190
　Fraser, Malcolm and, 38
　Kerr, Sir John and, 240
　Liberal Party and, 35
　loans affair, 113
　mandate, 49, 61
　Murphy, Lionel on, 46
　personality, 37
　Senate leader, 34
　Senate, and the, 35–8, 44–7, 49, 55, 60, 108, 142, 239–40
　　concedes cracking, 240
　　cracking possible, 236
　　positive majority, 109
　　tactics, 240
　Supply and, 36, 55, 114–15, 117
　　blocking of, 59, 111; 1974, 57–8
　　deferral, 49
　　secures Supply for Fraser, 268–9
　　vote for, 267
　　tactics, 115
Wood, Ian, 54
Wran, Neville, 120
　appointment of Governor, 82
Wriedt, Ken, 8, 109, 112, 117, 126, 129, 148, 176, 177, 222, 266–9, 289
　alternative financial arrangements, 176
　dismissal and, 268, 269
　Supply and, 118, 268
　swearing-in as Minerals minister, 129
　14 October, 126

Yarralumla, 41, 80–1, 85, 102, 120–1, 131, 139, 146, 152, 159, 163, 203, 208, 218, 241, 243, 248, 253, 255–6, 260, 266, 271–2, 275, 278, 281, 283–4, 298, 301–2
Yeend, Geoffrey, 118
Young, Harold, 239–40